FLOYD R. BOLTON
3101 SO. MAIN STREET
ELKHART, INDIANA 46517

July 6 198
Tuscon, Ariz

Guns and the Gunfighters

By the Editors of
Guns & Ammo

BONANZA BOOKS
New York

ACKNOWLEDGMENTS

A book such as this requires the assistance and cooperation of a great many organizations and individuals, and we, the Editorial Staff hereby acknowledge that help.

Angeles Shooting Ranges, Inc.;

Arizona Historical Society, Tom Peterson, Pierce Chamberlain, Jay Van Orden;

Armalite, Inc., Burt Miller, Erich Baumann, Fred Borcherdt, Bill Baber, Richard Ellis, Bob Nellis, Gordon Matson, Bob Sobolik, Lee Silva, Art Sowen, Gary Balthozor;

Colt Industries;

Dixie Gun Works, Turner Kirkland, Toby Bridges;

Kerr's Sport Shop, Jerry Knight;

King's Gun Works, Arnold 'Al' Capone, Bill Ward, Bill Capone;

Lyman Products, Ken Ramage;

Navy Arms Co., Val Forgett;

Pachmayr Gun Works, Frank Pachmayr;

Petersen Publishing Co., Photographic Department, Bob D'Olivo;

Pony Express Sport Shop, Ray Houser, Bob Ellithorpe;

Red River Frontier Outfitters;

Martin B. Retting, Inc.;

Sotheby Parke Bernet, Terry Parsons;

Wells Fargo Bank, Doug Murphey;

Jerry Crandall has contributed original art for use throughout the book on the titles of most of the stories.

This 1982 edition is published by Bonanza Books,
distributed by Crown Publishers, Inc.,
by arrangement with Petersen Publishing Company.

This book previously appeared in magazine form
under the title *Guns & Ammo Guide to
Guns of the Gunfighters.*

Manufactured in the United States of America

h g f e d c b a

Library of Congress Cataloging in Publication Data
Main entry under title:

Guns and the gunfighters.

   Originally published: Los Angeles: Petersen
Pub. Co., 1975.
   1. Crime and criminals—West (U.S.)—
Biography—Addresses, essays, lectures.
2. Firearms, American—West (U.S.)—Addresses,
essays, lectures. 3. West (U.S.)—History—
1848-1950—Addresses, essays, lectures.
4. West (U.S.)—Biography—Addresses, essays,
lectures.

F596.G92	1982	364.1'5'0922	81-21662
ISBN: 0-517-371545			AACR2

CONTENTS

JAMES BUTLER HICKOK By Jim Dunham.. 4
BONNIE AND CLYDE By H. Gordon Frost.. 10
JOAQUIN MURIETTA By Lee Silva 17
SERGEANT ALVIN C. YORK By Konrad F. Schreier, Jr................................ 25
THOMAS H. RYNNING By Phil Spangenberger 31
NED CHRISTIE By Clyde Good 39
WINSTON CHURCHILL By Garry James... 45
THE JAMES/YOUNGER GANG By Ron Terrell.. 53
DALLAS STOUDENMIRE By H. Gordon Frost 60
HECK THOMAS By Ron Terrell 63
THE PINKERTONS By Burt Miller 68
BILLY THE KID By E. B. Mann.. 74
JOHN WESLEY HARDIN By John Lachuk... 79
GEORGE ARMSTRONG CUSTER Staff Report... 86
JOHN DILLINGER By Lisle Reedstrom 94
FRONTIER GUN LEATHER By Phil Spangenberger 106
BLACK BART By Lee Silva 114
DOC HOLLIDAY By E. Dixon Larson.. 122
SIX-GUN TRICKERY By Jim Dunham 129
ARIZONA RANGERS By Burt Miller 134
BELLE STARR By Mary Elizabeth Good 140
THE DALTON-DOOLIN GANG By Ron Terrell 146
TEXAS RANGERS By Burt Miller.. 154
INTERVIEW WITH AN OLD TEXAS RANGER By Lee Silva 160
PAT GARRETT By Robert E. McNellis 163
HENRY STARR By Lee Adelsbach.. 169
JOHN SLAUGHTER By Allen Erwin 173
MELVIN PURVIS By Rick Fines 178
THE WILD BUNCH By Clair Rees 184
EYEWITNESS TO SIX-GUN LAW By Elmer Keith 188
JOHN HENRY SELMAN By Harlon Carter.. 193
TOM HORN By E. Dixon Larson 196
CHARLES A. SIRINGO By Konrad F. Schreier, Jr.................................. 199
FACES WEST—A Gallery of Gunfighters.. 202

Shooting Impressions

COLT 1851 NAVY REVOLVER By Phil Spangenberger 9
MODEL 1911 .45 AUTO PISTOL By Jim Woods 16
COLT 3rd MODEL DRAGOON By Phil Spangenberger 23
MISSISSIPPI RIFLE By Phil Spangenberger 24
MODEL 1917 U.S. ENFIELD RIFLE By Garry James................................... 30
COLT .45 PEACEMAKER By Phil Spangenberger 38
MODEL 1896 MAUSER PISTOL By Garry James 52
PERCUSSION POCKET PISTOLS By Garry James 72
MERWIN AND HULBERT POCKET REVOLVER By Phil Spangenberger 85
SMITH & WESSON'S SCHOFIELD AND RUSSIAN REVOLVERS
    By Phil Spangenberger... 92
A PAIR OF .32s FROM THE '20s By Jim Woods 102
DOUBLE 12-GAUGE PERCUSSION SHOTGUN By Garry James.............................. 119
THE WINCHESTER '95 By Jim Woods.. 139
MODEL 1875 REMINGTON REVOLVER By Garry James................................... 145
A TRIO OF .44 LEVER GUNS By Jim Woods 152
1874 SHARPS BUFFALO GUN By Phil Spangenberger 168
THOMPSON MACHINE GUN Staff Report.. 182

James Butler Hickok

Prince of Pistoleers

JC

By Jim Dunham

Hickok was a style-setter among the frontiersmen of the Old West. During his scouting days he dressed in buckskins and wore his ivory-handled Colt Navies reversed. Although it would be appropriate for Wild Bill to carry a fighting knife, the appearance of this one without a sheath leads one to believe that it may have been a photographers prop. (Kansas State Historical Society)

Born in Troy Grove, Illinois on Saturday, May 27, 1837, James Butler Hickok was the fourth son of William Alonzo and Polly Butler Hickok. Very few of the famous men or women of the American West were born in the west; rather, they were raised in the settlements of the East and Mid-west and catching the lure for adventure, followed Horace Greeley's advice to "Go West."

Young Jim Hickok displayed a yearning for the West and for adventure from his earliest days. Joseph Rosa, in his fine biography, *"They Called Him Wild Bill,"* says that even before the age of 12, Hickok owned a gun and showed a trait that was to mark him for the rest of his life: "An inborn fondness for handguns . . . and a desire for loneliness."

Although Jim became a skilled storyteller and a popular personality, he was never a good mixer, nor was he able to make friends easily. This was due, in part, to his reluctance to trust anyone which, in turn, had a bearing on the nature of the vocations he followed.

His family relates that his first gun was a flintlock and that soon afterwards he traded some furs for a second hand old pistol; perhaps, but not necessarily, a Colt.

Jim spent all his free time in the nearby forest practicing with his pistol. Although his parents would have much rather seen him devote more of his energies to his studies, he did keep the pot filled with wild game. Peters' *"Life of Kit Carson"* became his bible and he was soon winning shooting contests throughout central Illinois.

On one occasion, a fight between 18-year-old James Hickok and a Charles Hudson ended with both men falling into a canal and with Hickok fleeing under the mistaken belief that he had killed the man.

During the next few years Hickok served with General Jim Lane's Free State Army, "The Red Legs," and he met Will Cody, later to be "Buffalo Bill."

On March 22, 1858, Hickok was elected to the job of village constable of Monticello Township, Johnson County, Kansas. The fact that Hickok sought such a job is neither a major point in favor or against him as far as building any evidence to support or to debunk the myths. Being a small-town policeman was not a very dangerous job and certainly was not in the same category

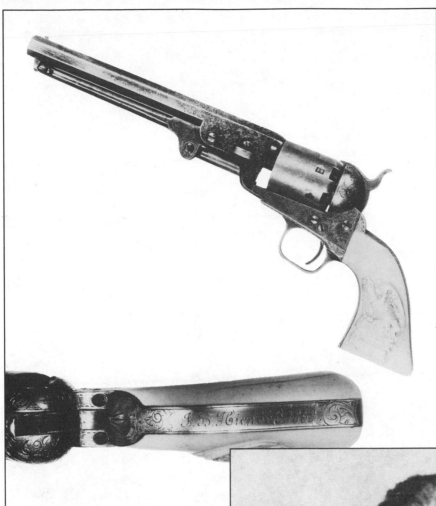

eral. Court records, local current newspapers and eye witnesses follow. However, much inaccurate information filters in from folk who reminisce 30 years later with comments such as, "Yep, I remember when old "Wild Bill" rubbed out the rebel gang of thieves headed by Dave McCanles."

The fictional concept of a fair fight as letting the other man draw first while standing 20 paces apart in the center of the street at noon or sundown, just can't be substantiated by facts. People bent on fighting to the death, do their best to put the advantage on their own side. The evidence indicates a kind of balance of blame in most Western conflicts, with usually more than just a "good guy" and a "bad guy" involved.

On the plus side for David McCanles, it was assumed he was trying to collect money owed him and long overdue. Also, he probably had a legitimate gripe with Hickok over the fact that Hickok had stolen

Wild Bill always wore his hair long, in the style favored by frontier scouts. It became one of his trademarks, as did his wide sash and pair of percussion .36 Navy Colts.

Upon returning from a hunting trip in the West in 1869 where Hickok had acted as a scout, Senator Henry Wilson of Massachusetts presented Bill with a pair of silver-plated and engraved 1851 Navy Colts. Detail on bottom reveals misspelled name on backstrap. (Photo by Gus Johnson)

as taming the later-to-be cow towns. However, it was not likely to be the kind of job that would appeal to the cowardly or timid.

After his stint as a peace officer, Hickok joined Russell, Majors and Waddell as a driver of freight wagons and in 1859 he met his boyhood hero, Kit Carson.

Sometime in 1860, Hickok had a run-in with a bear on Paton Pass, New Mexico, and was sent to Rock Creek Station, Nebraska to recover from his wounds and serve the company as a stable hand.

On July 12, 1861, Hickok killed his first man, David C. McCanles. Here is where historians seem to fall apart and appear to have what may be called an attack of brain fever. A number of sources are available in the research and the writing of history, but I believe that first and foremost is logic and the understanding of human behavior in gen-

James Butler Hickok

his girlfriend, Sarah (Kate) Shull, away from him. It seems likely that if he was looking for a gunfight, McCanles would probably not have taken along his young son, Monroe, to a shoot-out at the Rock Creek Station.

Nebraska History Magazine builds a pretty good case in defense of Dave McCanles and it seems quite possible that he was unarmed when he was shot by a rifle in the hands of Hickok. That rifle was donated to the Nebraska State Historical Society in 1931 by Mr. George

an argument over a card game, and most likely involved bitterness over a mutual girlfriend, Susannah Moore. Cards and women constantly meant trouble for Hickok throughout his entire life. The two men, James Hickok and Dave Tutt, agreed to settle their differences by shooting. They met at opposite ends of the city square, and as they moved towards each other, they both pulled pistols and both shots sounded as one. Tutt fell, having been shot through the heart. Without waiting to see if his bullet had hit its mark, Hickok turned about and brought his pistol to point at Tutt's friends and warned them not to try and get involved.

Colonel Nichols either elaborated greatly on what Hickok told him, or perchance "Wild Bill" was having a little fun with this newspaperman. In any event, the town of Springfield was not impressed enough with "Wild Bill" to elect him town marshal, a position which he conceded to Charles C. Moss.

When the "Harpers" article was published the story of Wild Bill immediately created great controversy in all parts where Hickok was known. Those people who wish to debunk Hickok hold up the "Harpers" article as evidence that Bill was a great fabricator. Others use the article to prove that Hickok was a kind of super hero. The truth of

Hansen. It was a half-stocked percussion plains-style rifle. Setting the rifle on the bed, Hickok stepped out of the cabin and pulled his Navy Colt 1851, .36 and wounded the two men who had come with McCanles. The two wounded men, James Woods and James Gordon, attempted to escape and were pursued by Hickok and his companions at Rock Creek, Doc Brink with a shotgun, and the station manager Wellman and even his common-law wife wielding a hoe, shouting, "Kill them, kill them all." Only the boy, Monroe, got away to tell what happened. There was a trial and it was judged that Hickok, Doc Brink and the Wellmans had lawfully acted in self-defense.

Then on July 21, 1865, came the classic gunfight. It was in Springfield, Missouri and was the result of

Each writer has a different opinion as to the weapons that were used in this duel. Hickok was known to have owned at this time a .32 caliber Smith & Wesson Rimfire No. 2 Army revolver and a .44 caliber Colt Dragoon and, of course, his pair of 1851 Colt Navies. Since he had time to prepare for this fight, my guess would be he used the larger caliber revolver.

While in Springfield, Hickok met Colonel George Ward Nichols and the consequence of this meeting resulted in one of the most amazing articles ever printed on any individual. Nichols' interview was printed in *Harpers New Monthly* magazine. He wrote about "Wild Bill" Hitchcock (using, of course, a nickname that would stick and misspelling his last name), killing hundreds of men with his own hands.

Following the murder of its first marshal, "Bear River" Tom Smith, Abilene, Kansas hired the most famous gunmen of them all, "Wild Bill" Hickok. This photo was taken in the main street about 1875. (Denver Public Library)

course is that the article was filled with un-truths but historians disagree on whom to place the blame.

In contrast to the fictional hero presented by "Harpers," rebuttal articles came from some of the frontier town newspapers. The *Springfield Patriot* of Jan. 31, 1867, says, "Wild Bill, as he is generally called, no finer physique, no greater strength, no more personal courage, no steadier nerves, no superior skill with a pistol, no better horsemanship than his, could any man of the million Federal soldiers of the war, boast of; and few did better or more loyal service as soldier throughout the war. But Nichols describes Bill's feat in arms, "We think this hero only claims to have sent a few dozen rebs to the farther side of the Jordan; and we never, before reading the 'Colonel's' article, suspected he had dispatched *several hundreds with his own hands*. This is no disparagement to Bill—Bill was the best scout, by far, in the Southwest."

Obviously the local newspapers considered Bill an important man among men, but not some kind of a god.

Hickok went from Springfield to Ft. Riley, Kansas, where he was recommended for the position of deputy United States marshal. The job

said to be gifts from Senator Henry Wilson of Massachusetts. The senator sent Bill a letter May 17, 1869, requesting Bill's as a scout on a private hunting trip to the Far West.

All the members of Senator Wilson's party were anxious to witness the famous scout's marksmanship and Bill performed a display of his shooting skills to the amazement of the senator's guests. Upon return to the East, the senator presented Wild Bill with two silver-plated engraved 1851 Navy Colts in .36 caliber.

August 23, 1869, Hickok became sheriff of Ellis County, Kansas. The county included Hays City, one of the most famous cow towns. Wild Bill killed two men in Hays during

with a salary of $150 a month plus 25 percent of all fines imposed in the town court.

On October 5, Wild Bill ordered gambler Phil Coe under arrest for firing a pistol within the city limits. Coe said he was merely shooting at a stray dog, but suddenly turned his pistol on Hickok. Wild Bill brought his gun up and placed two shots into Coe. Unfortunately, when the shooting started, one of Hickok's deputies, Mike Williams, ran around a corner to help and caught two more shots that Hickok had intended for Coe. The guns used by Hickok were 1860 Army Model .44 Colts and both Coe and Williams soon died from their wounds. Wild Bill

Hickok became sheriff of Ellis County, Kansas in 1869 and killed two men in Hays City that same year. This picture of Hays was taken a year before Hickok arrived. (Kansas State Historical Society)

involved only federal crimes and although Bill brought in a number of Army deserters and horse thieves, there is no evidence that he killed anyone in a gunfight during this time in his life.

The Western Plains were involved in serious Indian wars at this time and Wild Bill served the Army as a scout. Hickok served with George A. Custer as part of the 7th Cavalry, and Custer had this to say about Wild Bill's guns, "Wild Bill always carried two handsome ivory handled revolvers of the large size; he was never seen without them." The guns that Custer refers to are

1869. The first was Bill Mulvey (Mulrey) in that first month there, and the other was Sam Strawwhim on September 27.

Little is known of the surrounding events to these shootings. However, the story is that Bill Mulvey had the drop on Hickok and was ready to shoot him when Hickok looked over Mulvey's shoulder and said, "Don't shoot him boys!" One moment of distraction was enough for Hickok to get his own gun into action and end the gunfight.

Following the next election for sheriff, Hickok was out of work. Perhaps Wild Bill's use of guns to make arrests made him a little too wild for Hays. In any case he was soon requested to take the job of marshal of Abilene, Kansas. Abilene's founder and new mayor, Joe McCoy, swore in Wild Bill on April 15, 1871

suffered greatly from having killed his friend and eventually was removed from office.

Hickok next turned his attention to the theatre and joined his friend Buffalo Bill Cody in a stage show.

When Hickok got homesick for the West and wanted to return, his friends and fellow actors, Buffalo Bill and Texas Jack Omohundro each presented him with a revolver. Since both Cody and Omohundro were great admirers of Smith & Wesson revolvers, it is very probable that these were .44 caliber Model No. 3 Americans.

By 1876 Wild Bill had settled down somewhat and had married Agnes Thatcher Lake. Hickok left his new bride to seek his fortune in the gold fields of South Dakota and was killed on August 2nd, 1876 in Deadwood's Number 10 Saloon. Bill had

James Butler Hickok

been suffering from an eye ailment for some time and had taken to never sitting with his back to any accesible door.

He had been talked into playing cards and to take the only available chair which faced an open door. When Jack McCall saw his chance, he walked behind Hickok and shot him in the back of his head. In Bill's poker hand were a pair of aces and a pair of eights. These would become known as the *deadman's hand.*

We will never know for sure every gun that was owned by Hickok throughout his life, but surely he owned a variety of different kinds yet put his trust on only one or two types when a row had started.

A frontiersman called "Whiteeye" Jack Anderson said that most of Bill's shooting was done at 25 paces and by quickly pointing his revolver rather than taking aim. He said that Bill owned a Springfield rifle, which apparently was a custom

no equal when it came to shooting with a pistol. The undertaker who buried Hickok stated that he was buried with a "big Sharps rifle." However, when re-interrment was necessary years later, it was discovered that instead of a Sharps, the coffin contained a cavalry carbine of unreported manufacture, fitted into an old-fashioned Kentucky rifle breech, with the name J.B. Hickok engraved on the wood. There is good reason to believe that this may have been Hickok's own arm that he used to hunt buffalo before he became famous as a mankiller.

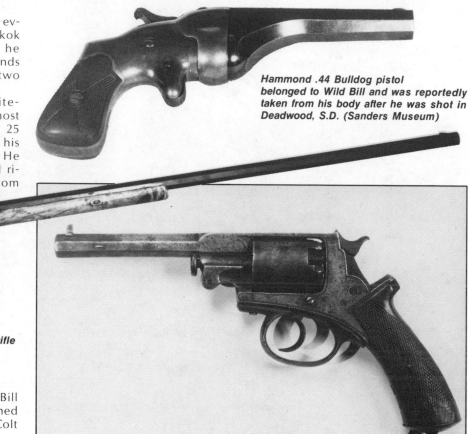

Hammond .44 Bulldog pistol belonged to Wild Bill and was reportedly taken from his body after he was shot in Deadwood, S.D. (Sanders Museum)

This half-stocked percussion plains rifle was reportedly used by Hickok in shooting David McCanles in 1861. (Nebraska State Historical Society)

Springfield sporter, 1870 pattern. Bill was also supposed to have owned two .38 caliber rim or centerfire Colt conversions. These were the new Richards or Richards-Mason conversions on patents of 1871-72. Also the Kansas State Historical Society has a photograph of an English-made Beaumont-Adams revolver claimed to have been owned by Hickok.

His close friend, "Colorado Charley" Utter, said Wild Bill could toss a tomato can about 15 feet into the air and draw his gun and place two bullets into the can before it hit the ground. Then drawing his other gun he could walk toward the can and keep it rolling ahead of him by alternating shots from both guns.

Although Hickok was not famous for using rifles, he sometimes took part in shooting matches with Doc Carver, billed as "Champion Rifle Shot of the World" by the Buffalo Bill's Wild West. Doc Carver could outscore Hickok with a rifle against targets, but said that Bill had

British Beaumont-Adams .442 revolver is reputed to be a Hickok gun. It is a double-action percussion arm of high quality. The side-mounted loading lever is missing. (Kansas State Historical Society)

The finest gun handlers since Wild Bill's first gunfight have wondered just how good Hickok really was. Legend and fact become almost impossible to separate when it comes to dealing with Hickok the marksman. All authorities agree that Hickok was very good with handguns, but often stories come down relating feats impossible to perform simply because they are beyond the limits of the firearms.

Certain tricks were, however, witnessed by responsible individuals. It is without doubt that Wild Bill was able to shoot very well with

either hand and that he could keep a can rolling in front of him as he walked towards it, shooting alternately with a gun in each hand. I own a .36 cal. 1851 Navy revolver and I know that with a little bit of practice I can do the trick with my right hand, so it couldn't be difficult for Wild Bill with both hands.

Hickok was also able to pull his gun and quickly place a shot into a telegraph pole and then spin around and hit the pole behind him. I have tried the trick using trees and know that if you don't try for ultra-fast draws, consistent hits are possible.

It is claimed that Wild Bill could shoot very small groups of 5 inches or less from distances of over 50 yards. This type of shooting is definitely beyond my skills of shooting from the hip and I would question whether Wild Bill might not have been a bit closer than the audience remembered.

However, Hickok was never afraid for people to see him practice with his guns and he did not merely sit back and live off his reputation. It is not hard to see why he was feared in a shootout.

Wild Bill Hickok was something more than being rapid and accurate with his guns. He was the first of a class of men that would live forever as the most storied and colorful individuals of the American West—the gunfighter.

Colt 1851 Navy Revolver

By Phil Spangenberger

The 1851 Navy, once again in production from Colt, could easily be termed the "Peacemaker" of the percussion era. This .36 caliber revolver was a scaled-up version of Colt's popular 1849 Model Pocket Revolver.

The '51 Colt Navy was a favorite arm of "Wild Bill" Hickok. He generally carried them in pairs as does the author here as he fires a 25-grain load.

One of the best balanced and easiest handling of the percussion handguns is the Colt Model 1851 Navy revolver. This cap-and-ball .36 caliber six-shooter could easily be called the "Peacemaker" of the percussion era.

It was not only a favorite of Hickok, but of many of his contemporaries who used firearms often. During the War Between the States, Confederate cavalrymen considered the Navy Colt to be the *supreme* pistol. Many troopers who followed the feather of Mosby were armed with as many as eight revolvers, and these were often '51 Navies. This same gun was a favorite in California during the decades following the discovery of gold at Sutter's Mill. Over 200,000 '51 Navies were manufactured from 1851 until 1873—certainly substantial proof of its popularity.

The '51 Navy was a beautifully designed gun. Its streamlined profile has endeared it to gun enthusiasts from its beginnings. The balance and feel of this revolver has led to tales of unbelievable shooting stunts performed by gunmen such as Hickok. "Wild Bill" earned the title "Prince of Pistoleers," while carrying his famed pair of ivory stocked and engraved Navies. Many of the "stunts" reportedly performed by men while using the Colt Navy revolver are well within the limits of the gun in a highly trained hand. The weapon had several things going for it that made it a good fighting handgun in the Old West. Balance has already been mentioned. Good pointing characteristics, ease of quick drawing and easy cocking are also features of the '51 Navy. The .36 caliber soft lead ball or even the conical bullet hits with quite a wallop and recoil is hardly to be considered in this sixgun.

One of the newly-made Colt Navy revolvers was chosen for this shooting impression. I figured that an original Colt Navy might be somewhat worn to enable me to get an accurate idea of its shooting capabilities and a modern replica, even a good one, would still be a different gun. Colt made them then and they make them now, so what better choice could there be than one of Colt's current manufacture?

Currently selling for around $200, the new Colt Navy is finished in the fine quality of the originals I have seen in new condition. After spending many enjoyable hours twirling and playing with this historic six-shooter, shooting it is likened to licking the icing bowl from one of your mom's home-baked cakes. I used a 25-grain load of FFFg black powder with a round ball, topped with a homemade variety of tallow to cover the chambers.

Once the nipples were capped, I was ready to fire. What a delight!

Shooting offhand at 50 yards at a man-sized target produced very satisfying results. The gun is sighted for 50 yards so shooting at a target at about 20 paces would necessitate shooting a little low to make your desired hit. This new Navy Colt shoots identically to the old-timers I have had the opportunity to fire. Functioning was smooth for about the first 12 shots, then as is common with all percussion revolvers, the rotation of the cylinder began to drag. This is caused by the carbons building up on the cylinder bolt. I experienced no misfires and ignition time was fast.

Colt's Model 1851 Navy revolver, again in production is a boon to not only black powder shooters, but to collectors and Western Americana buffs alike. They can experience the thrill of shooting an original type sixgun of the early frontier while firing a perfectly safe "brand new" gun, *by the same manufacturer too!* For further information write to: Colt Industries, Colt Firearms Div., 150 Huyshope Ave., Hartford, CT. 06102.

Bonnie & Clyde

Lawless Lovers.

By H. Gordon Frost

The elderly farmer screamed "Stop! Stop! In the name of God, stop," as he attempted to flag down passing motorists on the Dallas-Grapevine highway that Easter Sunday in 1934. Finally succeeding in his efforts, Will Schieffer ran to the halted car and pointed at the bodies lying halfway in the ditch. "They's dead! They's dead! I seen it with my own eyes! Run fetch the law," he panted excitedly.

The driver got halfway out of his car. Then sickened at the sight of two Texas highway patrolmen, their heads a gory, hardly recognizeable mush, got back in the vehicle and sped off to Dallas, where he notified the authorities.

As an ambulance slowly drove away with the bodies of officers E. D. Wheeler and H. D. Murphy, the farmer gave his eyewitness statement to the investigating officers: "I'd just finished eatin' Maw's fine cookin' and decided to amble over to my favorite oak tree yonder and set a spell so she could clear the table. I'd been there about ten minutes watchin' cars go by on the highway when this black Ford pulls off the road, about 40 yards away.

"There was a young feller and his redheaded gal in the car, talkin' and laughin' real loud," the farmer continued. "Pretty soon they throwed out a empty pint whiskey

bottle. It landed in the weeds yonder."

An officer walked to the designated area, briefly poked around in the tall grass and found the bottle. Sticking his finger down its mouth, he carefully carried the amber-colored container to a patrol car and placed it in an evidence bag.

"Well, they'd been there about a half-hour when these two officers came by on motorcycles, turned around in the middle of the road and pulled up behind the Ford,"

This .38 caliber Police Positive Colt, SN 505844, was taken off Clyde when he was apprehended by Sheriff Peavyhouse in May of 1930. The front of the trigger guard has been cut away for rapid fire and the hammer spur has been ground down to allow the gun to be drawn from the pocket quickly.

Schieffer went on. "They got off and went up to the car. I heard one of the officers say: 'Looks like you've got car trouble. Can we help?'

"Then all Hell broke loose. That boy and gal stuck guns out'a both sides of the car and commenced shootin' like I never heard before Pop, pop, pow! Pop, pop, pow! I reckon they fired more'n a dozen times. Those officers never had a chance; never even got their pistols outta the holsters!

"I got down on my belly and crawled over to that fencepost yonder to have a better look at what was goin' on. There wasn't a sound.

Then pretty soon the near-door of the car opens up and out steps this little bit of a gal. She was smilin' and walked over to the officer who was still movin' a bit. She rolled him over on his back with her foot, took a couple of steps back, then fired two point-blank shots in his face. She laughed real hard and yelled back to the car: 'Look-a-there! His head bounced just like a rubber

Clyde Barrow and Bonnie Parker.

Clyde Barrow was born on March 24, 1909, in Teleco, Texas. Moving to Houston with his parents, Clyde attended Houston schools through the fifth grade, then dropped out and began engaging in petty thefts. Neighbors of the Barrows recalled that the boy was quite sadistic, getting into trouble on several occasions for torturing various animals. On at least one occurrence he was observed trapping a bird, breaking its wing, then laughing at its painful attempts to fly.

In 1926, Barrow joined Houston's "Root Square" gang, a motley collection of smalltime punks who stole cars and held up filling stations. Bolstered by Clyde's braggodocious ways, the gang decided to take on a gambling joint in nearby Fort Bend County. Using an inoperative "Saturday Night Special" revolver, Clyde bluffed the gamblers into surrendering a large amount of money. Two guards from nearby Sugarland prison farm were shooting craps when the gang burst in, but

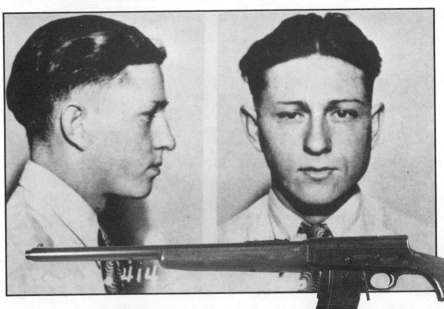

Clyde Barrow was arrested in Waco, Texas for a holdup just a month after he had met Bonnie. She smuggled a .32 Smith & Wesson revolver into his cell and he escaped, only to be quickly recaptured.

This .35 caliber Model 8 Remington semi-automatic rifle, was owned by Capt. Frank Hamer at the time of the killing of Bonnie and Clyde. It was modified to hold a 20-shot magazine. (Windy Drum)

This photo was taken shortly after a shootout, where Buck Barrow was wounded in Platte City, Mo. Buck's wife Blanch, is being held at the left, while Buck is on the ground to the right. Bonnie and Clyde escaped, leaving behind one of Bonnie's sawed-off Remington 20-gauges, a .30-40 Krag and several .38 revolvers.

ball!' Then she ran back to the car and they took off like a bat outta Hell towards Grapevine."

In spite of the farmer's good description of the car and its occupants, identity of the killers went unknown until the fingerprints had been processed. They belonged to

noting that Clyde had the drop on them, meekly surrendered their loaded revolvers to him. He contemptuously threw his broken pot-metal weapon at the peace officers as the gang left the premises.

Bonnie Parker's background was quite different from Clyde's. Born in

Bonnie & Clyde

Rowena, Texas, on October 1, 1910, she was known as a sensitive child who graduated with honors from high school. In 1925 she married Roy Thornton, a Dallas hoodlum who, five years later, was sentenced to life imprisonment as a habitual criminal. To please Thornton, Bonnie had a double heart with their names tattooed on the inside of her right thigh. This tattoo was to later serve as an identifying mark at a coroner's inquest when the inevitable event happened.

Bonnie met Clyde in 1930 and the couple fell in love at once, but their romance was short-lived, as Barrow was arrested and jailed a month later for a holdup. Bonnie smuggled a .32 Smith & Wesson revolver into his cell in early March and Clyde used the weapon to escape. Recaptured a few days later, he was sent to Huntsville prison. He was paroled two years later.

Out of prison, Barrow picked up Bonnie and their life of crime began in earnest. They began holding up small businesses, always exhibiting a great deal of bravado to their victims. Although Clyde was observed using a variety of weapons during these robberies, Bonnie seemed to prefer a 20-gauge, Model 11 Remington semiautomatic shotgun, with the barrel sawed off to about 15 inches and the stock cut to 2 inches behind the pistol grip. She is known to have owned several of these weap-

becoming better known with the passage of time.

A barn dance was held on the evening of August 5, near Atoka, Oklahoma. Among those present enjoying the loud music and rotgut booze were Clyde, Bonnie and Raymond. Hamilton made a pass at Bonnie and the jealous Clyde invited him outside to settle differences. As the two men were scuffling in

er Buck Barrow and his wife. The two couples traveled to South Joplin, Missouri, where they rented a small bungalow. Tipped off that the gang was holed up, a number of local and state Missouri lawmen surrounded the house. As Constable J. W. Harryman and Detective Harry McGinnis approached the front door, a shotgun was fired several times. Mortally wounded, Harryman

Two of Bonnie and Clyde's pursuers, Special Investigator Frank Hamer (left), and Sheriff Henderson Jordan. Hamer favored a .35 caliber Remington Model 8 autoloading rifle with a 20-shot magazine. Jordan used a semi automatic 12-gauge shotgun loaded with 00-buck.

An M-1917 .30-06 caliber Browning Automatic Rifle was used by Deputy Ted Hinton as a reserve gun when Hamer's group ambushed and gunned the couple down. Clyde was also known to have used a gun like this for his dubious activities.

ons, as at least three were recovered at various places where the couple had to leave in a hurry, with no time to take their guns with them.

Clyde acquired a partner whom he'd met in prison; Raymond Hamilton. On March 22, 1932, they attempted to rob a grocery store at Kaufman, Texas. The law was waiting, and though the two men escaped, Bonnie was captured, jailed and held for the Grand Jury. While she languished in jail, Clyde killed his first man, grocer J. W. Bucher, in Hillsboro, Texas, on April 28. A woman was with Barrow and some newspapers tried to implicate Bonnie, but this wasn't possible, as she remained in jail until June 27, when she was no-billed by a Grand Jury and released.

Joining Barrow and Hamilton, Bonnie helped rob many small stores, her sawed-off Remington ever-present as she matched nerves with their victims. The three were

the dirt, Deputy Sheriff E. C. Moore walked over to break up the fight. Bonnie attacked him, cursing and spitting. When he attempted to arrest her, Clyde shot him in the head with a .45 Colt automatic pistol. Sheriff John Maxwell was mortally wounded when Hamilton gut-shot him as the peace officer ran up to investigate the sounds of gunfire. The trio sped off into the night.

In the five-month period after the Atoka killings, three more men, including one Dallas deputy sheriff, were slain by either Clyde or Bonnie. Police traps were set to capture them, but the criminal trio always seemed to have incredible luck in evading the law.

Raymond Hamilton left the group when Clyde picked up broth-

fell, as McGinnis attempted to reach cover. He was cut down by a well-shot Browning Automatic Rifle. The foursome escaped in a rain of lead.

In the subsequent search of the hideout, officers found a roll of film and had it developed. It revealed an amazing set of photos, among which were those of Bonnie smoking a cigar while holding a Colt revolver; poses with various arms from their arsenal and one of Clyde standing on the roadside next to a "curve" sign, his arm hanging through a gaping, bullet-riddled hole.

The gang continued their activities, killing Alma, Arkansas, Town Marshal H. D. Humphrey on June 23, 1933, as he attempted to arrest them. But their luck was beginning to change, as Buck Barrow was mortally wounded in a Platte City, Missouri, shootout in which Bonnie and Clyde had to abandon one of her sawed-off Remington shotguns, a .30-40 Krag rifle and several .38 caliber revolvers.

Meanwhile, Raymond Hamilton had been arrested and sentenced to serve 263 years at the Eastham, Texas state prison farm. Clyde and Bonnie helped him and several other convicts escape in a spectacular prison break on January 16, 1934. Prison guard Major Crowson was shot and killed in the fusillade from the Barrow-Parker guns.

By this time the public was demanding that the killers be removed from the scene. The head of the Texas prison system was instructed by the governor to spare no effort

Appointed as "Special Investigator for the Texas Prison System," Hamer's first move was to visit Jake Petmeckey's sporting goods store in Austin, where he purchased a .35 caliber Remington Model 8 autoloading rifle, serial number 10045, selecting it as he felt the hard-hitting bullet's penetrating power would give him an advantage should he encounter the killers in their car. He then sent the rifle to the Peace Officer Equipment Company in St. Joseph, Missouri, where they removed the standard, 5-shot magazine and replaced it with a 20-shot clip. In effect, with this modification, Hamer had an accurate, lightweight, semi-automatic version of a Browning Automatic Rifle.

For 102 days the lawman

ways returning to Louisiana after killing someone. It is possible that, since they had killed no one in that state, they felt safer there.

It was at this time that the big lawman also got the most important aid in the case. The father of Henry Methvin, an escaped convict, was well acquainted with Clyde and Bonnie. He offered to "set up" the pair for the lawmen in exchange for executive clemency and a full pardon of his son's crimes in Texas. The governor agreed to this, and the wheels of criminal justice were set in motion.

Hamer knew that the chase was about to end, so he asked for some help. Consequently, Texas Ranger B. M. "Manny" Gault, along with Dallas Deputy Sheriffs Ted Hinton and

in the apprehension of the duo, so with *carte blanche* authority he asked one man to take on the job; Frank Hamer.

Described by J. Edgar Hoover as "one of the greatest law officers in American history," Frank Hamer had a reputation of being both feared and respected by the criminal element of the southwest. This former senior Ranger captain was well-known as being absolutely fearless; a crack shot with rifle, pistol and shotgun; and was a man of his word in dealing with criminals in over 30 years of law enforcement. Taking part in almost a hundred individual shootouts, Hamer was reported to have killed 53 men and was wounded 23 times. The choice was the right one; Bonnie and Clyde would eventually be eliminated.

Left: Clyde sits on the front of a stolen Ford V-8, displaying his armament consisting of Bonnie's 20-gauge and a .30-40 Krag rifle. Right: Though Bonnie was known to prefer a sawed-off 20-gauge, here she proudly displays two revolvers tucked into her belt.

dogged the trail of Clyde and Bonnie through Texas, Oklahoma, Arkansas, Missouri and Louisiana. The senseless slaying of the highway patrolmen near Grapevine caused Hamer to intensify his efforts, but the couple continued to elude him, killing yet another officer, Constable Cal Campbell, at Commerce, Oklahoma, on April 6. The perverse winds of fortune began to blow ill for Barrow and Parker after this last killing, though. Hamer detected a pattern in the couple's habits, by al-

Bob Alcorn were assigned to aid Frank. Also, since the trap was to be sprung in Louisiana, Bienville Parish Sheriff Henderson Jordan and Deputy Bryan Oakley joined the manhunters. The lawmen were ready, and got in touch with Methvin's father, who proceeded to bait the fatal trap.

Old man Methvin contacted Bonnie and Clyde, telling them a message was waiting for them at one of their secret "drops" next to a logging road near Gibsland, Louisiana, and early on the morning of May 23, they left to meet eternity.

The lawmen waited in their pine bough blind across the road from the "drop." As they whiled away the hours, they checked their weapons: Frank Hamer had his modified Remington Model 8; Manny

Bonnie & Clyde

Gault was using a 12-gauge Model 11 Remington shotgun loaned to him by Hamer; Henderson Jordan and deputies Alcorn and Oakley also had 00-buckshot-loaded semiautomatic shotguns; Deputy Ted Hinton had a .30-06 Browning Automatic Rifle. He was positioned farthest down the road to act as a reserve if the other lawmen were unable to stop Clyde and Bonnie.

The officers waited seven hours, then heard the sewing machine-

Top: Winchester Model 87 10-gauge shotgun belonged to Clyde; it has been sawed off and was in his possession when he died. Middle: Frank Hamer's Remington Model 11 12-gauge was his personal car gun. Bottom: Remington Model 11 20-gauge belonged to Bonnie. The barrel was cut to about 15 inches and the stock cut down to the pistol grip. (Windy Drum Photo)

Bonnie and Clyde look over their deadly arsenal of automatic and semi automatic shotguns and rifles.

Inspection of Bonnie and Clyde's car after their death revealed that it was an arsenal on wheels. Deputies found three stolen .30-06 BARs in mint condition, nine .45 caliber M-1911 Colt Autos, a Colt double action, a .32 and .380 auto, and two 10 and 20-gauge shotguns. Also included in the bounty were 100 loaded .30-06 20-shot BAR magazines, and 3000 rounds of ammunition in various calibers.

whine of a speeding car filter its way through the tall Louisiana pines. The lawmen tensed. The car drew nearer, then stopped opposite the blind and Bonnie and Clyde looked towards the "drop."

Hamer jumped from the blind into the road. "Stick 'em up! We're lawmen," he commanded.

The surprised couple jerked their heads around to see the 6-foot, 4-inch avenger standing 10 feet away. Bonnie brought her sawed-off shotgun up fast. It was the last living thing she ever did, as Hamer cut loose at her, his .35 caliber bullets slamming again and again through the windshield, each finding its mark with a vehemence. As the bullets tore into her, Bonnie was heard to scream like a panther.

Clyde jerked at his 10-gauge, Model 87 Winchester in vain, for as Hamer's bullets ripped into Bonnie, the 00-buckshot from the other lawmen's shotguns punctured him and the car again and again, raising great clouds of gory dust. And then all was quiet.

His 20-shot Remington empty, Frank Hamer drew his .45 Colt automatic and approached the car. Look-

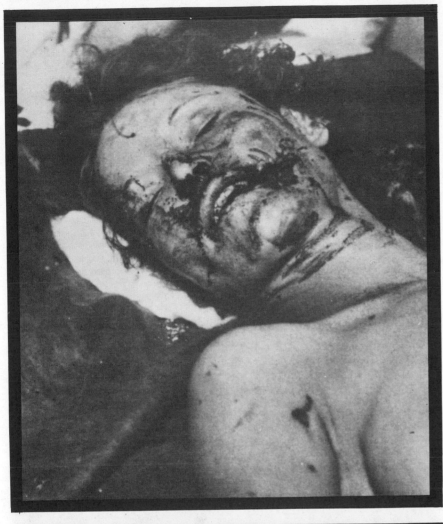

ing in through the settling dust and shattered windshield, he saw the couple awkwardly relaxed in death. Bonnie was slumped forward over her sawed-off shotgun, her head between her knees. Clyde leaned against the door, lifeless eyes staring with half-closed lids towards the spot where he first, and last, saw Frank Hamer.

Post-mortem inspection of the car and its contents revealed the car to be an arsenal on wheels. Besides the two shotguns covered with Bonnie and Clyde's blood, they found three, .30-06 mint Browning Automatic Rifles which were stolen from the Beaumont, Texas, National Guard armory; a loaded .45 M1911 Colt government issue pistol under each of Clyde's thighs; five more .45 Automatics in the trunk; a .45 Colt double-action revolver beneath the passenger side of the front seat and two other loaded Colt automatic pistols in the glove compartment: a .32 and a .380. In addition to the weapons, they counted 100 BAR

As Bonnie's body was being riddled with bullets and 00-buck, she is said to have "screamed like a panther." A double heart tattoo on her thigh was used to positively identify her body.

Clyde's bullet-riddled body as it appeared during the coroner's inquest. More than 200 shots were fired into their car by Frank Hamer's group in an effort to stop the couple.

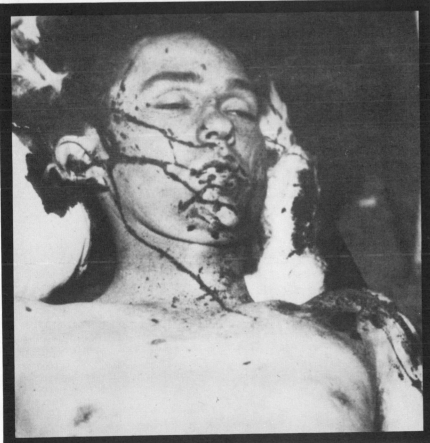

clips, each loaded with 20 rounds of .30-06 ammunition and 3000 rounds of various caliber ammunition scattered throughout the car.

Since Frank Hamer had taken a substantial loss in his Houston security service business income when he was tracking down Bonnie and Clyde, a grateful Texas legislature awarded him the weapons found in the car. The mothers of Clyde and Bonnie attempted to recover their children's guns from Hamer, but were unsuccessful. Hamer did give a few of the guns to some select friends, but kept the pair's most notorious ones. These included Bonnie's 20-gauge shotgun, serial number 1011222; and Clyde's lever-action Model 87 shotgun, serial number 72767. Both of these weapons were stained with the couple's blood, which Hamer never removed.

These guns, including Frank Hamer's modified Remington .35 Model 8 rifle and the Model 11 Remington shotgun, serial number 78121, which Hamer loaned Manny Gault to help end the careers of America's most infamous couple, are now on display at the Texas Ranger Museum at Waco.

Model 1911 .45 Auto Pistol

By Jim Woods

The Model 1911 .45 auto pistol and the current 1911A1 actually had their beginnings in the mind of John Browning in 1894. Some of Browning's patents were assigned to Colt who produced the early guns for the U.S. Army around the turn of the century. The Colt Model 1900 and the more important Model 1905 were the direct antecedents of what was to be described as "the most powerful automatic pistol made"—the Model 1911. Something slightly in excess of 6000 copies of the Model 1905 were sold, in contrast to several million of the Model 1911/1911A1.

Our test gun is a Model 1911 by Colt, one of almost 400,000 such guns manufactured in 1918. It was built for the U.S. Army, as were most of that year's production; however, some that year went to the U.S. Marine Corps, and were so identified. Model 1911s were continued until 1924 when, with modifications to sights, trigger, grip safety, mainspring housing and hammer shape, it became the Model 1911A1. At this point in its life, some 700,000 military units had been produced. Some of these were by Remington and Springfield Armory—about 50,000—and all the rest were by Colt. The Colt Company also produced commercial versions during the same period, designated "Colt Government Model."

Our shooting test was quite casual. Rocks, clumps of distant weeds and various other targets of opportunity were administered last rites by the big .45. Paper targets were recorded at 50-foot distances at the Angeles Range in San Fernando, California. Military hardball of various vintage was employed—no target ammo.

Firing offhand, 6 to 7-inch spreads were common. The more modern and effective 2-hand hold tightened those clusters considerably, to under 4 inches. I've seen many better groups, and even shot a few myself, using selected or carefully hand-loaded target ammo, but any time I can keep a 7-round magazine load from a G.I. .45 in the 6-inch black at 50 feet, I'm reasonably

The Model of 1911, U.S. Army .45 auto pistol has undergone several mechanical and minor cosmetic changes since John Browning conceived it, but millions of copies later, it's still the standard by which all other handgun designs are evaluated. Serial number of this test gun places its year of manufacture at 1918.

The G.I. .45 has a reputation for uncontrollability and inaccuracy, but in trained hands, it can be brought back to target while the just-spent brass is still being tossed aside. Off-hand groups at 50 feet, using G.I. 230-grain hardball ammo, stayed in or close to the 6-inch bullseye. Groups would shrink to about 3½ inches for the author, when the steadier two hand hold was used.

happy.

The guns from 1918's manufacture and other Model 1911s are somewhat rare, even though many were built. At least they're rare enough to be collectible, but also rugged enough to be shootable. However, the Model 1911A1 and the corresponding commercial versions are not so different in feel and operation than the M-1911s. I think my recommendations would be: Collect the old guns and acquire a current one if a lot of .45 ACP shooting is necessary to your lifestyle. But don't forget the old workhorses—take them out on the track for a brief workout occasionally. I don't believe that John Browning ever meant to be the father of just museum pieces when he begat his big bore auto pistol back in '94.

Joaquin Murietta

"Ghost of Eldorado"

By Lee Silva

The true story of Joaquin Murietta is forever lost in an era when legend was created by the romance of the word-of-mouth tale. Nothing was recorded for posterity except what was written in the newspapers of the time, much of this was based on hearsay.

The story of Joaquin Murietta is, without doubt, the bloodiest in the history of the West. There is no question that he did actually exist, but if he had had a thousand men and a helicopter, he couldn't possibly have committed all of the crimes and atrocities that have been blamed on "El Patrio," as he was also called.

Joaquin Murietta was a robber, a murderer and a man generally without morals, but he was also such a brilliant field general that even Bancroft, the most noted of Western historians called him "the Bonaparte of the West." At his peak, he commanded a robber army of over 100 men, and he cleverly spread them into raiding groups of half a dozen to 20 men, each group, in turn, commanded by a trusted lieutenant who was also named "Joaquin." These groups raided and roamed simultaneously all over central and Southern California and created so much confusion that, to this day, history can not even decide on how to spell his name.

The legend, however, goes something like this:

Joaquin Murietta was born to a Castillian family on their ranch near Hermosillo, Sonora, Mexico. He fell in love with a beautiful girl named

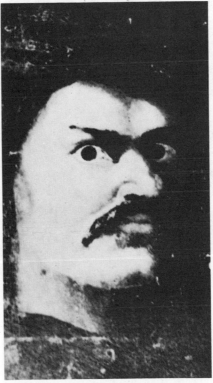

Besides two daguerreotypes, this painting, supposedly from life, is the only known likeness of Murietta. The picture was done by a priest while the bandit was hiding out in the Carmel Mission.

Rosita Feliz, who was, unfortunately, betrothed to an old "rico" of the town, as such was the custom of Mexico. One night Joaquin and Rosita rode off together to make a new life in California. It was 1849, and Joaquin was either 17 or 19-years old.

California, still predominantly populated by Mexicans, had just become a state on September 9, 1850, and there was no love lost between them and the "American" settlers.

One night, five miners broke into Murietta's cabin, caught him off guard, knocked him out, and raped Rosita. Most stories claim that Rosita died as a result of the attack, but others say that she lived.

Whatever the case, it was more than Joaquin could stand. Several days later, the bodies of all five men were found, brutally slaughtered in revenge by Murietta.

He quit mining and next turned up dealing monte in a saloon in Murphy's Diggings, where he became friends with Bill Byrnes, a veteran of the Mexican War and the frontier. They had originally met while Byrnes was a prisoner in Mexico during the war, and he was destined to play the most important part in the end of Murietta's bandit career.

When Murietta's brother, Jesus, was accused of stealing a horse that he had actually purchased, Byrnes tried to intervene and save them, but Joaquin was flogged and beaten and Jesus was hanged by a mob of about 20 men.

In the next few months, Murietta

Joaquin Murietta

if the story is to be believed, tracked down and murdered 18 of the 20 men.

From that time on, Murietta, like a man possessed, began his orgy of robbing and killing, and no mining camp or rancho in California was too small or too remote for his wrath.

At the height of his depradations in 1852, Murietta and his band stayed at a ranch near Salinas, California. Grateful for the lodging, they let the rancher live, and a few days later, the *San Francisco Herald* printed "Joaquin's Confession", as told from memory by the rancher: "The leader, according to the rancher's description, was young and handsome, and had four heavy revolvers

Murietta was viewed as a Robin Hood-type character by the Spanish-speaking inhabitants of California. A number of fanciful portraits were painted of him, including this one by Charles Nahl in 1859. (Wells Fargo Bank)

buckled around him. 'I am Joaquin,' he said, 'and no man takes me or comes within 100 yards of me as long as I have these good weapons. I was once a great admirer of Americans,' he said. 'I located first near Stockton. But I was constantly annoyed and insulted by my neighbors and was not permitted to live in peace. I then went to the placers and was driven from my mining claim.—At every turn I was swindled and robbed by the very men for whom I had had the greatest friendship and admiration. I saw the Americans daily in acts of the most outrageous and lawless injustice or of cunning and mean duplicity hateful to every honorable mind. I then said to myself, "I will revenge my wrongs and take the law into my own hands. The Americans who have injured me I will kill, and

those who have not, I will rob because they are Americans. My trail shall be red with blood and those who seek me shall die or I shall lose my own life in the struggle. I decided to submit tamely to outrage no longer. I have killed many; I have robbed many; and many more will suffer in the same way. I will continue to the end of my life to take vengeance on the race that has wronged me so shamefully.'"

Murietta's second in command was a Mexican barbarian called Three-Fingered-Jack, whose real name was Manuel Garcia. Garcia and Reyes Feliz, Rosita's brother, always rode with Murietta, but it was Garcia who added much of the blood to Murietta's legend, for his favorite method of killing was slitting throats. Garcia made himself a huge Bowie knife that was almost the size of a short-sword, and he literally used his bloody knife to cut a path of murder up and down the state of California.

The political climate of California during this time was torrid. The Mexicans wanted nothing to do with being a part of the United States, and they still felt that California belonged to Mexico. The Americans looked upon Murietta as a robber and murderer, nothing more. But though his ruthless killings shocked even his own countrymen, the Mexicans looked upon Murietta as the "patrio" who might overthrow the Americans and return California to the Mexican eagle. This general attitude was what enabled Murietta to create the confusion that he did. With half of his men running around claiming that *THEY* were "Joaquin," very few Americans really knew what Murietta looked like. With the Mexicans helping by calling everyone "Joaquin" also, and by letting Murietta hide safely away on their ranchos, he became the "ghost" bandit who was everywhere at the same time, yet nowhere.

Murietta's attacks were as diversified as they were ruthless. When the American miners left poor-paying claims for better pickings, the Chinese poured into them, and Murietta found the Chinese easy targets for his crimes of robbery and murder, leaving dozens of their dead behind him.

When two successful miners, loaded with $20,000 in gold, tried to

William Howard was the last member of the California Rangers to die. This portrait was taken just before his death at the age of 97—68 years after the group captured Joaquin.

sneak out of Stockton on a schooner, Murietta ambushed them in a rowboat, leaving six dead in the melee.

When the citizens of Stockton offered a $5000 reward for Murietta's capture, he rode into the midst of a crowd in Stockton and upped the ante on his own head to $10,000 and then galloped away before any of the startled witnesses could get a shot off at him.

Chased by a posse of enraged miners near the Mokelumne River, Murietta and his men doubled back on their pursuers, ambushed them and killed all 12 members of the posse, with the exception of one man who lived to tell the tale.

During a two-week period near Marysville, Murietta and his men took to lassoing and killing travelers and miners, leaving 17 bodies strewn across the countryside.

When local lawmen promptly hung several local Mexicans who were suspected of being members of Murietta's gang. Murietta, in revenge, answered by riding down the main street of San Andreas in broad daylight, shooting and killing three people at random. Awed by this brazen feat, the Alta California newspaper printed: "On Thursday, Joaquin rode through San Andreas at a gallop and shot three Americans as he passed through the street. Joaquin is a young man and must be one of the best shots with a revolver in this or any other country as all three men were shot through the neck."

A Los Angeles County deputy sheriff named Wilson, who had vowed to catch Murietta, was standing on a street in Los Angeles when a knife fight broke out between two Indians. When everyone ran to watch the fight, a single Mexican rider rode up to Wilson and shot him dead. When the shot rang out, the crowd turned from the fight, and the two "knife fighters" suddenly vanished.

Pursued by a posse of 25 men near San Luis Obispo, Murietta again used the tactic of circling around on them, ambushed them and left 11 of the posse dead, though he also lost nine of his own men in the battle.

And so it went. And these incidences that are mentioned are only some of the better documented happenings. Murietta and his band stole horses, cattle, gold, jewels and women, and they murdered anyone who looked at them crossways or who tried to stop them.

But there was a soft side to him too. He was a handsome Spaniard, and he loved to dance in the fandangos, slipping unrecognized in and out of dozens of public places in Los Angeles and the other larger cities of the state.

Though legend depicts him having a dozen mistresses and several wives, Murietta himself never harmed a woman, though it is said that he shot down a mistress who had been unfaithful to him.

Another time, he surprised his men by sparing the life of a man who had saved his own life when Murietta had first come to California in 1849.

Occasionally there was a light side to the depredations too. In the summer of 1852, when the good citizens of Saw Mill Flat, a predominately Irish settlement, heard that Murietta was planning to poison their water, steal their cattle and rob the general store where it's owner, Ira McCrea, weighed and bought gold dust. They decided to defend the town at all costs. "The work of cleaning and loading revolvers commenced, the little brass cannon (16-inch tube and 2-inch bore) was mounted on a pair of wheels." They descended on McCrea's store, feathers in their caps and guns ready. But after a lengthy and fruitless wait, the only attack that took place was when the hungry "defenders" de-

Patrick E. Connor was second in command of the California Rangers, with the rank of 1st lieut. This photo was taken when he was a major general of U.S. Volunteers. (California State Archives.)

voured about three dozen fresh pies. The "encounter" became known as the Saw Mill War, though the only "war" that occurred was waged on McCrea's pies.

By the end of 1852, Murietta's deluge of crime had created such a panic throughout California that Governor John Bigler decided to push an act through the congress, in a face-saving attempt to stop Murietta and his gang.

In December, 1852, a bill was submitted to the California congress which authorized a $10,000 reward for the capture of "the robber Joaquin," but is was defeated on the grounds that "we cannot legally at this time justify ourselves in placing a reward on the head of man whom we do not, in fact, even know to actually exist."

Finally, an amended bill was approved on May 17, 1893. The bill stated that: "Captain Harry S. Love is hereby authorized and empowered to raise a Company of Mounted Rangers not to exceed twenty men, and muster them into the service of the State for the period of three months, unless sooner disbanded by order of the Governor, for the purpose of capturing the party or gang of robbers commanded by the five Joaquins, whose names are Joaquin Muriati, Joaquin Ocomorenia, Joaquin Valenzuela, Joaquin Botelier, and Joaquin Carillo, and their banded associates.

"Said Rangers shall furnish, at their own expense, the necessary horses, arms, equipments, ammunition, provisions, forage, etc., for the purpose named in the first section, and shall receive from the State of California the sum of one hundred and fifty

Harry S. Love was the captain in charge of the California Rangers. Love was a hard-bitten ex-scout and Mexican War veteran who had made a name as sheriff of Santa Barbara County and deputy sheriff of Los Angeles County. He is wearing what appears to be an 1851 Colt Navy. (Wells Fargo Bank)

dollars, each, per month."

The bill also authorized a $1000 reward for the capture of Murietta.

The American citizens of California were screaming for Bigler's neck for not being able to stop Murrieta, and Bigler, in effect, gave Love *carte blanche* authority to bring back a Mexican, any Mexican, as long as Love could offer "proof" that the Mexican was Murrieta.

Harry Love was a hard-boiled ex-scout and veteran of the Mexican War. He had been a deputy sheriff of Santa Barbara County and was a deputy sheriff of Los Angeles County

Joaquin Murietta

at the time he was appointed by Governor Bigler to head the California Rangers. He was chosen because he was a seasoned frontiersman. But also because he had been on the trail of Murietta for a year, having taken it on his own to bring an end to the Murietta bloodbath.

With a few exceptions, the men who comprised the California Rangers were a motley crew, most of them veterans of the Mexican War, crack shots, hardened frontiersmen who walked a fine line between one side of the law or the other. They seem to have been chosen with the old axiom in mind that "it takes a thief to catch a thief."

For years historians have argued over who the 20 California Rangers really were, but in 1959 the original discharge muster roll turned up in the State Archives in Sacramento, having been misfiled and "lost for over one hundred years.

Though some die-hard historians still insist that the actual names changed several times during the Rangers' three months of existence as they rode all over the state of California in pursuit of Murietta, the muster accurately lists the Rangers who were active at the end, when they finally "captured" Murietta. Listed on the document are the names: Harry Love, Patrick Connor, William Byrnes, George Evans, William Howard, D.S. Hollister, Thomas Howard, William Henderson, DF. Bloodworth, Nick Ashmore, Lafayette Black, John Chiles, William Campbell, George Chase, Robert Masters, James Norton, John Nuttall, George Nuttal, John Sylvester, Edward VanBorn, John White. Of these men, four of them figured prominently in the Rangers' plans: Harry Love, of course, was captain and leader. P.E. Connor, as second in command, lent an air of respectability to the group, as he had been a captain in the Mexican War and was highly regarded in California.

William Wallace Byrnes was acting as first lieutenant and third in command, and proved to be the key to the Rangers' success. Of all the Americans in California, it was Byrnes who had been a close friend of Murietta when Murietta was still an "honest" monte dealer in Murphy's Diggins. Though many ranchers "knew" Murietta from giving him lodging, Byrnes was the only man who could really identify the real Joaquin.

The fourth man, William Howard, joined the Rangers with only

the rank of private, but Howard owned a ranch in Mariposa where he raised thoroughbred horses, and Love needed to mount his men on these horses if he had any hope of "catching" Murietta.

Howard, in his book, *"The Last Of The California Rangers,"* said of the Rangers: "Their traveling equipment was extremely light, each carrying his share of provisions and his cooking set behind his saddle in a piece of canvas, with a blanket

The Gold Rush of 1849 made for rich pickings—both for the miners and bandits. This rare daguerrotype depicts typical "diggings" of the 1850s. (Sotheby Parke Bernet, Los Angeles)

which constituted his sole bedding." All frontiersmen understand this phase of the situation and can appreciate the importance of packing as little weight as possible in a manhunt of this character.

The firearms consisted of old-fashioned muzzle-loading guns of every variety, and each man carried a Colt's Navy "six-shooter."

While Love and the Rangers were picking up the trail in Hornitos, Murietta and his men showed up at the Higuerra Ranch near San Jose in early June, 1853. The Higuerra was an original Spanish land grant, and it's "patrone" was sympathetic to Murietta. Murietta stayed hidden out there for two weeks, and when he left he told Three-Fingered-Jack to give the "patrone" one of Jack's own revolvers in appreciation for the lodging. This gun, a Colt Second Model Dragoon (1848), serial number 8315, is one of the few documented Murietta guns in existence today, and it adds credence to an early story about Mur-

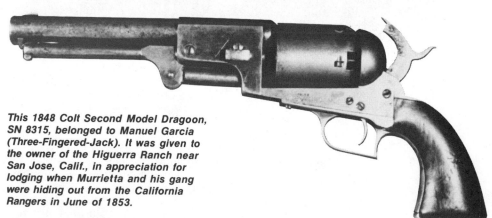

This 1848 Colt Second Model Dragoon, SN 8315, belonged to Manuel Garcia (Three-Fingered-Jack). It was given to the owner of the Higuerra Ranch near San Jose, Calif., in appreciation for lodging when Murrietta and his gang were hiding out from the California Rangers in June of 1853.

ietta which stated that "each of Murietta's men wore six of Colt's dragoon pistols; two in shoulder holsters, two in belt holsters, and two in saddle holsters."

The chase continued on and it netted the recovery of quite a few stolen horses, but no Murietta. The Rangers had been commissioned for only three months, and time began to run out on both them and the reward money.

In a letter to Governor Bigler dated July 12th, 1853, Love wrote, "I have arrested a Mexican, Jesus, a brother-in-law of Joaquin's. He says he will take and show us to Joaquin if we will release him."

Love began sending Connor and the other more "honest" men back to neighboring towns with the recovered stolen horses, and it was because of this that he had only seven men with him when the chase came to an end at the Cantuya Arroya, 80 miles East of Fresno, on July 25th, 1853.

The seven Rangers still with Love were Byrnes, Henderson, White, Black, George Nuttall, Chase and William Howard.

As related later by the Rangers, on the morning of the 25th, they spotted smoke from a campfire coming from a narrow draw in the arroyo. Brazenly, they filed into the draw with Love in front and Byrnes bringing up the rear.

They found seven Mexicans just rising from their blankets. One was an extremely ugly Mexican, with only three fingers on his right hand. Furthest away, a lean man with an air of importance about him, stood calmly next to his saddled horse.

When Love began to question the ugly one, the one beside the horse said, "Talk to me, I am the leader of this band."

At that moment, Byrnes, last of the Rangers to reach the camp, approached, and looking at the Mexican beside the horse, said, without hesitation, "That's Joaquin."

Henderson had a double-barrelled shotgun trained on Murietta, but, unbelievably, he fired and missed as Joaquin leaped into the saddle and galloped away.

At the same moment, Three-Fingered-Jack got off a quick shot at Harry Love, grazing his temple.

As William Howard said later, "The bandits were armed exclusively with six-shooters, whereas the Rangers, being fitted out with rifles, revolvers, and shotguns, had the advantage."

What happened next is lost in confusion because accounts of the incident as told by the intrepid Rangers (men who were trained to be keenly observant as a necessity for survival) all conflict with one another.

Howard always maintained that there were 15 Mexicans in the camp and that 12 were killed. The other raiders stated that there had been only seven in camp and that only two were killed (Murietta and Three-Fingered-Jack).

Henderson, White and Byrnes all claimed to have fired the fatal shot that killed Murietta.

What actually seems to have happened was that, after Three-Fingered-Jack's near miss of Love, Love shot him point blank in the face, killing him instantly. With lead apparently flying all over the place, the range was so close that no one else was injured, and two of the Mexicans surrendered, the rest escaping.

White, Henderson and Byrnes gave chase to Murietta, with either White or Henderson in the lead. Riding Murietta down on their thoroughbreds, either White or Henderson shot Murietta's horse out from under him. Murietta, badly wounded with a bullet in his back, staggered to his feet, trying to say something to White, who was first to reach Murietta. As White dismounted, keeping Murietta covered, Byrnes rode up and shot Murietta dead.

In a letter to Governor Bigler dated August 4, 1853, Love gives his personal account of the battle, stating, "Each of them being armed with two six-shooters, and three of their number killed, while the remainder escaped."

Having been given explicit orders by Governor Bigler to bring back proof of any capture of Murrieta, and fearing that the state wouldn't pay the reward and their wages if they didn't, the Rangers decided to take back the heads of both outlaws and also Three-Fingered-Jack's hand. It was Byrnes who performed the grisly task of severing the heads and hand.

However, because Three-Fingered-Jack's head was literally blown apart by Love's bullet, it was buried, and Joaquin's head and Three-Fingered-Jack's hand were taken on to Fort Miller where a Doctor Leach put them in bottles filled with alcohol.

Interestingly, one of the prisoners was drowned while crossing the Tulare Slough. The Rangers, straight-faced, said that it was suicide.

Taken to the jail at Mariposa and then Martinez, the second prisoner was promptly lynched by a mob of *Mexicans*, supposedly to keep him from "informing" on the local Mexicans who had been helping Murietta.

And so ended the short "successful" existence of the California Rangers.

They were mustered out of service at Quartsburg, California on July 28, 1853. They were paid their wages, plus the $1000 reward, and in 1854, they were voted another $5000 by a "grateful" governor and state.

The mass raiding and robbing stopped. However, the saga was just getting interesting. The "pickled" head was that of a Yaqui Indian Mexican and not a castillian Spaniard. The Americans who had "known" Murietta swore that the head was not his, but the Mexicans all swore that it was.

Political foes of Bigler screamed that Love and his Rangers had brought back a convenient head in order to stem the complaints that Bigler was losing control of the state, the Rangers being paid off for doing just that.

Then, John White was ambushed and killed at Fort Tejon, California, supposedly by Mexicans in revenge for Murietta's death.

The head even had a story of it's own. Thousands of people came to see it and the hand, which were exhibited throughout the West and the East. The head and hand ended up at Dr. Jordan's Museum of Anatomy in San Francisco. During the great earthquake of 1906, a policeman watched through the front door as they fell to the floor and burned. However, listed as #579 in Dr. Jordan's catalog was another head of a Mexican, which was also on display near Murietta's head, which was #563. It could have been #579 that the policeman saw burn, for "Murietta's" head turned up again in a museum in Almaden, California in 1961 and is now in a private collection, spurious or not, no one knows.

William Wallace Byrnes was committed to the insane-asylum in Stockton, California in 1873 and died there in 1874, a tormented man.

Henderson, also claiming to be haunted by Murietta's ghost, died of a heart attack at Coarse Gold Gulch, California on Dec. 28, 1882.

Patrick Connor rose to distinction as a general of the U.S. Volunteers, and had his own book written about him, while in command of Fort Douglas, Utah. He died in 1891.

William Howard lived to the ripe old age of 97, dying in Portland, Oregon on Jan. 4, 1924. (His book was published four years later in 1928).

Captain Harry Love died the most bizarre death of all. He settled in Santa Cruz, California and married a 350-pound woman who was 20 years older than he was. In a fit of jealousy in 1868, Love hid behind the fence of his own house and ambushed his gardener, a man named Elverson, and in the ensuing pistol fight, Love's right arm was shattered by a bullet. He was over-chloroformed by the doctors who were amputating his arm, and he never regained conciousness.

Joaquin Murietta

There is simply too much meat to fit into the larder for one article about Murietta and the California Rangers. The entire story of "Murietta's" demise stinks like a rotten cabbage patch. This author, for one, is convinced that it was not Murietta who was killed at the Cantuya Arroya. There is just too much evidence to the contrary.

For openers, Murietta was just too smart to be caught standing beside his horse by a posse of expert scouts that he *knew* was rapidly gaining on his heels.

Howard claimed to have known American friend that he had. As ruthless and as hardened as Byrnes was, it seems unlikely that Byrnes would have run Murietta into the ground for the $150 a month pay and his $50 share of the reward money. (He had no way of knowing that the state would grant an additional $5000 later).

It is my opinion that Murietta, taking advantage of the formation of the California Rangers as a way to get some of the pressure off his back, made a deal with Byrnes to identify the first convenient bandit that the Rangers caught up with, paying Byrnes to claim that the bandit was Murietta. Joaquin knew that Love was a good scout and that he fore he joined the Rangers, yet his own daughter, years later, stated that Byrnes was well off enough after the Murietta episode to never have to work again.

From John Rollin Ridge's first account of Murietta, published in 1858, (he was accused of creating Joaquin Murietta from fiction), to William Secrest's recent book, the trail of Joaquin Murietta still ends in mystery. Even the two known daguerreotypes of Murietta, though seemingly authentic, come under fire, and the mystery lives on.

Most modern "students" of Murietta lore concur that Joaquin Murietta probably died a rich man in Arispe, Sonora, Mexico in 1879.

This cut-down M-1833 Ames short sword was supposed to have belonged to Murietta and has his name scratched on the crossguard. (Wells Fargo Bank)

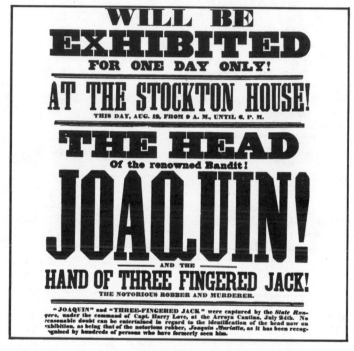

Murietta when Murietta first came to California. Why didn't he recognize Murietta instead of Byrnes recognizing him? Why did Howard's account of the capture differ so much from the others?

Why would a "faithful" Mexican relative suddenly lead Love *right* to Murietta?

If White was ambushed by Mexicans seeking revenge, why weren't any of the other Rangers ambushed?

Did the Rangers just "claim" that the dead Mexican had actually said that he was Murietta in order to give their stories credence?

If it wasn't really Murietta who was killed, then was it really Three-Fingered-Jack who was also killed? (Missing fingers actually were very common amongst vaqueros of the day because they were quite often caught up between riata and saddle horn while roping.)

The big clue, though, is Byrnes himself. Murietta is known to have said that Byrnes was the only true would eventually corner some of his band, and with Byrnes as a member of the Rangers, it would be a simple matter to "identify" Murietta and convince California he was dead.

If Byrnes really was being paid off by Murietta, it doesn't take much imagination to wonder why Byrnes rode up and killed the wounded "Murietta" when White had the drop on him. From there, it isn't inconceivable that Byrnes took Henderson and White into the plot with him, and that Byrnes, not Mexicans, killed White later when White got cold feet and was going to spill the beans.

There is one glaring "proof" to this conjecture. In an interview in 1879, Henderson stated that he and Byrnes lived at Byrnes' ranch in Mariposa county after the disolution of the Rangers. Did Henderson mistakenly refer to Howard's ranch, or did Byrnes suddenly become affluent enough to purchase a ranch? He was known to be stone broke be-

After Joaquin was killed, his head was severed and brought back to the authorities to verify his death. Three-Fingered-Jack's hand was also taken and the pair of grisly momentos were pickled in alcohol and displayed throughout the state. The head was supposedly lost in the San Francisco earthquake of 1906. (Wells Fargo Bank)

Because of Joaquin Murietta, the California Rangers were created, the only state Rangers that California ever had, the shortest existence of any state Ranger force in the West.

Today, the California Rangers are long forgotten, but the legend of Murietta lives on.

Perhaps some day, some concrete evidence will turn up, just as the Rangers' discharge muster roll did, that will offer proof of what really happened to Joaquin Murietta, or Murrietta, or Muriata, or however his name was really spelled.

Until then, he still remains the "Ghost of the Eldorado."

Colt 3rd Model Dragoon

By Phil Spangenberger

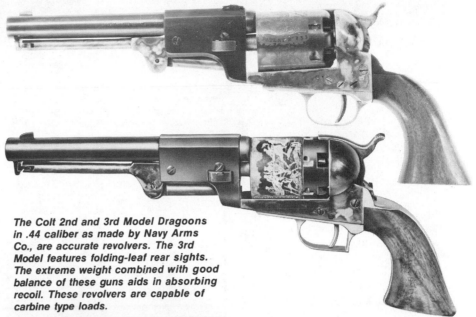

In the decade following the Mexican War of 1846-1848, Colt Firearms Co., manufactured a series of six-shot horse pistols that were then considered to be the ultimate in fighting handguns. These were the Colt Dragoon models. There were three basic variations, but really the weapons were almost identical to each other and were all improvements over the massive Walker model that Sam Colt had produced for the conflict. Today these revolvers are simply known as the 1st, 2nd and 3rd Model Dragoons.

The Dragoon Colt was a .44 caliber revolver. They were originally issued in pairs to the U.S. Dragoons to be carried in pommel holsters. These 4-pound, 1-ounce guns quickly found favor with the civilian population, especially in the Southwestern territories where they had seen service during the Mexican War. A Dragoon Colt pistol could pack all of the punch of the earlier Walker model, but had the advantages of a little bit less weight, better balance, and higher quality workmanship and materials, since these guns were now being made in Colonel Colt's own factory rather than being contracted out as he was forced to do with the Walker. Another advantage that this arm offered was a detachable shoulder stock. When fitted with this appliance, the 7½-inch barrel backed by a 50-plus-grain charge of black powder gave the pistol the qualities of a revolving carbine and was sometimes used as such.

It is reported that Joaquin Murietta and his men carried as many as six of these revolvers with them. There have been lawmen that have had Dragoons with lopped-off barrels stuck in their waistbands or trouser pockets for use as their "enforcers." Hickok is supposed to have used a Dragoon Colt in one of his shootouts. The Dragoon was no doubt a very popular sidearm during the 1850s and '60s.

Most gun collectors today have found that any model of the Dragoon Colt is just too expensive to even consider owning. Unfortunately, unless one turns up in somebody's attic or trunk, there is no hope for the average collector to obtain one. However, if you are a shooter, Val Forgett, of Navy Arms Co., has brought out a working replica of this old six-shooter. In fact,

The Colt 2nd and 3rd Model Dragoons in .44 caliber as made by Navy Arms Co., are accurate revolvers. The 3rd Model features folding-leaf rear sights. The extreme weight combined with good balance of these guns aids in absorbing recoil. These revolvers are capable of carbine type loads.

This "Californio" fires a 3rd Model Dragoon with a 40-grain charge of FFFg black powder and round ball, while a 2nd Model Dragoon is holstered and ready for use. Dragoons were favored by Joaquin Murietta and his band. (Holster courtesy Red River)

all three models of the Dragoon as well as the Walker model are available. They are priced realistically at around $115, and a shoulder-stock attachment is also available at extra cost.

I have never had the opportunity to shoot an original Colt Dragoon but from past experience with other Navy Arms replicas, I felt certain that one would shoot exactly like an original. I used Navy's 3rd Model Dragoon for the test. The action was smooth, with no hang-ups in cocking the pistol. Ignition was good and the recoil in this heavy gun is very mild. I used a moderate load of 40 grains of FFFg black powder with a round ball and tallow for most of my shooting. I did try filling the chambers so full that I had to shave the tops of the balls for a couple of shots. They went off as comfortably as the 40-grain loads, with just a bit more recoil. This Dragoon revolver is one of the most accurate pistols I have ever shot. I enjoy knocking over tin cans more than "punching paper," and at 40 yards, those cans are as good as dead with a big Dragoon and a two-hand hold. Offhand shooting with a pistol of this size is a bit difficult due to its weight. Sighting is easy with this revolver because of the long barrel and the folding leaf rear sight on this particular model.

The Colt Dragoon is an impressive looking handgun. Its massive proportions combined with the Colt "streamlined" look of the percussion era, gives it a strong suggestion of the powerful handgun that it is. The Navy Arms replica is a worthy addition to the line of gunfighters' handguns and should provide much shooting pleasure as well as historical interest. For more information on the Navy Arms Dragoon models, write to: Navy Arms Co., 689 Bergen Blvd., Ridgefield, NJ 07657

Mississippi Rifle

By Phil Spangenberger

One of the most accurate arms of the Mexican War and subsequently the "California Gold Rush" era was the U.S. Model 1841 Rifle, more commonly called the "Mississippi Rifle." This handsome muzzle loading arm earned its popular nickname through its distinguished service with Colonel Jefferson Davis' First Mississippi Regiment during the campaigning in Mexico in 1847 and 1848.

Also called the "Yager Rifle" which was adopted from the German word "Jaeger," meaning "hunter," the longarm was the standard issue rifle to the Regiment of Mounted Riflemen who stormed the walls of Chapultepec, Mexico armed with these guns.

The Model 1841 was originally issued in .54 caliber with open sights, and was designed to take a patched round ball backed by 75 grains of black rifle powder. The rifle was not designed for use with a bayonet, but in later years, alterations were made to many of them to accommodate this attachment as well as having them re-rifled to take the .58 caliber Minié ball.

Over 25,000 of these rifles were produced at the U.S. arsenal at Harper's Ferry, Virginia. From 1841 to about 1862 approximately an additional 70,000 weapons were produced for the U.S. Government under various contracts. Famous gunmakers such as Remington, Whitney and Tryon turned out these guns.

The rifle was popular with the early plainsmen and many of them saw use in the California gold fields as a sidearm or hunting rifle. During the Civil War, they were prized by many Confederate soldiers and were put to effective use by these rebel riflemen.

The test gun used for this shooting impression was not an original arm of the 1840s, but an amazingly close copy made by Navy Arms Company of Ridgefield, New Jersey. This rifle has the outward appearance of the gun as it would have been issued during the Mexican War with the open sights, but is rifled to take the .58 caliber Minié ball.

The Navy Arms rifle which currently sells for around $145, shoots and handles as well as the original

The U.S. Model 1841 "Mississippi" rifle was one of the most accurate and beautiful military muzzle loaders of the 19th century. This Navy Arms replica in .58 caliber is a faithful copy of the original.

Author enjoyed shooting the "Mississippi" replica using a .58 caliber patched round ball with an 80-grain charge of black powder. "Peace"-type powder flask is also a Navy Arms replica. (Shirt courtesy Red River)

1841 models I have fired in the past. Using both 70 and 80-grain charges of FFg black powder and a patched .58 caliber round ball, I was able to get good accuracy within reasonable distances of 100 yards. This gun is actually designed for use with the Minié ball; however, I wanted to try shooting the earlier style projectile in this test and was not displeased with the results. The sights are well cut and easy to use and the gun shoulders well. I feel that a little work could be done on the trigger pull to bring it up to snuff, although it was certainly acceptable.

One of the big thrills of shooting any muzzle loading arm is in the obsolete loading process, followed by a big boom with an abundance of smoke, settling to a lingering "aroma" of black powder. With this "Mississippi," the shooter is not cheated out of any of these pleasures. Light recoil in a large caliber weapon is another treat. Due to the

thickness of the barrel, this rifle will take a healthy charge of black powder, but be sure to use black powder *only* as these replicas are designed strictly for its use. The capping is easily accomplished because like any rifle musket, the gun uses the large "top hat" style musket caps which fit onto the nipple easily and shatter upon impact. Ignition time is as rapid as any modern arm I have fired, and shooting this gun is an enjoyable experience.

While the U.S. Model 1841 rifle is not generally thought of as a gunfighter's gun, the firearms historian may rest assured that in the days of the percussion weapons, when a reliable and accurate arm was needed, the "Mississippi" rifle was one that fighting men knew they could rely on.

For further information regarding the replica "Mississippi," write to: Navy Arms Co., 689 Bergen Blvd., Ridgefield, NJ 07657.

Sergeant Alvin C. York

Soldier, Gunfighter and Hero of the Great War.

By Konrad F. Schreier, Jr.

A .45 M-1911 Colt Auto, such as this, was York's sidearm during the famous Meuse-Argonne skirmish. With it, York shot seven men and subdued a captured enemy major, whom he needed to help bring in his prisoners.

In this U.S. Army photograph, York is shown standing at the foot of the hill where his famous fight took place. He was credited with killing 25 Germans and his patrol of seven men captured 132 enemy soldiers.

The number of gunfighters awarded medals for their exploits may be counted on the fingers of one hand. Sergeant Alvin C. York was one of the three greatest heros in the U.S. Army in France during World War I, and he earned this status from one of the most exceptional shoot-outs that ever took place—anywhere, or any time.

Sergeant York was a man from the mountains of Tennessee, where every man worth his salt knew how to use guns. His ancestors were pioneers when Tennessee was the wild western frontier in the decades following the American Revolution. When York was born in 1887, his hometown of Pall Mall was still a "far piece" from what many people called civilization.

As Alvin York grew up, one of the greatest delights of his life were the Saturday shooting matches, held weekly almost next door to his home. He was still quite young when he became known as one of the "win'n'est" shooters, and this ability would serve him well in his famous gunfight. Of course, York, like everybody in the Tennessee hills those days, did his target shooting with a caplock muzzle loading rifle.

The caplock muzzle loaders, like the one York mastered while he was still a boy, were used by the mountain farmers from his part of the country long after they had gone out of style in most places, and they were still using them up to the time of World War II! One reason was that they were very accurate guns. Another was that they shot loose powder, lead, and percussion caps which cost much less than metallic cartridges, and the people of York's homeland never had much "cash money."

The percussion rifle York learned to shoot with was what is called a "Kentucky rifle" today. These longarms were beautifully hand-crafted by mountain gunsmiths, and made to last several generations. When their rifling wore enough to affect their accuracy, they were re-cut, "freshed out," and brought back to their near original accuracy.

Most of the target shooting York and his fellows did with these rifles was for prizes: anything from money to livestock. The most popu-

Sergeant Alvin C. York

lar contests were turkey shoots, fired at 40 or 150 yards. For the long-range shooting, the turkey was tethered with a 2-foot string tied to one foot, and was free to move. A charge of ten cents a shot was paid to the man who offered the prize bird. Then, after the rifle was warmed up with a few shots at other targets, the riflemen stood up in turn and took their cracks at the bird. The first man who hit it won it, and York was noted for taking his share and more.

York and his fellow sportsmen also shot at targets for prizes ranging from a few dollars they pooled among themselves up to beef cattle from which each shooter got a part of the steer such as a quarter or hind according to his standing at the end of the contest. As in much of their shooting, a rifle support could be used, but when they shot offhand, the range at which they fired was cut to two thirds of the normal distance. York's hometown friends acknowledged he was one of the best-ever shots from those hills with any hold, and shooting was a sport he enjoyed all his life.

of roughnecks, and they engaged in a lot of pistol shooting from the backs of their steeds. They would gallop past a line of trees with spots cut in them, and try to hit them. York was the best of his crowd at this sport, and he got so he could even hit the targets from the hip. The pistol he used was an "old revolver," possibly an Army Model .45 Colt single action or a percussion arm of Civil War vintage.

Like every man from his locality, York was a hunter, and he did his part in keeping meat on the table.

While York was a man who knew how to use his guns, he had

In the 40-yard turkey shoot, the fowl was tethered behind a log so only its bobbing head served as the target. At 40 yards a moving turkey head is quite a challenge, especially since the other shooters were allowed to do almost anything they wanted to distract the shooter. They could talk at him, move around him, and even dodge under the muzzle of his rifle while he was trying to get the bird. York had an inner calmness and the self-control to withstand any amount of this hazing and still outshoot most of his friends.

U.S. troops on the move in France. Sergeant York was able to make the adjustment to this new environment fairly easily, but later said he didn't really care for it. York was a member of the All American Division which boasted men drafted from every state. (U.S. Army photo)

As a young man York was a bit on the wild side. His father died when he was young, and his mother couldn't restrain his high spirits. He drank too much, and gambled in places which his hill people considered "sinful." He rambled through the hills on horseback with a bunch

never used one on another man despite the "fussin' and feudin'" which went on in the back country where he grew up. About 1914 he "got religion," as they still say in that part of the country, and stopped being a wild young buck. This didn't stop him from his enjoyment of shooting, for this was a sport that was "considered highly" by everyone.

Communications being inadequate in the days when World War I started, the people of York's community didn't know much about it or understand it. This was true when York was drafted into the U.S. Army in November of 1917. After a long tussle with his religious beliefs, and with the help of his understanding home pastor and his Army commanding officer, York decided he should serve his country as a fighting man. This 6-foot, 170-pound mountain man was just the sort of intelligent, self-controlled individual who makes the best kind of American citizen-soldier. The Army recognized this and went far out of its way to make a soldier of him.

With his buddies in the American Expeditionary Forces, he was shipped to France, and underwent more training until his unit was considered fit for combat. York was made a corporal of Company G, 328th Infantry, 82nd Division, the All American Division made up of men drafted from every state.

Long before his famous fight, Corporal York's uncanny ability with either a rifle or pistol had made a deep impression on his buddies and officers. With a rifle he could get

little fighting except for a week during the St. Mihiel Offensive. In early October, the 82nd was moved into position for the Meuse-Argonne Offensive which ended the war a month later. The time for York's remarkable escapade had almost arrived.

On October 7, 1918 York's Company G was ordered to take a couple of hills the next day. They moved out through the morning mist behind the inevitable artillery barrage at 6:10 AM on the 8th, and immediately began taking very heavy German fire from the hills they were assigned to capture. Doughboys began dropping right and left, and the command was quickly pinned down. A sergeant then led 17 men, including York, to work their way around the left flank of the German position to see what they could do from that angle. They infiltrated into the German positions, and the first hostiles they encountered were two men wearing Red Cross arm bands.

ers of the enemy forces began firing at the Americans, and then, from just 40 yards up a hill, German machineguns were turned on the Americans. Almost at once six were killed, and three more, including the sergeant in command, were severely wounded.

York began picking off the German machinegunners on the hill with his Enfield. It was like his old turkey shooting days. York would fire a shot and a German would go down. Each of York's shots was carefully aimed despite the German fire pouring at him, and his aim was the best. His shooting was getting the enemy so rattled that they began to shoot wildly, which helped York, as did his calm disposition, and his ability to shoot with excitement all around him, even though this action was much deadlier than the old turkey shoots back home.

Then, when his rifle's magazine was almost empty, a group of seven Germans charged him with fixed

eight hits for ten shots on the difficult moving target course. Although long-range shooting was new to him, he quickly mastered the 600-yard target with the flat-shooting Army .30-06, Enfield M-1917 rifle. The .45 caliber Colt M-1911 service automatic pistol was a better handgun than the revolver he had used, and he was soon a master of it also.

The 82nd Division arrived in France in April through June of 1918, and took over a quiet sector of trenches in mid-July. From then until the end of September they saw

Over the top! American troops entered the First World War late in the conflict but proved to be excellent fighters, whose presence shortened the war significantly. (U.S. Army photo)

They fired at them and chased them since they had learned that any and every German was usually armed and dangerous.

The American patrol crossed a little creek, and came upon an enemy headquarters manned by about 20 Germans including a major. The surprised enemy surrendered, and the sergeant commanded his men not to shoot. At the same time oth-

bayonets. York's reaction was quick and effective. He laid his rifle aside and drew his .45 service automatic and began firing at the charging Germans. Each pistol shot hit a man, downing the rearmost man first, then the next and so on until all seven of the Boche bayonet squad were down. Seven rounds from a .45, seven enemy out of the fight. That is the kind of shooting that gunfighter legends keep talking about, but Corporal York may be the only man where witnesses prove that he actually did such a thing. It simply appalled the Germans, and

Sergeant Alvin C. York

made them ready to surrender.

York reloaded his rifle and resumed his sharpshooting, picking off more German machinegunners. His shooting, and he alone was firing, made the German fire slacken. Then York ordered the German major to tell' the men on the hill to surrender. Suddenly, a German soldier rose from some cover and pitched a grenade at the Americans, and a rifle bullet fired by one of York's buddies cut him down.

York, now the senior non-commissioned officer in command of the Americans, found the German major could talk English, and so he told him he would shoot him unless he told the men on the hill to surrender. York had already shot down so many enemies with his rifle and pistol, the major believed him, and ordered the Germans on the hill to give up. They began to surrender, and surrender, and surrender.

Corporal York and his seven unwounded buddies found themselves with over 100 disarmed enemies who crept from positions all around them. They lined the Germans up in a column of twos, and made some of the enemy carry the three American wounded.

They began to head back for the American lines, but all was not quiet. Bullets buzzed angrily past the small American contingent. Germans who could not see them, but could see the mass of prisoners, tried everything they could to draw

This German machine gun emplacement in the Argonne Forest is typical of the 35 machine gun positions York knocked out. The muzzle of a German MG-08 heavy Maxim gun can just be seen protruding from cover at the left side of the picture. (U.S. Army photo)

This column of German prisoners moving to the rear is close to what York's mass of captured soldiers must have looked like. (U.S. Army photo)

the Doughboys' fire so they could shoot them up. York maintained control and kept his men from answering the Germans, and issued the practical order: "Let's get 'em out of here."

York placed the three captive German officers around himself to keep the enemy from getting a shot at him, and had his men do the same thing with other prisoners. York put his .45 automatic to the German major's head and told him to order the prisoners to move toward the American lines. He used the lay of the land as he had learned to do hunting back home, and kept under as much cover as he could while moving back. As they went they picked up a few more prisoners.

One German showed fight, but by this time the prisoners were so scared that the major told the man to give up at once or he would be killed. The man submitted. Slowly the long column led by York moved to the American lines out of the vast hole they had cut in the German lines.

The German major tried to decoy York back toward the German lines, but York again nuzzled him with the cold muzzle of his .45. The column went on in the right direction, and soon met the challenge:

for it personally. His own outfit immediately promoted him to sergeant.

After the war General Pershing wrote in his book, MY EXPERIENCES IN THE WORLD WAR: "however, as typifying the spirit of the rank and file of our great army, I would mention . . . Sergeant Alvin C. York of the 82nd Division, who stood off and captured 132 Germans after his patrol was literally surrounded and outnumbered ten to one."

For his incredible performance with arms in the face of overwhelming odds, Sergeant York was awarded the highest medal for military valor the United States has: The Congressional Medal of Honor. He

cold. He had done his duty as he saw it, and he wasn't proud of having had to kill 25, and probably more, of his fellow men. Sergeant York went home to a farm at Pall Mall, and soon married his pre-war sweetheart. He lived a retiring life as a farmer, and continued to enjoy his favorite sport of shooting and hunting. You can bet he hadn't lost any of his ability in these.

When World War II came along, and the United States was again endangered, Sergeant York allowed Warner Brothers to make a motion picture of his early life and his great World War I gun fight. Gary Cooper played York, and portrayed him to perfection, but many a World War I

York's spectacular feat of markmanship was performed with a U.S. M-1917 Enfield in .30-06. These guns were produced as supplementary arms to the M-1903 Springfield rifle.

"Halt. Who goes there?"

"Corporal York bringin' in some prisoners."

The American rear outpost screen opened up, and York was told to pass through. When the Doughboys saw the long column of gray-clad Boche prisoners the call went up: "What you got there fella, the whole damned German Army?"

York soon found an American command post, and turned his prisoners over to an officer. They were counted and found to number 132, including three officers, one of whom was the major. After getting his receipt for the prisoners, York turned to the nearest officer and reported himself for duty. The officer told him he had done enough for one day, and relieved him and his men from further duty.

On hearing about the 132 prisoners, the officers of York's regiment went to see the place where they had been taken. On the ground where York had fought they found 25 dead Germans York was credited with finishing, and 35 abandoned enemy machine guns. There were other German dead, and the enemy wounded had either made it back to their own lines or had surrendered to other Americans. There were also the six Americans killed by the first blast of German machinegun fire.

Word of what York had done quickly passed from his regiment to his division's headquarters, and then to General John J. Pershing. Every command along the chain commended York's deed, and as many officers as could commended him got scores of other medals including

Sergeant Alvin C. York was one of the most decorated soldiers of World War I. He received the Congressional Medal of Honor and the French Croix de Guerre (both of which he is wearing) among numerous other American and foreign awards. (U.S. Army photo)

ones from the French Government and his home state of Tennessee.

While the medals and the fame they brought meant a lot to Sergeant York, they didn't go to his head. He came home to tremendous acclaim, parades and festivities in his honor. He received scores of offers to cash in on the heroism which made him a national celebrity, but he turned them all down

veteran who had known the redoubtable gunfighter never could figure out why Cooper didn't wear the moustache which York always wore on his open, pleasant face.

During World War II Sergeant York, who was then far too old to serve in the new citizen-soldier army, did his bit by going to Army training centers and telling the young fighting men of another generation how he did his bit in his war, and how they could do theirs in their war. To him, skill with arms in defense of his country was always a worthy cause, and he was with little doubt one of the greatest gunfighters of them all.

Model 1917 U.S. Enfield Rifle

Alvin York's Favorite.

By Garry James

When the United States entered the Great War in 1917, the country was dangerously short of the standard 1903 Springfield rifles. Plants were tooled up to produce the .280 rimless pattern 1914 Enfield, however, and with a few modifications the gun was easily converted to .30-06 and American use.

Redesignated the Model 1917, the .30-06 Enfield boasted one of the strongest military bolt actions ever produced. It was finished very well, in the manner of most American military arms, and featured a full-length walnut stock.

Manufactured by Eddystone Arsenal, Remington and Winchester, the 1917 was often criticized as being heavy and unwieldy—but it was rugged. It had a capacity of six rounds (five in the magazine and one in the chamber) and was designed to take a long-bladed Enfield-type bayonet.

The receiver, which had a distinctive "hump back" mounting for the rear sight, and the crooked "dog's leg" type bolt handle gave the gun a distinctive appearance.

Thousands of doughboys were issued the M-1917, including Sgt. Alvin York, who used it during his famous gun battle in the Argonne Forest. His shooting ability and the inherent accuracy of the gun accounted for a phenomenal number of captured and dead Germans.

Many 1917s have been converted to sporting rifles because of the strong action, and original military versions are becoming hard to find. Fortunately, we located one in the collection of Richard Ellis, and we took it to the Angeles Range in San Fernando, California, to give it a workout.

The M-1917 is loaded by withdrawing the bolt and placing a clip of five cartridges to the rear of the follower. With the thumb, the cartridges are forced down against the follower spring and into the magazine. The empty clip is then withdrawn and the bolt pushed forward to strip off and chamber a round.

The .30-06 is a beefy load. It was adopted in 1906 as a modification of the '03 .30 caliber service round, and American rifles were chambered for it up until the U.S. adopted the 7.65 NATO round in

The M-1917 U.S. Enfield was a more clumsy arm than its predecessor, the M-'03 Springfield, but its battle sights were far superior.

The M-1917 had an extremely strong action. The hump-back sight mounting and dog's-leg bolt were distinctive features.

the '50s.

Recoil of the '17 was heavy but not prohibitive. The plain steel buttplate did nothing to absorb the shock, but the heavy military tunic of the period helped to spare the shoulder a bit. The report, as with most big bore, smokeless powder rifles, was extremely sharp and loud.

The bolt could be worked very rapidly and it was possible to get off five rounds in about ten seconds. Deliberately aimed shots at 50, 100 and 200 yards produced excellent groups, and while I am no Sergeant York, I feel that the rifle was very capable of performing the chores he deemed necessary.

Despite its bulk, the Model 1917 handled very well. We ran a brief comparison test with the '03 Springfield, which is lighter and handier, but not really that much more accurate. The battle sights of the '17 are superior to those of its predecessor.

The Model 1917 was used by the United States until well into World War II, where it performed yeoman service as a training rifle. Great numbers of them were also used by the British after 1940.

While the '03 is a lighter, handier arm than the '17 Enfield, it is not that much more accurate. Alvin York dispatched a number of Bosch in the Argonne with his favorite '17.

Thomas H. Rynning

Adventurer With a Six-Gun.

By Phil Spangenberger

Ranger Webb cautiously entered the Cowboy Saloon in Douglas, Arizona Territory, to investigate the shot he had heard. As he did, the owner shoved a gun into his face so hard that he cut his cheek to the bone. Webb quickly shot him through the heart, turning the barkeeper's own trap against him. As the mortally wounded man spun around, Webb fired again, hitting him in the heart a second time. Almost immediately three more Rangers ran into the bar; one of them was a 6-foot-tall man by the name of Tom Rynning, then captain of the Arizona Rangers. As Rynning entered the bar, a half-breed dealer at a crap table to his right took a shot at him. The bullet missed and hit a fellow Ranger in the lung. Without turning, Rynning fired a back-handed shot at the dealer, breaking the man's arm and hitting him in the side with the single shot. Then it was over almost as quickly as it had started, with the opposition down, the place quieted, and the lawmen quickly took control of the situation.

The event just described was typical of the type of action that made up the career of Thomas H. Rynning, a man who, through a varied and colorful life, was often forced to resort to the use of a gun whether it be to keep the peace or to save his own neck. It was his able handling of firearms that helped to bring him through more tight spots than the average gunfighter could hope to survive.

Thomas H. Rynning was an all-round frontiersman, an excellent horseman and a crack shot with either pistol or rifle. He posed for this picture in 1903 while serving as captain of the Arizona Rangers. His saddle scabbard contains his M-1895 Winchester. (Arizona Historical Society)

Thomas H. Rynning

Tom Rynning was born in Beloit, Wisconsin in 1866. Both of his parents died by the time he was 12 years old and he went to live with his uncle at a lumber camp on the northern border of the state.

Young Tom found himself "frozen in" with his uncle that winter of 1878-79, but his restless spirit would not allow him to stay much longer than the first sign of the intense cold letting up. He made himself a pair of snowshoes and with the help of a French 'breed, made his way downriver to Marinette, Wisconsin. He stayed there until March when the waters in that part of the country were navigable and took a boat to Chicago to stay with his sister, where he began serving an apprenticeship as a stair-builder. This trade couldn't hold Tom back from fulfilling his childhood dreams of going

Rynning used Colt revolvers throughout his entire career. This example is the Single Action Army revolver in .45 caliber with a 7½-inch barrel and walnut stock, the standard issue cavalry sidearm. (Author's collection)

West and fighting Indians, so at the age of 16, he struck south and west for Texas, then the center of the many tales of Western adventure he had envisioned.

His journey took him to a little town named Cline, Texas, 73 miles west of San Antonio at the railhead of the Southern Pacific. His first job was as a bullwhacker with a local freighting outfit.

Though Tom Rynning was in the West, he still wasn't a cowboy until a local cattleman by the name of

Moulton took a liking to him and offered him a job on his ranch as a cowpuncher. He gladly signed on, finally beginning to realize his dreams.

Young Rynning had been working the frontier in his eastern duds up 'til this time, and his first appearance before the older hands around the ranch cost him his derby hat, which they immediately shot up as though it were some kind of monster. Tom didn't mind this playfulness much, as he was eager to adopt the clothing and equipment of the "cowboy" as soon as possible. Shortly after going to work for Moulton, Tom rode into nearby Del Rio and got his much-wanted and needed rigging of wide sombrero, chaps and other implements of cowboy life.

Tom Rynning considered his six-shooter the cowboy's most useful piece of equipment at this time. According to him, the punchers of the early '80s generally wore them in a .44-40 caliber with full belts of ammunition as well as a Winchester, (probably a '73 Model) in matching

Rynning served in the 8th U.S. Cavalry from 1885 to 1890. During this period the issue cavalry carbine was the M-1873 Springfield .45-70 "Trapdoor." Shown are the variations he probably used: (Top) 1879 model with folding buckhorn leaf rear sight and (bottom) M-1884 with Buffington type rear sight. This carbine has the sight-protecting barrel band introduced in 1890. (Author's collection)

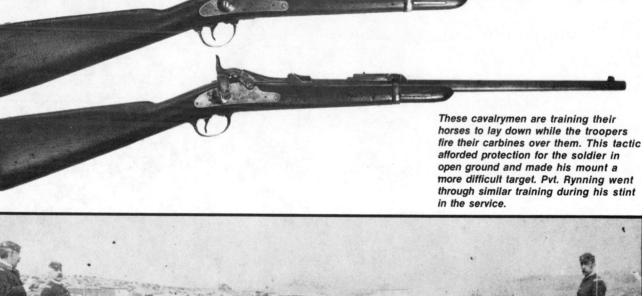

These cavalrymen are training their horses to lay down while the troopers fire their carbines over them. This tactic afforded protection for the soldier in open ground and made his mount a more difficult target. Pvt. Rynning went through similar training during his stint in the service.

caliber which was carried in a saddle scabbard. Their six-guns were used not only for protection against other men, red or white, but for such purposes as firing across the muzzles of lead steers in a stampede, in hopes that the flash from the shot would scare and turn them. They were also handy for shooting your horse if he got down on you and was thrashing and kicking about and you couldn't get free. Finally there was the old frontiersman's insurance policy against torture by the Indians—his last bullet was saved for himself.

As a young cowboy, Tom Rynning had many adventures with cattle rustlers, Indians, stampeding herds and the like on the range, but his first real excitemement and the one that he claimed stuck with him the most, was in 1883, in Dodge City, Kansas. His outfit had just completed a long trail drive up from Texas and was bedded down just south of the Arkansas River outside of town. Tom and another young

Some political string-pulling on the part of Theodore Roosevelt enabled the "Rough Riders" to receive the new smokeless powder M-1896 .30-40 cal. Krag carbines rather than the black powder Springfields that were standard issue to volunteer units during the Spanish-American War. (Courtesy Richard Ellis collection)

whole way with some of the town's inhabitants ducking for cover while others began to return fire.

When Rynning's outfit had reached the end of the street, most of them felt that they were just getting warmed up for the excitement and wheeled their ponies around, let out another yell and raced back through the street. This time they were greeted with heavy fire from peace officers, barkeeps, gamblers and anyone who could handle a gun. Several of the headstrong cowboys were done in on that second whirl through town as well as several of the citizens of Dodge. Tom and Sage had better sense than to go back for a second helping of trouble, so when they hit that west end of the street they just kept on riding. Rynning claimed that he doesn't think that either he nor Sage even drew their revolvers since they weren't expecting that kind of play.

The two scared punchers rode straight out of town and across the Arkansas River without going back to camp for their belongings, for fear of a posse being formed to round up their outfit. They continued their run for the next 3½ days without any sleep, very little to eat, and dodging trails and riding

were scheduled to be left behind. It did not set well with these ex-cowboys, who had enlisted for the sole purpose of fighting Indians, to be left out of the first chance for action. After much complaining, they succeeded in persuading their captain that they could ride and shoot as well as any man in the outfit and were taken along.

The U.S. Cavalry at this period was using the Springfield M-1873 "Trapdoor" carbine in .45-70 caliber and the Colt M-1873 "Peacemaker" in .45 caliber with the 7½-inch barrel. Some units were issued Smith & Wesson Schofield .45 caliber revolvers, but Rynning makes no mention of what he used, so it is fairly safe to assume that he carried the Colt which was the standard issue sidearm of the cavalryman.

The uprising of 1885 was put down successfully without starting another Indian war, but to Tom Rynning it was his first taste of campaigning with the Indian-fighting cavalry, and he loved it. There were plenty of tense moments during that reservation dispute. For a while it looked like the troops would be surrounded and annihilated. They were greatly outnumbered and there were many incidents of the Indians

The Colt New Army Model 1896 revolver in .38 caliber was the standard issue sidearm for U.S. Cavalrymen in 1898. Rynning would have carried one while serving with the "Rough Riders." (Courtesy Erich Baumann Collection)

companion by the name of Sage were too young to be served in the saloons so they just laid around camp and rested up. One evening an older cowboy rode into camp at just about dark, to get his six-shooter so he could go back and blast a group of gamblers he claimed had cheated him out of his earnings. It seems there was also a woman involved in the shenanigans, which meant that all hands would gladly be involved in saving their comrade's honor, for women were scarce in those days and it was worth the trip to town just to lay eyes on one.

The riled group of punchers rode into Dodge that evening, with Tom Rynning and his friend, Sage, riding drag. When they reached the scene of the supposed misdeal, the insulted cowboy drew his .44 and shot out the front lamp of the bar. Immediately all of the outfit let out a long howl and spurred their ponies into a gallop down the main street, shooting and hollering the

the bottom country for over 300 miles, until they were well within their home grounds of Texas, only stopping long enough to change horses. During this ride they were bedeviled by a cloud of dust in the eastern horizon which they figured was the law. It wasn't until about 15 years later that Rynning found out the posse actually had given only a short chase and the clouds on the horizon were probably made by the remnants of their own compadres fleeing for their freedom.

After a couple of years punching cattle, Tom Rynning still had not done any of the Indian fighting that he had come West for, so in February of 1885 he enlisted as a private in Troop D of the 8th U.S. Cavalry, then stationed at Fort San Felipe, Texas. In July of that same year, his regiment was ordered up to the Indian Territory (Oklahoma) to quell an uprising of Commanches and Cheyennes. He and his friends who had enlisted with him hadn't had sufficient military training so they

attempting to stampede horses from the picket lines and scattered shootings in the dark.

Upon their return to Fort San Felipe, Pvt. Rynning was sent to Fort Clark, Texas, to learn to become an army packer. He was soon told by his superior officers that he was an expert and was detailed to join C Troop, 8th Cavalry, at San Simon, Arizona to take part in the campaign then being waged against the renegade Apache, Geronimo. It was on this campaign that Tom Rynning got

Thomas H. Rynning

into his first real Indian fight.

Rynning was riding with his pack-train, well in the rear of two troops of cavalry when they were ambushed by the Apaches in the Mogollon Mountains of Arizona. The Apaches opened up on the troopers at about 150 yards distance, completely surprising the command. As fast as they could, the troopers dismounted and took up positions in a nearby gulch and in the rocks towards and below the Indians. After being forced to abandon their mounts in such a hurry, very few of the troopers had their canteens with them and the heat of the rocks quickly began to tell on them. Rynning complained that their heated condition and thirst was worsened by the gasses of the black powder arms they were using.

The fight went on throughout the afternoon with hardly any sighting of the hostiles other than an occasional death leap when one would be discovered in hiding and killed. One tactic used by the Indian fighters in that rocky terrain where

This stereoscope card shows a troop of "Rough Riders" standing to horse in full field equipment including 96 Krags & Colt D.A. New Army revolvers. The photo was probably taken while the outfit was training in Texas, as they are not yet wearing the tan cotton "tropical" uniforms used in Cuba. (Author's collection)

the opponent was hard to find, was to shoot at the side of a large boulder near where a hostile was suspected to be, and ricochet the bullet into him. It sometimes worked; however, the Apaches also tried this trick and for a while kept Rynning and his sergeant from returning fire while bullets were bouncing around their hiding spot. Once the firing ceased, Rynning placed his hat on the muzzle of his Springfield and slowly exposed it from behind his rock only to have the hat shot off.

Tom Rynning received a freak wound during this skirmish. While charging up through the rocks during the final rout of the hostiles, his revolver was shot from his hand. The bullet had struck the walnut grips and left him with a hand full of splinters.

As with most of the soldiers of the frontier army, the routine was not fight, fight, fight; rather, it was constant hard work, exposure to the elements and always keeping an eye peeled for the elusive foe. Rynning's experience was no different. He concluded the Geronimo campaign by packing for General Crook's headquarters mess in Mexico.

The rest of Tom Rynning's army experiences were pretty much routine duties for the period interspersed with Indian uprisings and reservation disputes in the central and northern plains.

He finally mustered out of the service in the winter of 1889-90 after, as he said in his life story, *Gun Notches,* by Frederick A. Stokes Co., Publishers, "I'd had a belly full of Indian campaigning. From the Sierra Madres down in Old Mexico up to the Canadian line where the Sioux broke out every winter..."

Rynning headed back to the country of his youth only to find that the rest of his family had died and his friends had all left that part of the world. In 1891, Tom answered an ad for 1800 ex-regulars to act as guards of the Chicago Worlds Fair. They were called the Columbia Guard. It was during his stay there that he met "Buffalo Bill" Cody and performed in his show.

Cody offered Rynning a job with his show and a chance to tour Europe, but Tom's heart still belonged to the west. He quit the Columbia Guard in 1893 and headed west for Los Angeles and finally to Tucson to work for the Southern Pacific Railroad, building bridges and other construction work. He soon left the railroad and started his own contracting business with a friend and partner, which proved quite a profitable venture. This business, however, gave way to the call of adventure when the Spanish-American War broke out in 1898. Tom quit his business, turning his share over to his partner, and travelled to Phoenix

Troop H—Captain Curry—"Rough Riders."
Copyright 1898 by Strohmeyer & Wyman

to enlist in the Arizona contingent of the "Rough Riders."

This unit shipped out for San Antonio, Texas for basic training before being sent over to Cuba. Rynning had enlisted in Phoenix as a private, but due to his past experience in the service, he was promoted quickly to sergeant and by the time the outfit had reached Cuba, he was again quickly commissioned as a lieutenant.

Through some political string-pulling, Theodore Roosevelt was able to procure the new smokeless powder .30-40 caliber Model 1896 Krag-Jorgensen carbines for his "Rough Riders," rather than the older black powder Springfield M-1873 .45-70 carbines that were being issued to the other volunteer regiments. They were also issued the Colt New Army Model 1896 .38 caliber revolvers.

The "Rough Riders" had a pretty active time of it in that war with Lt. Tom Rynning being in the thickest of the action. The unit took part in some pretty hot engagements, which led them to their famous charge up San Juan Hill. Lt. Rynning was in charge of his troop during that famous battle, as his commanding officer was suffering from heat fatigue.

During the advance, Rynning's troop was split up by the appearance of another troop, but throughout the assault, he kept his men moving forward. At one point, Rynning's men became mixed up with several members of the 9th U.S. Cavalry and they all continued the advance under his direction. After crossing Kettle Hill, which lay between the U.S. troops and the Span-

iards on San Juan Hill, the soldiers rushed San Juan Hill and took it with a hot fight.

That evening after the battle, the Spaniards attempted to retake San Juan Hill. All along the line there was heavy fighting. Rynning found himself firing with the American sharpshooters for awhile and on one occasion worked a Gatling gun. However, not being experienced with that sort of firearm, he quickly burned up a couple of barrels.

At the close of the war, Rynning visited Washington, D.C. and New York City before returning west. During his stay in the East, he received a visit from Dr. Gatling, the inventor of the famous gun bearing his name. Gatling was interested in Tom's opinion of the arm. Rynning told the inventor of his limited experience with the gun but mentioned that he had seen it perform in more capable hands, and was much impressed with the gun.

Tom Rynning's expertise with firearms also brought him together with the actor, Dustin Farnum, while he was playing "The Squaw Man." After an evening's performance, Rynning and his companion went backstage at the actor's invitation and taught him the proper way to wear a six-gun and belt—"cowboy" style—and how to walk like a plainsman. Farnum was very interested in doing it right, and was pleased to have such expert instructors.

By 1902, Rynning had married and settled down in Arizona Territory, when President Roosevelt and Governor Brodie of Arizona asked Tom to head up and reorganize the newly formed Arizona Rangers. At

Tom Rynning (sitting far left) and his Arizona Rangers posed for this photo during the Morenci, Arizona mine strike of 1903. They are armed with their issue 95 Winchesters and Colt Peacemakers. In the front row, however, one ranger still favors his 73 Winchester. (Arizona Historical Society)

this time the Rangers were 14 strong, but under Rynning's command they were expanded to a force of 25 men. These Rangers were issued Model 1895 Winchester carbines in .30-40 Krag caliber and Colt .45 caliber Peacemaker revolvers.

Turn-of-the-century Arizona was a raw country. Her citizens were hardened from over 50 years of Indian fighting and frontier living conditions, and the territorial status brought more than her share of unsavory characters within her borders. It would take a hard man backed by devoted deputies to keep the soon-to-be state in the hands of law-abiding people. Tom Rynning was just such a man. With his force of Rangers, he kept the territory clear of rustlers and other desperados who would have turned that land into a haven of crime.

The law of the gun prevailed and many times they were brought to play when no other course seemed open, but on more than one occasion, Rynning's word was enough to ease the pressure of a coming fight. Sometimes just the strength of his talk could avert trouble before it began.

One such incident occurred in 1902, in Douglas. A barkeep and pretty rough customer by the name of Walker Bush had forcibly kicked his (Bush's) wife out of their home.

Thomas H. Rynning

She complained to Constable Al Kerr, and he and two deputies, one of them a Ranger, went to Bush's Coney Island Saloon No. 2, only to walk into the wrong end of a double-barrel shotgun which Bush jammed into the belly of the officer closest to him. In this manner he backed the constables out of the bar and locked and barricaded himself inside along with two female hostages. Kerr decided to blow up Walker's saloon, so he planted dynamite around the building. However, since one of the men with him was one of Rynning's Rangers, he decided to wait for Rynning before he made his move.

Captain Rynning was away on a two-day trip, and upon his return, Kerr explained the circumstances. Tom felt that he could get Bush from the saloon and thus save the women and much gun play. He cautiously approached the adobe building and reached around the corner and knocked on the door, pulling his hand back quickly in case Bush

This Arizona Ranger (right) armed with a 95 Winchester and his companion who is using a lever-action Marlin rifle, are armed for a manhunt. They both rely on Colt Single Actions for their sidearms. Men such as these served with distinction under the able leadership of Capt. Rynning. (Arizona Historical Society)

off the second I stick my snoot out of here!'' Bush exclaimed.

"No, they won't. I'll take care of you if you come to court with me. You won't be in the least danger. It's pretty late now, but I'll come and get you in the morning if you promise that you'll come . . . ''

One of the women said, "You do it, Bush. Tom's word is good.''

"I know dam' well it's good.

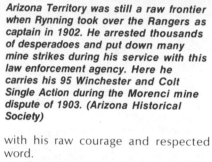

Arizona Territory was still a raw frontier when Rynning took over the Rangers as captain in 1902. He arrested thousands of desperadoes and put down many mine strikes during his service with this law enforcement agency. Here he carries his 95 Winchester and Colt Single Action during the Morenci mine dispute of 1903. (Arizona Historical Society)

with his raw courage and respected word.

Sometimes the six-gun was the only way out for Captain Rynning and his Rangers, and if that were the case, their ability to think cooly and handle their guns aptly usually made them the victors in any scrimmage in which they might find themselves.

The Chiricahua Mountains in Southeast Arizona was the scene of one incident that called for fast thinking and faster shooting. Rynning and fellow Ranger Dave Allison had been trailing a one-armed desperado who had killed a school teacher. They tracked the man to a rock cabin which he was using as a hideout. It was a small building with only one entrance; located in the front. The two Rangers didn't have the time to stay around long enough to smoke the bad man out so they slipped up to the door unnoticed and busted through it together. They surprised the outlaw, but he got his gun out instantly. The two men confused him so badly that he didn't know which one to shoot first, which allowed the Rangers enough time to fire the first shots. Ranger Allison's shot hit the man in the leg and Rynning's bullet went through the man's flank.

The desperado's comment, as taken from *Gun Notches*, was "God-

decided to send a load of buckshot through it. The following conversation from Rynning's life story, *Gun Notches*, was as follows.

"Who's there?'' Bush shouted.

"Tom Rynning'' was the captain's reply. "Come along out, Bush.''

"No, I'll be damned if I do. Them bastards'll blow my roof

What time does court open?'' Bush queried.

"Nine o'clock in the morning— I'll be here about a quarter to nine." was Rynning's answer.

The next morning Bush went with Rynning as he had promised. He received his fine and gave no more trouble after that. Tom Rynning had averted some real trouble damit, I was so rattled when I see two of you I didn't know which one to shoot first and you beat me to it."

Rynning's shooting became instinctive after his many years of handling guns. One such instance occurred when he was arresting a law-breaker. The man was sitting with his back towards Rynning, and when he was told that he was under arrest, he drew his pistol without turning in the chair, and being left-handed, fired it across his right shoulder. Tom Rynning immediately shot back, shooting off one of the man's fingers from his gun hand before he could get off another shot.

Rynning and his Rangers generally had *carte blanche* on crossing the border after villains and found it necessary to do so many times, with the thanks of the Mexican government. However, in the summer of 1906, Rynning, along with 300 men, crossed the border as civilians to volunteer for duty in the Mexican Army. Their mission was to help put down a revolt of Mexican miners who had a small group of American engineers under siege in La Cananea, a mining district in the Cananea Mountains of northern Mexico. Rynning was sworn in as a colonel and took charge of the American volunteers who acted under Mexican General Torres' orders.

The force moved by Mexican troop train down to the mining district and arrived on the scene during one of the assaults on the barricaded Americans. The relief force fought back the Mexican miners, quickly and restored order in short time. During the fracas, Rynning received word that there was some pretty heavy sniping going on over at the mining complex hospital. He double-timed it over to that spot to try to get some of the women, who were tending the wounded, to a safer spot. They refused to go as they said that the inside of the house was no safer than the porch where they were, due to the thin wooden walls. While Tom was talking to them, three Mexicans began shooting at him from about 200 yards away. Rynning quickly returned fire with his rifle, hitting the three snipers with as many shots.

Not long afterwards, with the revolt quieted and with the regular Mexican troops on the scene, the Americans moved out and returned to Arizona.

Rynning remained as captain of the Arizona Rangers until 1907, when Governor Kibbey asked him to take charge of the Territorial Prison at Yuma. Tom felt that most of his work with the Rangers was through by then, having cleaned up a good deal of territory, and he accepted the position.

He tackled this new challenge with the same old vitality that pulled him through every one of his earlier adventures. He had sent a lot of men to this same prison, and even though they were once his enemies, they quickly learned to respect this frontiersman who was now in charge of their lives.

He instituted many prison reforms based on hard discipline, tempered with an understanding of the rougher man's way of life. He built a new penitentiary at Florence, Arizona by using prison labor and paying them with two days off of their sentences for every day of work completed.

Rynning was able to complete the $1½ million facility for only $182,000 plus convicts' time off of their sentences. During the construction, there were many times when prisoners were miles away from any guarded area performing some duty, yet only one man really escaped.

Rynning never forgot his earlier training or the importance of firearms handling while serving as warden either. He took the shotguns away from the guards and issued them rifles, making them practice on a rifle range on Saturdays. Those who could not qualify were dismissed.

Tom Rynning died on June 18, 1941 at the age of 75. He was an adventurer, yet a man of peace, but one who was not afraid to step into a fracas with or without his guns when the need arose.

Few men have made vows to themselves during childhood that they have kept. Tom Rynning did. Impressed by the reports of the Custer battle in 1876, he promised himself that he would someday go west and fight Indians. Rynning not only kept that vow, but he became the sort of man that for ages to come, men will envy and respect, for what he did and what he was—cowboy, cavalryman, Rough Rider, Arizona Ranger, gunfighter.

Rynning "volunteered," and was made a colonel in the specially recruited American contingent of the Mexican Army in order to help rescue fellow countrymen during the La Cananea Copper Mine revolt of 1906 in Sonora, Mexico. Here Rynning (left center) with two fellow Rangers, parley with Col. Emilio Kosterlitzky and his Mexican Rurales. (Arizona Historical Society)

Shooting Impression

Colt .45 Peacemaker

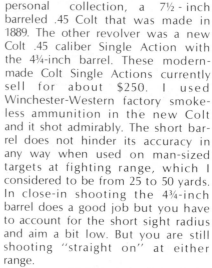

The legendary Colt .45 "Peacemaker" is by far the most popular handgun in the world. It is a reliable and powerful six-shooter that was the favorite of many gunfighters. (Author's collection)

By Phil Spangenberger

There are probably more photos of the 1873 Colt "Peacemaker" revolver in this book than any other gun. It was by far the most popular gun on the American frontier from the time of its introduction in the mid-1870s on. This revolver has become legendary. No other gun even comes close to the record of usage that the "Peacemaker" has.

First introduced in 1873, the weapon was strictly a military sidearm. It was issued to the U.S. Cavalry in .45 caliber with a 7½-inch barrel. The civilian population of the West did not have a chance to purchase one of Colt's new cartridge revolvers until the mid-70s. However, once it was made available to them, it caught on fast, and although the designers back in Hartford, Connecticut kept introducing faster-shooting sixguns, none of them ever really took the place of the Single Action revolver until well

Spitting flame and smoke, the "Peacemaker" Colt fires the cavalry load of 28 grains of black powder with a 250-grain slug. This gun throws its lead with great accuracy and a lot of punch.

after the Frontier had passed into memory.

The Colt Single Action Army revolver was the favorite of many of the most feared and/or respected gunmen in the West, including Wyatt Earp, Doc Holliday, the Daltons, etc. The list could go on and on and still only name a portion of the professional and part-time gunmen who chose this pistol as their fighting companion. By 1896, there were about 165,000 Single Actions circulating around the world and a large number of them went to the American West to make or break the law. They were available in a number of chamberings including .32-20, .38-40, .41, .44-40 and .45. The last being the most popular. This was the one used by the U.S. Army and was the first caliber that the Single Action was produced in.

Two guns were used in this shooting impression. One, from my personal collection, a 7½-inch barreled .45 Colt that was made in 1889. The other revolver was a new Colt .45 caliber Single Action with the 4¾-inch barrel. These modern-made Colt Single Actions currently sell for about $250. I used Winchester-Western factory smokeless ammunition in the new Colt and it shot admirably. The short barrel does not hinder its accuracy in any way when used on man-sized targets at fighting range, which I considered to be from 25 to 50 yards. In close-in shooting the 4¾-inch barrel does a good job but you have to account for the short sight radius and aim a bit low. But you are still shooting "straight on" at either range.

In my old Colt, I duplicated the period loads of 28 grains for the cavalry and 40 grains of black powder for the factory load with a 250-grain bullet. Both loads performed well, but the 40-grain charge is certainly noticeable after shooting the lighter load which I am used to. Cocking and firing the piece went smoothly, after I had put 40 or more rounds through the pistol. The gun just doesn't seem to want to jam.

Because of the "Peacemaker" balance, it is a fun gun to play with. It is easy to twirl and flip and after handling it for a while, one could easily understand how some of the gun tricks of the Old West could be performed. A practiced hand with a Colt Single Action can do wonders with it.

The Single Action Army, also known as the "Peacemaker," "Frontier," "Equalizer," "Hogleg" and a score of other affectionate terms was *the gun of the West*. It is by far the most popular handgun ever made, and I am proud to own one. For further information concerning the Colt Single Action Army revolver write to: Colt Industries, Colt Firearms Div., 150 Huyshope Ave., Hartford, CT. 06102.

Ned Christie

Determined Cherokee Renegade.

By Clyde Good

The triumphant deputies were proud to pose with the body of the man they called "the most dangerous outlaw in Indian Territory." Their rifles are all Winchester M-'73s and '86s, with the exception of one "trapdoor" Springfield. (University of Oklahoma Library)

Ned Christie, once a member of the Executive Council of the Cherokee Nation, became a hunted man the night he faced U.S. Deputy Marshal Dan Maples with a gun in his hand.

Maples, of Bentonville, Arkansas, was sent to Tahlequah, capital of the Cherokee Nation, Indian Territory, by Marshal John Carroll at Fort Smith to serve a whiskey warrant on an Indian named John Parris. The Federal Court at Fort Smith had jurisdiction over not only white offenders in Indian Territory, but also over any Indian committing a crime to, or in, the company of a white.

The deputy arrived in Tahlequah, made camp, and waited until dusk to begin his investigations. Restless, and seeking a better vantage point, the lawman worked his way to a spot where the clear waters of Big Spring surged over flint pebbles that lined the bottom of the creek, near the cabin of suspected whiskey seller Nancy Shell. It had been a hot, sticky day and the smothering humidity still lingered.

Dusk became darkness and the rasping sound of katydids muffled the deputy's footsteps as he finally began easing his way forward. Pausing at the single-log foot bridge over Spring Branch, Maples searched the yellow glow of light in Nancy Shell's cabin for any suspicious movement.

He slid behind a tree abruptly as the cabin door opened and two men came out—both were Indians and one was quite tall. For an instant, light from the cabin spilled

across their faces and Maples recognized one of them as John Parris, the known violator of the federal whiskey law. The other man—Ned Christie—was unfamiliar to him.

Unaware of the lawman's presence, the pair strode unsuspectingly along the well-worn path toward the foot-log. The tall man stumbled clumsily, then regained his footing.

With a quick movement, Deputy Marshal Maples stepped up onto the bridge and yelled at the two men to halt. Instead, they turned and ran. Maples pulled his revolver and fired a warning shot, but almost simultaneously a second gunshot thundered through the darkness as fire spurted from Ned Christie's gun.

The lawman toppled from the log and splashed face down into the

waters of Spring Branch. He was dead. Cautiously, the two men ran to the water's edge and one reached into the stream rolling the body over.

To their horror, they saw a silver badge pinned to his soiled shirt. Their panic-stricken footsteps thudded on the bridge as they ran for the woods.

It was May 5, 1885. Ned Christie had crossed over to the wrong side of the law.

The worried Indian left Parris and headed for the home of Ned Grease, where he was staying while the Executive Council was in session. He arrived breathless, now sober, and went directly to talk with a close friend who was a member of the Cherokee Senate. The senator advised that Ned say nothing, go about his regular business as usual, and wait to see what happened. Ned Christie, son of Watt Christie, was born into the prominent full-blooded Cherokee family on December 14, 1852. He was a highly respected member of the Cherokee

Ned Christie

government, even though had no formal education. He preferred to speak in Cherokee, but could communicate in broken English and he understood the language well. An excellent marksman, the 6-foot, 4-inch Indian served as a bodyguard to Principal Chief Dennis Bushyhead. He was, by trade, a blacksmith and gunsmith. Ned possessed a

the killer of Maples. The investigation quickly led to Nancy Shell, who in turn named John Parris as one of the suspects. She insisted she didn't know the identity of the tall Indian with him that night.

On a gamble, Deputy Thomas arrested a close friend of Parris'— Charlie Bobtail, who had just served a sentence in the penitentiary. Thomas was betting Bobtail knew where Parris was hiding and figured he was anxious to avoid going back to prison.

home in the Going Snake District, knew it had been done.

Ned went to his father's home and got two 44 caliber Colts his father had carried during the Civil War. Ned studied the technique used by the Colt factory to convert the cylinders from muzzle loading to breech loading. The Indian gunsmith worked carefully and before the day was out the Model 1860 Army revolvers would fire the modern metallic cartridges.

Christie used a reliable .58 cali-

Most of this group of ten deputy U.S. marshals who tracked down Ned Christie seemed to favor Model 1873 Winchester rifles. Two men sport the ubiquitous .45 Colt Single Action Army, while the deputy at the far right holds a .45-70 Springfield rifle. The lawmen seated in center and left of center appear to have M-1886 Winchesters. (Oklahoma Historical Society)

quick temper and he had developed a keen taste for whiskey.

The next morning, a somber Ned Christie went to the Executive Council meeting as usual. Tahlequah was alive with curiosity and excitement over the discovery of Maples' body. Even the Executive Council meeting closed early. Beset with inner turmoil, as calmly as he could manage, Ned mounted his horse and found the trail for home.

Dan Maples was well-liked and the town of Bentonville offered a $500 reward for the capture of his slayer. The governor of Arkansas also offered a reward.

U.S. Deputy Marshal Heck Thomas rode for the Cherokee Nation on May 16, 1885, to hunt for

He was right, as Parris was arrested and arraigned, along with Charlie Bobtail, on a charge of murder. When Parris finally talked, it was to implicate respectable Ned Christie as the killer.

At this point, facts become elusive, but by the time the murder warrant was issued, Ned Christie, at

ber Springfield musket as a shotgun, and later bought a new Model 73 Winchester in .44-40 caliber from Eli Wilson, a close friend. Ammunition for his new rifle was interchangeable with that of his pistols.

Judge Isaac Parker's deputies decided Christie was holed up in the rolling hills some 15 miles southeast of the Cherokee Capital, where Ned's cabin and blacksmith and gunsmith shop stood on the west bank of Bidding Creek.

Deputy Joe Bowers rode into the Going Snake District to serve Ned Christie with the murder warrant. As he neared, the Indian fugitive fired from the dense undergrowth of forest, and struck the lawman's leg. A charge of assaulting a

Ned Christie posed for an Indian Territory photographer holding one of his self-converted Model 1860 Colt Army revolvers, and wearing the other in a holster. The pair of pistols and the Model 1873 Winchester were all chambered for .44-40. (Oklahoma Historical Society)

bor children ran to the Christie homestead to gather the spent brass cartridges for Ned. He played marbles with the children and laughed warmly, while his son remained in the house, armed and ready should the posse return.

In 1889, Heck Thomas decided to get Ned Christie. Deputies L.P. "Bones" Isbel, Dave Rusk, and Salmon rode southward from Vinita, Indian Territory, to meet him. Leaving their horses in the hills, they carefully moved in on Ned's distant cabin. Their cautious approach lasted for three days, and they were not discovered by Ned's unseen sentries.

On the fourth morning before daybreak, they inched into position near the house. But Christie's watchdogs caught scent of them and started barking.

Ned ran to the loft, kicked loose a board at the gable end and started shooting. Thomas ordered Christie to surrender but silence was his only answer.

The marshal called for him to send his wife out, if he was going to fight and Christie opened fire.

Heck Thomas had taken cover behind a small outbuilding Christie utilized as a blacksmith and gunsmith shop. The deputies set it afire, hoping that would draw Christie out into the open.

Trying to get a better look, Isbel leaned out from behind a tree for an instant. Ned's keen eyes spotted him and a shot sent Isbel staggering back with a bloodied shoulder. As Thomas quickly pulled his long-time friend to cover, Christie's wife sprinted for the safety of the woods like a frightened rabbit.

The morning breeze blew the blaze toward the cabin and the flames danced higher as they engulfed the log structure. Christie's boy leaped from the smoke-blanketed structure and ran for the tree line. Thinking it was Ned, Rusk and Salmon gunned him down.

The deputies were attending to Isbel's wound when Christie jumped from the loft and made for the forest. Thomas leveled his rifle at Christie and it roared. Ned grabbed at his forehead and fell into the brush at the edge of the timber.

Thomas left Isbel in the care of Deputy Salmon while he and Dave Rusk searched the woods in vain for the fugitives. Indian friends located the wounded pair and took them to an Indian doctor.

Deputy Isbel lost the use of his right arm as the result of Christie's accuracy; Ned's boy suffered from wounds in the lung and hips, but eventually recovered.

Ned's injury was the most seri-

federal officer was now filed against Christie.

There was conflict in the Indian sense of justice and the white man's standard of law and order. Deputy John Fields understood this and decided to try to talk Christie into surrendering. Fields arrived early in the morning. Ned lunged out of the cabin door, his Winchester in his hand, and the sincere lawman turned his horse for a hasty retreat. The eagle-eyed marksman shot once, striking Fields in the neck. When he saw the deputy kept on riding Christie did not fire again. A third charge was filed.

It is told that Christie put out the word: "No want to kill another marshal . . . just want them stop sneaking around."

Meanwhile, back in Fort Smith, U.S. Marshal Carroll advised his deputies to "quit trying to take him alive." Aware of the coming change in tactics, Christie's neighbors be-

came his warning system. Christie knew of a stranger's approach an hour before he arrived.

At these times, Ned's wife brought up extra water from the rock-girthed spring, while Ned and his son filled leather pouches with extra ammunition, took positions and waited for the attack.

Once, as they waited, a large posse rode up. During the skirmish, Ned wounded three of them, but silenced his smoking '73 to allow the possemen to remove their battered comrades out of the range of fire.

When the gunfire ceased and the woods became silent, the neigh-

Ned Christie

ous. Thomas' bullet had ripped through the bridge of Ned's nose, torn into his right eye, then lodged itself just above the temple.

Christie was taken to a prominent hill, now known as Ned's Fort Mountain. It was about a mile north of his home, and there they kept him until he recuperated. Ned's loyal tribesmen built a stout stone and wood structure, camouflaged from view by massive boulders and dense foliage surrounding it. From the shelter at the crest of the hill, Ned and his allies could watch the only trails winding into the area. Fresh water could be easily obtained from the spring on the same plateau as Ned's make-shift hospital.

on the second floor small slits that a rifle barrel could be stuck through for shooting.

It was fear that pounded every hand-wrought spike into the sturdy logs—not a fear of death, but of the humiliation and shame of Parker's gallows and the hangman's noose.

Ned carefully cleared away brush and stones from around the area, that might afford a man cover. Ned told his family and friends: "I no give up, I die here fighting!"

Of all the lawmen, U.S. Deputy Marshal Dave Rusk was the most persistent in his attempt to capture Ned Christie. It was humiliating for Rusk and the other deputies that a single Indian had held off the entire force of Indian Territory lawmen for four years.

Rusk, in 1891, tried his hand at

Christie was receiving help from some cohorts.

Shortly after the shooting started, four Indian possemen fell wounded. A strange gobbling sound could be heard over the intermittent rifle blasts. The possemen recognized it immediately as the Cherokee death call. Rusk looked at his four injured men as the gobbling sound continued. There was no choice but to call off the fight.

On two other occasions, in a lone effort, the stubborn deputy crept into spying distance of Ned's fort. In each instance, the crack-shot Cherokee teasingly sent a bullet tearing through the crown of the old man's black hat.

Aware of the identity of the pesky deputy, Ned sent a young Indian boy to Tahlequah with a mes-

Very proud of his once-handsome features, the grotesque disfigurement of his face and his sightless right eye served as constant reminders; Ned grew vicious with his hatred of the white man.

When Ned regained his strength he returned the mile home, stared in silence at the ashes, crossed Bidding Creek to higher ground and commenced to build again.

After acquiring a steam-driven saw mill, the skilled craftsman constructed a two-story log structure. Its walls were two logs thick, and lined with oaken two-by-fours. There were few openings, only a door, and

The members of the posse that killed Ned Christie were photographed near the Indian's steam-driven saw mill. Their conglomeration of long arms includes (l-r) M-1873 Springfield rifle, M-1886 Winchester, another Springfield and a pair of double-barrel shotguns. A number of handguns are also in evidence, but are not identifiable. (Oklahoma Historical Society)

apprehending the wily outlaw Indian. He formed a posse of Indians known to be loyal to the federal government. As the posse took positions in the forest around the clearing, a barrage of rifle fire emanated from the cabin-fort. It was apparent

sage for editor Robert Fletcher Wyly to be printed in the *Cherokee Advocate:* "I thought I saw a big black potato bug in my garden, but it turned out to be the hat of that 'little marshal'—Dave Rusk!"

Rusk wisely gave up his single-handed pursuits, knowing full well that Christie could have as easily put the bullet through his head instead of his hat.

For added income, Rusk owned a general store in Oaks, a small community north of Tahlequah. Rusk's family lived in the town, and he began to fear for their safety. He moved them to Joplin, Missouri, to stay with relatives—and just in time. While the deputy was away, a group of Cherokees rode up to the store and dismounted, except for Ned Christie who rode his horse straight into the building.

The men ransacked the store while Christie held William Israel, a Cherokee clerk, at gun-point. The startled clerk was then forced out the back door. One of the desperados discovered a barrel of tar in the yard and came up with the idea to make good use of it. They tarred and feathered the helpless clerk and poured raw whiskey down his throat, sampling a little as they did. The bandits' shots then chased the drunken clerk into the woods.

Christie put the store to the torch. As the flames kindled and rose, his one good eye stared into the blaze, remembering the flames on another day when they had reduced his cabin and shop to ashes.

He turned and rode away down the dusty road, whooping. From this time on, Christie was accused of many crimes he never committed. Ned fought more battles and wounded more of Judge Parker's deputies than any other outlaw in the history of Parker's court.

Somehow through it all, Christie held to his intent not to kill another marshal. He continued to near-miss, or to graze a man, hoping only they would finally go away and leave him alone. His Cherokee mind could not comprehend that each injured man and each passing year that he remained at large, were a mounting disgrace to the lawmen. Even they began to wonder when he would come to understand, and change his point of aim.

The relentless marshals regrouped at Ned's fort on October 11, 1892. Deputies Rusk, Charley Copeland, Milo Creekmore and D.C. Dye were among the attackers.

Two men were wounded before the deputies risked taking a different approach than their bullets, useless against the formidable structure. They discovered an old wagon the outlaw had used to haul lumber for his log stronghold, and proceeded to fill it with brush and scraps of timber and set it ablaze. With a strenuous heave, the lawmen sent the flaming wagon rolling toward the fortress. To their dismay, the fiery cart smashed into Ned's outhouse, dumped the harmful cargo, and creaked to a halt.

In a final effort, the angered U.S. deputies threw several sticks of dynamite at the building, only to have them bounce off the wall, lose their fuses, and redden the ears of the fuming lawmen. Following this

After Christie's body was returned to Ft. Smith it was propped up and placed on the porch of the federal building for school children to see. His .44-40 Model 73 Winchester was placed in his hands for effect. (University of Oklahoma Library)

onslaught Ned lived in peace for three weeks.

Deputy Marshal Paden Tolbert led his large posse as they wound along the rocky trail, hidden by huge copper-leafed oaks. It was November 1, 1892, and this band, like the others came well armed. This time, they brought a three-pounder cannon which was shipped by train from Coffeyville, Kansas, then hauled laboriously by wagon into the rolling, rocky hills of the Going Snake District.

In addition to this, they carried 30 tins of black powder for the piece, fuses, three boxes of matches, and six sticks of dynamite. The posse arrived by nightfall, unnoticed. On November 2, in the dim light of the pre-dawn hours, the

men encircled the clearing and sought protection behind any available obstruction.

Then, through the murky light, they saw the cabin door open and a figure step out with a bucket in his hand. The lawmen centered him in their rifle sights and called for his surrender. Arch Wolf dived for the door as fire jutted from anxious Winchesters.

The battle raged on throughout the day, but the lawmen's bullets dropped harmlessly as snowflakes when they smashed into the tough log walls. Then the deputies readied their cannon, taking deadly aim. Again luck was with Ned. The projectiles left the cannon barrel with impressive force but hit the fort with a deafening crack, and bounced back into the clearing, leaving the logs skinned but the structure unmolested. After the 30th shot from the cannon, the tired breech split.

When darkness arrived, the lawmen retired deep into the woods to plan for the coming day. In their re-

Ned Christie

treat, they happened on the charred remains of the rear axle and wheels of Ned's old wagon used in the October 11 fight. The crafty deputies came up with an idea for their last-ditch effort. With oak planks found by the abandoned sawmill, the desperate posse built a thick wall buffer and mounted it upon the wagon axle. Taking another board they made a tongue to guide the rolling barricade.

The makeshift shield was completed shortly after midnight and the officers pushed it to the edge of the clearing.

Deputies Paden Tolbert, G.S. White, Bill Smith, Bill Ellis and Char-

against the bottom log.

The noisy staccato sound of gun fire echoed in the hills as lawmen made for the dim image of the tree line. As they went, the pounding of bullets could be felt as they thumped the strong oak boards, cut from the same native timber as those which protected Christie.

The eerie gobbling became audible above the consistent blasts. The men reached the forest safely as a jarring explosion occurred. The blast lit the sky and the posse watched as debris peppered the ground. As their eyes readjusted to the darkness, they saw a small fire in the cabin through a gaping hole in the south wall. The deputies readied their firearms and waited.

As Paden Tolbert searched

instantly.

Sam Maples, vengeful son of the slain deputy who had joined the posse at West Fork, ran up and emptied his six-shooter into the lifeless body of Christie. Ned was placed on the door of his cabin, which had blown free with the blast. He was loaded onto the lawmen's supply wagon and hauled down the lonely trail to Fayetteville, where Dr. H.W. Wood issued a death certificate. The triumphant group with their trophy boarded a train at Fayetteville and headed for Fort Smith.

Upon arrival, they took the body to the federal building and presented it to Marshal Jacob Yoes. A civic group asked if Christie's body could be put on display for

Christie's grave lies in a brush-shrouded family cemetery. The inscription reads: "He was at one time a member of the Executive Council of the C.N. He was a blacksmith by trade, and was a brave man."

ley Copeland, who was carrying six sticks of dynamite, manned the rolling wall as the remainder of the posse took positions around the clearing and commenced firing to provide diversion.

The dynamiters reached the cabin and began firing at the yellow flashes which surged from the gun ports on the second floor.

Meanwhile Copeland leaped for the wall of the cabin and placed the lethal bundle with its sizzling fuse through the hovering smoke for any

sign of Christie in the fiery cabin, he heard two quick rifle shots in a direction away from the fort. He went to check them out, but on the way six more sounded from the place Wess Bowman had been posted. He began to run.

Tolbert arrived to find Bowman nursing a wound on his face, and on the ground lay Christie, dead. As the story goes, Ned had followed the lingering smoke and was running frantically when he came charging out of the haze into young Bowman. The startled Indian let off a shot in the lawman's face. Only powder burned by the close call, Bowman quickly spun and fired at the outlaw as he passed, striking him behind the ear and killing him

This is all that remains today of the stone and wood structure built by Christie's allies on the crest of Ned's Fort Mountain. This is the spot where his Indian friends brought him after he had been shot and cared for him until he was healed.

the school children of Fort Smith. The deputies placed it on the federal building porch and there it remained for the afternoon. Ned's family came that evening and claimed the body.

After being pursued for 5½ years, and at the age of 39, Ned's watchful days were over. Ned Christie, an outlaw by accident, fell victim to the white man's whiskey and the white man's law. 🦅

Winston Churchill

Soldier, Adventurer, Statesman.

By Garry James

Winston proudly posed in his 4th Hussars full dress uniform after being gazetted to that regiment in 1896. He is holding a pattern 1822 Light Cavalry Officer's Sword.

The boy sprawled on the floor taking stock of his battle lines. Several hundred of Britain's finest were lined up against a polyglot horde of Sudanese, Zulus and Afghans, and the commander of the defenders was taking no chances on heathen surprises or weaknesses in his troop dispositions.

Suddenly the door to the nursery opened and a dignified, mustacheoed gentleman somberly dressed in a morning coat entered and surveyed the scene. Silently he made a formal inspection of the battle array, until after a full 20 minutes he spoke. "Winston, would you like to go into the Army?"

"Oh, yes please," the boy unhesitatingly answered.

From that inauspicious occasion began the career of one of the most famous statesmen in history, Sir Winston Churchill.

Winston Leonard Spencer—Churchill was born at Blenham Palace, ancestral home of the Dukes of Marlborough, in 1874. His father, Lord Randolph Churchill, was the second son of the Duke, and his mother was the American socialite Jenny Jerome. Lord Randolph was a promising Tory Member of Parliament, whom it was rumored would one day be prime minister.

In the manner of the times, young Winston was sent off to a series of boarding schools, where he displayed a profound lack of ability. As a lad he was considered too dull to learn Latin and Greek and was put with the bottom form boys to study English. He later admitted that this was the best thing that could

have happened, and his mastery of his mother tongue has been responsible for a wealth of literature.

Winston had supposed that his father had seen some germ of military genius in the small boy's array of toy soldiers, but in fact, Lord Randolph considered his son unfitted to the Bar and felt that the Army was an honorable, intellectually untaxing vocation.

Winston was sent to the exclusive Harrow boy's school where he studied in preparation for the entrance examination at the British Military Academy at Sandhurst. After two failures he finally managed to pass the test and was admitted with the provision that he be placed in the Awkward Squad for those who needed extra instruction.

To everyone's surprise, the young cadet began to apply himself, and soon became a model student. He relished strategy and musketry, and bemoaned the fact that the Brit-

Winston Churchill

ish army had not fought a "white" enemy since the Crimean War of 1854-56. He sincerely wished that he had lived 100 years earlier so that he could have been a subaltern of 19 with 20 years of fighting Napoleon ahead of him. Winston particularly excelled at horsemanship, and later offered the sage advice to parents, 'Don't give your son money. As far as you can afford it, give him horses."

He graduated in December of 1894, and was slated by his father to join the 60th Rifles, an infantry regiment. While still a cadet, however, he had been invited to dine at the Regimental Mess of the 4th Hussars. The dash and glitter of the officers dressed in their finery and the table set with souvenirs of 200 years of honorable and exciting duty had a heady effect. He conducted himself well and was invited to attend several other dinners. Colonel Brabazon of the 4th wrote to Winston's mother that he would be glad to have her son in his regiment, but his father was adamant that the boy should join the infantry. At this time Lord Randolph was suffering from the final stages of syphillis. His ca-

Hussars," he wrote; but Winston's head *was* turned.

Lord Randolph died in December of 1895, and Winston's remote, yet loving mother expressed no objection to her son's joining the cavalry. In March of the next year he was gazetted to the 4th Hussars and set off to undergo the strenuous Recruit Officer Training. The young officer loved the cavalry, but was realistic enough to realize that its days were numbered. He knew that all of Europe's fine columns of lancers, hussars and dragoons could be swept from the field by a "half dozen spoil-sports" in a trench with a Maxim gun.

Each British officer was granted two and a half months leave per year and the greater portion of this was usually spent on the hunting fields. Churchill had "invested" most of his allowance on polo ponies and consequently could not afford to join the sporting set.

Itching for action he, and a brother subaltern, received permission from his regiment and the Spanish Government to join the

Churchill (far right) and comrades as prisoners of the Boers. After his escape from the camp at Pretoria the Boers put out a reward for his return—dead or alive.

in selecting his pistol, with the major stipulation being that it chamber the .455 Service ammunition. While Churchill's memoirs do not mention a specific handgun, we can assume that it was more than likely one of the various models of the splendid Webley revolver then in favor with the British Army. At this time the official models were the Mark I and II. The Mark I was accepted in 1887 and was officially superseded in Oc-

Churchill as he appeared during the Boer War as a lieutenant of the South African Light Horse. He used the small pockets above his breast pockets to store loaded 10-round .30 Mauser clips.

tober 1894 by the Mark II. Both revolvers were in .455 caliber (although the Mark I was also chambered for the .476 and .442) had hinged frames, 4-inch barrels and were double action. The guns were blued with black vulcanite bird's head grips.

Webleys could be loaded very quickly and ejection was simultaneous upon breaking the gun. The .455 round, while not as powerful as the .45 Colt, was a sure man-stopper. Many officers purchased this type of revolver from such retailers as Boss & Co., Wilkenson or Westley Richards. Generally these were of superior finish, and might even be of earlier patterns such as the fine Webley-Green. Barrel lengths were not standard, and often 6 or 7½ inches was chosen. Adjutant General, Field Marshal Lord Wolseley suggested that a nickel-plated finish was superior to a blued one in tropical climates, and for this reason many officer's Webleys were nickeled. Grips might have been either checkered walnut or vulcanite.

Winston spent an interesting but unstimulating several weeks

reer was ruined and the family's financial situation was perilous. At this time, the British officer's pay was such that he could not be expected to maintain himself in the proper manner without outside income—usually from family allowances. An infantry officer's kit was far cheaper to maintain than a cavalry officer's and this had a great deal to do with Lord Randolph's desire that his son join the 60th Rifles. "Brabazon, who I know is one of the finest soldiers in the Army, had no business to go and turn that boy's head about going into the 4th

Spanish forces in Cuba as observers. The Spanish Army had been engaged in an interminable conflict with rebel forces, and a shipment of 80,000 fresh troops to the island indicated that the insurgence might be becoming more serious. Winston and his colleague packed their kits and set off for Havana in November of 1895.

At this time British officers were not issued sidearms, but they were required to purchase swords of the proper pattern as well as acceptable handguns. The War Department offered the officer a degree of latitude with the Spanish. He went on a long march in which some 4000 government forces were constantly sniped at by small bands of rebels as they wound aimlessly through the jungles. He was "under fire", and on one occasion a bullet passed within a foot of his head, striking a horse behind him. He noted that the rebels were primarily armed with single-shot Remington Rolling block rifles, while the Spaniards were using the superior M-1893 7x57mm Mauser magazine rifle, which, due to the Government Forces' cumbersome tactics, offered them little advantage.

ent minor injury which was to affect the future course of his service life.

The 4th Hussars were posted at Bangalore, and the easy life, coupled with cheap labor and platoons of servants and interminable polo games agreed with the young officer, although he soon began to yearn for action.

During a sojourn in London in 1897, Winston heard that there was trouble brewing with the Pathan tribesmen on the Indian Frontier. He cabled the commander of the British Field Force, Major General Sir Bindon Blood, with whom he was acquainted, and was allowed to join

young *Daily Telegraph* correspondent joined the Jeffreys force in the early evening, and spent a restless night as the Mamuds kept bullets whistling through camp until daybreak.

The next day found Winston accompanying a detachment of 85 men and five officers of the 35th Sikhs on their attempt to punish a village at the head of the valley. At first the mud houses looked deserted, but suddenly gunfire and shouts arose from the mountain side. The troops took cover and Churchill borrowed a .577-450 Martini-Henry single-shot rifle from the nearest

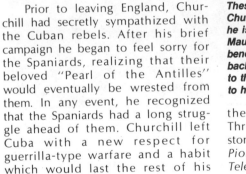

Prior to leaving England, Churchill had secretly sympathized with the Cuban rebels. After his brief campaign he began to feel sorry for the Spaniards, realizing that their beloved "Pearl of the Antilles" would eventually be wrested from them. In any event, he recognized that the Spaniards had a long struggle ahead of them. Churchill left Cuba with a new respect for guerrilla-type warfare and a habit which would last the rest of his life—a taste for Havana cigars.

In the spring of 1896 the 4th Hussars prepared to sail for India. The regiment would be posted there for at least a dozen years, and the officers were given ample opportunity to settle their affairs before leaving. Six months were spent in Hounslow, Middlesex in luxuriant idleness, with the major activities being the daily polo matches to which Churchill became addicted.

The regiment finally left for India, and after a voyage of about a month, the troop ship arrived at Bombay. While disembarking Winston strained his shoulder, an appar-

These two photos were taken after Churchill's escape from the Boers. Note he is wearing his .30 caliber M-1896 Mauser in a shoulder-stock holster beneath his right arm. In the background is an armored train, similar to the one Churchill was riding in prior to his capture. (Bettmann Archives)

the force as a correspondent. Through his mother's efforts Winston was retained as a writer by the *Pioneer* newspaper and the *Daily Telegraph*.

He rushed to the front and was forced to wait at the summit of the Malakand Pass for five days while Sir Bindon subdued the Bunerwals, another tribe with a valley of their own to protect. During this time Churchill put his kit in order and visited the officers mess where he developed another taste for which he would later become famous— whisky.

When Sir Bindon returned, the force of three brigades was ordered to move through the Mamud Valley where sniping by the Mamud tribesmen led Blood to send in a punitive force under General Jeffreys. The

soldier, in order to return fire. The Sikh was very content to hand Churchill cartridges while the young officer fired at the attackers. By now bullets were buzzing like hornets, but the soldiers found that by laying flat they were fairly safe.

It was finally decided that the detachment should retreat and as they arose and turned several officers and soldiers were hit. As it was a point of honor on the Indian Frontier not to leave wounded comrades, the able-bodied soldiers, including Churchill, grabbed the nearest wounded and dragged, pushed or pulled them along as best they could. Suddenly a dozen Pathan swordsmen rushed from a mud hut. Churchill, who had won honors in fencing, drew his sword and made ready to receive the leader of the

Winston Churchill

tribesmen. When the savage was about 20 yards away, he stopped and hurled a large stone. This gave Churchill a moment for reflection, and he decided that his revolver would serve better in this situation. Returning his sword to its scabbard, he drew his Webley, took deliberate aim and fired three rounds at the Pathan, who promptly stopped, ran back several yards and took cover behind a large rock.

Churchill glanced around and realized that he was alone. Quickly he ran to the nearest knoll where the Sikhs had taken cover. Bullets were still flying in all directions but miraculously, Churchill was unhurt.

Winston served for the remain-

Kitchener's staff. Kitchener, however, had different ideas. He was not pleased with the young subaltern's comments about his superior officers in *The Malakand Field Force* and felt that Churchill was strictly a glory hunter. Despite pressure brought to bear by high government officials, Kitchener insisted that there was no place on his staff for Churchill.

Finally he managed to arrange an attachment to the 21st lancers, and received this rather pessimistic message from the War Department: "You have been attached as a supernumerary Lieutenant to the 21st Lancers for the Soudan Campaign. You are to report at once at the Abassiyeh Barracks, Cairo, to the Regimental Headquarters. It is understood that you will proceed at your

mounted in front of the trigger guard which held 10 rounds of 7.63mm (.30) Mauser that were loaded by a strip clip. Its round, ribbed walnut grip gave the gun its nickname, the "broomhandle."

Churchill also arranged with the *Morning Post* to send back dispatches for which he would be paid £15 per column. This would help him defray expenses somewhat. Armed with his Mauser, his correspondent's assignment and the highest hopes for a new adventure, he proceeded to Egypt.

At daybreak on September 2, 1898 Kitchener's Anglo-Egyptian Army, including officers and men of the 21st Lancers, found themselves near Omdurman—only three miles from a force of 60,000 Dervishes. Churchill and seven troopers were

der of the expedition and then returned to Bangalore and Calcutta where he spent the winter writing his fascinating, controversial book, "The Malakand Field Force." The book was a runaway success with the public, but was viewed with a jaundiced eye by many of the older members of the Military Establishment—including the influential Sir Herbert Kitchener.

As soon as the Indian Frontier had quieted down, news reached Churchill that a new expedition was to be mounted in the Sudan. Its purpose was to capture Khartoum from the Khalifa and free the area from the control of the powerful Dervish Empire. Naturally Winston wanted to accompany the Army and tried to wrangle an appointment to

Churchill (rear, second from left) posed with Lord Kitchener (center, seated) and staff officers in South Africa in 1899. Earlier, Kitchener had refused to take Churchill to the Sudan because of a book the Young officer had written which criticized the high command. (Bettmann Archives)

own expense and that in the event of your being killed or wounded in the impending operations, or for any other reason no charge of any kind will fall on British Army funds."

Before leaving, Winston stopped in at the London store of Westley-Richards and purchased one of the new Model 1896 7.63mm Mauser automatic pistols and a wooden shoulder-stock holster. The Model 1896 was one of the first practical autos. It featured a box magazine

sent on an advance patrol, and his group carefully mounted a ridge and found considerable number of the fanatics awaiting them. They watched the enemy for some time, advancing at one point to within 400 yards of the gigantic force where they provoked a few stray shots. After potting with his Mauser at a patrol of Baggara horsemen, Churchill decided discretion was the better part of valor, and he only just got his men back to the infantry lines before the battle proper began.

Although Kitchener's force numbered only 20,000 as opposed to the enemy's 60,000, the Dervishes possessed but 20,000 rifles of varying makes, calibers and quality. Soon the contestants were battling it out and the 21st was ordered to ride out and determine how many of the Khalifa's forces stood between the British/Egyptian Army and Omdurman. The horsemen rode away in a southerly direction and soon found itself within sight of the city. Churchill commanded the second troop from the rear which included about 25 lancers.

The regiment continued to move forward over the hard ground, until about 300 yards away a large force of Dervishes suddenly appeared. The cavalry wheeled into line and sounded the bugle call for the charge.

Due to Churchill's earlier shoulder dislocation, he decided to use his Mauser instead of his sword, and prior to the gallop, he returned the edged weapon to its scabbard and drew his pistol. He had practiced

trigger. He was so close that the gun actually touched the man. Winston looked up just in time to see a chain mail-clad Arab horseman moving toward him about ten yards away. Again he fired the Mauser and the rider pulled off to the side.

By this time the 21st was completely enveloped by the enemy and troopers were fighting for their lives. Churchill soon found himself cut off from his comrades—everywhere he looked were rifles, spears and swords. Having no other choice, he hunched down in the saddle and spurred his horse forward. The remnants of the 21st were attempting to regroup themselves and he happily moved toward what was left of his troop about 300 yards away. Suddenly an unnoticed Dervish jumped up in the midst of the British horse-

Churchill's famous M-1896 .30 Mauser automatic pistol was left on the armored train prior to his capture and returned to him by the engineer of the train following his successful escape from the Boers. The gun was retailed by Westley-Richards and has "W.L.S. Churchill" engraved on the front of the magazine. (Sotheby Parke Bernet)

with the handgun during the campaign, and was fairly sure of its reliability and his own accuracy.

Suddenly he found himself and the regiment at a gallop, charging toward the awaiting crouched multi-colored figures, who were by now firing volleys at the onrushing horsemen. The two forces clashed and Churchill was surrounded by scores of Dervishes, their swords flashing and rifles firing. He glanced to the side in time to see a man raise his sword for a ham-stringing cut on his horse, and moved out of the way, simultaneously firing two shots at his attacker. Immediately another Dervish advanced and Churchill aimed the Mauser and pulled the

men. Several troopers wounded him with their lances, but the man rose and came at Winston with his spear. Churchill pointed his Mauser and shot the man at a distance of less than a yard.

Up to this time, Churchill thought the 21st had inflicted heavy damages upon the enemy. He looked back at the severely wounded men and horses, and realized that the affair had actually been a disaster. Omdurman was to be the site of the last formal British cavalry charge in history, and like the Charge of the Light Brigade 40 years earlier, it was a glorious failure. One-fourth of the Lancers were lost at the onset of the charge, and the whole action had lasted but three minutes.

With Kitchener's eventual defeat of the Dervishes Churchill resolved to leave the army and enter politics, as his finances were in a sorry state. He decided to write a book about the Sudanese Campaign, and the *River War* became as great a success as the *Malakand Field Force*.

Churchill now devoted his energies to campaigning as the Conservative candidate for Member of Parliament at Oldham, Lancashire. Unfortunately this strong working-class area had traditionally voted Liberal, and Churchill lost by a wide margin. Storm clouds were gathering in South Africa, however, and the young correspondent would not be idle long.

When the Boer War broke out in late October of 1899, Churchill already had an offer to go to the seat of war as a correspondent for the *Morning Post* at the not insubstantial salary of £250 per month. He left for South Africa immediately and arrived in Durban after a two-week journey, during which the passengers were cut off from all news of the war. They disembarked to

Winston Churchill

find out things were not going well for the British.

Churchill, dressed in a quasi-military khaki uniform and sporting his Mauser (it was technically forbidden for correspondents to be armed, lest they be regarded as spies) boarded an armored train bound for Ladysmith, the scene of most of the action. Accompanying Churchill on the train was a company of the Durban Light Infantry and a 6-pound naval gun with a detachment of sailors to service it.

After an uneventful journey of about 15 miles the train was suddenly jarred to a stop and a force of Boers opened up with their M-95 7mm Mausers, two light cannon and a pom-pom gun. Churchill gathered his wits, looked over the steel-clad sides of the car in which he was riding, and saw scores of Boers running towards the train, throwing themselves on the ground and pouring in a heavy rain of accurate rifle fire.

He determined to dismount and

British officers were not issued sidearms, but were required to purchase handguns privately. Two popular models at the time of Churchill's graduation from Sandhurst were the .455/.476 Webley-Green revolver (top) and the .455/.476 four-barrelled Lancaster. Although he does not mention what specific model of handgun he had during the Cuban and Malakand adventures, Churchill does state he carried a revolver. One can assume that it was one of the many fine types of Webleys then available.

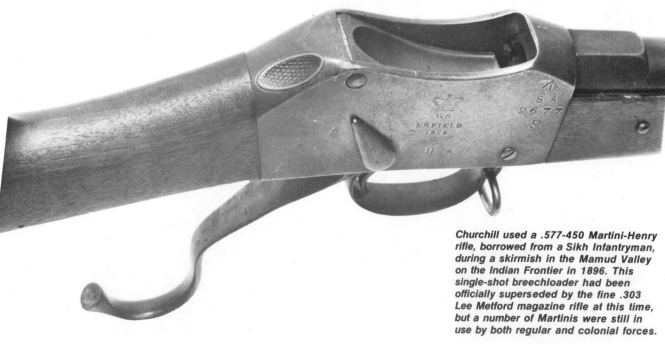

Churchill used a .577-450 Martini-Henry rifle, borrowed from a Sikh Infantryman, during a skirmish in the Mamud Valley on the Indian Frontier in 1896. This single-shot breechloader had been officially superseded by the fine .303 Lee Metford magazine rifle at this time, but a number of Martinis were still in use by both regular and colonial forces.

see what damage was done to the train. As he ran forward, towards the engine, he noticed a number of wounded British troops weakly returning fire. The Boers were continuing their onslaught and bullets and shrapnel pelted the hapless defenders. Churchill conceived a plan whereby the damaged cars could be removed from the tracks and the train be freed. While he was running the length of the train to coordinate plans and assist wounded soldiers he looked up in time to see two Boers. Quickly he withdrew, their 7mm bullets spattering the iron plates as he ran. He dove behind a bank along the rail lines, determined to run for the Blue Krantz River about 200 yards away. As he made his move he noticed a lone Boer galloping toward him. The horseman stopped within 50 yards and ordered Churchill to halt. The young correspondent reached for his Mauser, only to realize that he had left it behind on the train. With no other alternative, Churchill surrendered. His captor was Louis Botha, one of the best shots on the Boer Army, who was destined to be The Republic of South Africa's first Prime Minister.

Winston walked along next to Botha, noticing that a number of the British forces were also prisoners. Churchill's heart gave a sudden jump. He remembered that he still had two 10-round Mauser clips in small pockets above his breast pockets and could be considered a spy rather than a reporter. Carefully he managed to remove one and drop it to the ground, but as he attempted· to lose the other, the Boer barked, "What have you got there?" Keeping his head, Churchill answered, "What is it? I picked it up." Botha grabbed the clip, examined it and tossed it away, urging his prisoner forward.

Churchill was sent to a State Model School in the Boer capital of Pretoria which had been converted into a prison. His days as a captive passed slowly, and boredom, mixed with a desire to get back into action soon led to a plan for escape.

An open circular latrine near one of the outer barbed wire-covered walls provided the opportunity. One evening, Churchill hoisted himself over the wire and lay in the shrubbery of an adjoining garden. He waited there for a short period, and even though two brother officers inside the fence suggested that he would be found out and should return, Churchill was resolved to make the escape. Coolly he stood up, strolled casually across an open area which was blazing with flood-

Churchill was a member of an 85-man detachment of the 35th Sikhs during an assault on a small village in the Mamud Valley. This soldier is a subadar (sergeant) in the 35th. The Sikhs were a powerful Indian military sect.

lights, and walked out the gate within 5 yards of a sentry. He wandered through the streets of Pretoria and formulated a plan to catch a train to Portugese East Africa—some 300 miles away.

Winston made his way to a train station and as a waiting freight began to move, he dashed for one of the cars and boarded. He slept for some time, and rather than be discovered, when the train stopped to pick up coal, he dove from the slowing car. He now found himself in the middle of a large valley, and eventually made his way to the mining district of Witbank and Middleburg where a number of English mining engineers had been allowed to remain by the Boers to keep the coal mines in operation.

Fortunately Churchill chose a house occupied by Britisher John Howard, manager of the Transvaal Colleries. Howard supplied Churchill with food, clothes, lodging (while the furor of Churchill's escape subsided) and a small revolver. He helped the fugitive clandestinely board a train which, after a journey of three days, landed him at Lourenco Marques, Portugese Territory.

Churchill presented himself at the British Consulate where he was delighted to discover that he was a national hero. Winston read the accounts of his escape with relish, but was unhappy to hear of numerous British defeats. He decided that his place was back in the Army.

Befitting his predilection to the cavalry, Winston accepted a lieutenancy in the South African Light Horse, a regiment of 700 men which also included a flying battery of Maxim guns. Churchill attached his rank insignia to his correspondent's uniform, and adopted a slouch hat decorated with tail feathers from a *sakabulu* bird. His M-96 Mauser had been returned to him by the engineer of the armored train, and he eagerly slung its cross strap over his shoulder.

Churchill took part in actions leading to the relief of Ladysmith and was involved in fighting and correspondent work in the Orange Free State, Johannesburg, and Pretoria. The capture of the latter marked the virtual end of the war.

Because of his two books, adventurous escape and war dispatches Churchill returned home to England a national hero. His second attempt to gain the post of Conservative MP from Oldham met with a resounding success, and Winston the soldier became Winston the politician—his battles were just to begin.

Model 1896 Mauser Pistol

The First Practical Military Auto.

By Garry James

In 1897 the highly-respected German arms firm of Mauser introduced what was to become one of the first, and most popular of their wide line of semi-automatic pistols.

The M-1896 7.63mm (.30) caliber Mauser was a 10-round handgun with a box magazine located in front of the trigger guard. It incorporated an adjustable tangent rear sight, and provision for a wooden shoulder stock. The round, rat-tailed walnut grips gave the gun its nickname of "Broomhandle."

The M-96 was complicated but beautifully made. With its wooden shoulder stock holster, it was an accurate arm and the .30 Mauser round was a fairly potent manstopper. Later the gun was also offered in 9mm Parabellum.

Immediately it became favored with military men, and achieved quite a vogue in England, for it was introduced just in time to take part in the Boer War. As British officers were allowed to purchase their own handguns, many departing members of Her Majesty's Army, including a youthful Winston Churchill, took M-96s along with them. British-retailed Broomhandles are often found with the name of the dealer engraved on the box magazine, and they will exhibit British Proof marks. Most were blued, but nickeled versions were also available.

The Model 1896 Mauser was loaded by first pulling the bolt to the rear until it was secured by the bolt stop. This allowed access to the magazine. A metal strip clip, loaded with 10 rounds, was inserted into a slot at the rear of the magazine, and the 10 cartridges were then pushed down, against the follower into the magazine. When the empty clip was withdrawn, the bolt would move forward, and strip off and chamber a round, readying the gun for the first shot. When the last round was expended, the bolt remained open ready for another clip.

The Broomhandle we used for test came complete with its wooden shoulder stock holster (although the stock could not be attached as the connecting iron had been removed in accordance with federal regulations). The gun was loaded in the prescribed manner, with the first 10-shot string consisting of deliberately aimed shots. Twenty-yard groups measured around 3½ inches—certainly combat accuracy.

We now tried several rapid fire shots and found, as might be expected, that the pattern spread out somewhat. The shots were still in the vital areas, however.

The gun functioned flawlessly through about 100 rounds. Recoil was minimal and the round grip allowed for a good degree of controllability.

It is very easy to see how a young officer, such as Winston Churchill, could become enamored of the M-1896. Given the other crude automatics of the day, as well as many of the heavy service revolvers, the Broomhandle was indeed a superior weapon.

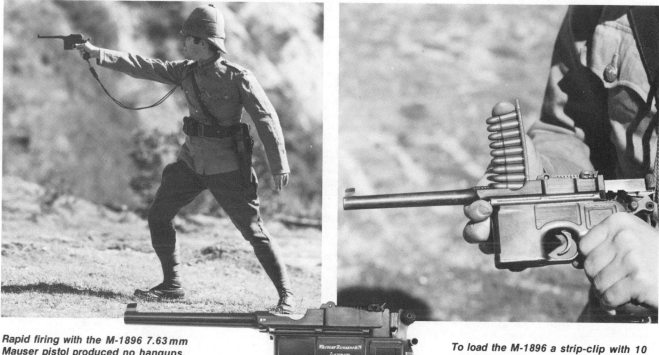

Rapid firing with the M-1896 7.63mm Mauser pistol produced no hangups. Although the gun looks ungainly, it points naturally and balances quite well. Accuracy was very good.

The M-96 Mauser was one of the earliest automatics. It found acceptance with military men, civilians and police alike, and was a particular favorite of Winston Churchill. With its attached holster/shoulder stock it was capable of good long-range accuracy.

To load the M-1896 a strip-clip with 10 rounds is inserted into a notch at the rear of the magazine. The cartridges are then forced down with the thumb.

The James/Younger Gang

"The Boys."

By Ron Terrell

There has been more material printed about the James/Younger gang than any other outlaw band in history. With all the reams of copy that have been produced by writers' pens, it would seem logical to assume that all the facts about these men, their lives and activities would be known. Not so! Even today, one can still engage in heated arguments with pro or anti-James/Younger "historians"

Never has more confusion about an individual or group's activities been evident than exists with this most widely publicized gang of outlaws. When the factors of era, locale and historical events are considered, we can perhaps understand this confusion a little better. And, as the personalities of the principals themselves are scrutinized, we gain even more insight into the factors that kept them out of the hands of the law for almost 20 years.

It is difficult to look at these well known western figures as individuals, with the exception of Jesse. Yet, in order to see them properly as members of a gang, we must look at them separetely in order to see their places within the structure of the gang. Then we are better able to see the roles they played as members of that band that attracted so much local and national attention during its years of operations. Since the name of Jesse James commands more attention and interest, we'll save him until last. So, let's start with the Younger brothers.

The Civil War came as a result of strong feelings on both sides of the slavery issue. These feelings had built up over a period of years until they brought on the War Between the States and continued for years after the close of official hostilities. In the Western or frontier states, these feelings were often accompanied by violence and atrocities. Missouri was the jumping off place for the Western movement and became a focal point for pro and anti-slavery factions. Kansas was about to enter the Union and these slavery forces battled each other trying to get Kansas' representatives as "free" or "slavery" votes. Eastern states and cities emptied many of their jails and prisons and sent their occupants to Kansas with instructions to keep Kansas free from pro-slavery forces. Missourians and other Southern sympathizers fought back. The resulting Border warfare recorded numerous attacks, murders and burnings on both sides.

Henry Washington Younger was born in Crab Orchard, Kentucky, of a strongly Southern family. He was related to Robert E. Lee and the Younger family owned a number of slaves. His family moved to Jackson County, Missouri, when he was a young man and, in 1830, he married Miss Bursheba Fristoe of nearby Independence. Her father had fought

This "mature" photo of Jesse James was taken around 1875 and was authenticated by his wife. At the time of this picture, Jesse was 28—he had seven more years to live. (Bettmann Archives)

The James/Younger Gang

under General "Andy" Jackson at the battle of New Orleans and it was he who named Jackson County in honor of his leader.

Henry Younger acquired the honorary title of colonel during the early years of his married life due to his activity in political affairs. Among other things, he served as judge of the Jackson County Court, served in the state legislature and was in control of the federal mail lines in that frontier region. He managed to own and operate farms and raise a family of 14 children during those turbulent years just prior to the outbreak of war.

The oldest Younger son was Richard, who died at the age of 23 in 1860. This was the start of tragedies that resulted in heartache and disaster for this influential and respected family.

Colonel Younger, himself a slaveholder, spoke openly on the issue of holding the Union together during the months before secession. After he was killed by a Union soldier named Walley (in retaliation against Cole who had fought him over Walley's advances to one of Cole's sisters), the family was harassed, attacked and humiliated. They were forced to turn to their relatives and friends for protection and sanctuary.

During this time, Thomas Coleman "Cole", who had been born in 1844, joined William Clarke Quantrill's guerrillas. The original purpose of this band was to fight against Kansas Jayhawkers and Redlegs, freebooters who were raiding into Missouri. This noble purpose got lost somewhere along the way.

Cole rode with Quantrill for several years and also wore the gray uniform of the regular Confederate army. He participated in the Confederate victory at Lone Jack, Missouri, in August of 1862 and gained favorable recognition for his courage, coolheadedness and leadership qualities in several engagements during the Civil War years.

James Henry "Jim" Younger shared Cole's January 15 birthdate, four years after his older brother's entry into a troubled world. The humiliation forced on his mother and sisters, finally got too much and caused him, at the age of 15, to join Quantrill as a means of fighting back. He participated in the August 21, 1863, raid on Lawrence, Kansas, in which over 150 men were killed and the town wiped out.

Cole was promoted to the rank of captain in the Confederate Army and, at war's end, had just reached

Frank was the elder of the James brothers, and although he took part in a number of the gang's escapades, he was never brought to trial. He is wearing what appears to be a .36 Colt Navy.

the port of San Francisco with his company on a recruiting trip. Jim had gone with Quantrill to Kentucky and was captured during the battle in which Quantrill was wounded, dying four weeks later. Jim was held prisoner in the Alton, Illinois, military prison until the summer of 1866.

When Cole and Jim returned home after Lee's surrender ended the Civil War, they found their mother and brothers and sisters living in poverty. They and other Quantrill and Confederate fighters were constantly in danger from Union forces or pro-Unionists who wanted all Southerners moved out of the region. It was difficult, if not impossible, for these men to even earn a living from their farms as many were taken from their fields and hung or shot

In retaliation and revenge, the Youngers joined with some of their war time compatriots in earning a living in the way they knew best—with a gun in their hands. John, born in 1851, and Robert Ewing, born in 1856, had been too young to fight during the War but now they

joined brothers Cole and Jim in their outlaw activities. There were 15 bank and train robberies, along with an occasional interruption of a stage coach schedule, attributed to the James/Younger gang between the years of 1866 and 1875, and the Youngers were involved in most of them.

The only Younger killed during these years was John, considered the coldest and fastest gunman of the gang, in a shoot-out with lawmen in 1874. Jim and John became involved in a gun battle with two Pinkerton detectives and Sheriff Ed Daniels near Monegaw Springs, Missouri. John was fatally hit in the neck but stayed in the saddle long enough to shoot Pinkerton Captain of Detectives Louis J. Lull and Sheriff Daniels before dying. Both his victims died at a nearby cabin a little later. Jim was wounded in the arm during this gunfight.

The physical and personality characteristics of the outlaw Younger brothers were such that, even after their final capture in Minnesota, people who met them were favorably impressed. So much so, that many of those who worked for their pardon ranged from the president of the Northfield bank to the governor of the state. Cole stood almost 6 feet and weighed 215 pounds (he gained up to 15 more pounds during his prison years), had curly light auburn hair in his earlier years, but started balding by the time he was 30, a reddish beard and freckles. He was an incurable joker, intelligent, very well read and dressed conservatively and tastefully. During a stay in Texas between robberies, he even worked as a government census taker and sang in a church choir.

At the time of their capture, Colonel Vought, who owned a hotel where Cole had stayed while posing as a cattle buyer before the raid, was one of the possemen in at the capture of the bandits. In fact, it was he who fired some of the shots that dropped Cole. Vought was one of the first to reach the downed outlaw and, when Cole greeted him with a bloody, extended hand and a "howdy, landlord," he shook hands with him warmly, recognizing this notorious outlaw as one of his tenants with whom he had recently shared pleasant conversation.

Jim was the loner of the group, being less gregarious than Cole and not as physically impressive as Bob. He stood 5 feet 10 inches and weighed about 160 pounds. His hair was a darker brown and he usually wore an almost sullen expression. His upper jaw was shattered by a bullet during the final gun battle in Hanska Slough where the Youngers' outlaw activities ended and he suffered with that wound for several years.

The bullet that shattered Jim's jaw had imbedded itself just in front of the lower part of his left ear and remained there for several years, causing almost unbearable pain. He finally persuaded a prison hospital attendant to dig it out through the roof of his mouth. The result was impaired speech and a disfigured face which contributed to an already degenerating mental attitude. That, plus a refusal of permission to marry after his release from prison

in 1901, caused him to commit suicide October 19, 1902.

Bob was regarded as an excellent specimen of manhood. He stood 6 feet 2 inches, weighed about 190 pounds, had sandy hair and light blue eyes. He was well educated, personable and a good conversationalist. His polite manners and good looks attracted the attention of many women and, even while in jail before his trial, was the recipient of gifts of fruit, flowers and baked goods from some of the women who had been to see the notorious Youngers. A portion of a newspaper account of Bob's impression on the ladies and his response to them appeared in St. Paul's *Pioneer Press* shortly after his transfer from the Madelia jail to the one in Faribault: "Bob Younger had his bouquets in Madelia, and he has his cigars, oranges and nuts in Faribault. We haven't a doubt that Bob could marry the handsomest woman who confers these palatable luxuries on him, if he himself did not despise the whole simple and gushing set. Bob's sentiment, it should be remembered, doesn't get above a bawdy house."

It was Bob's wound that was largely responsible for the capture of the Youngers and the death of Sam Wells (alias Charlie Pitts) in Hanska Slough, near Madelia. Bob's right elbow was shattered by a bullet from the rifle of 19-year-old Henry W. Wheeler, a medical student home on vacation from Ann Arbor, Michigan. The gun Wheeler used to good advantage from a second story hotel room across from the bank, was an old Army carbine that used paper cartridges. Although underpowered by today's standards, it was adequate to finish an already wounded, but still mounted, Clell Miller and cripple Bob's arm as described above.

Bob, as were most men of his

profession, was brave and courageous in a gun battle, even if he was on the other side of the law and order fence. When Wheeler's bullet rendered his right arm useless, he switched his pistol to his left hand and retained it as he was helped into the saddle of Clell's now riderless horse.

A total of eight men made the trip North from Missouri to Minnesota but six of them were all that left Northfield. Frank and Jesse James were the other two who left with the Youngers and Sam Wells. Jesse and Cole were not particularly close but each man respected the other's fighting abilities. After some difficulties in finding their ways out of the heavy timber and swamp areas (Bill Stiles, alias Bill Chadwell, had lived in Minnesota, knew the country and was to have guided them in their escape back to Missouri but he died in the streets of Northfield), Jesse suggested that Bob be left behind so they could move faster. After passing through Mankato, Jesse's temper erupted and he stated they all would have a better chance of escaping if Bob were eliminated. A showdown (which would have meant a shootout) would have come between Cole and Jesse if the others had not interfered. It was agreed that they split so the Youngers (except Jim, for some reason) and Wells gave Frank and Jesse all their money and valuables, thinking their chances of getting away were better.

Frank and Jesse made good their escape to Missouri but it was some

These photos of (l-r) Jim, Cole and Bob Younger were taken in prison following the trio's capture after the Northfield, Minnesota bank raid. All three were wounded during the gun battle at Hanska Slough, and Bob later died in prison from the wounds he received. The other two brothers served 25-year sentences.

The James/Younger Gang

time before Jesse's ego recovered from the humiliation of Northfield. The Youngers were all captured and Sam Wells was killed during the final gun battle in Hanska Slough. Cole was wounded 11 more times (at his death, 17 bullets were still in his body), Jim suffered five more wounds, the worst being a bullet through his upper lip and jaw and another slug that stopped just under his spine. Bob remained untouched except for his earlier arm wound until all the others were down and he waved a white flag of surrender. As he did so, someone fired and hit him in the chest, the bullet passing through his lung and out his back. This would would turn into tuberculosis (then called consumption) and claim his life in prison 13 years later.

The Youngers were model prisoners at Stillwater prison and were liked and respected by officials and prisoners alike. After the first eight years, they were allowed to visit with each other at regular intervals. Then, attempts which were to stretch from 1889 to 1901 were started to obtain their pardons. Bob was never to see that day for he died in September of 1889. Cole and Jim were to finally leave Stillwater's bars

and walls July 10, 1901. Jim was to commit suicide in October the next year and Cole was to finally return to Missouri a few months later—February 16, 1903. He lived with relatives in and around Kansas City until his death March 21, 1916.

There has been more information—and misinformation—printed about Jesse James than all of the others of this gang combined. Even older brother Frank was left on the sidelines of history in comparison to Jesse.

So much material has been printed about "the boys" as their supporters and friends still call

them, that it would be repetitious to recount all the events of their younger days. We will hit some of the highlights but, then, we'll take closer looks at some of the less publicized aspects of their activities.

Alexander Franklin James was born January 10, 1843, and Jesse Woodson James was born September 5, 1847. Their mother was a strong willed, dominant woman who defended her sons against all charges and attacks, even to the day of Jesse's death.

Frank James and Cole Younger were about the same age and had similar experiences in their early gun-fighting training. Both rode with Quantrill and were proficient with a variety of weapons. Jesse's first taste of warfare was also with Quantrill where, at 16, he was considered a fullfledged fightin' man, according to most reports. There are several stories of his exploits during those years but one that might be of interest to today's gun enthusiast is one relative to an accident with his revolver. The story goes that, during his early Quantrill days, Jesse accidentally shot the tip off one of his fingers while handling a pistol (he preferred the Colt Navy .36, but used a variety of others over the years). Religiously trained Jesse is supposed to have exclaimed something like: "By Dingus, I've shot myself!" and was stuck with the nickname "Dingus" from then on.

Jesse apparently had his "blood bath" at Centralia, Kansas, (Frank was on the Lawrence raid but apparently Jesse was not,) where he was "second in command" (at 16, on one of his first raids and new in Quantrill's forces, it is a little hard for this writer to accept that position for Jesse,) and helped kill 75 Union soldiers. He apparently formed his own band when Quantrill went to Kentucky in 1864, and led raids into Texas and back to Missouri where, in 1865, he was shot in the right lung and chest three times as he rode in to Lexington, Missouri, under a flag of truce.

Jesse was nursed through his almost fatal wounds by his cousin, Zerelda Mimms, whom he later married (April 24, 1875). They had two

children and his family was in another room of the house when he was killed by Bob Ford April 3, 1882, in St. Joseph, Missouri.

Frank and Jesse and the Younger brothers started their trips down the outlaw trails about the same time and for approximately the same reasons. The James brothers continued their activities until 1882, but the Youngers had their careers shortened by the gun-owning citizens of Northfield, Minnesota. There is no accurate record of how many robberies or murders were committed during those years, but most authorities agree on at least 17 robberies, netting a reported $200,000.

A total of 16 men rode in the James/Younger gang at one time or another, some only briefly. Several were killed, others arrested and a few of the wiser ones quit while they were ahead—free and alive. Most of the non-relatives of these two principal families had ridden with Quantrill. All were Missourians and Southern sympathizers.

While each of these men was well-acquainted with firearms, it's doubtful if any of them, including Jesse, could be classified as a "fast gun." Their technique was to take their victims by surprise, with pistols drawn, and retain control by not giving anyone a chance to arm themselves.

Cole Younger's nickel-plated, ivory-gripped .45 Colt SAA was captured from him at Madelia, Minn. and sent to Belle Starr at his request.

The first robbery of this gang was the First National Bank of Liberty, Missouri, in 1866. Visitors to this bank today, which is operated as a museum, can almost hear the thunder of hooves, wild guerilla yells and roar of gunfire as the bandits race down the hill from the scene of their crime. They were encouraged by the success of this means to fast money, and other robberies soon followed.

Citizens exposed to today's modern methods of law enforcement, radio equipped patrol cars, telephone and teletype systems find it hard to understand how these men could escape and remain at large for such a long time. Students of American history during that era understand better, but even they have problems sometimes. Briefly, the factors of politics, frontier inde-

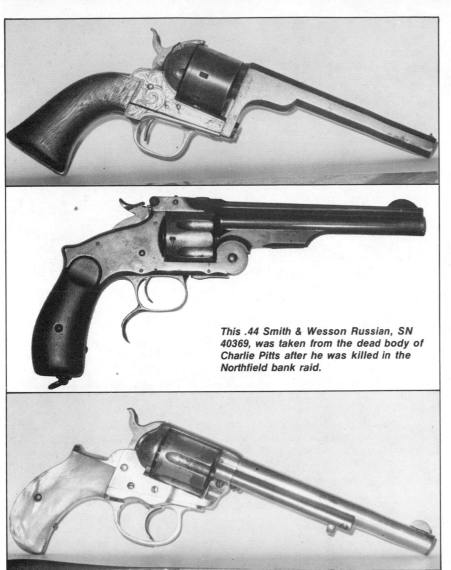

This .44 Smith & Wesson Russian, SN 40369, was taken from the dead body of Charlie Pitts after he was killed in the Northfield bank raid.

This nickel plated Colt .41 Lightening revolver with pearl grips was given to the Schilling Museum by Cole Younger after his release from prison in 1901.

sanctuary until things "cooled down". There are reports that Frank and Jesse made it as far West as Arizona and New Mexico and there are confirmed reports of Cole, Jim and Bob spending some time in Texas.

There is a fairly well-grounded story that Cole and Belle Starr lived together for a while in Texas and that Cole fathered Belle's daughter, named Pearl. Supporting this story is the fact that Belle later named the outlaw headquarters she and her lover Sam Starr established in Indian Territory as "Younger's Bend".

Belle herself told the story in later years that a "blinking, blue eyed quiet man who refused to hang up his guns" was "an old friend from Missouri"—Jesse James. This was not too long after Jesse and Frank returned from a not too profitable trip to Minnesota. Jesse's blinking problem stemmed from a childhood disease of the eye commonly called "sleepy eye".

In addition to their travels West and South, some of the gang members went East. Frank and Jesse had gone to Tennessee to make a new start for themselves and their families. Frank had married, too, and they tried to leave the outlaw life. They lived respectable honest lives as farmers for about three years before Jesse got restless and decided to go back to earning his living with a pistol instead of a plow. He convinced Frank to join him and some of the other gang members who had come to Tennessee to take on a stage coach job near there. They did and then returned to their old stomping grounds—Missouri.

There are probably more James/Younger firearms floating around the country than any other "famous" guns. It seems that someone is always coming up with a new discovery. It is doubtful that all these guns are authentic, yet there is a very good possibility they could be. These men were accustomed to owning and carrying a number of different arms—sometimes simultaneously. They apparently relied more on revolvers than long guns and this was probably due to their training in mounted warfare. A handgun in Civil War times was easier to use and reload than the muzzle loading rifles available. Many of their battle engagements were after cavalry type charges and at close quarters. Those conditions were best suited to handgun use.

Not only did these men rely more on revolvers than rifles, they

pendence, inept (and often corrupt) local law enforcement officials and family loyalties were responsible. The reconstruction years were hard for those on both sides but especially on Southern sympathizers. Missourians were often abused, attacked and forced from their homes by those who had the political support of pro-Unionists. Farmers could not tend their crops and ex-Confederates were forced to flee their homes or, many times, be killed or see their families killed.

So it was that, during those early years of activity, the James/Younger gang was looked on as heroes by many who would have liked to strike back themselves. The money taken from the banks was not theirs for very few pro-Southerners had *any* money, let alone enough to keep in a bank. The trains and stage coaches were also looked on as tools of or conveniences for the Unionists.

In time, many of these attitudes changed but the loyalties of the people living in and around the gang's home ground were such that

no one would betray them. Those who might have considered it were usually too afraid of reprisal to follow through with any such idea.

As surprising as it might seem to modern travelers who would not think of going more than a block if they couldn't get in a car and drive, many of the people living during the last half of the 1800s traveled widely. In fact, those who lived on the frontier—as Missouri was still considered—were movers. It took a special personality to settle new frontiers and there were some who could not stay in an area once it became "civilized" but felt compelled to move on to new areas with more elbow room.

This knowledge gives us more of an insight into the widespread activities of these Missouri outlaws. Their usual practice was to split up after a robbery and move across country to predetermined areas of

The James/Younger Gang

This Army issue Colt .45 SAA, SN 1222, was taken from Jesse at the time of his death and given to U.S. Marshal Fred Sutton by St. Joseph City Marshal Enos Craig.

This .44 Starr percussion revolver was used by Jesse James in a gunfight with lawmen near Joplin, Mo. He reportedly killed a number of his assailants and gave the gun to a negro cook to hide.

Frank James surrendered this Remington .41 RF double derringer to Major John M. Edwards when he turned himself in to the law.

usually carried more than one at a time. During their time in St. Paul, just before their abortive Northfield raid, Bob and Sam Wells became involved in a poker game. As the evening wore on and temperatures warmed up in the small room, their coats were removed. "The proprietor and several onlookers beheld the unveiling of two living arsenals, having exposed an array of guns, knives and cartridges," according to printed reports after their identities were known.

About that same time, Frank, Jesse, Jim and Clell Miller arrived in St. Paul. Stiles (alias Chadwell) knew the town and some of the long time residents of a bawdy house and they all apparently accompanied him on a visit to one of these residences. Stiles familiarly went upstairs to see a former acquaintance. She noticed, in addition to the roll of money he displayed, that "he was carrying three or four large revolvers." This was not uncommon for these men and was one reason they usually wore linen dusters on their raids. They helped conceal their heavy armament.

Shortly after this writer moved from Colorado to West Central Missouri (almost in the center of the James/Younger territory), many reports of guns that belonged to these

men were received. One individual just a few miles from my home posesses two Colt Navy revolvers that have been passed down to him. The story behind those guns is that Frank and Jesse were visiting friends in a small town when a gun salesman passed through peddling his wares to the local hardware store owner. Jesse asked his friend if he would buy four of the best pistols the salesman had. The Colt Navies were left in return for the favor.

There is a family in Liberty, Missouri, that has a picture of Frank and Jesse with a relative of theirs. These three men had been hunting and posed for a picture of themselves with their guns, camping gear and game. All are wearing Colt Navy revolvers and holding muzzle loading rifles. This writer was allowed to see this unpublished picture but not to copy it since they are among those who think "the boys" were not all that bad but don't want to have attention drawn to their family due to a predecessor's association with the James boys. The most impressive thing about the picture, to me as an outsider, was the appearance of Frank and Jesse—they were what our womenfolk would most likely consider "handsome specimen of manhood"

There are other firearms record-

ed as belonging to members of the James/Younger gang, some of which have been completely authenticated. There is a Colt Single Action .45, serial number 13757, with a 7½-inch barrel, in the Missouri State Historical Society's Museum, located in the state capital building, Jefferson City, Missouri, that belonged to Cole Younger. There are other James/Younger items in this display, too, but this is the only firearm.

There are several firearms in the Schilling Museum at Northfield, Minnesota. These are completely authenticated, having been taken from their owners shortly after their demise or capture. Two of these belonged to Cole. One is a nickel-plated self-cocking Colt .41 with pearl handles. The other Cole Younger pistol is a .32 RF D. Moore 5-inch barreled, engraved single action with serial number 880—It was taken from Cole by Captain Walsh when Cole was captured.

The third pistol in the Schilling Museum is a Smith & Wesson .44 Russian Model single action with spur trigger guard; serial number 40369 and 6½-inch barrel. This pistol was taken from the body of Sam Wells (Charlie Pitts) after he was killed in Hanska Slough.

Frank James also used a Smith & Wesson .44 Russian at one time. His pistol is now in the Saunders Museum, Berryville, Arkansas, which houses one of the more impressive gun collections in the Mid-West. There are also some other pistols that belonged to some of these gang members in the Saunders Museum. There is an engraved Starr percussion revolver Jesse used in killing some lawmen who tried to arrest him near Joplin, Missouri. This pistol has the initials "J.J." stamped on the left side of the frame, near the bullet seating lever, and features a miniature dagger of pearl inlaid in the right grip.

There is also a nickel plated Colt .45, serial number 19242, with 7½-inch barrel and ivory grips in the Saunders Museum. This pistol was also taken from Cole at his capture and he requested that it be sent to Belle Starr at Fort Smith, Arkansas. She used it for several years and then gave it to Texas Jack who used it with the Buffalo Bill Wild West Show for some time before selling it to Colonel Saunders.

There is one other pistol that belonged to one of these gang members: a Colt .45 Single Action with 5½-inch barrel, blued and with standard Colt grips. This was carried by Jim Cummings during the time he rode with Jesse and Frank. Cummings saw the light of day about the time two other gang members, Wood Hite and Dick Liddell, shot it out—with Hite ending up dead. Cummings quietly left the country and later presented his pistol to Colonel Saunders.

Two handguns authenticated as belonging to the James brothers are in a private collection in Arkansas but now on display at the Museum of the Great Plains, Lawton, Oklahoma. One is a 7½-inch barreled Colt Single Action .45 that belonged to Jesse. It is nickel plated and has walnut grips. An interesting facet of this pistol is that it is stamped with a four digit serial number—which

has been obliterated by someone using a steel punch. An attempt was also made to wipe out the "U.S." marking stamped on the side of the grip frame. The numbers 1222 are still present on the loading gate, however. This Colt was presented by St. Joseph City Marshal Enos Craig to Fred E. Sutton, a former deputy U.S. marshal in Kansas and the Indian Territory. According to Sutton's letter of authentication with this Colt, the exact mate of this pistol is owned by Governor T.T. Crittenden's descendants.

The other pistol in this private collection is a Remington .41 double derringer that was given by Frank James to Major John M. Edwards of St. Joseph, Missouri, when Frank surrendered himself to the law. The serial number on this engraved two-shooter is 5462.

Undoubtedly, there are many other James/Younger gang member firearms in private collections and on public display. There are bound to be others that turn up in the future, too. Authenticating these arms has always been a problem and will be increasingly difficult as time passes. Perhaps someday each state will make the necessary efforts to collect many of these items from its past and preserve them for future generations to see and relate to this part of their own history.

As long as historians write and gun enthusiasts dig, there will be an interest in the guns used by "the boys." For, even though they were outlaws and killers, public opinion—now as well as then—has been divided. Some still feel these men were driven to their lives of crime. Perhaps.

There is no question that such a gang could not operate as freely with the same public support today that these men received. Granted, there are criminals who continue to operate because of intimidation of average citizens but they are not ac-

corded the defense given these "Robin Hood" types of 100 years ago. Neither is there division of opinion concerning the personalities of today's outlaw, the organized criminal element. One thing we can all agree on is that, whether or not we are James/Younger fans, we have to concede that they hold a unique place in the history of our country. Never before, or since, has there been the public support of an outlaw gang's activities as these men were given during the early years of their operations. And, even after their capture and deaths, there were many who rallied to their support and defense. For, in spite of all else "the boys" were considered "good ole boys" by most of their victims and associates.

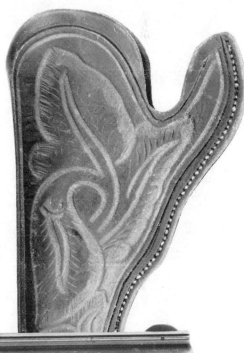

This heavy saddle-leather holster, which belonged to Cole Younger, was kept by Frank James until his death. (Gordon Matson Collection)

This fine .45 Smith & Wesson Schofield revolver, SN 3444, remained in Frank James' possession until his death in 1915, when it was given by his widow to an old friend, C.M. Polk. (Gordon Matson Collection)

The year 1880 was a violent one in El Paso. During the first six months, at least 57 men and women lost their lives in shootouts, stabbings and beatings. Since law enforcement was non-existent, the word was out that this West Texas border town was the place where "everything goes and nobody really gives a damn!"

Of course, there were many God-fearing, respectable people living in this Hell-hole, but their efforts to provide a decent environment for their children were mostly in vain. Four city marshals were hired in succession; four were fired as their involvement with various forms of vice and corruption was uncovered.

As often happened in cases such as this, the city council decided it was time to employ the services of a no-nonsense town tamer. This proved to be an unpopular move with the "sporting crowd," an unruly group of hard-drinking, mean-tempered hell raisers, led by the Manning brothers: Jim, Felix, Frank and John. They liked El Paso the way it was, and warned everyone that all reform movements would be violently resisted. Ominous threats notwithstanding, the city council began the search and four months later found their man in San Antonio.

He arrived in early April, 1881. Stepping down from the Butterfield-Overland stage onto the rutted dirt thoroughfare which served as El Paso's main street, he knocked the travel dust from his clothes, then introduced himself to the anxiously waiting mayor and councilmen. The 6-foot, 2-inch gunman was Dallas Stoudenmire.

Well-qualified for the city marshal's job, Stoudenmire had both the looks and reputation of being a deadly killer. The auburn-haired *pistolero* was born in Macon County, Alabama, on December 11, 1845. Serving in the Confederate Army only whetted his taste for adventure, so after the Civil War, Dallas Stoudenmire drifted south to Mexico, where it is said he served Emperor Maximilian as a mercenary.

When the emperor was overthrown by Benito Juarez' forces, Stoudenmire re-entered the United States, settling near Columbus, Texas, in 1867 as a farmer. His agricultural activities were not as peaceful

Dallas Stoudenmire

A Man to Reckon With.
By H. Gordon Frost

Dallas Stoudenmire stood 6'2" and was acknowledged as being "a man to reckon with." Following service with the Confederate Army, he joined the Texas Rangers and then became city marshal of El Paso, Texas. He was killed a year later by the Manning Brothers.

"X" marks the spot where Stoudenmire was killed during a gun battle with Felix and Jim Manning. This photo of El Paso Street was taken in 1882.

as one might think, since the ex-Confederate volunteer let his proud temper involve him in several local shootouts.

Tiring of his pastoral life, Stoudenmire enlisted in Captain J. R. Waller's Company A of the Texas Rangers, serving as a second sergeant for the better part of 1874. Resigning his commission, he took up residence in Mentz, Texas, working as a wheelwright. While living there, Stoudenmire enlarged his reputation as a gunfighter by killing at least three men. During this time he reputedly trained his stallion to attack adversaries on command with slashing hooves and snapping teeth.

Beginning in 1877, Dallas Stoudenmire drifted from place to place in Texas, engaging in various occupations while enjoying hard liquor, fast horses and soft women. When contacted by the El Paso city council, he was visiting friends in San Antonio. His acceptance of the city marshal's job was to write the final chapter in Stoudenmire's full life, but not before he made a lasting impression on the pages of southwestern history.

Almost immediately after taking the oath of office on April 12, 1881, Stoudenmire made enemies in El Paso. Asking for the city's jail keys, the new city marshal was told they were in the possession of his alcoholic predecessor, Bill Johnson. Locating Johnson in front of Frank Manning's

saloon, Stoudenmire demanded the keys. In his pathetic stupor, Johnson was slow to comply, so the marshal shook him violently and tore the keys from his hand.

This unnecessary action was observed by many members of the Manning faction, and as the tall lawman stomped away an idea began forming which was to bring sudden death once more to the dusty streets of El Paso.

Dallas Stoudenmire had been El Paso's chief lawman a scant three days when unrestrained violence erupted, giving him the opportunity to show the "sporting crowd" that he was a man to reckon with. On April 15, a buckboard was driven into town bearing the bullet-riddled bodies of two Mexican cowboys who had left several days earlier, trailing some stolen cattle. Practically every man in El Paso knew the animals had been rustled by henchmen of the Manning brothers, so suspicion was readily levelled in their direction.

A coroner's inquest was conducted into the double-slaying, during which time accusations were vehemently hurled between the Mannings and Constable Gus Krempkau, who attempted to have murder indictments drawn up against the two suspected killer/rustlers. Unable to secure the necessary court action, the constable angrily left the coroner's office and pre-

Stoudenmire's favorite handguns were a pair of S&W .44 Americans. This one of the pair is nickel-plated with ivory grips; Serial no. 7056.

pared to mount his riding mule.

At that moment, drunken John Hale gave vent to pent-up hatred for Krempkau. Pulling his .45 Colt single-action, the rustler shot the constable through the lungs. Krempkau staggered backwards and sagged against a saloon door casing.

Stoudenmire was eating a late lunch across the street at the Globe Restaurant. On hearing the shot, he raced from the restaurant with his twin Smith & Wesson .44 American revolvers ready for action. Seeing Hale holding his smoking handgun, the marshal snapped off a shot which missed the gunman but hit and mortally wounded an innocent Mexican bystander.

The lawman's second shot was more carefully placed and Hale dropped, a .44 bullet in his brain.

George Campbell, another Manning cohort, drew his pistol and stepped into the street. Krempkau

Dallas Stoudenmire

saw him and weakly pulled his .45 Colt. Slowly sliding to the ground, he squeezed off shots at Campbell, hitting him in the wrist and foot.

Stoudenmire turned and gut-shot Campbell, who dropped his gun and fell to the ground. Rolling over, the painfully dying gunslinger grasped his stomach and gasped between clenched teeth: "You big son-of-a-bitch, you murdered me!"

In less than ten seconds, Dallas Stoudenmire had added the names of three more men to the roster of those who stood before his guns.

The killing of two Manning men infuriated the "sporting crowd" leaders. Not only were good friends lost, but Texas Rangers were sent to help Stoudenmire control the saloon crowd. This hurt the Mannings where it counted; in the pocketbook. Consequently, the brothers decided to have Bill Johnson assassinate the marshal.

Two evenings after the April 15 shootout, Stoudenmire and his brother-in-law, S. M. "Doc" Cummings, were walking the lawman's rounds. As they passed a large pile of bricks in front of the State National Bank, Bill Johnson drunkenly fired his double-barrelled shotgun at Stoudenmire and missed. Johnson's battle with the bottle ended the next instant as eight bullets from the Stoudenmire-Cummings revolvers buried themselves in his body.

Several Manning gunslingers across the street attempted to carry out Johnson's job. They began firing wildly at the brothers-in-law, hitting the marhal in the heel. Stoudenmire

whirled, let out a roar and charged the group, firing his Smith & Wessons. His opponents scattered into the night, unable to cope with such a display of sheer courage.

For the next ten months El Paso's more stable citizens were able to relax a bit, as Stoudenmire's law enforcement caused the wilder element to pull in its horns. There was still plenty of action for those who sought it, but the border community was beginning to assume some trappings of respectability. But Marshal Stoudenmire began drinking heavily during this period, and often staggered down the street, firing his .44's at whatever target caught his fancy. His verbal feud with the Mannings continued and apprehension of a showdown fight grew.

Stoudenmire left El Paso in February, 1882, to get married in east Texas. During the marshal's nuptial absence, Doc Cummings was killed by Jim and Felix Manning in a drunken shootout. The town anxious, held its breath.

On returning from his wedding, the marshal was told of his brother-in-law's death. What had been repressed contempt turned into fiery hatred. The city council became highly alarmed at the situation and persuaded the Mannings and Dallas to sign a well-publicized peace treaty. But neither side really intended to keep the terms. The marshal was asked to resign, and on May 27, he assumed the duties of deputy United States marshal for the western district of Texas, with headquarters in El Paso. He served this position with distinction for four months.

On the evening of September 18, 1882, Dallas Stoudenmire decid-

Stoudenmire's "hideout" gun was a Model 1860 Colt Army, SN 6904, converted to chamber .44 cartridges by the Mason-Richards system. The barrel was shortened to 2⅞ inches, and the gun was carried in a special leather-lined trouser pocket.

ed it was time to end the many rumors circulating about his difficulties with the Mannings. Strapping on his two .44 Smith & Wessons, he slipped an additional persuader into his leather-lined lefthand pants pocket: a model 1860 Colt Army revolver. This handgun had been converted by the Richards-Mason system from percussion to centerfire, handling a .44 caliber cartridge. Bearing serial number 6904, Stoudenmire's "belly gun" had its barrel shortened to 2⅞ inches, and the ejector removed. Although the weapon couldn't be reloaded very

easily, its six extra shots could become a very handy "ace in the hole" when needed.

Fortifying himself with a last shot of whiskey, Stoudenmire walked to the Manning's saloon. There he and Felix Manning got into a violent argument. Words turned into frantic action from which there would be no second-place winner.

The two enemies faced each other, then in one insane moment each drew his gun. Felix was quicker, his .45 Colt clearing leather first. The revolver bucked in Manning's hand, its slug hitting Stoudenmire in the left arm, entering his chest. Dallas' nickle-plated revolver was partially drawn and went spinning across the barroom floor. Once again the Colt fired, the bullet knocking the cursing, bleeding lawman into the street. The bullet was absorbed by a thick layer of papers and a tintype photo carried by Stoudenmire in his breast pocket.

Getting to his feet, the marshal tortuously managed to draw his "belly gun" and shot Felix in the right hand. His .45 dropping in the dust, Manning whipped off his hat and rushed the lawman, beating Dallas in the face. Throwing his arms around the big man, Felix defensively pinned Stoudenmire's arms to his side.

Jim Manning rushed up. Pulling his triggerless, sawed-off Colt .45, he thumbed a shot at the marshal, which missed, the slug shattering a nearby barber pole. He fired again, this time eight feet away from the men locked in their danse macabre. The bullet struck Stoudenmire in back of the left ear. With a mighty groan the lawman collapsed to the street. The feud was over.

The absolute power of the Manning brothers over the legal affairs of El Paso was revealed in the coroner's verdict of the killing. Accordingly, Dallas Stoudenmire's death was caused "from a shot fired by a six-shooter .44 or .45 caliber in the hands of party unknown."

The .44 Colt Richards-Mason "belly gun" and tintype photo which deflected Felix Manning's second shot were picked up by a bystander and kept as mementoes until given to an El Paso sporting goods store owner in the 1930s. Today they are prized items in the collection of an El Paso historian.

Stoudenmire's nickel-plated .44 Smith & Wesson "American" Model revolvers remained in the possession of his sister, Doc Cummings' widow, until 1889, when she sold them to saloon keeper George Look. Only one is still known to exist, having the serial number of 7056. It, too, is in a private El Paso collection. ♣

Heck Thomas

Fearless Frontier Marshal.

By Ron Terrell

This photo of Thomas was taken in 1892 when he was acting as deputy U.S. marshal at Arkansas City, Kansas. He was working with Chief of Dectectives Fred Dodge of Wells Fargo in trailing the Doolin Gang.

The weather was typical for a late August night in Oklahoma—only in 1896 it was still Indian Territory—when the posse quietly moved into position along the road leading to the house on the hill. A bright moon lit the scene, causing the lawmen to choose their waiting spots carefully.

A tip had come to the marshals that Bill Doolin, considered the most dangerous criminal on their wanted lists, would be coming to the house about midnight and they wanted to be in position well in advance of that time. Doolin's wife and young son were at the home of her parents and Doolin was reportedly coming to take them out of the country.

Some accounts indicate that a few of the local young men had been keeping an eye on the house for the marshals—in fact, they are the ones who tipped off the lawmen that Doolin was going to be there this night—and Doolin wanted to get revenge on them before leaving the area. It was with considerable surprise that the waiting marshals saw a man they recognized as Doolin emerge from the house and start down the road leading his horse. His ever-present Winchester was held in both hands, ready for immediate action, the tips of his bridle reins held in the hand grasping the forearm.

Heck Thomas, the 46-year-old deputy U.S. marshal leading the posse, had given strict instructions for the other possemen to hold their

Heck Thomas

fire until he had called on Doolin to surrender. One of the men had apparently neglected to cock the hammer of his Winchester before this time, and the night's stillness magnified that unmistakable sound to Doolin's ears.

Reflexes of both outlaw and lawmen took over as Doolin swung his rifle and snapped a fast shot at the ominous sound he had just heard. Thomas quickly stepped into the road and commanded Doolin to throw up his hands and surrender. By prearrangement, Thomas had another marshal repeat the command from the other side of the road almost simultaneously. Doolin, knowing he had no chance of living beyond a hangman's noose in Judge Isaac Parker's court in Ft. Smith, Arkansas, gambled on the slim chance of surviving a shoot out with the marshals.

In Thomas' own words: "He came straight down the lane, leading his horse by the tip ends of the bridle reins, walking slow in the bright moonlight, Winchester in both hands, well out in front of him, nearly in position to shoot. He was walking slow, looking first to one side and then the other. He was sure on the prod for the neighborhood boys who had been spying on him, intending to shoot them up a little, when I hollered to him and had one of the boys on the other side of the road to holler to him right after I did.

"He shot at me and the bullet passed between me and the Dunns. I had let one of the boys have my Winchester and had an old No. 8 shotgun. It was too long in the breech and I couldn't handle it quick, so he got another shot with his Winchester and as he dropped his Winchester from glancing shot, he jerked his pistol and some of the boys thought he shot once with it . . . . About that time I got the

shotgun to work and the fight was over."

The killing of Bill Doolin has been considered the crowning achievement of a conspicuously exciting and dangerous career for Heck Thomas. His career as a law officer stretched from 1868 to 1912 with very little time spent in other professions.

Henry Andrew Thomas was born January 6, 1850, at Oxford, Georgia—not far from Atlanta. The youngest of 12 children born to Colonel Lovick Pierce and Martha Ann Thomas, Henry grew up surrounded by and involved in the use of weapons for war and self-defense. His uncle was the famous Confederate General Ed P. Thomas, and, at the tender age of 12, Heck went to war as courier to his uncle's 35th Regiment of Georgia Volunteers, a part of Stonewall Jackson's Corps.

Glenn Shirley, a Stillwater, Oklahoma, historian and western authority, in his book on Heck Thomas, states: "The day after Heck reached Lee's army, the second battle of Manassas was fought, and he was assigned a duty that contributed his first paragraph to history. The one-armed Mexican War hero, Major General Phil Kearny, of the Federal Army, was killed by a member of Uncle Ed's brigade, and his horse, saddle and sword turned over to Heck for safekeeping.

"Then Lee's army started its big raid down the valley of the Virginia, capturing Harpers Ferry and 14,000 prisoners. Uncle Ed's brigade was detailed to hold these prisoners while the rest of the command went on to fight the battles of Chantilly and Fredericksburg. While they were guarding the prisoners, General Lee ordered Kearny's horse and gear sent through the lines under a flag of truce to his widow.

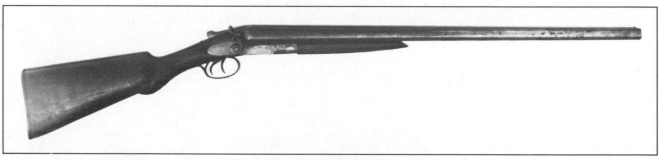

Thomas used this 12-gauge L.C. Smith to end the life and outlaw career of Bill Doolin in 1896. (Museum of the Great Plains)

Heck posed for this photo while deputy U.S. marshal at Ft. Smith, Arkansas in 1886. During this period he was responsible for bringing in a number of outlaw bands which operated in the Indian Territory.

"Heck took them through. Kearny's mount was a big black, very 'showy' horse and Heck hated to give him up. But it was the proudest moment of his life."

Typhoid fever caused the young Thomas to be returned home in the winter of 1863 in a dying condition. By the time he recovered, the war was all but over. The next few years were difficult for the Thomas family as for most other Southerners.

The nickname "Heck" appears to have been bestowed on Henry Thomas while he was studying for religous work at Emory University. His mild manners and quiet, gentlemanly ways apparently brought some kidding his way and "Heck" was the name from this time on.

A life of religious work was too tame for Heck after his taste of military life, so when his father was appointed Atlanta City marshal, he joined the force as a policeman—he was 18-years-old. Race riots were becoming severe and this young man received his first two bullet wounds while he and four other officers fought back an angry mob trying to take a Negro prisoner from them. Heck's bravery, coolness and good judgement during this and other such riots earned him the kind of recognition and respect that was to be the standard of his career for the next 44 years.

Thomas married Isabelle Gray, a minister's daughter, and entered into partnership with two other young men in a wholesale grocery business, thus assuming the quiet, calm and peaceful life his new bride preferred over law enforcement work. Heck's adventurous spirit didn't allow him to stay out of law work long, however, for by 1878 he had taken his wife and two children to Texas where his cousin Jim had recommended him to his own employer, the Texas Express Company, as a messenger—or, guard.

Heck Thomas' interest in and use of guns was much deeper than just considering them as necessary tools of his trade. He seemed to have an appreciation and enjoyment of guns that extended beyond the use of them as a lawman. On the occasion of Bill Doolin's escape from the Guthrie jail, Heck was at home with his wife. According to her report of that evening, given to a newspaper's magazine section in 1939, this conversation took place: "After hearing the news of Doolin's escape, he said: 'Doolin has escaped. I've got to go after my posse and go after him.' He strapped on his pistols, grabbed up his Winchester and hurried from the house. But when he had finished saddling his horse, he came back to the house. 'You had better hide my guns. That bunch will know I have some fine guns and they might find out where I live and come by here. You take my pistols and rifles and hide them.' I took the weapons and hid them in the tall grass and brush near the house. The next evening Heck returned—and found that his precious guns had been left out in the dust and weather. 'Why, woman', he said, 'I wouldn't have had you put those guns out there for anything!

They might have rusted!' And he spent hours polishing and cleaning the guns that night."

Thomas' early exposure and use of firearms was with muzzle loaders. He may have come across some Colt revolvers during his Civil War years and it's possible he took part in some skirmishes. Although, due to his age, the fact that he was under the eye of his uncle and his responsibilities as courier, that is doubtful. There is no doubt, however, that he saw a variety of handguns used in combat. Confederate soldiers were poorly armed but many were able to pick up Colt pistols from the battle fields and others may have been fortunate to have obtained a Griswold & Gunnison or Spiller & Burr pistol made specifically for the Confederacy. These were in short supply but some found their way into the hands of foot soldiers as well as the cavalrymen for whom most were intended. Of all the contractors who hopefully signed agreements to produce as many as 15,000 revolvers apiece within three years, only five succeeded in making any consider-

able number of weapons at all. These were: Griswold & Gunnison, Leech & Rigdon, Rigdon & Ansley, Spiller & Burr and the Columbus Firearms Company. Harassed by manufacturing problems, material shortages, a lack of skilled labor and the need for frequent movement to avoid advancing Union troops, the total production of all five firms was less than 15,000 revolvers.

Thomas' years as a policeman in Atlanta brought him into several confrontations in which his gun skill played a big part in keeping the peace. These years were still before Sam, Colt's introduction of the Single-Action Army .45 so it is possible he was carrying a .44 cap and ball revolver—or one of these cap and ball models that had been con-

This Colt New Service .44 with the barrel cut off to 2 inches was carried by Thomas during the time he worked with Wells Fargo dectives in trailing the Dalton-Doolin gangs. (Museum of the Great Plains)

verted to handle a brass cartridge. While many of his contemporaries preferred the .36 Colt or one of the copies of that pistol, Heck seemed to prefer the bigger bores.

Thomas' move to Texas and his work as an express guard, and later, U.S. marshal, was in the mid-1870s and his preferred sidearm for the next 30-odd years was the Colt .45. In addition, he chose a Winchester '73 in .44-40, for deliberate and/or long-range shooting.

The reputation Heck had earned in Atlanta didn't carry much weight in Texas when he first started with the express company. Those character traits that had earned him that reputation, however, coolness, courage and resourcefullness, soon showed themselves in his new job—and against the Sam Bass gang, no less.

Jim Thomas was robbed on February 22, 1878, and Heck made plans to outsmart any outlaws who stopped a train on which he was riding as express guard. He made up some bundles of paper the size of currency packets and carried these with him on each run he made. The

Heck Thomas (left) posed with his first police force at Lawton, Oklahoma Territory following the Kiowa, Commanche and Apache opening in 1901. Also pictured are (l-r) Leka Hammon, Harry Foster, Bill Bruce and Colonel Hawkins.

Heck Thomas

Heck Thomas (seated center) and a group of Texas Express officials in 1878. This was the crew that trailed Sam Bass.

evening of March 18, gave him a chance to prove his boast that he wouldn't let the robbers get money for which he was responsible.

His train left Denison en route to Galveston and about 10:00 p.m. pulled into the little station of Hutchins, near Dallas. As soon as the train stopped, three masked men captured the engineer and fireman and marched them, along with the station agent, porter and two printers who had hitched free rides up front, back to the express car. The mail clerk opened the door about that time to toss out the mailbags and saw the small group of men approaching. He slammed the door shut and yelled to Heck that robbers were on the platform. Heck blew out the lamp and drew his revolver—apparently a Colt Single Action .45—and waited. The robbers used their hostages as shields and the station agent called on Heck not

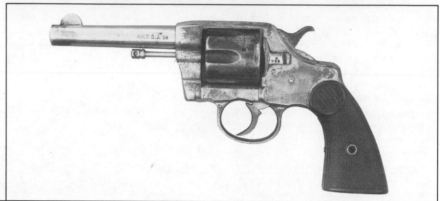

Top: Colt New Navy Model 1892 .38 revolver with 4½-inch barrel, is believed to be the gun carried by Thomas during his hunt for Bill Doolin. He later gave it to a posseman. (Museum of the Great Plains) Bottom: Heck apparently favored the double action .38 revolver. This New Navy Model with a 6-inch barrel is one of the last handguns to be used by Thomas and was given to his son shortly after the turn of the century. It is currently on display at Bianchi's Gunfighter Museum in Temecula, Calif.

to shoot for fear one of the hostages might be hit.

Heck had barricaded the door, and when ordered to open up, plainly told the outlaws where they could go. Their response with lead caused him to seek the protection behind heavy boxes of freight.

This was not the first robbery committed by the Bass gang and a proven method of convincing recalcitrant guards before had been to disconnect the express car from the train and smoke the guard out by placing oil soaked rags under the car and lighting them. This they did, to convince Heck to open up. While they had been doing this, Heck managed to transfer the shipment of about $20,000 from the safe to the ashes of the heating stove—not in use on this run because of mild

weather. The dummy packages of money were put in the safe and the safe door was closed and locked.

After some exchange of shots and threats, the smoke got to Heck and he opened the door after the robbers said they wouldn't shoot him. He reluctantly allowed himself to be forced to open the safe and dropped a bag of silver in the cloth sack first so the robber could hear the clink of coins. The dummy currency packages went in next. He was then marched outside to join the others under guard of a robber's rifle.

Meanwhile, the conductor and brakeman had left the train and run to the hotel to get help. None was immediately available, but they found a shotgun and opened fire on the bandits with it. In the confusion,

Heck took off at a run for the disconnected engine where he knew the engineer kept a revolver hidden—this might be his chance to capture the outlaws! A slug from one of the outlaw's rifles caught him in the neck, cutting the cheek to the bone under his left eye, leaving him partially blinded in that eye for the rest of his days.

Heck was forced to change his mind about going for the engineer's pistol, and when the outlaws gave up their plans to look for more loot and rode off into the darkness, he told the engineer to hurry out of there for he had saved the money. He refused help with his wound and tore a sleeve from his shirt to stem the flow of blood. He had to stop and see a doctor at Corsicana, but continued on to Houston where he turned the money over to Express Superintendent C. T. Campbell.

Heck's description of the leader of the gang firmed up the opinion

"First City Officers of Perry, Oklahoma."
Deputy U.S. Marshal Heck Thomas (left
in white hat) and Bill Tilghman (left of
center post in white hat) were sent to
establish law and order in the newly
created town of Perry in 1889.
(Oklahoma Hist. Society)

that Sam Bass was the man responsible and a concentrated search was begun. On July 19, 1878, the last gun fight between lawmen and members of this gang took place, ending with Bass' death. His promise to "kill Heck Thomas if it's the last thing I ever do," for tricking him with the dummy currency was not kept.

In appreciation for his efforts in protecting the money during the holdup, Heck was presented a gold watch and $200. He was also promoted to chief agent at Fort Worth and spent the next seven years in the Dallas—Fort Worth area in that capacity. His associates were men like T. I. "Longhair Jim" Courtright, a well-known, highly-respected gunman who was marshal of Fort Worth.

Thomas and Courtright had met while in posses searching for Sam Bass, and reestablished their contact in Fort Worth. From Courtright, Heck learned a great deal about the science of frontier law enforcement.

After seven years with the Texas Express Company, Heck resigned his job, and in 1885 ran for city marshal of Fort Worth. Elections during that period of history were boisterous and often violent affairs. Guards were stationed a half-mile from polling places to collect the revolvers and bowie knives usually carried by voters. Even unarmed, however, voters often expressed their political preferences in a physical way. A fight that broke out at one polling place caused it to be closed nine minutes early—with 41 men in line waiting to vote for Heck. He lost the election by 22 votes!

Two more children had been born into the Thomas household during these years in Texas. With four mouths to feed, Heck opened a private detective agency and was al-most immediately contacted by a wealthy Texas cattleman who wanted his brothers' murderers captured.

The tracking and killing of Jim and Pink Lee is another important step in Heck Thomas' career, but for our purposes here, we will only mention the highlights. Heck contacted a friend, Jim Taylor, who was a deputy U. S. marshal in the Chickasaw Nation, Indian Territory, and they agreed to stay on the trail of the Lee brothers until they could be captured. Or, if they refused the order to surrender, killed. Many lawmen, bounty hunters and posses had tried to bring the Lees in, but they didn't stay in the hills as long as Heck and Jim planned to.

For three months, Thomas and Taylor lived out in the hills on the trail of the Lees. Their chance came when the two lawmen saw the brothers camp in a pasture for the night. This was not far from the Texas line, and they would have a chance to get them across into Texas and away from the tribal authorities (Jim Lee had married an Indian girl and this gave him rights and protection from the U. S. marshals as long as he was in the territory). At sunup, Heck and Jim were on a small knoll about 75 yards from the Lee's camp, armed with their Winchesters. When Jim and Pink Lee started stirring around, Heck shouted for them to surrender—they ignored it and grabbed for their guns. Shots were exchanged and the Lee brothers ended up dead. They were loaded in a borrowed wagon

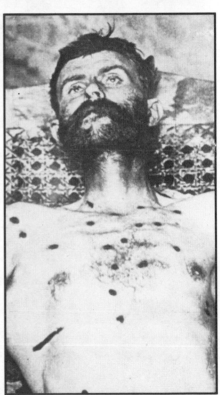

Bill Doolin was photographed in the Guthrie, Oklahoma morgue in 1896 after he was shot and killed by Thomas at Lawson (now Quay).

and taken to the Gainesville, Texas, sheriff's office where they left them and claimed the $2000 reward from Alva Roff. Heck later collected another $500 reward from the state of Texas.

Heck's success in bringing in Jim and Pink Lee, where so many other lawmen had failed, brought many offers from the councils of tough towns that needed taming, a request from Texas' Governor Ireland to join the Rangers and support of the Democratic Association of

Continued on page 210

The Pinkertons

"We Never Sleep."

By Burt Miller

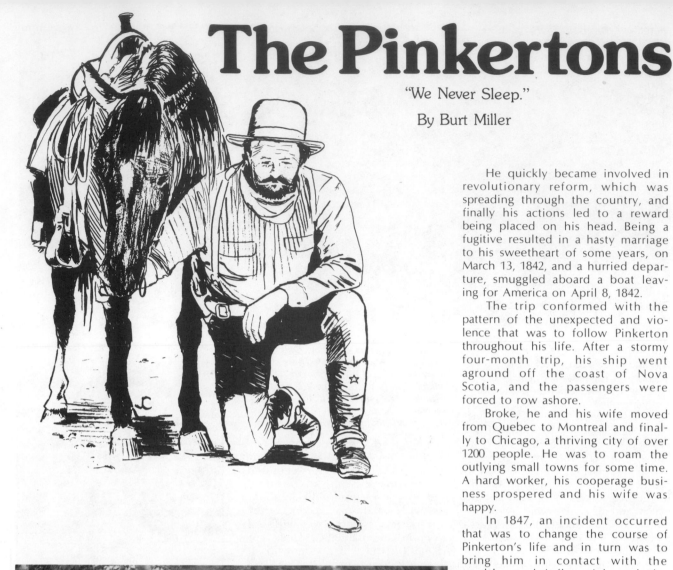

He quickly became involved in revolutionary reform, which was spreading through the country, and finally his actions led to a reward being placed on his head. Being a fugitive resulted in a hasty marriage to his sweetheart of some years, on March 13, 1842, and a hurried departure, smuggled aboard a boat leaving for America on April 8, 1842.

The trip conformed with the pattern of the unexpected and violence that was to follow Pinkerton throughout his life. After a stormy four-month trip, his ship went aground off the coast of Nova Scotia, and the passengers were forced to row ashore.

Broke, he and his wife moved from Quebec to Montreal and finally to Chicago, a thriving city of over 1200 people. He was to roam the outlying small towns for some time. A hard worker, his cooperage business prospered and his wife was happy.

In 1847, an incident occurred that was to change the course of Pinkerton's life and in turn was to bring him in contact with the wealthy and influential, and the country's most notorious criminals of the time.

Searching a small island for lumber he needed for his cooperage business, he noted the surreptitious actions of two men. His curiosity and suspicions led him to notify the

Alan Pinkerton was the son of a Scottish blacksmith who grew up in the poor section of Glasgow. After immigrating to the United States Pinkerton resumed his trade as a cooper until his aprehension of a counterfeiting gang led to a job as deputy sheriff of Kane County Illinois. He later founded The famed detective agency and set up the Secret Service during the Civil War. This photo was taken by Alexander Gardner after the battle of Antietam. (Betmann Archives)

It would appear most unlikely that an emigrant from Glasgow, Scotland was destined to become the greatest detective the world has ever known.

Born on August 25, 1819, Allan Pinkerton grew to manhood in a crowded tenement section of that city. The large family, a mixture of half-brothers and sisters, lived in a third-floor flat. The father, William Pinkerton, was a blacksmith by trade.

A miserable poverty stricken part of the town, overrun by criminals and unsafe at night, the area could hardly fail to influence the future of young Pinkerton.

He became an itinerent cooper (barrel maker), traveling about the countryside finding work as best he could.

sheriff, ending with the apprehension of a gang of counterfeitters.

The die was cast. Publicity of the gang's arrest led to requests for further sleuthing in relation to counterfeitting. He became a deputy sheriff of Kane County, Illinois.

Offered a job as deputy sheriff of Cook County, he sold his cooperage business and moved to Chicago. In 1849, he was appointed the first detective of Chicago by the mayor.

His career established and a reputation spreading, he set up a private detective agency in 1858 at 100 Church St., in New York. It was a time when there was little, if any, coordination between law enforcement agencies, either local or national. Crime and corruption was also becoming rampant in governments throughout the country. Success in his profession was to add two new words to the American vocabulary: a "Pinkerton" became synomonous to "detective," and the agency's trade mark,—a wide open eye with the slogan "We never sleep"—resulted in the expression "private eye."

Early in his career the Illinois Central Railroad became one of his clients. Pinkerton's work—providing protection and efforts in the apprehension of hold up men—was to result in direct and continuing confrontation with possibly the most notorious outlaw of that century, Jesse James.

an agent named John Scully was to be a notorious exception.

Pinkerton developed a blind faith in General McClellan and tied his own career to that of the general, who was to become better known for his reluctance to engage the enemy than any contribution he ever made to winning the war.

During the war, Lincoln gained a great respect for the detective's abilities. Working under McClellan's command, he formed a spy organization that infiltrated the south and reported back on matters of military intelligence. An extremely hazardous assignment at best, Pinkerton was not above going behind enemy lines himself.

The names and work of his operatives became an important part of Civil War history. Pryce Lewis, Sam Bridgeman, George Bangs, Hattie Lawton, Tim Webster, John Scully, John B. Babcock, Seth Paine and G.H. Thiel to mention only a few.

His Rogue's Gallery, a collection of portraits and facts on known

Scully were sent across the enemy lines to Richmond, Pinkerton, known as "Major Allan" in military intelligence, provided each with an adequate bag of gold coins and a .36 caliber Model 51 Navy Colt. In spite of the number of Pinkerton operatives used over the years and the evident fact that they were always armed with the best guns available, only an occassional reference was ever made to any specific model. The Navy Colt was the one exception that was mentioned several times, with the implication that it was a more or less standard arm for the Pinkerton for that period proceeding the development of the cartridge revolver. One other arm mentioned, and a logical replacement for the Navy Colt, was the Number 2 model Smith & Wesson in .32 cali-

General George B. McClellan first hired Pinkerton as Chief of Secret Service for the Army of the Potomac. When McClellan was removed from command, Pinkerton returned to Washington to set up the government Secret Service.

Here Pinkerton poses with President Lincoln and General McClernand. Pinkerton always claimed that had he been in Washington in April of 1865 he could have prevented Lincoln's assassination.

His association with the Illinois Central led to his initial contact with Abraham Lincoln, then counsel for the railroad and George B. McClellan, its vice-president. These contacts were to influence history. In one instance he was to prevent an assassination attempt on Lincoln. He established a spy system for the North under General McClellan and organized the first "secret service" to operate behind enemy lines.

Pinkerton had an uncanny ability to select proficient agents and few ever brought disrepute to the organization. During the Civil War,

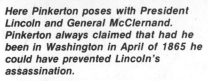

criminals was the first of its kind, and he was first to establish the custom of protecting informers—a police procedure still practiced.

At a time when most men went armed, it was a custom that Pinkerton's men usually had their arms concealed.

On what turned out to be their last mission, Pryce Lewis and John

Pinkerton provided his operatives Pryce Lewis and John Scully with a bag of gold coins and an 1851 .36 Colt Navy revolver when they were sent across the enemy lines into Richmond.

ber. Smaller than the .44 Army model, these conformed better with the role the operative had to play.

Their trip ended in disaster. Webster, another operative already in the city and seriously ill had been tentatively identified as a spy and Lewis and Scully were also under suspicion. Scully, weak at best, frightened and in an attempt to save his own skin, confirmed the identities of all three and Hattie Lawton

The Pinkertons

A favorite early hideout gun with Pinkerton agents was the Smith & Wesson .22 No. 1 First Issue. This was the first practical revolver using a bored-through cylinder and rimfire ammunition. This specimen is complete with its original gutta-percha case. (Sotheby Parke Bernet, Los Angeles)

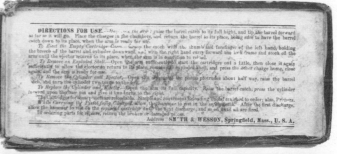

Small revolvers were favored with agents and policemen because they were easily concealed. These .36 percussion Cooper Pocket Police revolvers would have been ideal pistols for a Pinkerton man of the 1860s. (Sotheby Parke Bernet, Los Angeles)

deadly feud than the usual search for a criminal and his accomplices.

History reflects that the bitterness generated started with what must be considered, a stupid and cowardly act on the part of Pinkerton operatives, although local officers were also present at the "bombing" of the Dr. Samuel's home.

Long since established in the annals of history as the nation's most notorious outlaws and train robbers, the James brothers, after several successful holdups and heavy pressure from the law, decided to lie low for a time. During this interval both were to marry.

The Pinkertons were close on the trail, watching every possible contact. On January 26, 1875, they were tipped off that the brothers were visiting their mother's farm, the "Samuel place" as it was known. Afraid to make a direct attack on the cabin, they tossed a flare through a window, which exploded and tore off Mrs. Samuel's right arm and killed Jesse's 8-year-old half-brother.

The affects of that inhumane action was to have a lasting impact

Smith & Wesson .38 Fifth Model hammerless revolver was very popular with Pinkerton agents. It was small enough to be carried in a pocket, and its streamlined shape enabled it to be drawn quickly. The grip safety afforded extra protection against accidental discharge. (Sotheby Parke Bernet, Los Angeles)

as well, who had been nursing the sick Webster.

Webster was hung; Hattie spent a year in prison before being exchanged and Lewis and Scully were imprisoned until the end of the war. Pinkerton did all he could to obtain their release, but to no avail. Webster's death, however, did result in the hanging of two Confederate spies two years later in retaliation.

With McClellan's removal from command of the Army of the Potomac, Pinkerton returned his operatives to the more prosaic jobs of running down war profiteers and ordinary criminals.

Later, Pinkerton was to bitterly insist that if he had not been away he would have prevented Lincoln's assassination. As it turned out, his agency contributed little in the apprehension of the perpetrators.

The man Pinkerton was now to encounter, and probably who was to cause him and his organization the most trouble of all the desparados of the day was Jesse James, his brother Frank and their various gang members. In reality, the patient and prolonged search was more of a

on the agency, engendering instinctive hatred and aversion to both the railroads and their "hirelings," the Pinkertons. In spite of romantic stories about the outlaws, they were nothing more than a band of murderers, bred during the turmoil, created by the reconstruction period in the border states where, at least in Missouri, local sympathy was with the Confederacy. Thus the James boys, their friends, Cole and Jim Younger passed off their depradations as a continuation of the War.

Allan Pinkerton probably never realized for a number of years that his life hung on a thread after Jesse's mother lost her arm. The James brothers placed the blame on Pinkerton himself and swore to kill him in spite of the fact that Pinkerton denied that his people had thrown the bomb.

The famous Pinkerton "Hands Up!" poster was a popular advertising device around the turn of the century. This particular version is printed "Compliments of Wm. A. & Robert Pinkerton." (Lee Silva collection)

reference to the fact that Jesse, Chet Miller and a local friend had killed a Pinkerton a month later.

Just after the war, Allan Pinkerton suffered a stroke which left him partially paralyzed. His doctors believed that he would never recover, at least not to the extent that he could carry on his business.

Typically, he refused to accept their consensus and painfully set up his own program to restore his health. In five years he was able to

The Model 1907 Savage automatic in both .32 and .380 was a runaway favorite with police and agents alike. It was reliable, concealable and held 10 rounds.

ment, an effort that was to last only two years. On October 6, 1866 they made history by executing the first train robbery. They were to rob one train of $96,000, a sum never exceeded by even the James brothers.

Their end can be credited to the Pinkertons, who set a trap by spreading word of a $100,000 train shipment of gold. When the bandits stopped the train and opened the doors, the hidden posse opened fire. Those captured were placed in jail, but were later hung by vigilantes on December 11 1868. The communityy was fed up with their robberies and murders.

Although most of the information found seems to pertain to Midwest desparados, during this same period less spectacular crimes were just as numerous in the East.

Local customs, dress and activities influenced the arms used by peace officers and the criminals. During, and some time after the Civil War, considerable reference was made to the .36 caliber Navy Colt revolver, implying that it was a near standard arm of the Pinkertons. Indications are that this was the arm provided by the agency.

Unless acting a part, the concealable Navy was a compromise in size, yet considered effective enough in its relatively small caliber. This did have one advantage, it permitted some criminals to live to hang, that the .44 Army model would possibly have finished off!

Shotguns were generally provided in those instances where the operatives had occasion to join a local group of officers when closing in on holed up bandits.

During mounted pursuits, which were common, the Pinkertons obtained rifles, usually from local sheriffs or police. As might be expected, these were probably not the best available and some, undoubtedly, hardly justified being taken along.

Ten or 12-gauge shotguns, such as this Colt, with the barrels shortened to 18 or 20 inches were used by Pinkerton agents when they had to move a prisoner. Loads of 00-buck were good insurance against rescue attempts. (Sotheby Parke Bernet, Los Angeles)

Jesse shadowed the Pinkerton family and easily could have killed its younger members, but he wanted only Pinkerton; under circumstances so that he would realize by who and why he was to die. Otherwise, Jesse felt there was no point in killing him! In spite of spending four months trailing Pinkerton, Jesse never got the opportunity just as he wanted it, and gave up for the time, but fate dictated that he would not live to try again.

Frank James complained that the Pinkertons were hounding his family and that they had killed John Younger during a shootout with two Pinkerton operatives. He made no

move about fairly well, although he used a cane. He forced himself to walk daily until he could cover several miles. Finally he could walk as far as 12 miles in one day.

During that period he built a family "castle" called the Larches, after the 1800 larch trees he had shipped from Scotland. His sons ran the business and continued to conduct the agency in the same manner as their father had established. In temperament, they were much like their father.

It was during this time that the Reno brothers of Indiana made their bid for glory with the criminal ele-

Pistols were essential when transferring prisoners by train or stage coach. Unlike the bandits, the operative had to worry about innocent bystanders. It was not unusual to lose some non-participants in the hostilities!

Even so, a shotgun such as the Remington, LeFever, Parker and others, charged with black powder and 00 buck, either 12 or 10-gauge and barrels sawed off to 18 or 20 inches was the best insurance against an attempt to free a prisoner. In those days a Pinkerton moving a prisoner was more often than not on his own. Local police were too often directly involved with, or part of, the

Continued on page 224

Percussion Pocket Pistols

Small pocket pistols have been popular with lawmen, bandits and adventurers ever since a reliable ignition system was first perfected about 400 years ago. Their concealability and light weight made them perfect for hideout guns, or as primary weapons for those not used to packing heavy hardware.

When Sam Colt developed his percussion Paterson revolver in 1836, he offered "Baby Paterson" pocket pistols in .28, .31 and .34 calibers although these, like the other Patersons, were not well received.

Colt's later group of fine .44 percussion Dragoon revolvers spawned a fine little pocket pistol, the .31 "Baby Dragoon." This five-shot revolver was available with either 3, 4, 5 or 6-inch barrels and was extremely popular with police, civilians and those going to California for the Gold Rush. In 1849 a modification of the Baby Dragoon superseded its parent and was designated the M-1849 pocket pistol. With a few minor variations it was identical to the Baby Dragoon.

The limitations of the rather anemic .31 caliber round ball was all too evident, and Colt, realizing this, brought out a .36 caliber version of the M-1849. Finally, in 1862 the firm introduced a fine five-shot .36 revolver designated the 1862 Police Model. It followed the classic streamlined shape of the .44 M-1860 Army and was destined to be the last percussion revolver made by the company.

The Police Model found instant popularity with metropolitan police, Pinkerton agents, and Civil War officers. It was lightweight and relatively compact, but it still packed a wallop of the larger .36 Navy.

Navy Arms, 689 Bergen Blvd., Ridgefield, NJ 07657, offers quality replicas of the Baby Dragoon pocket pistol and 1862 Police revolvers, so for this shooting impression it was not necessary to fire any of the valuable originals.

First we chose a 6-inch barrelled version of the .31 Baby Dragoon. This little pistol is basically a scaled-down copy of its bigger brothers, and the grips are reduced as well. They are small enough to be almost lost in a big mitt, but are large enough to be satisfactorily gripped in the average hand.

To load the Baby Dragoon (and this procedure goes for the Police Pistol as well) one must first snap caps on each of the five nipples to clear the vents of any oil which may be creating a blockage. Charges of 15 grains of FFFg black powder may now be loaded into each chamber by a small flask and five .31 round balls rammed down on the charges

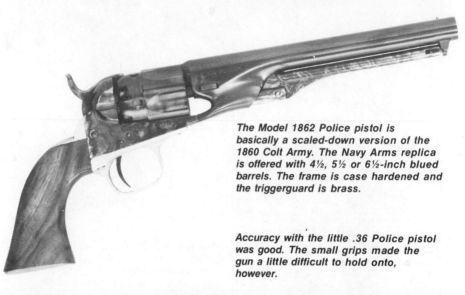

The Model 1862 Police pistol is basically a scaled-down version of the 1860 Colt Army. The Navy Arms replica is offered with 4½, 5½ or 6½-inch blued barrels. The frame is case hardened and the triggerguard is brass.

Accuracy with the little .36 Police pistol was good. The small grips made the gun a little difficult to hold onto, however.

The Baby Dragoon was a mini-version of the larger .44 Colt Dragoon revolvers. It was superseded by the 1849 Pocket Model, which was also in .31 caliber.

The .31 Baby Dragoon was a delight to shoot. It is accurate and has little recoil. The small grips are good for concealment but not conducive to serious target work.

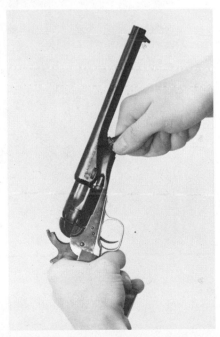

To load the small percussion revolvers, a lead ball of appropriate caliber is forced down over the powder charge by means of the loading lever.

by the loading lever located beneath the barrel. Heavy grease should be placed over the balls to provide lubrication and to eliminate the chance of any chain fires (flash from one chamber setting off others.) Finally, percussion caps are placed on all of the nipples.

As early Colt revolvers do not have top straps, it was necessary to incorporate the rear sight as a notch in the nose of the hammer. This means that when the pistol is full cocked, the shooter lines the front sight up with the hammer groove. Needless to say, this was not conducive to match-type accuracy, but it was sufficient for the combat-type shooting the pistols were designed for.

The recoil of the little .31 was virtually nil. It was very comfortable to shoot, and the report was a sharp crack rather than the bass bark of the larger .44s. Accuracy was quite good, and all five balls were kept within a 4-inch circle at 25 yards— certainly combat accuracy. No mis-fires were experienced, and the gun functioned flawlessly.

Next, the Police Model was loaded for a comparison firing. It uses .375 balls and 22 grains of FFFg. The recoil was noticeably sharper, and the pistol had a tendency to rock upwards. This apparently comes with the heavier charge coupled with the small grips. Accuracy was about the same as the Baby Dragoon, but we had a bit of trouble with a fired percussion cap which had fallen off a nipple and managed to relocate itself in the bowels of the pistol, jamming the mechanism. It required some shaking and probing to dislodge it. This was a problem with all Colts, however, and was not peculiar to just the M-1862.

Both replica pistols functioned well and would have been a welcome piece of armament for anyone "going West." Popularity of the originals of both guns did not end with the cartridge era, for numbers of them were used well into the 1870s and even '80s in their original forms.

The Navy Arms replicas sell for about $95 each and a selection of 4, 5 and 6-inch barrels are available for the Baby Dragoon and 4½, 5½ and 6½ inches for the 1862 Police.

Billy The Kid

Teen-age Killer.
By E. B. Mann

Billie the Kid, a copy a very old tin-type.

What William Bonney "Billy The Kid" looked like, and what manner of boy he was are disputed. He is described as a buck-toothed lout, a monster, a psychopathic murderer; and he is lionized. The picture most commonly published as Billy the Kid is of a boy in rough, ill-fitting clothes, armed with a rifle and a revolver.

But ladies of social status in the Territory, ladies young and not so young—Mrs. John Chisum, wife of New Mexico's wealthiest cattle baron, and Mrs. James Brent, wife of one of Pat Garrett's deputies, among others—described Billy as "a nice looking boy," "well-mannered," "almost handsome." Massachusetts-bred General and New Mexico Teritorial Governor Lew Wallace made a similarly favorable description a part of the official record. Ash Upson, Silver City newsman, described Billy as "bold, daring, reckless, open-handed, generous-hearted, frank, manly, loved and admired, a benefactor, never seen to address a lady but with his hat in his hand;" strange words from the pen of the ghost-writer of *The Authentic Life of Billy the Kid,* by Pat Garrett! But the rest of that book is not impeccably "authentic" either.

Another newspaper man wrote and published in the Las Vegas (New Mexico) Gazette, his own description—better at least to the extent that it includes specifics: "He is about 5'8" tall, slightly built and lithe, weighing about 140, with a frank and open countenance... roguish blue eyes, light hair and complexion. He is in all quite a handsome looking fellow...and he had agreeable and winning ways."

Is this Billy the Kid? This disputed photo has long been used as evidence to prove that Billy was left-handed. In fact, the picture is printed in reverse, as were many of the period. The loading port on the M-1873 (?) Winchester is obviously on the wrong side. This photo has been repeatedly retouched and the revolver cannot be properly identified.
(Bettmann Archive)

That much-published picture is the source of the claim that Billy was left-handed—a deduction based on the fact that the picture, as usually published, shows Billy supporting a rifle with his right hand and wearing a holstered revolver on his *left* hip.

The catch is that the picture, so printed, is reversed. Study the print under magnification and it can be seen, in spite of bad retouching, the ejection port appears on the wrong side of the rifle. Hold that picture up to a mirror and the ejection port is where it should be, and the revolver is where it should be also—on the boy's right hip.

One writer brands the picture as "entirely phony," since the rifle is

Pat Garrett (left) was sheriff of Lincoln County when he shot Billy the Kid. He was succeed by sheriffs John W. Poe (center) and James Brant. The photo was taken in 1883 or 1884. Poe accompanied Garrett the night he killed Billy.

obviously a Winchester Model 94, not issued until years after Billy's death." The picture is so heavily retouched that nothing about the guns is "obvious." But there were several lever-action rifles (carbines) Billy could have owned, including the Winchester Model 66, Model 73, and even earlier Henrys.

At any rate, nobody who knew Billy ever reported that he was left-handed. He was probably more or less ambidextrous with revolvers; most practiced pistolman are; but he was *not* a southpaw.

What guns did he use? Many. This would be true of any gunman. At least two of his better chroniclers

say that he favored Colt Single Action revolvers and Winchester lever-action rifles or carbines, both in .44-40 caliber for convenience in carrying ammunition. Many south-westerners liked this combination, including Pat Garrett. Billy is said to have carried a .41 Colt double-action "Thunderer" the night of his death.

How good a shot was he? He was at least a good shot with either handgun or rifle; was deadly at least once with a shotgun. One writer tells of his riding a horse at a dead run, a gun in each hand, knocking snowbirds off fence posts with unfailing accuracy. I doubt it; and if you've ever tried shooting from horseback, so will you. But he did quite well leaving the McSween

house, on the run, two guns blazing, as we'll see later.

How many men did he kill? *Quien sabe?* Not "one for each year of his life;" that is ridiculous. The tale that, at the age of 12, he "killed a man who insulted his mother" is purest fiction, refuted by all credible informants. And what about the alleged killing of the Texan called, by some writers, Joe Grant?

The story is that Grant—a fancy dresser, wearing a fancy gun, boastful of his prowess—met Billy somewhere, and granted Billy's request to "let me see that pretty gun." Billy admired the gun, turned the cylinder so the hammer would fall next on an empty chamber, gave the gun back, and then challenged Grant to a shoot-out. Grant drew; the gun misfired, and Billy killed him.

The story has no authentication other than hearsay. Believing it means believing that a gun-proud

bravo posing as a killer would hand his gun over to a stranger, much less to a man reputed to be a killer. It's more than I can swallow. But if you like it, take it. Billy was a killer; no one denies it; nor was he bound by any Hollywood code of gunfighting behavior, as will be shown. But even so, he deserves to be judged on reasonable evidence.

The legend reverts to fact, however, in crediting Billy—teenager though he was, and surrounded by older, more experienced men—with a major role in the Lincoln County War. Space forbids any detailed history here of that war; weighty tomes have been written about it, including endless pages in the Congressional Records in Washington; but we must sketch it if we are to gain any understanding of Billy's role.

At that time, Lincoln County,

This Colt .44-40 SAA, SN 0361, is said to have been taken from Billy the kid at the time of his capture at Stinking Spring. The name "Billy" is engraved on the backstrap. The gun is from the collection of early western movie star, William S. Hart.

Territory of New Mexico, was bigger than several of our eastern states; approximately the size of Pennsylvania. Its county seat was Lincoln, a one-street village in a pleasant, verdant canyon-valley. It's one hotel, best bar, and only general store were owned by a partnership composed of L.G. Murphy and James Dolan. Murphy and Dolan also dealt in cattle.

It has been said that the Lincoln County War was between ex-Texas cattle baron John Chisum and rival ranchers Murphy and Dolan. It is true that Chisum accused Murphy and Dolan of handling mostly cattle that wore, or should have worn, Chisum's own Long Rail brand and Jinglebob earmark. But Chisum was not a fighting man; in a land where most men went armed, Chisum never carried a gun. Men who had worked for Chisum—Billy the Kid, among others—fought in the war;

Billy The Kid

but Chisum himself never pulled a trigger nor led a war party. The war was sparked by other frictions.

Billy Bonney-Antrim-McCarty arrived in Lincoln County in the mid-1870s. He worked briefly for Chisum; left Chisum to ride for John H. Tunstall, a wealthy young Englishman who, like so many of his countrymen, was enamored of the country and believed that fortunes could be made in western cattle. A close friendship grew between Billy

Brewer deputized ten men as his posse. One of those men was Billy. The posse headed for the Murphy-Dolan ranch, "flushed" a party of five men, gave chase, captured two: Frank Baker and Billy Morton. On their return to Lincoln, the posse reported that the two captives had tried to escape and were shot. Some say Morton and Baker were summarily executed; some say that Billy the Kid killed both men; some say the whole posse shared the shooting at the fleeing pair and nobody could say who hit whom. In any case, the Lincoln County War was "hot."

Soon thereafter, the Brewer

Bowdre was quicker, that he shot Roberts through the body. But Roberts, mortally wounded, managed to hole up with a heavy rifle and the posse found itself "with a bear by the tail" trying to dislodge him. Roberts shot posseman John Middleton in the belly, shot off Coe's trigger finger and killed Dick Brewer with a bullet through the head. Then, after consultation, the posse decided to withdraw and let the old wolf die whenever it pleased him. Roberts is another name usually added to Billy's record. According to Coe's and other testimony, it doesn't belong there.

Garrett claimed that this .44-40 M-1873 Winchester rifle (top), was found among Billy's belongings after the gunman's death. The shotgun is a Whitneyville s/s double 10-gauge, SN 903. It was the property of Bob Ollinger, and the gun with which Billy killed Ollinger from the window of the Lincoln Courthouse. The small of the stock has been repaired with copper wire. (Robert E. McNellis)

and Tunstall, and that friendship was a primary reason for Billy's role in what followed.

Tunstall was also drawn to a man who recently had come to Lincoln; a man named Alexander McSween, a lawyer, educated for the Presbyterian ministry, deeply religious, prayerfully non-belligerent, who would be trapped like a white moth in a flame of violence. For when Tunstall and McSween opened a rival general store in Lincoln, trouble with the Murphy-Dolan "crowd" was inevitable. There were law suits, charges and counter-charges; and, finally, there was murder. Ten or more Murphy-Dolan men rode out from Lincoln, met Tunstall on the trail, shot him down, and made drunken sport over his body. Various versions are told of the killing, but no one denies that it was cold-blooded murder. As to whether Billy the Kid, kneeling beside Tunstall's body, swore to kill every man who had a part in the killing, who knows? It is a part of the legend.

A man named Dick Brewer was (legally) appointed special constable to run down the Tunstall killers.

Billy the Kid shot guard Bob Ollinger from the window (marked "x") of the Lincoln County Courthouse. The outlaw escaped from his jailroom, and shot guard J.W. Bell as he tried to escape down the front stairs. He then ran to the window and blasted Ollinger with his own shotgun as the deputy returned from lunch.

posse, now somewhat enlarged, were engaged in another skirmish, this time at Blazer's Mill on the Tularosa. There they encountered a man named Bill "Buckshot" Roberts. Roberts had had no part in the Tunstall killing, but there was bad blood between him and Charlie Bowdre, one of the possemen, and when the two men met, both "went for their guns." George Coe, now also a member of the posse, says that

Things moved rapidly from bad to worse in Lincoln County. The citizenry seems to have been pretty much equally divided between the McSween and Murphy-Dolan factions. Neutrality was hazardous, if not fatal. The county was a powder-keg, the fuse burning.

Sheriff Brady was the law in Lincoln County. He was a friend of Murphy's, and was appointed sheriff through Murphy's political efforts. Unquestionably partisan, he may nevertheless have believed himself on the side of right. But Billy the Kid and others believed that Brady had sent the posse to kill Tunstall. Billy hated Brady.

On the morning of April 1, 1878, Sheriff Brady and two deputies, George Hindman and Billy Mathews, left the Murphy-Dolan store to walk to the courthouse. Lincoln was an armed camp, so all three men carried rifles and sidearms. The Tunstall store and residence stood midway between the Murphy-Dolan store and the courthouse. Beside the McSween store, a low adobe wall, part of a coral, faced the street. Be-

New Mexico Territory Governor Lew Wallace (shown in Civil War Major General's uniform) offered Billy a pardon, but the Kid rebelled when he was told he would have to leave the territory. Wallace then issued a Wanted notice.

hind the wall, six men—Billy the Kid, Charlie Bowdre, Tom O'Folliard, Jim French, Fred Wayte, and Frank McNab—waited. The McSweens were visiting friends in Roswell.

As Brady and his deputies came opposite the corral wall, six rifles blazed at them. Brady fell, riddled.

Hindman ran, but a flurry of bullets cut him down instantly. Miraculously, Mathews won the safety of another house.

They name Brady and Hindman as two more tallies for Billy. Well, Billy was there; he was shooting; he was a good shot. No doubt he scored. There were no heroics here, it was cold-blooded ambush-murder. But there were six men shooting, all practiced shots, all equally guilty of murder, but—one-sixth of two should be the extent of Billy's "credit" toward that legendary 21-man tally.

Alexander McSween was appalled by Brady's murder. He is said to have lectured the killers, sworn to see them punished when the war was over. But Brady's death gave McSween an opening to place a friend in the position of law enforcement in Lincoln County, and

he persuaded the County Commission to appoint John N. Copeland sheriff. Copeland was ruggedly honest, but he had no experience as a lawman, was easy going, unlikely to earn the respect or fear of veteran fighting men on either side.

Murphy and Dolan, of course, had other opinions. They made their voices heard all the way to Santa Fe, to the offices of Territorial Governor Axtell. Axtell summarily rescinded Copeland's appointment and named George W. "Dad" Peppin, sheriff of Lincoln County. Peppin seems to have been honest, too; but like Brady, he was honest on the Murphy-Dolan side.

This appointment backfired on Governor Axtell. President Rutherford B. Hayes disapproved of this and other Axtell actions in New Mexico Territory, removed Axtell from office, and appointed General Lew Wallace to replace him, with specific instructions to end the war. Wallace could do little to end the war; it ground on to its own bloody conclusion. What Wallace did do in Santa Fe was to finish the writing of "Ben Hur," the great novel for which he is famous. But again, the question of which side was on the side of the law was a matter of partisan opinion. The McSween faction had claimed legality under Brewer, and under Copeland. The Murphy-Dolan faction had claimed legality under Brady, and claimed it now under Peppin. It was, still is, a "Mexican stand-off."

The climax came with the three-day siege of the McSween house in Lincoln.

It was mid-July, 1878. As if by agreement, the opposing armies were gathering in Lincoln. The distribution of forces was: McSween men in the Montana and Patron houses in the east end of the village; George Coe, Hendry Brown and Charlie Bowdre in the McSween store; and in the McSween residence, McSween himself, complete with Bible, his wife, her sister, Mrs. Elizabeth Shield, Mrs. Ealy, wife of the Presbyterian minister, Billy the Kid, Tom O'Folliard, Doc Skurlock, Francisco Semora, Ignacio Gonzales, Harvey Morris, Jose Chaviz, Jim French, Vincente Romero and Ygenio Salazar. Murphy forces held the Murphy-Dolan store and hotel, both some 50 yards west of the McSween residence; and from the steep hillsides to the south, Murphy-Dolan riflemen commanded the entire village. The stage was set. Ammunition was plentiful, supplied for each side from its own store.

The early fighting was desultory; much shooting but, with both sides

Billy The Kid

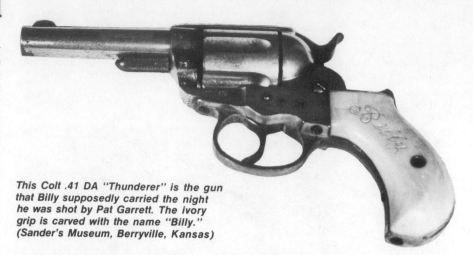

This Colt .41 DA "Thunderer" is the gun that Billy supposedly carried the night he was shot by Pat Garrett. The ivory grip is carved with the name "Billy." (Sander's Museum, Berryville, Kansas)

shooting from cover, few or no casualties. Some Murphy men did reach the walls of the McSween house and its back door courtyard, and it was one of these who finally thought of setting fire to the house.

Perhaps the most noteworthy single shot of the war was made by Fernando Herrara, a McSween fighter, from the Montana house. Harassed by Murphy sharpshooters firing from rocky covers on the south side of the canyon, Herrara provided himself with a "bench rest" for his big "Buffalo" Sharps rifle, timed the

Billy the Kid's grave in Fort Sumner, New Mexico's, old cemetery has been chipped and disfigured by tourists over the years.

re-appearance of a target above its boulder, and squeezed the trigger. The body of a man named Montoya came tumbling down, shot through the body. The shot has been reported as having been scored at "900 or more yards." William Brent says, in his book *The Complete and Factual Life of Billy the Kid* that "the miraculous shot was, years later, measured airline with surveyor's instruments and found to be exactly 787 yards." Miraculous indeed, considering the rainbow trajectory of any of those big Sharps slugs!

A strange interlude in the battle occurred with the arrival in Lincoln

of a company of U.S. Cavalry—black soldiers with white officers, known in the West as "buffalo soldiers"—under the command of Colonel N.A.M. Dudley. Two Gatling guns rumbled on their caissons behind the troopers.

Alexander McSween heaved a sigh of relief. Surely, with the U.S. Army in command, the battle was over. All would be well now; justice would prevail.

It was strange justice. Colonel Dudley and his aides discussed the situation with Sheriff Peppin and others in front of the Murphy-Dolan store. Presently, troopers swung the two Gatlings to face the McSween forces. They were never fired, but their position left no doubt as to which side they supported.

The temporary cease fire provided opportunity for Mrs. McSween, her sister, and Mrs. Ealy to leave the McSween house. Mrs. McSween went immediately to Dudley and made an empassioned appeal for her husband, their friends, and their

Continued on page 212

John Wesley Hardin

"Over 40 Men Killed—Not Countin' Mexicans or Injuns."

By John Lachuk

house. And those still sympathetic to the Southern cause knew that they were in for some bad times! Thus it was that James G. Hardin, Methodist preacher, attorney, teacher, sent his son into hiding rather than have him face a kangaroo court.

Before long, the authorities discovered Wes' hideout, and three Union soldiers came to arrest him. His brother Joe got wind of the posse, and warned Wes to flee. The natural inclination of a 15-year-old boy should have been to run, but Wes was obstinate and totally without fear. As he said, "Nothing could

Hardin often makes mention of a Winchester, without further clarification. Considering the dates of much of his activity, the Model 1866 in .44 rimfire would be the rifle he referred to. (Sotheby Parke Bernet, Los Angeles)

The guns of John Wesley Hardin could well have numbered a hundred or more. He was in no way a gun buff. Hardin Regarded firearms merely as tools, albeit tools that he used exceedingly well! He often lost guns, or simply wore them out, but he always seemed to have several at hand during times of need.

Hardin's latter-day biographers, and there are at least as many of them as there were victims of his shootin' irons, are no help at all in narrowing down the possibilities. Hardin himself, in his famous autobiography, is less than specific about the arms that he used during his exploits. It does appear, however, that he had an understandable prediliction for Sam Colt's revolvers. In his first death encounter, Hardin speaks of his gun first as, "...my pistol," and later described it as, "...a Colt's .44 six-shooter." Young Wes killed his first man, a freed Negro slave, when he was only 15 years of age. After a previous argument, the pair met by accident on the trail. As Hardin tells it, "I stopped in the road and he came at

me with his big stick. He struck me, and as he did it I pulled out a Colt's .44 six-shooter and told him to get back. By this time he had my horse by the bridle, but I shot him loose. He kept coming back, and every time he would start I would shoot again and again until I shot him down." This one act, which might have been excused as self-defense in normal times, put John Wesley Hardin permanently outside of the law. "Law" in that time and place meant the rule of occupation soldiers from the North, with little sympathy for "Johnny Reb," old or young, and the appointed officials of quisling Governor Edmund J. Davis. To enforce his edicts, Davis had a State Police Force consisting of more than 150 men. About one-third were Negros.

Young Wes was fiercely dedicated to the cause of the Southern Confederacy. He, and many others of Texas' 818,579 residents, didn't consider the war ended with Lee's surrender at Appomattox Court-

scare me but a ghost." Instead of running, Wes rode to the spot where the posse would have to cross a deep creek bed. As he candidly described it, "I waylaid them, as I had no mercy on men whom I knew only wanted to get my body to torture and kill. It was war to the knife with me, and I brought it on by opening the fight with a double-barreled shotgun and ending it with a cap-and-ball six-shooter. Thus it was that by the fall of 1868 I had killed four men and was myself wounded in the arm."

By adding up all of John Wesley Hardin's descriptions of his handgun, we come up with a Colt .44 cap-and-ball revolver, which had to be the 1860 Army Model, widely used by both sides during the Civil War. About a quarter-million of these excellent handguns were produced, and many of them made their way to the Western frontier. For most people, thoughts of the Western frontier conjure up visions of the Single Action Peacemaker .45 Colt revolver. Few seem to realize that the era of the gunfighter was actually ushered in by the 1860 Army Model Colt cap-and-ball. The Peacemaker was patented in 1873, but only 200 were produced that year. Over 14,000 were manufactured the next year, but that was reduced to half the year following. From

John Wesley Hardin

then on, production teetered from a low of 4000 units to a high of 17,000 in 1883. With this limited production, it took time for the new-fangled cartridge revolvers to seep in and displace the well-entrenched cap-and-ball variety. When he was finally captured and sent to prison in 1877, Hardin was carrying a Colt .44 cap-and-ball!

The streamlined, superbly-balanced 1860 Army Model with its 8-inch barrel, weighed just 2 pounds 11 ounces. It is reliably reported that young John Wesley Hardin could perform sheer magic with one of these in each hand. Doubtless he practiced fast draw, spinning and twirling the revolvers, doing the "border shift," that is switching two guns from one side to the other simultaneously, as well as the "road agent's spin," which consisted of offering the guns to an adversary butt-first, then suddenly whirling them around to aim the muzzles at him.

Hardin tells of using the trick to back down the vaunted Wild Bill Hickok, then marshal of Abilene, Kansas. As Wes tells it, "I spent most of my time in Abilene in the saloons and gambling houses, playing poker, faro, and seven-up. One day I was rolling ten pins and my best horse was hitched outside in front of the saloon. I had two six-shooters on, and, of course, I knew the saloon people would raise a row if I did not pull them off. Several Texans were there rolling ten pins and drinking. I suppose we were pretty noisy. Wild Bill came in and said we were making too much noise and told me to pull off my pistols until I got ready to go out of town. I told him I was ready to go now, but did not propose to put up my pistols, go or no go. He went out and I followed him. I started up the street when someone behind me shouted out, 'Set up. All down but nine.'

"Wild Bill whirled around and met me. He said, 'What are you howling about, and what are you doing with those pistols on?'

"I said, 'I am just taking in the town.'

"He pulled his pistol and said, 'Take those pistols off. I arrest you.'

"I said alright and pulled them out of the scabbard, but while he was reaching for them, I reversed them and whirled them over on him with the muzzles in his face, springing back at the same time. I told him to put his pistols up, which he did. I cursed him for a long-haired scoundrel that would shoot a boy with his back to him (as I had been

told he intended to do to me). He said, 'Little Arkansas, you have been wrongly informed.'

"I shouted, 'This is my fight and I'll kill the first man that fires a gun.'

"Bill said, 'You are the gamest and quickest boy I ever saw. Let us compromise this matter and I will be your friend. Let us go in here and take a drink, as I want to talk to you and give you some advice.'"

According to Harding, Wild Bill and John parted in guarded friendship, that was little more than an

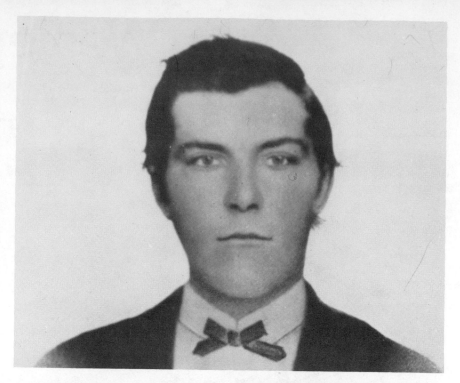

armed truce. While the author has yet to turn up any eyewitness corroboration for the above incident, he does not doubt that it happened just as Hardin described it. Certainly young Wes possessed the skill and outright audacity to pull it off. And Wild Bill was too careful to take the risk of letting the cocky teenager from Texas kill him on the streets of his own town. Better to pose as the patronizing "Big Brother," to both stay alive and save face.

Although backing down Wild Bill was certainly dramatic enough, Hardin used the road agent's spin

on a later occasion with still more telling effect. Young Wes was again being sought by a posse of Texas State Police. As he picks up the narrative, "They found me at a small grocery store in the southern portion of Gonzales County. I really did not know they were there until I heard someone say, 'Throw up your hands or die!'

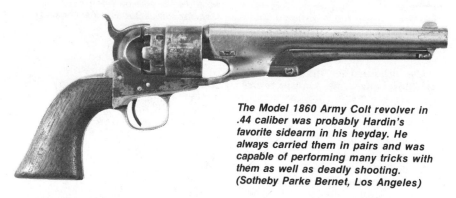

The Model 1860 Army Colt revolver in .44 caliber was probably Hardin's favorite sidearm in his heyday. He always carried them in pairs and was capable of performing many tricks with them as well as deadly shooting. (Sotheby Parke Bernet, Los Angeles)

"I said, 'Alright,' and turning around saw a big black Negro with his pistol cocked and presented. I said, 'Look out, you will let that pistol go off, and I don't want to be killed accidentally.'

"He said, 'Give me those pistols.'

"I said, 'Alright,' and handed him the pistols, handle foremost. One of the pistols turned a somersalt in my hand and went off. Down came the Negro, with his pistol cocked, and as I looked outside, I saw another Negro on a white mule firing into the house at me. I told him to hold up, but he kept on, so I turned my Colt's .45 on him and knocked him off his mule on my first shot. I turned around then to see what had become of No. 1 and saw him sprawling on the floor with a bullet through his head."

It seems that Hardin shot most of his unfortunate opponents through the head! Throughout his autobiography, he never mentions whether he used round balls or the pointed picket bullets in his .44 revolvers, but when placed neatly between a man's eyes, as was Hardin's habit, either should have proved instantly fatal.

Hardin normally carried two Colt revolvers, thereby providing 12 shots before necessitating the painfully slow process of loading powder, ball and caps. For Hardin, the issue was usually settled before both pistols were empty! On two occasions, when he was caught with a single revolver, he had reason to regret it. The first incident occurred while Hardin was driving a trail herd north from Texas to Kansas. Another

the meanwhile, Jim Clements, hearing that I was in a row, had come to my assistance. I was riding a fiery gray horse and the pistol I had was an old cap-and-ball, which I had worn out shooting on the trail. There was so much play between the cylinder and the barrel that it would not burst a cap or fire unless I held the cylinder with one hand and pulled the trigger with the other. I made several unsuccessful attempts to shoot the advancing Mexican from my horse but failed. I then got down and tried to shoot and hold my horse, but failed in that, too. Jim Clements shouted at me to 'Turn that horse loose and hold the cylinder.' I did so and fired at the Mexican, who was now only ten paces from me. I hit him in the thigh and stunned him a little. I tried to fire again, but snapped."

It seems that Clements' pistol was not loaded, so he couldn't shoot. Had he been carrying a cartridge revolver, it would have taken only moments for him to get into action. As it was, both men fled

ican Hotel to retire for the night. We soon got to bed, when presently I heard a man cautiously unlock my door and slip in with a big dirk in his hand. I halted him with a shot and he ran; I fired at him again and again, and he fell dead with four bullets in his body. He had carried my pants with him and so I jumped back, slammed the door, and cried out that I would shoot the first man that came in. I had given one of my pistols to Manning the night before, so the one I had was now empty.

"Now, I believed that if Wild Bill found me in a defenseless condition, he would take no explanation, but would kill me to add to his reputation. So in my shirt and drawers I told Gip to follow me and went out on the portico."

So it was that John Wesley Hardin, still only 19-years-old, but one of the most famed gunfighters on the frontier, was forced to flee in his skivvies, pursued by Tom Carson, one of Wild Bill's deputies, and two others. Wes commandeered a horse and beat the posse back to his cow

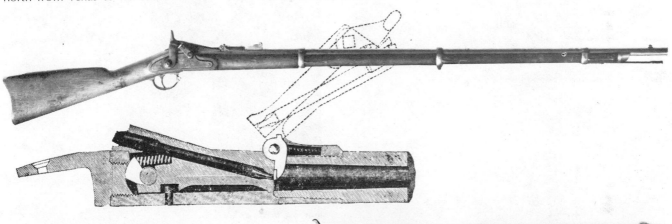

Hardin makes reference to a "needle gun." This would be the Model 1866 Springfield .50-70 Allin conversion, so called because of the long needle-like firing pin as illustrated by this old engraving.

One of the civilian versions of the M-1860 Colt .44 Army featured a full-fluted cylinder. Hardin easily could have used a number of these models during his career.

herd, driven by a group of Mexicans was crowding him from behind, and an argument ensued. In Hardin's words, "The boss Mexican rode back up to where I was and cursed me in Mexican. He said he would kill me with a sharp-shooter as quick as he could get it from the wagon. In about five minutes I saw him coming back with a gun. He rode up to within about 100 yards of me, got down off his horse, took deliberate aim at me, and fired. The ball grazed my head, going through my hat and knocking it off. He tried to shoot again, but something got wrong with his gun and he changed it to his left hand and pulled his pistol with his right. He called up his crowd of six or seven Mexicans. In

back to camp, where they, "...loaded two of the best pistols there." Now better armed, Hardin and Clements returned to the fray, which ultimately ended with six of the Mexican herders dead.

Later, in Abilene, Wes was caught one-pistol short again. "In those days my life was constantly in danger from secret or hired assassins, and I was always on the lookout.

"On the 7th of July, Gip and I had gone to our rooms in the Amer-

camp on the north bank of North Cottonwood River. There he armed himself with two six-shooters and a Winchester, the better to greet his pursuers! He sent the trio back to Abilene sans boots and clothing.

In his autobiography, Hardin often speaks of Winchesters, but they were usually in the hands of others. He preferred to use handguns for combat. The year was 1871, so the Winchesters referred to had to be the Model 1866 .44 rimfire. At one point, he mentions firing at a pursu-

John Wesley Hardin

ing posse with a "needle gun," a frontier term for the .50-70 Springfield Allin conversion rifle.

Hardin used a shotgun in his first encounter with the Texas State Police. He mentions using a scattergun on several other occasions. For example: "I looked around and saw Jack Helms advancing on Jim Taylor with a large knife in his hands. Someone hollered, 'Shoot the damned scoundrel.' It appeared to me that Helms was the scoundrel, so I grabbed my shotgun and fired at Capt. Jack Helms as he was closing with Jim Taylor...He (Helms) fell with 12 buckshot in his breast..." The shotguns he used had to be muzzle loading cap locks. This is born out by another Hardin encounter with pursuing lawmen. "It was now about 9 a.m. and drizzling rain. Capt. Waller apparently con-

turn. "He told me he would arrest me for interfering with him in the discharge of his duty. I told him he could not arrest one side of me, and the boy laughed. Spites started to draw a pistol. I pulled a derringer with my left and my six-shooter with my right and instantly fired with my derringer. The dauntless policeman ran to the courthouse and asked the judge to protect him." Derringers of the day were too numerous to allow educated speculation on the breed or bore.

Hardin never alludes to the manner of holster or "scabbard" that he used to hold his guns. Certainly he was canny enough to seek out the best leather goods then available, something that would aid rather than hinder his draw. In his book, "Triggernometry," (Caxton Printers, Ltd. 1941) Eugene Cunningham credits Hardin with developing a unique holster vest. The soft calf-skin skele-

Later, when he was being transferred to Waco, he contrived to get at the gun, killed one of the deputies and escaped. After his final capture, on July 23, 1877, Hardin was found to be carrying a Colt .44 cap-and-ball, stuck in the waistband between his shirt and undershirt.

After almost 17 years of confinement, John Wesley Hardin emerged from Rusk Prison a different man. It might not be correct to say that his spirit was broken, but it was sorely tried. His beloved wife, Jane, had died a little over a year before his release, denying him the one anchor that might have held him steady in the strife to follow. Granted a full pardon by Governor J. S. Hogg, Hardin passed the bar and became an attorney, taking up residence in Gonzales with his son and two daughters. All might have gone well, but he again became embroiled in politics, unfortunately on

Colt .38 caliber double action "Lightning" revolver, with nickel finish and mother-of-pearl grips, along with Elgin pocket watch, both presented to Hardin by Jim B. Miller.

ceived the idea of running on us and turned his horse loose after us for that purpose. I told Jim to hold up as I wanted to kill him. I wheeled, stopped my horse, and cocked my shotgun. I had a handkerchief over the tubes to keep the caps dry, and just as I pulled the trigger, the wind blew it back and the hammer fell on the handkerchief. That saved his life. Waller checked up his horse and broke back to his men."

Hardin mentions using a derringer on one occasion. Hardin came upon the scene of an argument between a 10-year-old boy and Sonny Spites, a Texas state policeman. Spites was threatening to whip the boy when Hardin arrived, and events followed their inevitable

ton vest had two holster pockets sewn on the front, holding a brace of six-shooters, butts inward, muzzles pointed toward the hipbones. Doubtless, John Wesley Hardin could whip those two pistols out in a twinkling, but when James B. Gillette became police chief of El Paso, and was presented with such a vest, he found himself all tangled up trying to draw the guns across each other, forcing him to relegate the vest to purely ornamental status! It appears that Hardin often depended upon surprise or deception, rather than pure speed of draw, to give him the edge. When but 17-years-old, Hardin already had a price on his head. He was captured and jailed at Marshall, Texas, where he managed to purchase, "...a .45 Colt with four barrels loaded." Wes tied the revolver with a stout cord under his left arm, beneath his shirt, with a vest and heavy fur coat over that, certainly no rig to offer a fast draw

Warrant for Hardin's arrest after his holdup of the dice table at the Gem Saloon, along with the pearl-handled .41 Colt "Thunderer" taken from him during the arrest.

the losing side. He moved abruptly, and opened a law office at Junction, Texas. He married a much younger girl, but couldn't hold her, probably adding to his inner bitterness. However, Wes was embarked upon one project that brought him pride. He was writing his memoirs.

About this time, Wes received what amounted to a clan call. Jim Miller, brother-in-law of Manning Clements, Hardin's cousin, needed an attorney. Miller, himself a notorious killer, wanted Hardin to aid him in prosecuting Bud Frazer, the man who had crippled Miller in a shootout! Hardin had never refused help to a kinsman before, and he couldn't start now. The first trial of Frazer resulted in a hung jury. The second one absolved Frazer. All the same, Miller was grateful to Hardin for his help, and presented him with a Colt double action .38 caliber "Lightning" revolver, serial number 84304, and an engraved Elgin pocket watch, serial number 4069110. Denied satisfaction under the law, Miller took matters into his own hands, and emptied a shotgun into Frazer, in Toyah, Texas.

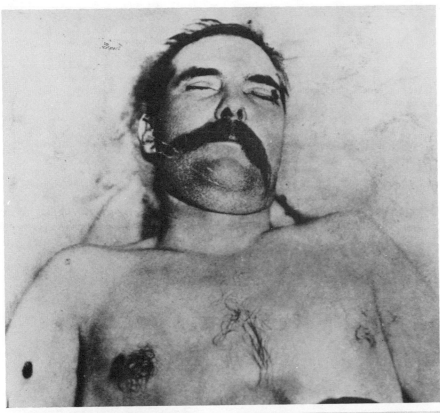

John Wesley Hardin was shot in the back of the head by John Selman. Four shots were fired. Exit wound of killing shot is visible on lid of left eye. Two other hits can be seen in right arm and chest. One bullet missed completely.

During this litigation, Hardin was called upon to go to El Paso, perhaps the one town in Texas that he should have avoided! Because of its strategic location just across the river from Juarez, offering an emergency haven in Old Mexico, El Paso acted like a magnet to all of the riff-raff driven from the rest of the Southwest by stiffening law enforcement. Among El Paso's bars and pool halls, Hardin soon discovered that his reputation as a killer still evoked murmurs of admiration from the crowd. Once more, he was a celebrity! Here, he acted out the last few melancholy months of his turbulent career.

Soon after he arrived in El Paso, in April 1895, Hardin was employed by Mrs. Beula Monrose (AKA "McRose" and "M'Rose") to aid her husband, who was jailed by Mexican authorities in Juarez, awaiting extradition proceedings. Before long,

Hardin and Beula were openly living together, and henchmen of Monrose were vocally threatening his life.

Hardin cited these threats upon his life as his reason for carrying a pistol when he was arrested several weeks later. The incident actually stemmed from Wes' increasingly heavier drinking and gambling. In his cups, he became belligerent and

This .45 slug, worn by the fondling of many hands over the years, took the life of America's most famous gunfighter. It was displayed for many years in a glass jar at the Acme Saloon in El Paso, Texas.

overbearing. One night he felt that he had been cheated in a dice game at the Gem Saloon, and reclaimed his $95 stake at gun-point. A few weeks later, he surrendered to a

warrant charging him with, "unlawfully carrying a pistol," dated the 6th of May, and signed by George Parker, Clerk of El Paso County Court. Hardin appeared before Justice of the Peace Walter D. Howe, and was fined $25. The arresting deputy Will TenEyck, confiscated the gun used by Hardin, a double action .41 caliber Colt "Thunderer," factory engraved, with mother of pearl grips, Serial No. 73728. TenEyck sold the revolver to George Look, owner of the Gem Saloon. Later, it found its way into the Tom Powers Collection and was displayed at the Coney Island Saloon. Robert E. McNellis, of El Paso, Texas, to whom the author is obliged for much of the material and photographs used herein, is currently engaged in writing a definitive biography of John Wesly Hardin. Judging by the depth of his research on the project, it should bring to light many facts heretofore unknown about the famed gunfighter. McNellis wrote to Colt to trace the .41 "Thunderer," and was told that it was a part of a shipment of some 15 guns shipped by Colt on December 30, 1889, to Ketelsen Digetau, El Paso, Texas.

The stage was now set for Hardin's last involvement with violence. While he was out of town, his mistress, now the widow Monrose (Martin having been killed by El Paso Police Chief Jeff Milton), was arrested by a young officer, John Selman, Jr., for brandishing a firearm in public. Upon his return, Hardin took this as a personal affront, and openly threatened young Selman. The elder Selman, then 58-years-old, was himself a gunman of some repute, and he took his son's argument upon himself. He also had the power of the law on his side, inasmuch as he was a Constable of Precinct No. 1 in El Paso. On the night of August 19, 1895, Selman and John Wesley Hardin met and exchanged angry words. Sometime between 11 and 12 o'clock that night, Hardin was standing at the bar of the Acme Saloon, throwing dice with grocer Henry S. Brown. His back was to the front door of the saloon. John Selman stepped quietly through the swinging doors, and at point-blank range, fired a .45 caliber slug through the back of Hardin's head. He fired three more frenzied shots at Hardin's inert body, as it lay prostrate on the floor. One bullet penetrated Hardin's right arm, another struck his right breast. The third was a clean miss. Of course, Hardin was already dead from the first bullet that according to the autopsy, "... entered near the base of the skull posteriorly and came out at the upper corner of the left eye."

John Wesley Hardin

The spent bullet struck the frame of the bar mirror and dropped to the floor, where it was recovered by bar owner R. B. Stevens. He displayed it for many years in a glass jar in the bar. The bullet is now in the possession of Bob McNellis.

Selman's claim of firing in self-defense may appear somewhat thin under the circumstances, but he was ably defended by A. B. Fall, later to become Secretary of the Interior. Fall stated that the antagonists saw each other in the bar mirror, and that Hardin reached for a gun, a

Courthouse as curiosities until 1908, when they were purchased by Manning Clements, Hardin's nephew, for $24. Clements sold them the same day to Tom Powers for $100, for his display in the Coney Island Saloon. They hung on the wall in a wooden shadow box, with a city marshal's badge affixed in the middle.

In the final summing up, we find the statement of J. L. Whitmore, "Temporary Administrator of the Estate of J.W. Hardin," addressed to the Honorable F. E. Hunter, County Judge, listing a less than imposing array of books, clothing, and one .41 Colt pistol number 68837 (this was

and later returned to his relatives).

There are conflicting reports on just how good Hardin really was. The truth is that in an era of fast guns and tough men, Hardin stood out. He was respected by his contemporaries as one of the best with a sixgun, and finally met his fate in the same way as another controver-

This display hung in an El Paso saloon for many years. Top gun is the Smith & Wesson .44-40 with nickel finish, taken from Hardin's body. Bottom is the .45 Colt Peacemaker used by Selman to shoot Hardin through the back of the head. Between the revolvers is a city marshal's badge.

Selman at 58 years, pictured after he killed Hardin, presented an imposing picture. He was himself something of a notorious killer, but he didn't have long to glory in his victory over Hardin. Within months he was also shot down.

declaration not supported by the evidence.

The gun used by Selman was a Colt Peacemaker .45 caliber, serial number 141805. It was taken from Selman the night of the killing and held as evidence by the court, along with the break-top .44-40 double action Smith and Wesson revolver taken from Hardin's body, serial number 352. The Smith and Wesson was sold to Hardin along with the Colt .41 "Thunderer," by Arthur R. Kline & Co., Commission and Custom House Brokers, El Paso, sometime in April 1895. The "Thunderer" was taken from Hardin after he held up the dice game, but he kept the Smith until his death. Hardin's Smith and Wesson, and Selman's .45 Peacemaker remained around the District

Ivory-stocked Colt Peacemaker, SN 126680, listed among Hardin's effects by the administrator of his estate. The ejector and housing are missing. (University of Oklahoma)

apparently another "Thunderer," now lost), one .38 Colt pistol number 84304, white handle (the Colt "Lightning" given to Wes by his grateful client "Killer Jim" Miller), one Colt pistol .45 number 126680 (a Peacemaker belonging to Hardin

sial gunfighter, James Butler Hickok—shot in the back! A sure way not to take a chance on a man that you know is good with his gun. John Wesley Hardin lived and died by the gun, but while he lived he tallied perhaps the largest record of kills. Whether all of his stories can be believed or not does not matter. The fact remains . . . he was one helluva gunfighter!

Merwin and Hulbert Pocket Revolver

By Phil Spangenberger

The Merwin & Hulbert revolvers certainly have an interesting frontier history. Back when the gun's inventors were trying to promote it, they decided that one man should stay in the East and produce the hardware while the more personable partner went West to obtain sales or perhaps some sizeable contracts. While scouring the Great Plains, the traveling inventor was captured by a band of hostile Indians and subsequently burned at the stake. The firm didn't last too long after that, even though one of their larger revolvers was considered for use by the U.S. Army and a few of them were purchased for trial use by the troops. These guns did enjoy a certain amount of popularity however, Henry Starr reportedly used a Merwin & Hulbert open top revolver, and Pearl Hart, the lady bandit, used a Pocket Army revolver during her outlaw career.

Manufactured by Hopkins & Allen Manufacturing Co., of Norwich, Connecticut, the Merwin & Hulbert's were odd looking affairs that were uniquely different in their operation from other guns of the era. The caliber is as marked on the side of the frame "Calibre Winchester 1873." This was accepted in the 19th century as meaning .44-40. Merwins are not just top-break revolvers, they could best be termed as "Top-break-turn-to-the-side and pull forward" single or double action guns. The aforementioned process would unload the piece while loading was done through the side loading gate which slid down.

A Pocket Army was used in this shooting impression. It is truly a "Bulldog" pistol. It seems to have some advantages for use as a pocket or concealable type revolver. It is fairly compact with a 3.3-inch barrel, and the healthy .44-40 cartridge speaks for itself. I fired this mini-blunderbuss with a load of 40 grains of black powder and a 205-grain slug. The revolver kicked like a mule! You can really feel that big cartridge going off in that short barrel. Accuracy was good with a two-hand hold and shooting single action. But double action is another story. The pull is so hard that the gun weaves all over creation. Rapid firing is all but impossible. Once the

The stubby proportions of the Merwin & Hulbert .44-40 Pocket Army revolver gives it a true "Bulldog" appearance. It is an accurate and powerful little handgun. (Author's collection)

"Pinkerton agent" Phil Spangenberger fires the Merwin & Hulbert using the double action. Trigger pull was so heavy that rapid fire was impossible. Single-action trigger let-off was smooth and crisp, however.

gun is fired, the recoil throws it out of alignment in your hand and your trigger finger is not in place to provide a squeeze powerful enough to discharge the weapon again. After several unsuccessful attempts at double-action shooting, I changed over to strictly single action. The gun is certainly enveloped in a cloud of smoke when it is fired. It is no wonder when the size of the barrel in ratio to the cartridge is considered.

An interesting drawback in the author's opinion is that the revolver cannot be reloaded when in the broken-open position. This would tend to slow one down in an emergency as it requires too much thinking in times of stress. This was probably a major consideration for the Army when they tested and finally refused the gun for their use.

Since my life doesn't depend on it, I can and did enjoy shooting the Merwin & Hulbert Pocket Army. It is a straight-shooter and functioned without any misfires or hangups, but this is one "Pinkerton Agent" who will stick to his Colt. 🔫

George Armstrong Custer

Gun Enthusiast, Hunter, Indian Fighter.

Staff Report

Custer poses with one of his favorite hunting rifles, a .50-70 sporterized "trapdoor" Springfield. He often donned buckskins for hunting expeditions or campaigns.

People are often surprised to find out that George Armstrong Custer had an almost boyishly simple character. He was a man who wanted little more than to be able to pursue the military life—preferably an active one—in whatever capacity it presented itself. He was a "Beau Sabreur" in an age that lionized military achievements. Custer was a hyperactive outdoorsman who, when not fighting the enemy, turned his pursuits to hunting, camping, taxidermy and writing.

"Autie," as his family called him, was born in New Rumley, Ohio on Dec. 5, 1839. George was an apt but impatient student with a marked preference for spelling, at which he excelled. He managed to wangle an appointment to West Point in 1857, at the age of 17.

A fresh-faced, blue-frocked figure scaled the steps of the War Department building in July, 1861. Second Lieutenant George Armstrong

Custer, Co. G, 2nd U.S. Cavalry, was given dispatches to take to the Army of the Potomac commander General Irwin McDowell, told to find a horse and ride with all possible haste to Centerville.

"Autie" arrived at McDowell's tent the next morning just in time for the fateful Battle of Bull Run, and delivered the dispatches. He then made his way to the 2nd Cavalry and assumed his command.

An incident which illustrates Custer's growing adeptness with the handgun occurred in an encounter at White Oak Swamp, August 7, 1862. Capt. Custer found himself in pursuit of two Confederate officers whom he discovered as they were riding clandestinely through the bushes. Custer drew his horse within ten yards of the first man, pointed his .44 M-1860 Colt Army revolver and ordered the man to surrender. The "Secesh" officer paid no heed, so Custer threw a ball over his head and shouted "If you don't stop I'll blow your damned head off."

The rebel spurred his horse and this time Custer took aim, fired and the rebel slid from his saddle. Custer grabbed the reins of his victim's horse and took off after the other man. He fired two shots, bringing the Confederate's horse down. The officer reached for his Sharps carbine but decided at this point that discretion was the better part of valor and surrendered to the wild-eyed young Yankee. Custer captured a fine silver-studded black morocco saddle, an engraved double-barrelled shotgun and a fine Solingen straight sword engraved in Spanish, *No me saques sin razon, no me enbanes sin honor.* (Draw me not without reason, sheath me not without honor). This was to be one of many edged weapons Custer would own.

Through making himself known to the right people such as Generals Alfred Pleasanton and George B. McClellan, and through many valorous episodes, George Armstrong Custer was made Brigadier General of U.S. Volunteers in June of 1863.

At 24 he was the youngest general of the war! He was given command of the 2nd Brigade, 3rd Division, U.S. Cavalry Corp., comprised of the 1st, 5th, 6th and 7th Michigan, as well as M Battery of the 2nd U.S. Artillery. Immediately he adopted a resplendent blue velvet uniform.

He personally acquitted himself well at Gettysburg, but circumstances, not always of his own making, caused his command to take heavy casualties. His Battle Honors after Gettysburg read like a particularly pregnant page from the *Official Records of the Civil War:* Rappahannock, Brandy Station, Yellow Tavern (where Custer's troops were responsible for the death of the Confeder-

Custer had come out of the war a national hero—a role in which he unconceitedly revelled. He had come to believe in the "Custer Luck", and felt that his star was, if not at its zenith, at least on its upward rise. He was offered many political jobs which were obvious and unabashed stepping stones to the White House, but he passed them all up, favoring the hardy life of active service.

Second Lieutenant Custer grips his M-1860 .44 Colt Army revolver as though he were about to club someone with it. This photo was taken near Yorktown in 1862.

Even though the Texas reconstruction duty was demanding on Custer as a commander, life had its compensations. His father had been appointed provisioning agent for the unit, and brother Tom Custer was his aide. There were many family outings on the Texas plains, riding to hounds, 19th Century American style. Both whitetail and mule deer were "run", as were bear and a few buffalo. Tom Custer once accidentally shot one of Armstrong's dogs, in a close tangle with game, and was never permitted to forget it. The dogs and other pets had already become a passion with Armstrong Custer, a passion which would last out his lifetime.

acy's pet cavalry officer James Ewell Brown (Jeb) Stuart, Trevilian Station, Shenandoah Valley, Winchester, Cedar Creek, Five Forks, etc.

By the end of the war, Custer's troops (and the whole Federal Cavalry) were the best equipped, hardest fighting and riding horse troops in the world. With their Colt or Remington Army revolvers, Spencer repeaters, Sharps, Maynard, Burnside and numerous other well-made carbines, they were irresistable. Although the Confederate trooper was generally a better horseman than his Federal counterpart, the ravages of war had taken it's toll.

At the orders of his mentor and idol, General Phil Sheridan, Custer was assigned to policing both sides of the Texas Reconstruction plan—one method of occupying a defeated land that appeared to be uniformly distasteful to the occupier and the one being occupied. To make things worse, the troops which Custer had been given to do this delicate job were little more than a pack of rowdies in the main. Yet, he managed to do as well as any post-Civil War commander of reconstruction forces, while whipping his command into a semblance of professionalism.

Political interests in the administration—perhaps fearing his appeal as a presidential candidate, back-stabbed Custer out of his Civil War generalcy. His cavalry captain's pay dropped from $8000 a year to $2000 (multiply by about four, for current values), at the age of 26. Custer was however, returned to the active list and given the Lt. Colonelcy of the recently organized 7th.

Taking his wife and others of his family with him, Custer gladly returned to the outdoor life. During his Texas stay, he had become exposed to every type of sporting and military firearm. As a cavalryman,

George Armstrong Custer

and one who had gone far to prove to the entire military world the worth of the revolver as opposed to the saber, he was pistol-conscious. Along with his Colt .44, he had a beautifully cased, engraved .44 Remington New Model Army. He also took along a Spencer repeater, done

Custer bagged this elk with his .50 Remington Rolling Block rifle during the Black Hills Expedition of 1874. (South Dakota Historical Society)

up as a sporter. Since he rode his game down and shot from close range, the mediocre power of any of the Spencer loads was less of a handicap than a modern hunter would think.

An exact record of the caliber of the Spencer that Custer carried for almost a decade is hard to find. There were four popular Spencer loadings, three of which were common in manufacture until after the turn of the 20th century. First came the .56-56 Spencer, used in the butt-magazine-fed lever action Spencer military rifle. It fired a .56 caliber, 350 grain conical ball ahead of 45 grains of black powder, rimfire primed. Custer would have been most familiar with this round from his Civil War service. However, since the Spencer shown in several of his pictures is definitely a sporter, other possibilities exist. The Spencer factory-made sporter was sold in .56-46 Spencer, designed as a sporting cartridge. This one is similar to .44-40 WCF in power, but using a 320 grain bullet (also a conical ball) with 45 grains of black powder. This

round originated in 1866, when Armstrong could have purchased his rifle chambered for it. A third, and somewhat more logical choice lay in the Springfield Armory-designed .56-50 Spencer round begun in 1864. Many of the Spencer repeaters issued to post Civil War troops of the early Indian campaigns were chambered to this cartridge. Because of this, Custer would have ready sup-

One of Custer's favorite rifles was his Spencer repeater. Here he brandishes it at the entrance to his Sibley tent near Fort Dodge. He is surrounded by his ever-present pack of dogs and a pet pelican (far right.) (Custer Battlefield Museum)

plies of ammunition. The 20 or 22-inch barrelled carbines so chambered were designated Model 1865, using a new magazine cutoff device. This was as effective as any other Spencer or Henry repeating rifle

round, and had the advantage of greater ballistic coefficient for accuracy at longer range. The .50 caliber conical ball weighed 350 grains and was powered with 45 grains black powder. It is described as being able to penetrate 12 inches or more of solid pine at 50 yards. The deeper into the plains that the troopers progressed, the more demand there was for a round that was effective on horses and men at long range.

The .45-70 Springfield was actually a magnum in comparison to Spencer cartridges, as it fired 100 grains more lead at 300 to 400 fps greater speeds. But, for a time, the Spencers gave good service. It is interesting to conjecture what the outcome of the Battle of the Little Big Horn might have been, had the troopers carried carbines that could deliver eight rounds of .44 Magnum-power with adequate accuracy to 200 yards—in 12 seconds or less as the Spencer repeaters could. The .45-70 was fine for open plains work, by expert marksmen against small groups of distant opponents, but useless against the "human waves" that swept over all three flanks of Custer's command.

Duty on the Western frontier enabled the Custer family to indulge in much hunting, although little else in the way of sport, when on campaign. Whole troops of cavalry—including marching bands—were put into the field to ride down game behind Custer's 40-hound pack. The buffalo was the favored quarry. This was no mere chore, however. Clearing out the buffalo meant that the trooper's enemy, the Indian brave, had no ready supply of food to enable him to range far and wide over the plains. In addition, it was both diversion and training for the mounted command. As Custer himself wrote: "To break the monotony and give horses and men exercise, buffalo hunts were organized, in which officers and men joined heartily. I know of no better drill for perfecting men in the use of firearms on horse-back, and thoroughly accustoming them to the saddle,

Cheyennes, and small marauding bands of Arapaho, Kiowa and Comanche, Custer led a column of the 7th Cavalry, including the regimental band, through the brisk morning air of the Washita Valley, armed with his favorite Spencer sporter repeater.

Women and children were killed along with the braves, as in many cases they were as deadly as the men. When the last of the braves had been killed or escaped, Custer slaughtered almost 900 ponies and set fire to the village.

Custer had at last found the solution to Indian fighting, and although to the 20th century mind this sort of tactic seems unconscionable, to the 19th century soldier who had lost men through unspeakable torture and had seen broken, captive white women, it was justifiable. To Washington, which saw the Indian as a troublesome nuisance to "progress", it was an acceptable mode of conduct. Although the Eastern drawing-room liberals assailed his "blood-thirsty" attack, he was amply defended by his old cronies Phil Sheridan and William T. Sherman.

Custer was not an Indian hater. He had a profound respect for the valor, spirit, endurance and indomitability of the Redman. On one occasion he noted, "If I were an Indian, I often think I would greatly

Custer took his first grizzly near Bear Butte Creek. With Custer are (l-r) Bloody Knife, Pvt. Noonan, and Cpt. William Ludlow. (South Dakota Historical Society)

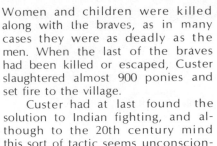

Custer considered shooting buffalo from horseback with service revolvers excellent training. On one such hunt, Autie accidentally shot into his horse's brain and found himself unhorsed, facing a bull buffalo. The pair stared into each other's eyes for a short time, and the beast finally galloped away.

than buffalo hunting over moderately rough country. No amount of riding under the best of drill-masters will give that confidence and security in the saddle which will result from a few spirited charges into a buffalo herd."

The one event in Custer's career that has caused more dispute than any other was the Battle of the Washita., Custer's troops were constantly out-ridden and out-fought by the fine Indian "light cavalry." Too often he had chased braves only to have them disappear like will-o-the-wisps. He decided, as a pragmatic soldier, that the best place to stop them would be in their own villages. It was difficult for white men to understand the philosophy and tactics of the Indian. Indians had little or no concept of territory, and a treaty signed by a chief was recognized by the braves as binding only on the chief and not on the tribe as a whole.

In response to alleged depredation by Chief Black Kettle's

As the column approached Black Kettle's lodges on the Washita River, Custer ordered the band to strike up the Regimental song, "Garry Owen", and led the troops into the middle of the village.

The Indians were caught sleeping and the troopers rode them down as they stumbled from their shelters. Sabers flashed and carbines and revolvers opened up as the soldiers were met with the knives, spears and arrows of the Cheyenne.

prefer to cast my lot among those of my people who adhered to the free open plains rather than submit to the confined limits of a reservation—there to be the recipient of the blessed benefits of civilization with its vices thrown in without stint or measure."

Much to Custer's unhappiness, the 7th Cavalry was ordered back East, early in 1871. He spent two years in Elizabethtown, Kentucky, going through the motions of civi-

George Armstrong Custer

lized cavalry duty. A portion of his 7th galloped around the South Carolina hills chasing the Ku Klux Klan one way and the illegal whiskey still people the other.

Although on duty away from his beloved plains, Custer was still looked upon correctly as an expert on plains sport. He was detailed to help entertain one of the most important visitors to the plains: the Grand Duke Alexis Romanoff of Czarist Russia. Congress laid out the

leans, where the Russian fleet lay at anchor, awaiting the Duke's return.

Out of this lavish American safari came one of the most colorful stories of U.S. arms production in the 19th century. The .44 American revolver made by Smith & Wesson had begun to be issued to Plains campaign troops. Although not as widely sold commercially as Colts, the S&Ws had several advantages over the open-topped 1871 Single Action Army. Not the least of these was the break-top action that ejected all six empties when snapped open and permitted reloading with-

out the necessity of injecting single rounds through a loading gate. The extra power, great durability and fine handling qualities of the solid-frame 1873 Colt Frontier would soon eclipse all other handguns in the West, but when Alexis saw "Buffalo Bill's" .44 S&W American, he was impressed.

The .44 American was a single action revolver which fired a 250 grain outside-lubricated conical ball from a straight-walled, cup-primed brass case loaded with 21 grains of FFg black. Its 650 fps speed supplied about 220-ft-lbs of energy at close

Autie and wife Libbie in their study at Fort Lincoln. The walls are festooned with game trophies, as well as portraits of Custer and his old crony, Gen. Phil Sheridan. A gun rack at the far right contains what appears to be a Webley RIC revolver and a pair of Smith & Wessons. (Custer Battlefield Museum)

hunting party of all hunting parties to cultivate the already friendly Russian royal family, beginning in January of 1872.

Four U.S. Generals and Custer were detailed to coordinate the entertainment of the Ducal party. Nothing was spared; "Buffalo Bill" Cody, past Chief Scout of the 5th Cavalry, was hired to guide the hunt. Two companies and the 2nd Cavalry band accompanied the party to its first base, Camp Alexis on Red Willow Creek in Nebraska. The hunt itinerary went through Denver, Topeka, Forts Wallace and Hays, St. Louis and back to base at Louisville. However, Alexis insisted that Custer accompany the party on to New Or-

This portrait of Major General Custer was taken by Matthew Brady in 1865. Custer was 25 years old! (National Archives)

Custer sported a full beard, buckskins and a muskrat cap on the Washita Campaign. (Custer Battlefield Museum)

a sale of some 250,000 revolvers, plus perhaps several thousand separately numbered guns identical to the "American" model without Russian markings. The Russian model is easily told by its second-finger spur on the trigger guard, and lanyard ring, plus "Russian Model" markings. The Russian Model and cartridge went on to set most of the late 19th Century's hand-gun marksmanship records, as well as being awarded a gold medal at the Moscow International Exposition of 1872.

Soon after this international event, Custer's series of articles entitled "My Life On The Plains" was begun in Galaxy Magazine. These covered mainly his experiences on the Indian fighting trail, but showed that he was a keen observer of the nature and ecology of the Great Plains. He remarks at the close of these that he had been asked many times to also chronicle his shooting and sporting days. At a later date, he wrote that he would detail his hunts and taxidermic efforts. But fate intervened. Still, his wife's and other writings hand down a picture of Custer as the student of Nature and preserver of specimens.

By 1873 most of the personal arms known to have belonged to

scription giving October, 1869 as the date. Thus, these too could have gone along on the Duke Alexis buffalo hunt. Since the .32 Short Rimfire introduced for the S&W New Model No. 2 Hinged Frame revolver was a very light load for plains duty, these may have seen most use as target pistols. The cartridge put nine grains of black powder behind an 80 grain outside-lubricated bullet. The whole round looked like a scaled-up .22 RF Short, and would do just about the same damage as a standard .22 LR.

Yet, weak as it was, the Model No. 2 was also known as Smith & Wesson Army Revolver No. 2, because so many were carried during the Civil War. Certain authorities describe this pistol as a U.S. secondary martial revolver. The No. 2, with 6-inch barrel and loaded, weighed less than 30 ounces and was quite accurate at 50 yards and beyond. By breaking open the frame at the front, removing the cylinder and knocking empties out with the integral ramming pin under the barrel, a respectable rate of fire could be kept up. A pair of such pistols in the hands of an expert shot like Custer would not be trivial, but cavalryman's sidearms they weren't.

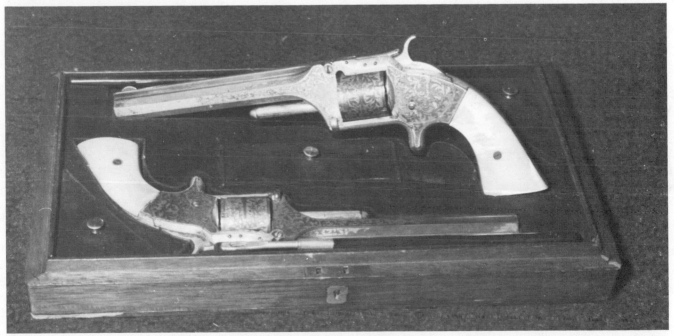

General J.B. Sutherland presented this cased pair of pearl-handled, engraved, silver-plated .32 Smith & Wesson No. 2 Old Issue revolvers to Custer in the late 1860s. (Greg Martin collection)

range. Alexis, as soon as he saw the fine manufacture, accuracy and firepower of the U.S. Army's S&W Model No. 3 First Issue .44, determined that the Imperial Army would have it also. The model which S&W supplied is now called the Model No. 3 .44-Caliber Single Action Russian-First Issue.

Probably owing to the skill with which Custer and "Buffalo Bill" Cody used these pistols, S&W made

George Armstrong Custer were in his possession. These included a matched pair of Smith & Wesson .32 rimfire spur-trigger revolvers. These 6-inch barreled pistols were presented to him in a cased set by Major General J. B. Shutherland, with an in-

Perhaps because of seeing little use, this pair has survived to this day.

Other arms in Custer's personal battery included his .44 1860 Colt Army revolver, and engraved, cased .44 Remington, and a pair of double-action Webley, Royal Irish Constabulary model revolvers with 4-inch barrels and ivory stocks. These last two were chambered for the .450 Webley centerfire round. It was

Continued on page 214

Smith & Wesson's Schofield and Russian Revolvers

By Phil Spangenberger

In 1869, the firm of Smith & Wesson brought out the first substantial cartridge revolver. This was the Model No. 3, .44 caliber Single Action American. A few of these guns were put to trial use by the U.S. Army, and while the American was popular in its own right, it was responsible for two other famous Smith & Wesson pistols: The Schofield .45 and the .44 caliber Russian Model.

The Schofield is basically an "American" with a 7-inch rather than the 8-inch barrel of the American. It also featured an improved top latch for breaking the gun open to load or unload and the bore size was increased to .45 caliber. The im-

the Grand Duke Alexis of Russia noticed the Smith & Wesson American revolvers carried by "Buffalo Bill" Cody and was favorably impressed. Eventually a contract was signed with the Russian government and the pistols were made with a few modifications such as chambering the pistol for a slightly different cartridge than the "American" used and the addition of a spur which

intriguingly attractive. They appear to be poorly balanced due to their long barrels and the fact that the cylinder sits in front of the triggerguard, but this is not so. These Smiths are as well balanced as any gun of the period, and better than many. With a little practice, spinning tricks and border shifts can be accomplished easily with a pair of Smith & Wessons.

The .45 caliber Smith & Wesson Schofield was originally issued to the U.S. Cavalry in blued finish. This example was nickel plated in later years. Frank James was one of the many Western gunfighters who used a Schofield. (Courtesy Art Sowen)

proved latch was invented by Major Schofield of the 10th U.S. Cavalry. While the .45 Schofield is a martial arm, it saw much use in the civilian world. Frank James used a Schofield, and Wells Fargo & Co., purchased many of these guns as government surplus and issued them to their guards.

The Model No. 3, .44 caliber Single Action Russian revolver was also a direct offspring of the "American." On a buffalo hunt in 1872,

was extended from the triggerguard. The cartridge and gun became known as the .44 Russian and went on to win many international shooting events in the late 19th century.

Both of these big frontier Smith's were favored by many shooters and were reliable guns with an admirable record of use behind them.

The Smith & Wesson revolvers of the Old West have a somewhat awkward look about them, yet are

Armed with a pair of .45s, a Schofield and a Colt "Peacemaker", author fires a volley from the hip. The Schofield proved to be a well-balanced and good shooting revolver using the same load as the Cavalry Colt.

They are reliable shooters also. I used a 250-grain bullet (the army used a 230-grain slug) backed by 28 grains of FFg black powder in .45 Colt casings which had been cut to size. The cylinder on the Schofield is shorter than the Colt Single Action, so it will not chamber the Colt cartridge although the Colt will take the Schofield cartridge.

The Schofield shot as well as the Peacemaker at 25 to 50 yards and functioned smoothly. The conformation of the Schofield is different than the Colt and I had a little

to be a good six-shooter.

The Russian model is another good handgun in my estimation. The .44 Russian ammo is difficult to get these days so I used .44 Special casings cut to size with a 235-grain slug and 25 grains of FFg black powder. They worked well. In shooting the Russian model, I experienced

the same difficulty with aligning my sights as with the Schofield. I know this was my fault and not the gun's. Once I corrected my problem I was able to knock over can-sized articles 40 to 50 yards away with little difficulty. I think the Russian is sighted for longer range shooting as it seemed to shoot a little high at

Like the .45 Schofield, the .44 Russian was an offspring of the .44 American revolver. It proved to be one of the most accurate target pistols of the 19th century. This ivory-stocked specimen retains much of its original nickel finish. (Author's collection)

The Frontier Smiths were quicker to unload than were the Colts as illustrated by this Russian model. Cases are thrown well away from the cylinder so that there is no interference in reloading.

Author found the S&W .44 Russian Model to be an accurate and smooth functioning arm. The spur extending from the trigger guard was an aid in controlling recoil and steadying shots.

trouble getting my thumb up to the hammer to recock for each shot. I think that rapid shooting from this revolver would be a difficult feat unless the shooter had large hands. Recoil is identical to the Colt Single Action with the same load. The big difference in the two revolvers is in the loading and unloading. The Smiths break open, and by flipping the barrel downward while moving the handle forward and slightly up, the empties are ejected, and live ammo can be inserted. The big drawback is when you don't fire all six shots, and want to reload the empties only. Then you get to play "one-to-six pick-up." This is one reason the army preferred the slower loading Peacemaker. I like the Schofield, however, and consider it

these ranges, but this is easily adjusted by the shooter. Like any gun, it is a matter of becoming familiar with each individual gun. The spur on the triggerguard was very helpful in shooting as the recoil in this arm was stronger than the Schofield. The Russian model gave no problem with the cylinder rotation after a few rounds of black powder had been put through it, but the Schofield did give me a little trouble. Perhaps this was the fault of the individual gun used.

It's too bad that there are no remakes or replicas being made of any of the old frontier Smith & Wesson revolvers. I think they would be accepted as well as the modern Smith & Wesson revolvers. I know I would be a customer.

John Dillinger

Public Hero and Public Enemy.

By Lisle Reedstrom

The author wishes to thank Joe Pinkston, curator of The John Dillinger Museum, Nashville, Indiana, for assistance in this article.

Following the early depression years, prohibition, jazz tunes, bathtub gin, speakeasies and movie heroes set a new mood for the American public. It also changed the gun-toting modern outlaw of the 30 s, who equipped themselves with fast cars and automatic weapons while adopting regimental techniques in bank robberies. Newspapers followed the exploits of these motorized bandits, romantically building up their dare-devil adventures for a depression-weary public. Some were even thought of as heroes or Robin Hoods, who stole from the banks what the banks allegedly took from the people.

John Herbert Dillinger's fame and high adventure was spread throughout the world by radio and press. His infamous career was unparalleled in the annals of criminology and journalism. Not even Al Capone contributed more to Chicago's scandalous reputation for gangsterism. During his short-lived career, Dillinger was rated Public Enemy Number 1 by the FBI. Prior to 1935, the FBI was known simply as the Bureau (or Division) of Investigation of the Department of Justice. In this article, for the sake of convenience, "FBI" is the term used when referring to that Bureau previous to 1935.

Dillinger and his gang had killed four policemen, three FBI agents, one sheriff, and an undetermined number of holdup victims. Within this traumatic 12-month period (June 1933 until June 1934), Dillinger broke out of three prisons, looted three police station arsenals and robbed 13 banks of nearly $500,000.

Born in Mooresville, Indiana, June 28, 1904, "Johnnie" and his father, John Dillinger, Sr., a farmer, attended a nearby Quaker church. When he was three, his mother died after a long illness. Soon after her death, Dillinger's father packed up and moved to Indianapolis, where he opened a grocery store in a poor section of the city. Johnnie grew up with reckless, uncontrollable hoodlum youths. Here he attended high school, played on the baseball team, and helped his father at the store. In 1920, the Dillingers moved back to Mooresville and opened another grocery store. Johnny, 16, was already showing signs of restlessness.

During the next three years, Johnnie fell in and out of trouble with juvenile authorities. His father tried everything he could to instill in the youngster his own stern religious and moral principles, sometimes punishing the boy for the slightest offense. In 1923, young Dillinger enlisted in the Navy, having been jilted by a high school girl friend. Six months later, he deserted in Boston but returned voluntarily after he learned that a $50 reward was posted for his apprehension. No surprise to him, the Navy gave him a dishonorable discharge.

A year later, Dillinger married a 16-year-old girl from his hometown, Mooresville, Indiana. Times were hard and jobs were scarce. When he finally got a job in a Mooresville furniture factory, he worked hard as an upholsterer. He was later rated an expert at the job by his employer and was praised as an affable worker. With a steady income, Johnnie began staying out late at nights with an old cronie, Ed Singleton. Ed, who was ten years older and a heavy drinker, persuaded Dillinger that married life was not for him. Seeking a little high adventure, the two robbed 65-year-old Frank Morgan, proprietor of the West End Grocery store. Dillinger, wielding a .32 caliber Colt revolver in one hand and a bolt wrapped in a handkerchief, demanded the day's receipts. Morgan, who offered no resistance but who recognized his assailant, shouted a cry of distress. Dillinger began beating the old man on the head with the bolt. During the scuffle, the gun accidentally discharged, and Dillinger, thinking he had shot his victim, fled the scene. Morgan later identified both men as the assailants. Singleton pleaded guilty and testified against his partner in that it was Dillinger who instigated the robbery and carried it out; Singleton only admitted to driving the getaway car. Dillinger was sentenced to serve 10 to 20 years in the state reformatory at Pendleton. Ed Singleton received a lighter sentence.

From the beginning of his term at Pendleton, John Dillinger bore a grudge against society. Feeling rejected, he became a troublesome prisoner. His bitterness was so apparent that when brought before Superintendent A. F. Miles, he boasted of attempting to escape. After two unsuccessful attempts to break out, he was transferred to the Indiana State Penitentiary at Mich-

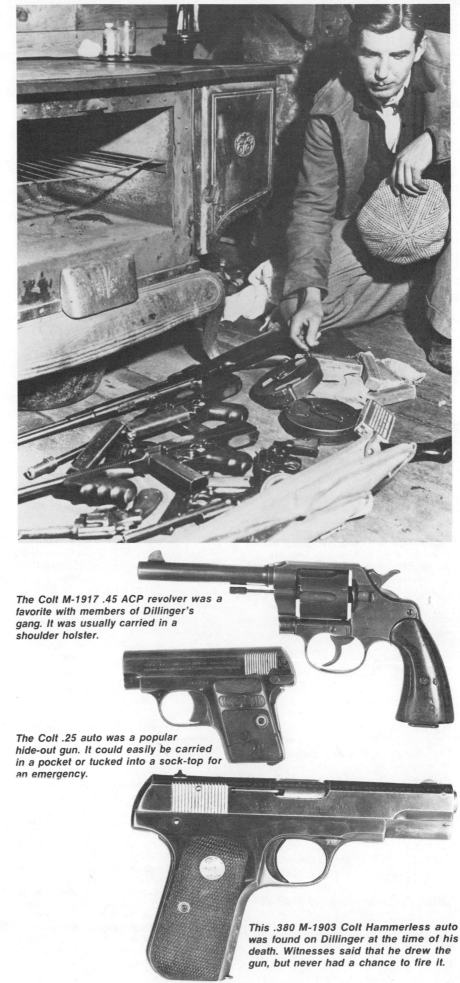

This cache of weapons was captured by the FBI during the raid on Little Bohemia. It includes a pair of Thompson submachine guns, a Model 94 Winchester lever action and .351 Winchester Automatic rifle, several handguns and boxes of government and commercial ammo. (Wide World Photo)

igan City, where he studied methods of criminal procedures under the direction of "long termers" John Hamilton, Russell Clark, Harry Pierpont and Charles Makley, all members of the fraternity of experienced bank robbers.

After nine long years of prison life, all those who were responsible for sending him there signed a petition for his parole. Indiana's Democratic Governor, Paul McNutt, granted the petition, not knowing how costly an error he had made in terms of loss of human life by releasing Dillinger to society. On May 23, 1933, just 14 months before he was shot to death by FBI agents, John Dillinger walked through the gates of the Indiana State Penitentiary, a free man. In those 14 months that were to follow, he rivaled the new depression era President Franklin D. Roosevelt, as a subject of front page news.

Before Dillinger was released from prison, he had promised to arrange for weapons to be smuggled into the penitentiary for his hoodlum mentors. This same group cultivated Dillinger as their future contact man on the outside. It would be his job to organize a group to rob a string of small-town banks from a list furnished by Pierpont and Hamilton. The funds from the robberies would finance a massive break from prison.

Several weeks later, Dillinger recruited two hoodlums, William Shaw and Paul "Lefty" Parker, to share in robbing small stores and companies, besides using Pierpont's list of potential and ripe banks. However, most of these ripe banks had already failed during the depression, and the Dillinger gang was met with boarded up buildings and locked doors. They were, however, successful in obtaining enough money to supplement the escape funds for his friends still in Michigan City, besides recruiting a healthy and deadly gang.

On September 26, 1933, Dillinger kept his promise. Clark, Hamilton, Pierpont and Makley, along with six other convicts, shot their way out under a heavy curtain of fire, severely wounding one prison guard. During their escape, they stopped long enough to break into the prison arsenal, arming themselves with Thompson submachine guns, Colt .45 caliber automatics,

The Colt M-1917 .45 ACP revolver was a favorite with members of Dillinger's gang. It was usually carried in a shoulder holster.

The Colt .25 auto was a popular hide-out gun. It could easily be carried in a pocket or tucked into a sock-top for an emergency.

This .380 M-1903 Colt Hammerless auto was found on Dillinger at the time of his death. Witnesses said that he drew the gun, but never had a chance to fire it.

John Dillinger

and various makes of .38 caliber pistols.

Dillinger's identity as a daring, counter-leaping bank robber, with nerves of steel, soon spread throughout the state of Indiana. The police were desperately searching for him and his gang. Wearing straw hats and expensive gray suits, they would storm into banks, waving machine guns at guards and panic-stricken employees. Dillinger would usually call out, "Stand back, everyone . . . this is a stickup!" Vaulting over counters or high railings to ran-

Dillinger's .45 Thompson submachine gun, .45 Colt M-1911 auto and bullet-proof vest were recovered from Lake Michigan at Chicago after his death. (Wide World Photo)

sack the tellers' cages was usually his trademark. Although he was ice cold, flint hard and trigger sensitive, his courtesy with the ladies was very chivalrous.

After a series of bank robberies in Indiana, Dillinger drove to Dayton, Ohio to see a girl friend, Mary Longnaker. Unknown to the Indiana bankrobber, his girl friend's plush rooming house was staked out by Dayton police detectives and Dillinger was quietly taken into custody on September 22, 1933, without a shot fired, and transferred to the county jail at Lima, Ohio.

Hearing of Johnnie's capture, Pierpont, Makley, Clark and Hamilton, newly liberated from prison, resolved to return the favor and help their pal escape. Speeding to Dillinger's rescue, the gang stopped long enough to pick up stolen funds to outfit Pierpont and his men with clothes, a new car and an arsenal of weapons. Making certain they would have enough traveling money, they knocked off the First National Bank in St. Mary's, Ohio, carrying off

$14,000 in a sack without firing a shot.

On October 12, Pierpont and his men entered the office of Sheriff Jesse Sarber and stated they were police officers who had come from Michigan City to return Dillinger for violating his parole. When the sheriff asked to see their credentials, Pierpont drew out a pistol from his expensive suit and said, "Here is our credentials." Upon resisting, Sheriff Sarber was shot twice. He sank to the floor, mortally wounded, before he could draw his own weapon. After hearing the shot, Mrs. Sarber and a deputy sheriff who rushed into the sheriff's office were placed in a cell and locked up. Pierpont rushed down the corridor of cells, looking for Dillinger. "Over here . . . ," came a call over the clattering cell doors of other inmates who begged to be freed. "Shut up, you bastards, we came for Johnnie," yelled Pierpont as he nervously unlocked Dillinger's cell door.

Two weeks after Dillinger's escape from Lima, two police stations were boldly raided of their arsenals, machine guns being the most sought after arms. They were now going to live up to the outlaw image created by newspapers and a hysterical public.

As in any profession, tools of the trade are very important. In this case, weapons of various calibers were essential to Dillinger's gang and were carefully chosen. During police arsenal robberies, machine guns were the likely primary choice. As early as the 1920's, submachine guns were established in the public mind as gangster weapons. Anyone who followed the newspaper articles on the national crime wave would believe that only gangsters had these deadly weapons. By far, it was the Tommygun that gained much reputation in the years that followed, next to the bandits who terrorized the country during the 1930s.

Neatly tucked into a shoulder

holster beneath the armpit, these depression desperados most often carried a .45 caliber automatic Colt, U.S. Army model 1911. Crime statistics compiled during those years found that larger caliber revolvers and automatics were found on criminals because of the knock-down and killing power. Usually smaller caliber pistols were carried as second guns, either jammed in waist belts in the small of the back, pocketed or slipped into a sock for an emergency.

John Dillinger went into winter headquarters in Chicago, Illinois, changing addresses at several North Side apartments. While visiting a dentist's office on November 15, he eluded a trap set for him by Chicago police. On December 14, John Hamilton, leader of the ten convicts whom Dillinger had helped to escape from Michigan City, shot and killed Police Sgt. William T. Shanley while having a fender straightened at an automobile repair shop on Broadway Avenue. While Chicago was ringing in the New Year, Dillinger and six other hoodlums held up the Beverly Gardens night club on South Western Avenue. During the gun battle that followed, two policemen and two gangsters were critically wounded.

On January 15, 1934, Dillinger and Hamilton, armed with .45 caliber machine guns hidden in trombone cases, casually walked into the First National Bank of East Chicago, Indiana, just before closing time. Dillinger announced in a loud voice that he was robbing the bank. Walter Spencer, vice-president who was talking on the telephone, quickly hung up and pressed the bank alarm buzzer. Dillinger politely told the customers that he knew the alarm had been set off and quickly herded them into a corner for their own protection. He noticed a man standing at the cashier's cage, frozen in his tracks. He had just cashed a check and the cash was lying on the counter. "Is that your money or the

This kitchen tabletop at the Little Bohemia Lodge has become a temporary resting place for the Dillinger gang's arsenal. Their varied selection of arms includes: 1. Thompson .45 submachine gun with beavertail forend; 2. Colt .45 ACP M-1917 DA revolver; 3. Thompson .45 M-1928 submachine gun; 4. Colt .45 M-1911 automatic; 5. Colt .32-20 Army Special DA revolver; 6. Ortgies .32 auto; 7. Winchester 12-ga. M-1897 pump shotgun. Guns 1, 2, 3 courtesy Burt Miller, Gun 4 from Pony Express Sport Shop, Gun 5 courtesy Bill Baber, Gun 7 from Sotheby Parke Bernet, Los Angeles. Photo by Mike Parris.

John Dillinger

bank's?", Dillinger said calmly. "M-m-mine," the man stuttered. "Keep it," the outlaw smiled, "...we only want the bank's."

Hamilton was already scooping money into a sack when Dillinger noticed a policeman at the front door. (Three others were in plain clothes, answering the alarm set off by Spencer.) As the patrolman entered the bank alone, Dillinger herded him into the corner with the others. Seeing that the plain clothes officers outside had already flashed their guns, Dillinger decided to use the bank's vice-president and the uniformed policeman as hostages. As the group walked out of the bank, Patrolman William Patrick O'Malley, who was standing in an entrance next door, spotted the attempted kidnaping. The police hostage dropped to the sidewalk, giving O'Malley a clear shot at Dillinger. O'Malley's bullets glanced off Dillinger's bullet-proof vest. The bandit returned the fire, hitting O'Malley in the leg. O'Malley fired again, and once more bullets glanced off the vest. Dillinger opened with a short burst from his machine gun, dropping O'Malley. Pushing Spencer aside, Dillinger and Hamilton made tracks to a car nearby. Suddenly Hamilton dropped. A bullet had found its way through his vest. Under a heavy hail of lead, Dillinger returned to his friend's side, helped him to his feet, and raced toward the getaway car parked in the middle of Chicago Avenue. After returning to Chicago, an underworld doctor was summoned for the badly wounded Hamilton. It was later learned that the loot came to $20,376; the Irish officer who fell in a barrage of machine gun fire, died.

Tucson, Arizona was still bathing in its historic past, but now catering to tourists as a health spot. It was decided that this was as good a place as any to enjoy the climate and lay low for a while until things cooled off. Dillinger was now wanted in a number of states and often reported having been seen in several places at the same time. While staying at the Congress Hotel in Tucson, a fire broke out on January 22, resulting in the capture of Dillinger, Clark, Makley and Pierpont. Firemen became suspicious when they found machine guns and other gangland articles in the bandits' rooms, and later identified the desperados from photographs. Three days later, Clark and his mistress, Opal Long, were arrested. On the same day, Pierpont was captured at a tourist camp with

Dillinger struck this chummy pose with Prosecutor Robert Estill of Lake County, Ind., while he was awaiting trial for murder. The picture was widely circulated by the press and proved very embarassing for Estill.

Dillinger supposedly used this carved wooden pistol to bluff his captors when he escaped from the Crown Point Jail. A Department of Justice report stated that a real automatic was used, but one of the hostages acknowledged that the gun was a mock-up. (Wide World Photo)

his moll, Mary Kinder. He offered no resistance until he was brought to the police station, where he suddenly reached for his gun. Half a dozen guns were leveled on Pierpont before he could draw. When searched they found two more guns, one in a shoulder holster and another tucked snugly in his sock.

Makley and Dillinger were both arrested without difficulty. Officers waited for the pair at a bungalow rented three days earlier, and were able to casually take them into custody when they drove up. Evelyn "Billie" Frechette, Dillinger's half-breed Indian sweetheart, was also arrested.

Pierpont, Clark and Makley were charged with the slaying of Sheriff Sarber and the breakout of Dillinger at Lima, and were turned over to

the Ohio authorities. Pierpont was later electrocuted; Makley was sentenced to die but was mortally wounded in an escape attempt. Clark was sentenced to life imprisonment. Both women, Billie and Mary, hoodlum sweethearts, were sent back East to face punishment.

Dillinger was flown from Tucson, Arizona to Chicago, and then taken by a motorcade of 13 cars and a dozen motorcycles to Crown Point, Indiana, their sirens shrieking almost continuously. Lodged in the Crown Point jail, which was termed "escape-proof", Dillinger couldn't help noticing a group of vigilantes roaming the grounds outside the jail, cradling shotguns and machine guns in their arms—just in case any of his old cronies might decide to spring him. Even though Dillinger's gang was behind bars, they weren't taking any chances.

While awaiting trial for the slaying of Patrolman O'Malley in the East Chicago bank robbery, Dillinger was persuaded to pose for news photographers with Robert G. Estill, Lake County prosecutor, with their arms around each other. Estill vowed earlier that he would send Dillinger to the electric chair; but what the prosecutor thought was a harmless photo, out-of-town newspapers blew out of proportion, calling it a brotherly embrace. The so-called disgraceful incident assumed more significance on March 3, when Dillinger carved a wooden pistol, blackened it with shoe polish, and walked out of the Crown Point jail.

Herbert Youngblood, a Negro criminal who was killed two weeks after the Crown Point jail break while resisting arrest in Port Huron, Michigan, had accompanied Dillinger. Two machine guns and several smaller weapons were taken from the jail's arsenal, as well as the sheriff's automobile which was parked in a garage next door. Two hostages were also taken, Deputy Sheriff Ernest Blunk and a mechanic, Ed Saager. A statement from Saager to the author is as follows:

"While we were driving through Crown Point, we passed the First National Bank. Dillinger said he'd take that bank because all he had on him was $15, but he didn't know where two other deputies were at that time. Dillinger knew where he was going because we took the back roads to St. John. Ernie Blunk was driving while me and Youngblood sat in back. When we came to 41 [Route 41], Dillinger got a little nervous; I guess he figured on a road block. On the way going to Peotone, Illinois, he asked me and Ernie, how'd we like to go to Lima, Ohio. He said he had some buddies in jail there, and he wanted us to help get them out. Just two miles this side of Peotone we stopped. Dillinger looked around, he didn't see any telephone lines. He told me and·Blunk to get out and handed me $4 to get back on. 'I'd give you more,' he said, 'but I only got what I took off them birds back in Crown Point. And if I live through Christmas, I'll get you a present'."

As for the much disputed wooden gun used in the break, Saager said Dillinger showed it to him and Blunk, saying, "Ya think that would of done it." As the convicts drove off, leaving the two hostages behind, Dillinger was heard singing, "I'm headin' for the last roundup."

Dillinger was wanted by state authorities for murder and bank robbery, which was of comparably small consequences, but by transporting a stolen automobile in interstate commerce he had committed a federal crime. On April 22, Melvin Purvis, head of the FBI office in Chicago, received a tip from a resort owner in Rhinelander, Wisconsin, that Dillinger, five members of his gang and four women were staying at Little Bohemia, on Little Star Lake. Dozens of agents from Chicago and St. Paul converged upon the lodge within hours, only to find that their presence was announced by watchdogs barking continuously, warning the gangsters. Purvis failed to cover the back of the building, assuming that escape there would be impossible because of the lake.

As agents were being deployed around the front and sides of the

lodge, five men came through the front door. Only three ran from the doorway to a parked car nearby and started to drive away. After repeated warnings from the agents for the car to stop, firing broke out, smashing glass and peppering the moving vehicle. One man was killed and two others were wounded. These men, it was learned later, had only come to Little Bohemia to drink beer. After

several minutes, a machine gun burst came from a second-story window, another from the roof. A few yards from the lodge was a dark cabin. From it also came a grand chorus of machine gun chatter. George "Baby Face" Nelson tarried in the cabin long enough for his pals' exit through the rear of the lodge, holding agents in check until he, too, disappeared.

Dillinger was shot in front of the Biograph theatre in Chicago by FBI agent Melvin Purvis. After the shooting, crowds gathered in the alley where he lay and mopped up the blood with their handkerchiefs as souvenirs.

This photo of Dillinger was taken at his father's home in Indiana while police were searching for him. He holds his favorite Thompson, minus buttstock, and the wooden pistol he claimed he used in his escape from the Crown Point Jail. (Wide World Photo)

After the shooting, tear gas shells were thrown through windows of the lodge and cabin, but the bandits had gone. At a neighboring house, down the road, it was later learned that another gun battle had taken place, leaving an FBI agent dead, killed by one of the escaping gangsters. Tear gas did bring forth Marie Conforti, girl friend of Homer Van Meter; Helen Gillis, wife of Baby Face Nelson; and Jean Delaney, Tommy Carroll's moll. As they staggered out, they coughed and mopped their tear-filled eyes. The Little Bohemia, raid was a tragic one, its net result being the death of one federal agent and one innocent native, the wounding of several others, and the capture of three gangsters' molls.

John Hamilton, leader of the massive breakout at the Michigan City prison, also escaped Little Bohemia with the other members, but was mortally wounded in a gunfight several days later by a deputy sheriff. Dillinger nursed the dying gangster and later buried him in a gravel pit at Oswego, Illinois, throwing lye on Hamilton's hands and face, to

John Dillinger

prevent identification. Tommy Carroll was killed 15 days after the Little Bohemia incident by two detectives in Waterloo, Iowa.

Dillinger's exploits created public clamor, and FBI Director J. Edgar Hoover placed a "shoot to kill" order out on the desperado, with a $10,000 reward on his head. From five other states where Dillinger had robbed banks, another $10,000 reward was offered. During the next several months, dozens of men looking like the bank robber were arrested or almost gunned down by agents. Dillinger had seemed to disappear. Yet additional bank robberies committed throughout the mid-central states and investigated by local police were thought to have been the responsibility of Dillinger and his gang.

Meanwhile, Dillinger was hiding out in Chicago where, on May 28, he submitted himself to face surgery with hopes of disguising his features. Attempts were also made to alter his fingerprints beyond possible identification. Dillinger paid handsomely for the operation, to the tune of $5000, with the permission to use the hide-away for the operation and convalescing period. Confident of his new image, Dillinger struck again with four members of his gang at South Bend, Indiana, where they relieved the Merchants National Bank of $29,890, killing one policeman and wounding four other men. The license plates on the same car used in the South Bend holdup also had been used on a car driven by three machine gun bandits who robbed the First National Bank of Fostoria, Ohio of more than $10,000, killing Police Chief Frank Culp on May 3. Homer Van Meter, one of Dillinger's expert machine gun artists, was identified as the leader of the Fostoria bank job. Van Meter was destined to fall under police bullets in St. Paul, Minn., August 23.

Far better men in our West's history praised themselves for their achievements and illusiveness from the law, yet fell by making the fatal mistake of trusting a woman. Such was the case with John Dillinger. He was betrayed by 42-year-old Anna Sage, a former brothel keeper in Gary and East Chicago, Indiana, where Dillinger knew her well. It is a general assumption that no respectable "madam" would "squeal" on an old customer simply for his reward. But Anna had good reason. Under orders of deportation to her native Romania, she had hoped that the United States Government might

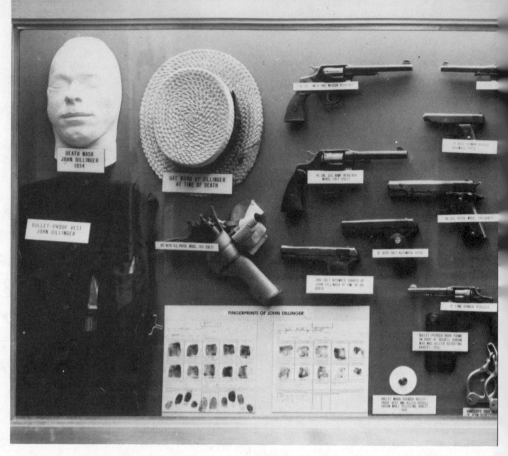

work a deal wherein by helping to capture Dillinger, they would permit her to remain in the States. Anna kept an apartment almost directly behind the Biograph Theatre on Halsted Street in Chicago, which Dillinger had used on several occasions to entertain his girl friends. The flat provided meals, living room, kitchen privileges, bedroom and

John Dillinger was the most famous of the depression-era desperados. His short career lasted only 14 months but in that period he established a reign of terror that earned him the FBI's rating of Public Enemy Number 1. (Wide World Photo)

bath facilities. Unknown to Dillinger, Anna confided in an old friend, Martin Zarkovich, a detective sergeant in East Chicago. Zarkovich made arrangements for Anna to meet with Agent Purvis on July 21, to formulate a plan to capture Dillinger and arrange for a large part of the $25,000 reward to be turned over to her after he was in custody, dead or alive. Satisfied with the assurance of the reward money, she also asked for immunity from deportation. Purvis could make no promise because of certain jurisdictions with the immigration authorities, but he would do all in his power to prevent her deportation.

Polly Hamilton, a waitress in a Wilson Avenue restaurant, knew Dillinger only as Jimmy Lawrence. She had been going out with him on a number of dates and had no knowledge of his profession.

Dillinger kept his northside hide-out and identity secret. He told his new girl friend that he worked as a clerk at the Board of Trade Building downtown. Anna was convinced that Dillinger would show up from uptown and take his new girl friend to the Marbro Theater at 4110 Madison Street, or the Biograph Theater at 2433 Lincoln Avenue, where she had gone with the pair on many Sundays before. The problem was, which one were they going

This arsenal was captured by the FBI in a series of raids on the Dillinger gang by law enforcement officers. It includes a number of unusual weapons including a .45 M-1911 auto with extended magazine and front hand grip and a sawed-off and shortened Model 11 Remington auto shotgun. Dillinger's death mask, and bullet-proof vest are also displayed. (FBI Photo)

to, and when? Anna agreed to let Purvis know which theater was scheduled. She would wear an orange skirt, which would be a code message meaning, "Here he is."

On Sunday, July 22, 1934, Purvis received a call from Anna Sage at about 5:00 p.m. "He's here; he's just come. We're either going to the Marbro or the Biograph." Purvis immediately sent several agents to the Marbro, he and another agent going to the Biograph. Before splitting up, they agreed to call the office every five minutes. At approximately 8:30, Dillinger and the two women arrived at the Biograph. Purvis recognized the outlaw, who wore dark glasses, gray trousers, a straw skimmer no coat. While Dillinger purchased the tickets, both girls went into the theater lobby. Overhead, the marquee read, "Manhattan Melodrama," starring Clark Gable and William Powell. The film was a gangster picture, but near the end Powell betrays his old buddy Gable,

sending him down the last mile to a silverscreen death. Had Dillinger believed in omens, the episode on screen would have warned him to make tracks out of there, leaving the women. But apparently he was content and felt safe as he sat there watching his favorite movie idols.

Meanwhile, Purvis planned to go after Dillinger in the theater, locating several seats behind the bandit, from which the agents could pin his arms and head. But it was too dark and they couldn't find Dillinger. There was nothing else to do but wait for him to come out after the show. About half an hour after Dillinger disappeared into the theater, FBI agents from the office and the Marbro stake-out arrived. Purvis stationed his men up and down the streets, at exits from the theater and in the nearby alleys. Two East Chicago policemen were also stationed at the north end of the theater. All eyes were to watch Purvis. He would signal by lighting a cigar if Dillinger was sighted.

At approximately 10:40 p.m., Dillinger was sighted in the crowd, exiting from the theater entrance with both women. Anna Sage's orange skirt looked blood red under the marquee lights. Women and children were all around. Purvis and his men had to wait for the crowd to thin out. The trio turned south on

Lincoln Avenue, passing a tavern next to the movie house. Dillinger glanced casually at Purvis standing in the doorway, as he and the girls passed by, but did not recognize him. As they neared an alley, Purvis lit his cigar and then raised his hand. As the agents were closing in, Polly Hamilton tugged at Dillinger's shirt, as if in warning; then Purvis nervously commanded, "Stick 'em up, Johnny, we have you surrounded." Dillinger lunged forward, at the same time drawing a .38 caliber Colt automatic from the side pocket of his trousers, but he never had the chance to fire it.

The dimly lit street flashed with gun fire; women screamed as Dillinger fell, his head in the alley and his feet on the sidewalk. In falling, his right elbow struck the sidewalk with a hollow thud, and bounced. Purvis immediately extracted the gun from Dillinger's upthrust gun hand.

Polly Hamilton and Anna Sage, tagged as the "Lady in Red" by newspapers, disappeared into the crowd that was now closing in to see what had happened.

The ricocheting bullets fired by the FBI accidentally hit two women bystanders, lodging in the fleshy part of their bodies.

When Purvis knelt to speak to Dillinger, there was no answer. The desperado was dead. ♛

Shooting Impression

A Pair of .32s

The Ortgies Auto Pistol and the Colt Army Special DA Revolver With Their Origins Miles Apart, Both Found Favor With American Gunmen.

By Jim Woods

The Prohibition era gangsters and the lawmen who opposed them are associated largely with some of the more glamorous guns of the period. However, life of the times was not all Thompsons and

The Ortgies auto pistol is clean of projections on its exterior and generally is characterized by simple construction and flawless workmanship. The pistols were produced in Germany between 1920 and 1926, in .25, .32 and .380 calibers.

BARs. A couple of lessor knowns are the Ortgies pocket auto pistol and the Colt Army Special double action revolver.

The Ortgies auto pistol was designed by Heinrich Ortgies and produced by Deutsche Werke of Erfurt, Germany, from 1920 through 1926 in

caliber 6.35mm (.25 ACP), 7.65mm (.32 ACP) and 9mm Corto (.380 auto). Our test gun is the mid-range .32 caliber and is a particularly fine example of the German-made pocket pistol.

The Ortgies is a pocket pistol in a most practical sense. Its deep-blued surfaces are free of any projections that would impair its accessibility by way of coat or pants pocket. Sights are fixed and small, and grip panels are affixed by use of hidden spring clamps so that not even the usual screwheads show there.

The only projection in the gun's flat construction is the pushbutton

After moving close enough to the target (15 yards) to pick up the X in the small sights of the Ortgies, acceptable 8-shot, 3-inch groups could be repeated. This test gun, or possibly the shooter-author, needs a bit of windage correction.

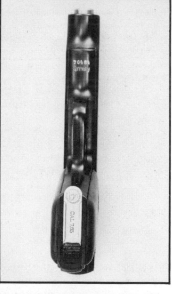

Serial number of the Ortgies, along with the word "Germany", are stamped on the underside of the frame on this import gun. Serial number is repeated inside the slide and on the barrel. Base of the 8-round magazine is stamped with the trademark, a stylized, crouched lion forming the letter "D" (Deutsche), and the legend, "CAL. 7,65."

that sets the grip safety and also permits release of the slide from the frame to start the disassembly operation. The 8-round magazine is held in place by a knurled spring-loaded rocker button on the end of the butt.

With the slide pulled fully rearward and the aforementioned pushbutton release operated, the slide may be removed by lifting it up away from the frame and forward over the muzzle. The coiled recoil

The test-gun Ortgies digested both factory loaded hollow point and jacketed round nose bullets, without malfunction. Recoil was minimal and control, at short ranges, was excellent.

spring then may be slipped off the barrel. The barrel is set into place by means of a quarter-turn key stud. When the barrel is turned in the mating key slot to right angles to the frame, pointed to the left side, the barrel is simply lifted off the frame. The only other readily removable piece is the firing pin assembly. The barrel and slide are stamped with the same serial number as the frame.

Functional tests were conducted at the Angeles Range in San Fernando, California. A series of shots were rapid-fired at 6-inch bullseye, 25-yard paper targets. Acquisition of the target at the prescribed distance of 25 yards was difficult and inconsistent due to the diminutive sights, so the range was shortened to 15 yards. From there, a 3-inch group was achieved, and repeated, firing offhand, rapid fire. A 2½-inch diameter pipe target was repeatedly rung at the same distance with both hollow point and jacketed round nose bullets.

Perhaps it was this short-range controllability that made the Ortgies

from the '20s

pistol attractive to the John Dillinger gang. One was recovered from their possessions, in caliber .25, and is on display along with other Dillinger guns at the Department of Justice Building in Washington, D.C.

The Ortgies pocket pistol seems almost out of place in a time

Colt Army Special models in 4-inch barrels were so identified in order to interest the U.S. Army in the revolver when the gun was introduced in 1908. The model designation was changed to the Colt Official Police Revolver in 1928.

here was also chambered for a .32—the Colt Army Special double action revolver in caliber .32-20.

The Army Special was so designated by Colt in an effort to interest the U.S. Army in its new medium frame revolver. Guns identified and barrel-stamped "Army Special" were introduced in 1908 in calibers .32-20 WCF, .38 Special and 41 Colt, and production was continued under that label until 1928. The same gun was manufactured after that date but was identified as the Colt Offi-

The Colt Army Special double action revolver of the 1920s is an unmistakable ancestor to today's Colt revolvers. The recognizable family resemblance has changed little over the years. Ejector rods on the Army Special were unshrouded as are certain Colt models of current manufacture. Fixed sights on current

Basically, little has changed in Colt's fixed sight revolvers since the Army Special model. It was recognized, however, that six shots of the somewhat anemic .32-20 cartridge could be improved. Originals were chambered also for .38 Special and .41 Colt. Comparable Colt models of today are chambered for the .38 Special, still considered by many to be a minimal defense cartridge.

The Angeles Range, San Fernando, California, was employed for testing of the Colt Army Special by the author, shown here firing off-hand at the range's 25-yard targets.

Double action, off-hand deliberate fire at 25 yards with the Colt Army Special produced this 3-inch, 6-shot group. Recoil effect of the factory-loaded .32-20 cartridge was negligible.

marked by the influence of larger guns and calibers—the 1911 .45 auto, the Thompson machine gun and the BAR—but the back-up gun for modern gangsters and lawmen alike, tends to the small caliber, concealable models. Although not commonly available today, the Ortgies was imported in substantial numbers, and it's a good bet that many of them saw duty on both sides of the law.

It is certainly not inconceivable that the .32 caliber guns and cartridges played a definitive role in the crime era of the 1920s and '30s. The other test gun for examination

cial Police Revolver, to properly reflect the actual market. The Army, at the time, was more interested in its brutish .45 auto.

The Colt Army Special is equipped with a tall blade front sight and a square notch rear sight milled in the top strap. Such sights are adequate for offhand shooting at the 25 yards at which the tests were conducted.

Firing with deliberate aim, 6-shot groups would spread to about three inches. Recoil effect was minimal.

Some long-range shooting was attempted, but the lightweight 100-grain bullets refused to kick up enough dirt to indicate the strike. No paper targets were recorded at ranges over 25 yards.

Colts are of the same type as used on Army Special models of 50 or more years ago. The still familiar rampant colt emblem is set into the checkered walnut grip panels of the Army Special as well as stamped into the side plate, just as are the Colts of today.

The Colt Army Special never made it into the U.S. Army uniform for which it was designed, but became a part of the many Colt police models instead. As a civilian gun, it, like the Ortgies auto pistol, also found its way to the other side of the law.

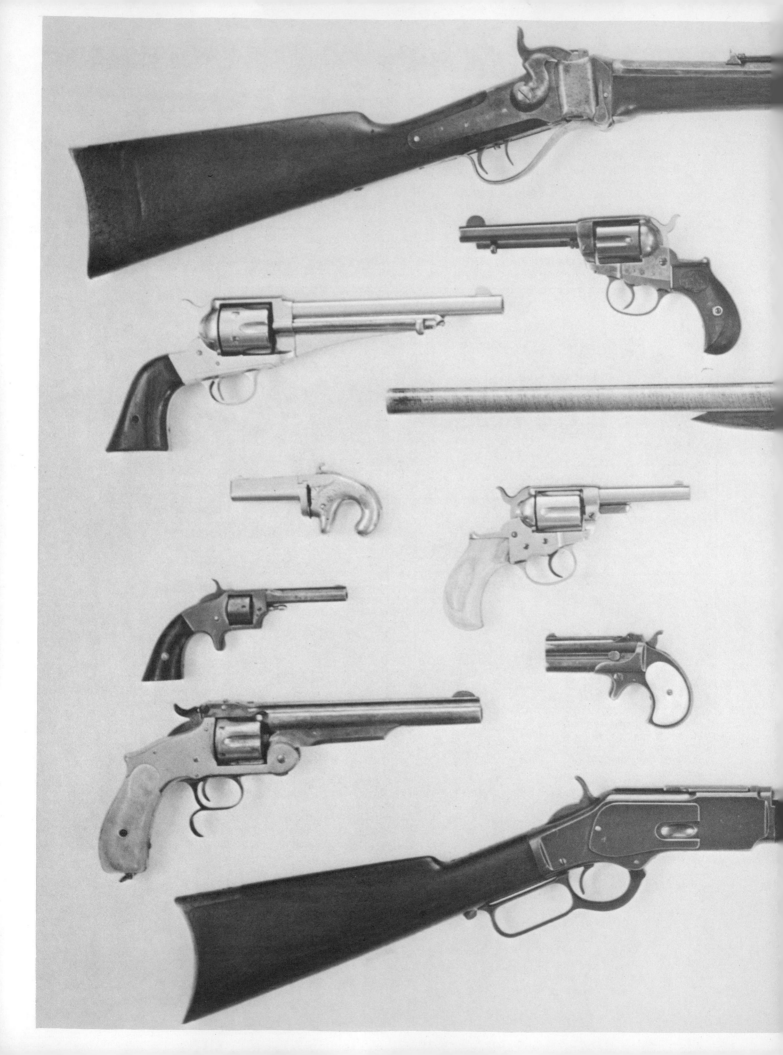

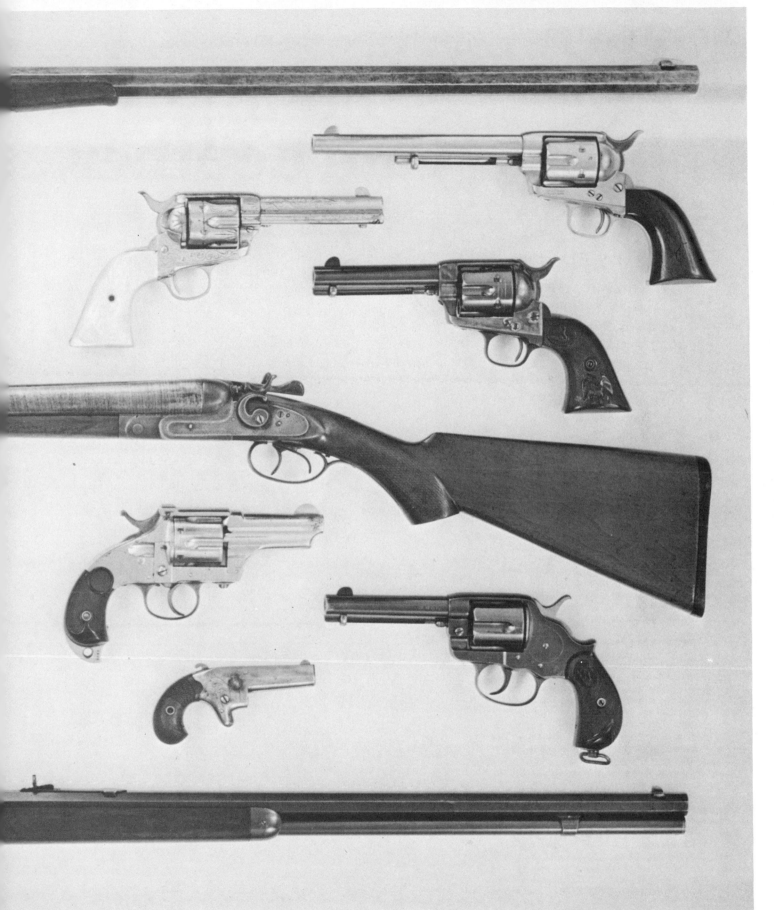

Frontier Gun Leather

By Phil Spangenberger

This Frederic Remington sketch from an 1888 issue of Century Magazine illustrates the typical fashion of the day in frontier gun leather. Double-loop holster worn over a belt full of cartridges which is slanted loosely but not too low for comfort or practicality.

Much has been written about the guns of the Old West, but it seems that very little is known about the leather that was used to carry these arms. What did these holsters, belts and scabbards look like? How were they worn? Were they similar to the rigs used in modern western films, or by the fast-draw artists of today? Let's take a closer look at this much ignored but important part of firearms history.

The primary purposes of a holster are protection and transportation of the gun to which it is mated. During the frontier period of the American West, both of these needs were magnified by the extreme weather, and long distances traveled. Unlike many modern holsters, especially the fast-draw type, the holsters of the Old West served their purposes very well. They were simply constructed, gave ample protection to the arm, and provided a secure place to carry a gun during travel.

Holsters made before the era of the six-gun, consisted mainly of a leather frog or socket that one could slip his horse pistol into. Belt hooks which were integral parts of many pistols in the days of flint and percussion lock arms were another way that one could transport his sidearm; however, this method left the gun exposed to the elements, which was extremely hazardous for a flintlock pistol. Mounted men often relied on pommel holsters; that is, a set of holsters that attached to the front of the saddle.

With the coming of the revolving pistol, holsters began to come into their own, so to speak. The basic construction of a revolver is more compact than a single-shot pistol of the old side-hammer-lock style. This fact alone makes it more likely to be worn in a scabbard-type arrangement because it doesn't have any appendages which will cause it to snag or grip the inside of a holster as it is being withdrawn.

Revolvers made their appearance in the American West in the mid-1830s with the Colt Paterson Model. These guns were often carried in the old style of simply being tucked into one's belt or sash. When a holster was worn, it was usually not much more than a boot-

This selection of original cartridge handguns and long arms of the Old West represents a spectrum of firearms popular with gunfighters from the 1860s to the turn of the century. It includes: 1. Sharps M-1874 .45-100 Old Reliable; 2. .41 Colt New Model Thunderer; 3. .44 Remington M-1875 Army; 4. Colt .41 RF No. 1 derringer; 5. Colt .38 Self Cocking Revolver; 6. Smith & Wesson .22 RF No. 1, Second Issue; 7. Remington .41 RF double derringer; 8. Smith & Wesson First Model .44 Russian; 9. Winchester .38-40 M-1873 rifle; 10. Colt .45 Single Action Army, 11. Engraved Colt .38-40 Peacemaker; 12. Colt .44-40 Frontier; 13. 12-ga. American Gun Co. Shotgun; 14. .44-40 Merwin & Hulbert Pocket Army; 15. Colt .38-40 M-1878 Double Action Army; 16. Colt .41 RF No. 2 derringer.

Photo by Mike Parris. Guns No. 2, 3, 5, 9, 10, 11, 12 and 15 courtesy Erich Baumann. Guns No. 4, 6 and 16 courtesy Sotheby Parke Bernet, Los Angeles. Gun No. 7 courtesy Pony Express Sport Shop, Encino, Calif. Guns No. 1, 8, 13, and 14 from Phil Spangenberger.

From pages 104 and 105

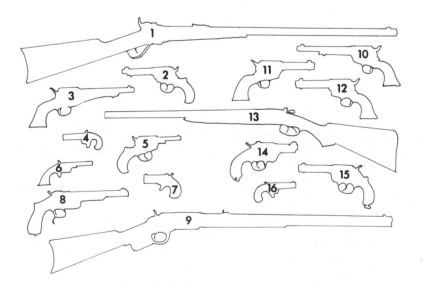

The flap holster was common during the percussion era as the flap top would protect the powder and caps from foul weather. This English-made black holster was designed for a Model 1849 Colt Pocket Revolver. (Author's collection)

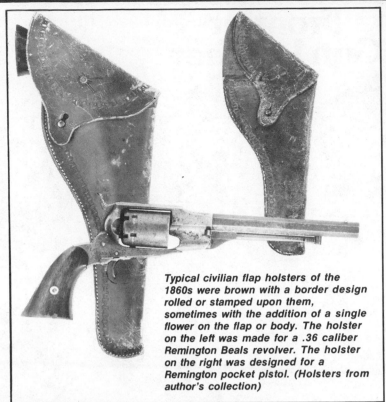

Typical civilian flap holsters of the 1860s were brown with a border design rolled or stamped upon them, sometimes with the addition of a single flower on the flap or body. The holster on the left was made for a .36 caliber Remington Beals revolver. The holster on the right was designed for a Remington pocket pistol. (Holsters from author's collection)

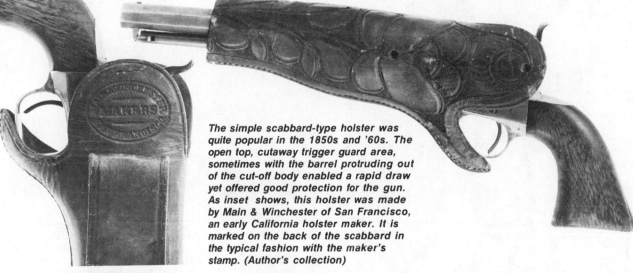

The simple scabbard-type holster was quite popular in the 1850s and '60s. The open top, cutaway trigger guard area, sometimes with the barrel protruding out of the cut-off body enabled a rapid draw yet offered good protection for the gun. As inset shows, this holster was made by Main & Winchester of San Francisco, an early California holster maker. It is marked on the back of the scabbard in the typical fashion with the maker's stamp. (Author's collection)

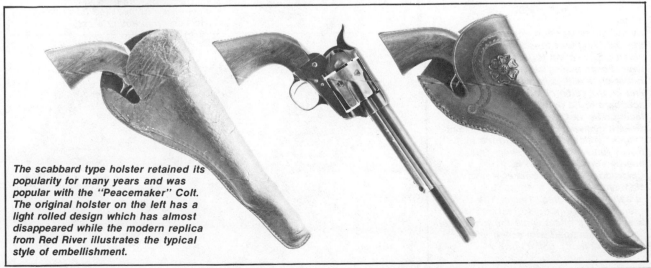

The scabbard type holster retained its popularity for many years and was popular with the "Peacemaker" Colt. The original holster on the left has a light rolled design which has almost disappeared while the modern replica from Red River illustrates the typical style of embellishment.

Frontier Gun Leather

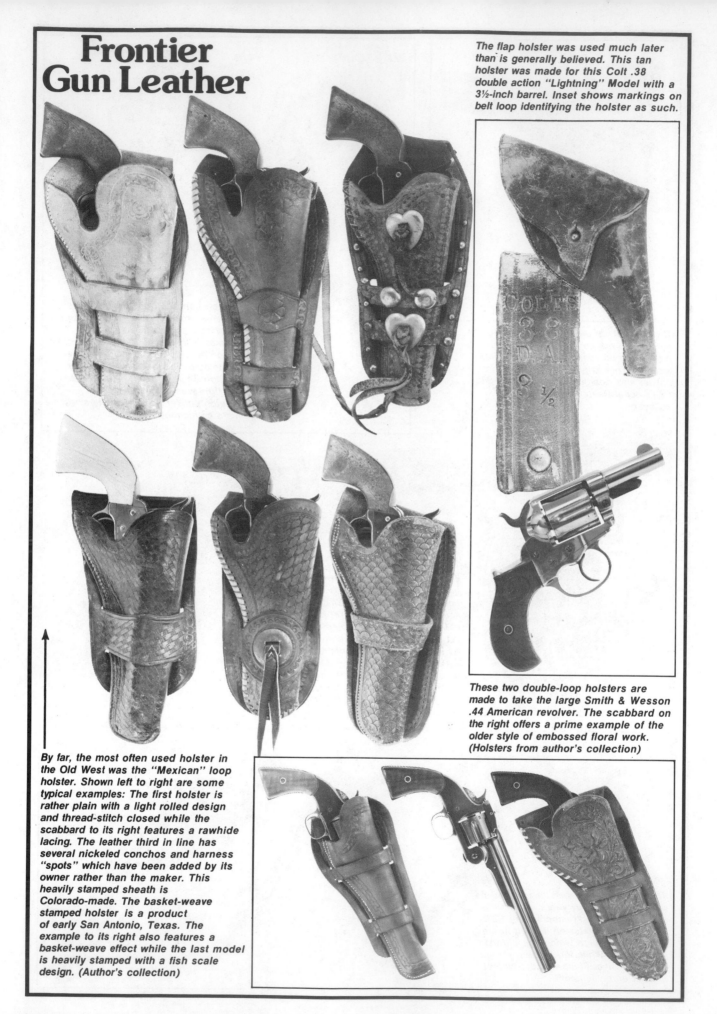

The flap holster was used much later than is generally believed. This tan holster was made for this Colt .38 double action "Lightning" Model with a 3½-inch barrel. Inset shows markings on belt loop identifying the holster as such.

These two double-loop holsters are made to take the large Smith & Wesson .44 American revolver. The scabbard on the right offers a prime example of the older style of embossed floral work. (Holsters from author's collection)

By far, the most often used holster in the Old West was the "Mexican" loop holster. Shown left to right are some typical examples: The first holster is rather plain with a light rolled design and thread-stitch closed while the scabbard to its right features a rawhide lacing. The leather third in line has several nickeled conchos and harness "spots" which have been added by its owner rather than the maker. This heavily stamped sheath is Colorado-made. The basket-weave stamped holster is a product of early San Antonio, Texas. The example to its right also features a basket-weave effect while the last model is heavily stamped with a fish scale design. (Author's collection) type affair that conformed to the general shape of the arm. Oftentimes, these holsters would be made with a protective flap to prevent foul weather from ruining the percussion caps. A loop sewn or riveted to the back of the holster would serve to attach it to a belt.

Colt's Dragoon and pocket pistols of the late 1840s as well as their 1851 Navy Model were the first truly practical revolvers for a man to carry on himself. Although the big Dragoons were primarily repeating horse pistols and were meant to be carried in pommel holsters, many of them were worn on the persons themselves. It was during this era that holsters began to take on some character of their own with distinctive shapes. They also began to utilize the cutaway trigger idea of construction due to the easy handling of guns of this configuration. One could draw a Navy Colt or pocket revolver, cock, and fire it with one hand, unlike the more cumbersome pepperbox style arms, or any of the variety of oddball multiple shot weapons which existed then.

Holsters were usually made of one thickness of 7 to 9-ounce leather as opposed to the two-layer stitched-together method of the present day. They were made to cover most of the weapon. This holds true in the cartridge, as well as the percussion era. Tooling usually was limited to a continuous stamped or rolled design running around the border of the holster and perhaps with an added single flower stamped into the body. Occasionally one would see a carved or embossed holster, but the design was not like the modern large petalled flowers and leaves. Designs of this period often consisted of elongated vines with smaller flowers, leaves or blossoms at the ends. Fancier varieties could even sport silken or metallic thread embroidered into a floral motif on the body. Most of the holsters of the frontier era seemed to share these common characteristics.

In the 1850s and '60s, it was common for a man to wear his revolver in cross-draw fashion. A right-handed man would generally wear his six-gun on his left side with the butt facing forward. This method enabled him to draw the pistol easily while sitting and was preferred while on horseback. It was not uncommon, though, to see a fellow wear his revolver on his right side (assuming he is right-handed) with the butt forward in the military style. This style of wearing your iron was largely due to habit. At the close of the Civil War, thousands of

ex-soldiers of both sides flocked to the frontier for fortune, adventure, or both. They naturally reverted to wearing their sidearms in the manner that they had been used to for the past several years. Many of the men were carrying their issue weapons in military belts and holsters which they had purchased upon mustering out of the service.

The stereotyped version of the West has it that upon leaving the service, these veterans immediately cut the flaps off of their holsters and cut away the trigger area. Nonsense! Some of them did, but many more of these fellows were just average young men who weren't out to gain reputations as gunmen. They just simply needed a firearm to survive the wild frontier. Besides, as

Cross draw was a commonly used method of wearing handguns on the frontier. Here Ed Schiefflin, a prospector who founded Tombstone, Arizona, carries what appears to be a pair of Smith & Wesson ivory stocked revolvers along with his big "Buffalo" Sharps rifle. (Arizona Historical Society)

mentioned earlier, the flaps served a very useful purpose with percussion arms. Many civilian holsters were made as exact copies of the military style, flap and all, with the possible exception of being brown rather than black. The exposed top holster was gaining in popularity though, and by the early '70s, it was by far the most common type of handgun leather.

Belts of the percussion era were generally plain and about two

Frontier Gun Leather

inches wide. Sometimes they would contain the border tooled design or light floral work. They sported simple iron buckles, often of the roller or frame type, or even a belt plate such as the military used. Accoutrements were not worn often on the belt in civilian life as they were in the army, because prolonged fights were not expected as were anticipated in a military battle. If any accessory was worn, it might have been a small flap pouch designed to carry an extra cylinder, though these were not very common. It was far easier to carry an extra revolver if it was felt that more than six quick shots were needed.

Sometime during the early to mid-'70s, the loop holster made its appearance. Also called the "Mexican" loop holster (probably denoting its origin), this arrangement consisted of a scabbard where the top and back is not cut off, but simply folded over and down behind the holster portion to form a belt loop and skirt between the body of the wearer and the holster. This backing has one or more slots cut into it which the scabbard portion passes through. Sometimes these loops were sewn or even riveted rather than cut. These loops could be straight cuts or curved. Some were cut with scalloped edges and contained a bit of tooling, or perhaps a concho which was laced on for extra embellishment. On holsters made for long barreled revolvers, two or sometimes three loops were

used. Shorter barreled six-guns usually sported a single loop. The loop holster was by far the most commonly used holster on the frontier.

It's anyone's guess as to how early shoulder holsters were used, but one thing is certain; they were quite common with lawmen as well as those on the other side of the law. With the taming process slowly civilizing the frontier towns, anyone who might feel the need to carry a gun without calling attention to its presence relied more and more upon the concealable shoulder holster. City ordinances against carrying firearms within the town limits were imposed quite early in many frontier communities.

There were other forms of concealing a gun, however, but these do not fall into the category of typical holster leather but rather as novelty ideas. Some men carried one or more revolvers in pants, vests or coat pockets. The Colt Peacemaker with a lopped-off barrel and removed front sight was ideal for this simple setup. By simply thrusting the gun in your pocket and flipping the loading gate out, you had your weapon concealed, yet ready to draw quickly. Don't forget—this was the age of loose-fitting bulky clothing and it was no rough task to conceal a hunk of iron like a Peacemaker under a woolen frock coat. Wyatt Earp is reported to have had a special canvas-lined, wax-rubbed pocket sewn into his overcoat. There were also special holsters designed to fit inside one's trousers and were held up by attaching to the suspender buttons located on the inside of the waistband. Some cowboys had hol-

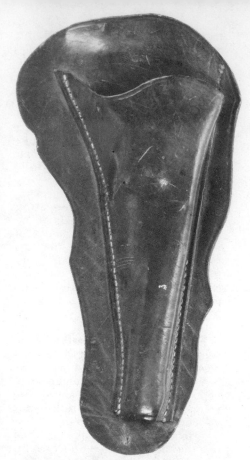

A seldom-seen style of holster nowadays is this one with the body sewn to a flat backing. It is attached to the belt by means of a belt loop riveted to the backing. This example appears to be made for a Smith & Wesson Army Revolver No. 2. (Author's collection)

sters or pockets sewn to the inside of their chaps in order to conceal their shootin' irons. The list of ingenious inventions could go on indefinitely, stretching as far as the imagination or individual situation

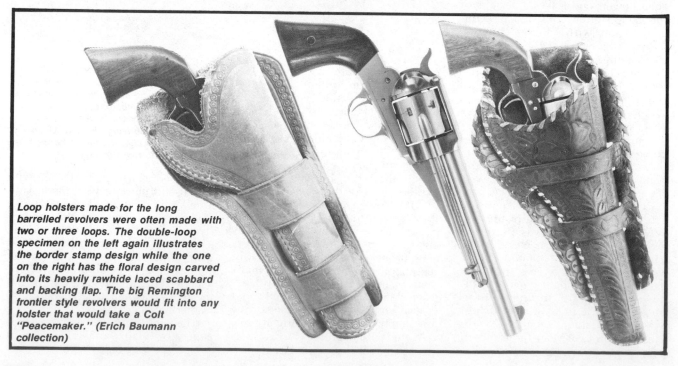

Loop holsters made for the long barrelled revolvers were often made with two or three loops. The double-loop specimen on the left again illustrates the border stamp design while the one on the right has the floral design carved into its heavily rawhide laced scabbard and backing flap. The big Remington frontier style revolvers would fit into any holster that would take a Colt "Peacemaker." (Erich Baumann collection)

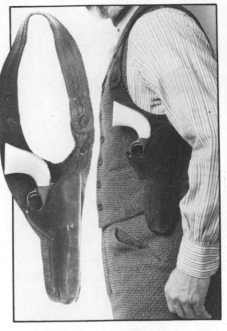

might dictate, but this piece will concentrate on the commonly used methods rather than the one-of-a-kind contraptions.

One commonly used shoulder-harness rig was of the pouch-type holster. This was simply a boot-type of scabbard attached to a strap which went around the shoulder, sometimes adding a strap to the bottom of the holster which would go around the chest for added support. The one drawback to this style is that withdrawing the gun can only be done by pulling it upwards, out of the top. This could slow the user down enough to cost him plenty in a split-second situation. Two alternatives that were used were the clip-spring system and the half-breed holster.

The clip-spring holster consists of the holster backing with the front covering flap taken off, and in its place, a steel spring which would support the frame of the weapon while the muzzle is held in place by a small socket at the base of the backing.

The half-breed holster is similar to the pouch type except that the

Holsters were worn over the cartridge belt in the Old West, not hanging from a slot cut into the bottom of it as in modern rigs, and the belts were generally worn high on the waist, not hanging off of the hip.

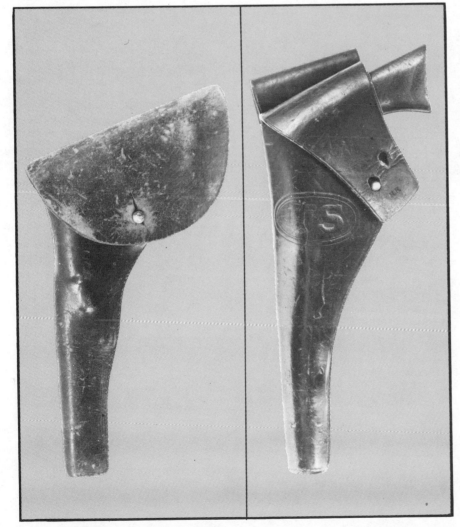

The Army of the frontier years used two basic models of holsters. They were: (Left) The full flap style of the Civil War period and used through the mid-1870s and (right) the half-flap style, which was first introduced in 1874 and used until the turn of the century in different configurations. The holster pictured is a variation of the M-1885 which was designed to hold either the Colt Single Action or the Smith & Wesson Schofield and was probably made around 1886 or 1887.

seam that faces the front of the wearer is left open. It also contains the same type of spring as in the clip-spring model. This holster allows protection against snagging on clothing and allows for a quick draw by simply pulling the gun forward.

Regardless of the type of shoulder holster used, they were pretty handy to gunmen on both sides of the law. A constable in a relatively peaceful community could give the appearance of tranquility while being fully prepared for trouble, and a lawbreaker could go about his "business" without drawing suspicion to himself, at least not until the shooting started. Such holsters served their purposes and were used often.

The final type of holster rig that was not really common but was used enough to warrant space here was the belt with the slotted metal plate affixed to it. The gunman could add an elongated hammer screw to his revolver with a broadened head similar to a nailhead. This

Continued on page 208

Black Bart
The Bloodless Bandit

REWARD!

WELLS FARGO ... EXPRESS ... CON-
taining $160 in Gold Notes ... was robbed this morning by one ... on the route from Sonora
to Milton, near top of the Hill, between the river and ... crossroad ...

$250

By Lee Silva

The history of California's gold rush is written in blood, bandits, villains, vigilantes, and violence. During a period that spanned less than 50 years, names like Murietta, Vasquez, Sontag and Evans, and Bláck Bart became household words, but only the name of Black Bart stands alone amongst the violence and mayhem.

In an era that was best known for the greed and avarice that the lust for gold created, the fruits of a day's toil in the goldfields could result in a bullet in the back faster than any other "reward" for labor. Black Bart became known as the bloodless bandit and won the hearts and fancy of everyone in California,

with the obvious exception of Wells, Fargo & Co., and its chief of detectives, James Hume.

On July 26, 1875, the Sonora stage, bound from Copperopolis to Milton, struggled slowly up Funk Hill from the Stanislaus River and came to a sudden halt, its path blocked by one of the strangest looking highwaymen that John Shine, the stage driver, had ever seen.

The bandit held a double-barreled shotgun that pointed convincingly at Shine, and sported another double-barreled shotgun strapped across his back. He wore a dirty linen duster, his boots were covered by socks to disguise his footprints,

Wells Fargo issued this wanted poster the day following Bart's first robbery. The substantial reward indicated that the company considered the bandit a threat even at this early date.

and for a mask he wore a flour sack with eye holes cut into it.

"If he dares to shoot, give him a solid volley, boys," the bandit said. At least half a dozen rifle barrels pointed menacingly from the bushes beside the road.

Shine tossed the metal strongbox onto the road, and as the bandit removed the gold from the box, a panicked lady passenger threw her purse from the stage.

From pages 112 and 113

The Wells Fargo coach rumbled its way through the gold country—its destination, Angels Camp. As it rounded the bend at the 10-mile point, the driver was confronted by a masked desperado leveling a sawed-off 12-gauge American Gun Co. shotgun, a brace of .45 caliber Colt "Peacemakers" and the command "Stand and deliver!" The bandit stood on the reins of his bay horse which was carrying his back-up gun, a M-1881 Marlin in .45-70 caliber. From out of the trees to the coach's right appeared another highwayman, mounted on a big sorrel horse and wearing a linen duster. He cocked and aimed his Colt .45 Single Action at the unarmed driver. The

buckskin-clad guard didn't have a chance to reach for his nickel plated Smith & Wesson Schofield .45.

As the passengers climbed out of the big Concord, the guard threw down the mail pouch, driver's gear box and his 12-gauge Remington shotgun. It was unloaded by the "road agent" in the duster, whose face is concealed by a hood indicating that these are not his first customers. He wears his Colt .45 in reverse draw fashion and has his 10-gauge Remington scattergun pointed menacingly at the guard.

The "drummer" standing below the guard finds himself in the role of a customer, and has himself been thoroughly fleeced for a change, while the visiting

Englishman ponders over the wisdom of his trip out to the American Frontier. The banker stands by his ruffled-through carpet-bag where a withdrawal has been made. The fashionable lady looks as if she wishes she were brandishing the nickel plated .44 cal. 1875 Remington instead of the frock-coated robber who has just discovered an "ace in the hole" on the shady gambler, in the form of a shoulder holstered .44-40 Merwin & Hulbert Pocket Army revolver. The San Francisco merchant nervously looks on as he anticipates the loss of his investment capital.

Stagecoach, team and driver courtesy of the Wells Fargo Bank, San Francisco, Calif. Photo by Mike Parris.

The bandit politely returned the purse to the lady, saying, "I don't wish your money—, only Wells Fargo boxes."

With that, the robber told Shine to drive on, and the stage lurched forward as the bandit disappeared into the brush. When the robber did not reappear, Shine stopped the stage again and went back to get the new empty strong box. Suddenly

Charles Bolton, alias Charles Boles, alias Black Bart, terrorized the California Wells Fargo stage line from July of 1875 until November of 1883. He accounted for 29 successful holdups. Bolton later acknowledged that his double-barrelled shotgun was never loaded, because he didn't want to take a chance on hurting any of his victims. (Wells Fargo Bank)

he noticed that the rifle barrels still pointed at him from the brush. But they didn't move. Proceeding with suspicious caution, the stage driver discovered that the rifle barrels were actually sticks placed into the bushes in such a way that they resembled guns from a distance.

The bandit got away clean, but the clever trickery and the bandit's chivalrous refusal to accept the woman passenger's money became instant front page copy in all of the gold country newspapers.

The same daring, polite bandit struck the Wells Fargo stages again on Dec. 28, 1875, and again on June 2, 1876.

The name of Black Bart was thrust dramatically upon the California goldfields on Aug. 3, 1877 when the same strange-looking bandit held up the Point Arena stage, near the Russian River, and though he got only $300 in cash for his troubles, he began to create what is still a legend in California.

The bandit left a piece of paper, weighted down by a rock, stop a stump near the road, and on the paper was written a poem which read:

"I've labored long and hard for bred For honor and for riches But on my corns too long you've tred You fine-haired Sons of Bitches."

The poem was signed, "Black Bart, the Po8."

The local newspapers pounced on this delightedly fresh fodder of

Wells Fargo Detective James Hume, was one of the most respected criminologists of his day, and his failure to capture Bart became a source of embarrassment. Hume finally tracked the desperado down through a laundry mark on a handkerchief left at the scene of a robbery. (Wells Fargo Bank)

news, and almost overnight the name Black Bart was wagging tongues and bringing chuckles of delight around every campfire in California.

Black Bart, the daring bandit, did not let his public down.

On July 25, 1878, he robbed another stage and left behind some more verses to add to his legend:

"Here I lay me down to sleep To await the coming morrow Perhaps success, perhaps defeat And everlasting sorrow.

"Let come what will, I'll try it on My condition can't be worse And if there's money in that box Tis munny in my purse."

When Henry Wells and William Fargo created Wells, Fargo & Co., in 1852, they had done so with the intent of monopolizing the express company business by offering the public the fastest and cheapest rates in the West—and they had succeeded in doing just that. Wells Fargo hauled everything from passengers to ice, and even succeeded in undercutting the speed and rates of the U.S. mails. Its major source of business, however, was in shipping the gold and silver bullion from the mines of Nevada and California to the rail spurs which were just beginning to reach their tentacles from San Francisco and Los Angeles.

In the 1860s, Wells Fargo was shipping amounts of silver and gold that ran from $150,000 to $200,000 per week, on its major routes such as the one from Virginia City, Nevada. Between 1858 and 1861, Wells Fargo shipped 15 tons of gold out of its Sonora, California office alone, and in 1866 it shipped over $14 million worth of bullion from Nevada to San Francisco.

The Wells Fargo strongboxes became not only the favorite targets of

Black Bart

shotgun-wielding highwaymen, but also the targets of Wells Fargo's own employees, too, many of whom found that they could not resist the apple of temptation that one of the chock-full strongboxes offered them.

One of the keys to Wells Fargo's success was its guarantee that it would, with its own money, reimburse to any shipper, all shipments of money or bullion that was lost to

bery, and few pleasures to smile about. So it came as no surprise to Wells, Fargo & Co., and to James Hume in particular, when Black Bart suddenly became a folk hero to the miners of the mining country, instead of just another robber.

For this reason, James Hume set his sights on capturing the clever Bart, for unlike other previous thorns in Wells Fargo's side, Bart was causing too much public sympathy on the side of the bandit.

of some of the best detectives in the West.

Fortunately for Wells Fargo, Black Bart started his 8-year attack on its strongboxes in the waning days of the gold boom when train robbing instead of stage robbing was becoming the fashion for the men who took the "easy" road to money. By the 1870s many a highwayman went to the trouble of waylaying a stage only to find that the strongbox was empty.

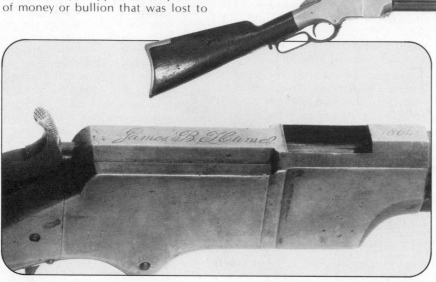

One of Hume's favorite rifles was his .44 Henry. It is engraved on the top of the receiver "James B. Hume 1864." (Wells Fargo Bank).

bandits or stolen in any manner. To survive the losses, Wells Fargo depended on an elite detective force to track down and recover enough stolen money and bullion to still show a profit, and also to hopefully provide enough of a psychological deterrent to would-be robbers to at least hold the number of robberies down to a reasonable level.

However, during the 1860s it began to look as if stagecoach robbers outnumbered farmers in California, and Wells Fargo was forced to raise its freight rates astronomically to offset the losses.

As a result, Wells Fargo's public image changed from one of benevolent service in the 1850s to that of just another money-grabbing monopoly by the late 1860s. By the 1870s, too many citizens of California and Nevada looked upon the robbery of a Wells Fargo strongbox with the attitude that it was just a case of one thief robbing another.

By then, the gold boom and the days of overnight riches were considered to be over, and the name of Black Bart suddenly brought levity to lives that were too filled with 20-hour work days, murder and rob-

Hume carried this cut-off M-1860 Colt .44 revolver as a hideout gun. It is not known whether it was used at the time of Bart's arrest. (Wells Fargo Bank).

Hume had been hired as Chief of Detectives by Wells Fargo in 1873. He was an able investigator, one of the top criminologists of his day, and one of the first detectives to utilize ballistics to convict a criminal. Though good detectives were about as scarce as a beautiful virgin in California, Hume had also managed to assemble him a small staff

Though Black Bart, or whoever he really was, was not gleaning much profit from Wells Fargo's nearly empty strongboxes, it soon became too apparent to Hume that Bart was not just another everyday stage robber.

By his fifth holdup in 1878, Black Bart had not only established a pattern of robbery that never changed, but he also had painted a picture of himself that was just downright weird. He said "please" to the driver whenever he stopped a stage, he refused to rob the passengers, and he thus far had not fired a shot. What puzzled Hume the most

was that Black Bart seemed almost to have a psychological desire to be caught.

Though his holdups were professionally and artfully planned out well in advance, Bart began to leave tracks and clues all over the state of California, almost as if he was thumbing his nose at Wells Fargo and daring it to catch him.

Only five days after his fifth holdup, Black Bart struck again on July 30, 1878.

His M.O. was always the same. He evidently carefully selected each

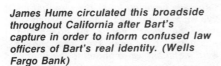

Wells, Fargo & Co's Express,

J. B. HUME,
Special Officer.

OFFICE, ROOM 3, WELLS, FARGO & CO'S BUILDING,
Sansome and Halleck Streets.

RESIDENCE, 810 McAllister Street.

San Francisco, Nov. 26th, 1883.

To Agents of Wells, Fargo & Co.:

Since the conviction and incarceration of CHARLES E. BOLES, *alias* CHARLES E. BOLTON, *alias* "BLACK BART, the Po 8," for robbing WELLS, FARGO & CO'S EXPRESS, numerous inquiries have been received from Sheriffs and other officers, inquiring as to the identity of BOLTON *alias* "BLACK BART." This inquiry has doubtless been occasioned by the statement of the prisoner when pleading guilty before the Court, to a particular robbery—that it was his first offence, and that he was not "BLACK BART." All officers will readily understand the reason of such a statement, viz: To excite judicial clemency. The man CHAS. E. BOLES *alias* BOLTON (of whom we herewith append photograph and description) is " Black Bart, the Po 8."

DESCRIPTION.

Received November 21st, 1883.

Number of Commitment—11,046.

Education—Liberal.

Nativity—New York.

Crime—Robbery.

Term—Six years.

County from—Calaveras.

Age—50 years.

Occupation—*Mining.*

Height, 5 feet 8 inches, in stockings.

Complexion—Light.

Color of Eyes—Blue.

Color of Hair—Iron Gray.

Heavy Mustache—Nearly white.

Heavy Imperial—Nearly white.

Size of Foot—No. 6.

Weight—160 lbs.

Size of Hat—7¼.

Does not use Tobacco in any form.

Does not use Intoxicating Liquors.

Respectfully

James Hume circulated this broadside throughout California after Bart's capture in order to inform confused law officers of Bart's real identity. (Wells Fargo Bank)

holdup location after first spending days watching the route and the schedules of the stages. He always used a double-barreled shotgun, pointed readily, and he always stood between the lead horses so that a shot at him would be difficult, for good horse flesh was too highly prized to be shot accidentally. When cutting open the purloined mailbags, Bart always made a T-shaped slit at the top that became an instant trademark of his work. His getaways were expertly planned, and he never used horses, always escaping on foot over miles of terrain that only a man in perfect physical condition could have covered in the short times that it took him to get clear of any pursuit. Somehow, at the end of every trail, he just seemed to vanish, probably falling into the safety of a previously established and reputable identity.

On Oct. 2, 1878, he held up a stage near Ukiah, Calif., and then, on the very next day, he held up another stage miles away from the site of the previous day's holdup.

Then he vanished completely

This stage robber was not as lucky as Black Bart. He was shot down and killed by a guard during an attempted holdup. (Wells Fargo Bank)

until June 21, 1879, when he robbed the Oroville-bound stage. Seeming to play games almost at will, he then struck again on Oct. 25, 1879, and again, Oct. 27.

Growing bolder as the months and years stretched on, Black Bart robbed four stages during 1880, again supplying front page copy to the local papers when, during a holdup in September, he politely asked the stage driver to give James Hume his compliments.

Wells, Fargo & Co., offered a $300 reward for Black Bart, the state of California matched the amount, and the U.S. government chipped in

$200, since Bart also had a habit of lifting the U.S. mail along with Wells Fargo's strongboxes.

Hume, in the meantime, was completely unsuccessful in catching up with Black Bart. But he was beginning to piece together a physical description of the wily bandit, because Black Bart mockingly walked about freely while casing each holdup, leaving behind not only hundreds of footprints but lots of people whom he ate with, visited with, and generally charmed with his quiet friendliness.

Hume learned that Black Bart wore a size 6 or 8 boot, was middle-aged, sported a thick but neatly trimmed mustache, was slightly built, was about 5 feet 8 inches tall, had blue eyes, and had two front teeth missing. But he still couldn't catch up with him.

Black Bart robbed five stages during 1881, all of them carried out methodically like the previous ones, never firing a shot, but never bagging an overwhelming amount of money either.

He casually carried out his 21st and 22nd holdups in 1882 before he finally ran into a bit of bad luck. On July 13, 1882, still mocking Wells Fargo, he chose to rob the same stage route that he had robbed two times already. The stage ground to a dusty halt at Black Bart's usual command of "Please throw out the strongbox," but instead of the box, he was met by a bullet from the rifle of the man riding shotgun, George Hackett. Hackett had been held up by Bart before and was finally pushed far enough to put bravery before the silent muzzles of Bart's scattergun.

Fortunately for Black Bart, Hackett was a lousy shot at close range. The bullet only nicked the star-crossed bandit in the scalp, and once again he managed to disappear into the brush, this time, though, not only leaving a trail of blood, but thwarted for the first time in 23 at-

Black Bart

These lawmen were all involved in the pursuit of Bart. They are (l-r): Tom Cunningham, sheriff of San Joaquin County; Captain Stone, San Francisco Police; Ben Thorne, sheriff of Calaveras County; and Jonathan Thacker and Harry Morse of Wells Fargo. (Wells Fargo Bank)

and no one after Hackett chose to test his mettle against Black Bart's ever-present shotgun.

Perhaps the cagey old bandit finally got bored with it all, for his next holdup was to be his last, only because he did everything to get caught except to walk right into James Hume's office and announce himself.

On Nov. 3, 1883, Black Bart casually, again mockingly, held up the

go hunting. At the base of Funk Hill, Rolleri dropped off the stage, his Henry rifle over his shoulder.

Just as he had done eight years previously, Black Bart stopped the stage just before it reached the top of the hill. The usual flour sack was over his head, and his ever-present shotgun was leveled cooly and squarely on McConnell.

"Who was that man who got off the stage?" Black Bart demanded. It was obvious that he had been lying in wait for the stage and had seen Rolleri get off with his rifle.

"He's just a friend," McConnell explained, "out looking for some cattle."

Incredibly, instead of being spooked off by the knowledge that there was another armed man just down the road, Black Bart nonchalantly asked McConnell to get off the stage.

When McConnell refused, saying that the brakes were bad and the stage might roll, Black Bart chocked the wheels himself with rocks from beside the road. That done, he made McConnell unhitch the horses and take them on his way over the hill.

Black Bart knew there was a man just down the road, armed with a rifle. He knew that he had just sent another man over the hill who

Generally believed to be the strongbox, this wooden box was actually carried under the driver's seat of the coach and was used for his gear. True strongboxes were metal and were bolted to the floor of the passenger compartment. (Sotheby Parke Bernet, Los Angeles)

tempts to get away with any of the Wells Fargo money. As usual, all he left was a trail, and Black Bart vanished once again—but not for long.

Much to the chagrin of Wells Fargo and James Hume, Black Bart held up the stage bound for Redding on Sept. 17, 1882, and promptly followed that with another in November, cooled his heels through the beginning of 1883, and then struck again in April and June of 1883.

As persistent as a flea on a hound-dog, Black Bart was barely slowed down by the bullet wound.

He still had never fired a shot,

exact same stage, on the exact same route, at the exact same spot in the road that he had held up in his first stage robbery in 1875.

The driver of the stage was a veteran driver named Reason McConnell, and the Wells Fargo strongbox contained about $4000 in gold. At the Reynolds Ferry river crossing, McConnell gave a ride to Jimmy Rolleri, the ferry operator, who was on his way to Funk Hill to

was now out of sight not more than a couple of hundred yards away. But ignoring both of them, he set to work inside the stage, hammering away at the strongbox, which, by then, Wells Fargo & Co., had taken to bolting and strapping down to the floor of the stage in a somewhat successful attempt to at least slow down its constant popularity with highwaymen.

Continued on page 216

Double 12-gauge Percussion Shotgun

By Garry James

The Navy Arms double percussion shotgun functioned extremely well. It has the pointing characteristics of the original English versions and throws acceptable patterns at the requisite distances.

barrels would be cut to 18 or 20 inches to aid in maneuverability and to increase the shot pattern at short ranges.

The famous California stage robber, "Black Bart", always brandished a shotgun. He recognized the terror it struck in the people facing the business end, although he later confessed that his guns were never loaded for he didn't really want to hurt anyone.

While percussion guns were widely used in the early days of the West, by the 1870s and '80s they had become more or less passe. Scores of inexpensive cartridge hammer double flooded the market and the convenience of self-contained cartridges was just too much of an attraction. Still, caplock shotguns were used to some extent, both by hunters and lawmen, and they certainly figured heavily in the Gold Rush Era.

A number of original and replica shotguns, double-barrelled percussion and cartridge shotguns, suitable for shooting, are currently available at reasonable prices. One

the gun was ready to fire.

A target board was set up at about 15 yards—approximately the distance a robber would keep between himself and the stage coach driver. The hammers were put on full cock, the gun shouldered and the trigger for the left barrel pulled. The loud, booming report and clouds of white smoke certainly indicated that the gun meant business. Recoil was not heavy, and the black powder "push" was more or less similar to what we have become used to with other muzzle loading longarms.

Fifteen-yard patterns measured about 15 inches—certainly a damaging radius. The gun was quite easy to control and had the natural pointing characteristics a good shotgun should have. Several from-the-hip shots were easily kept on the target area, indicating that accurate emergency snap-shots were well within the capability of the Western marshals and badmen.

The MPSD-100 sells for about $140 and Navy offers a complete line of accessories to service the arm.

The lines of the Navy Arms double, are very close to the fine English and French originals. The 29-inch barrels are warmly browned and the half-length walnut stock features a checkered pistol grip.

Highwaymen, especially stage-coach robbers, seemed to favor scatterguns. Many lawmen preferred shotguns as well, for at reasonable ranges, multiple hits with buckshot were sure and deadly. The gaping muzzle of a 10 or 12-gauge also had a considerable psychological effect.

In the early days of coaching, especially in England, short barrelled flintlock blunderbusses were carried by drivers as a deterrent against the Dick Turpins and Captain Lightfoots. This custom carried over into the New World and in the American West percussion, and later cartridge, shotguns were de riguer. Often their

of the best of the percussion replicas is offered by Navy Arms Co., 689 Bergen Blvd., NJ 07657. The Model PSD-100 is an Italian-made copy of an 1850-60 period fine English, percussion double-barrelled shotgun. The 29-inch, 12-gauge barrels are warmly browned and choked improved and modified. Twin lockplates and hammers exhibit good cast engraving and the half-length walnut stock features a checkered straight pistol grip

To load the Navy double we first snapped caps on the nipples to clear the vents and then fired light black powder squib charges to clear the tubes of any oil that might retard proper ignition.

Sixty-grain charges of FFFg black powder were poured down each of the barrels, and then Federal fiber shotgun wads were tamped down firmly on the charges. A 1¼ ounce load of No. 6 shot was dumped on top of the wads, and the shot was kept in place with shredded tissue. The nipples were finally capped and

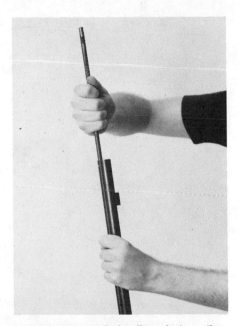

In loading a muzzle loading shotgun the wad should be tamped down on the charge hard enough to "spring" the ramrod. The shot is held in with a covering of shredded paper.

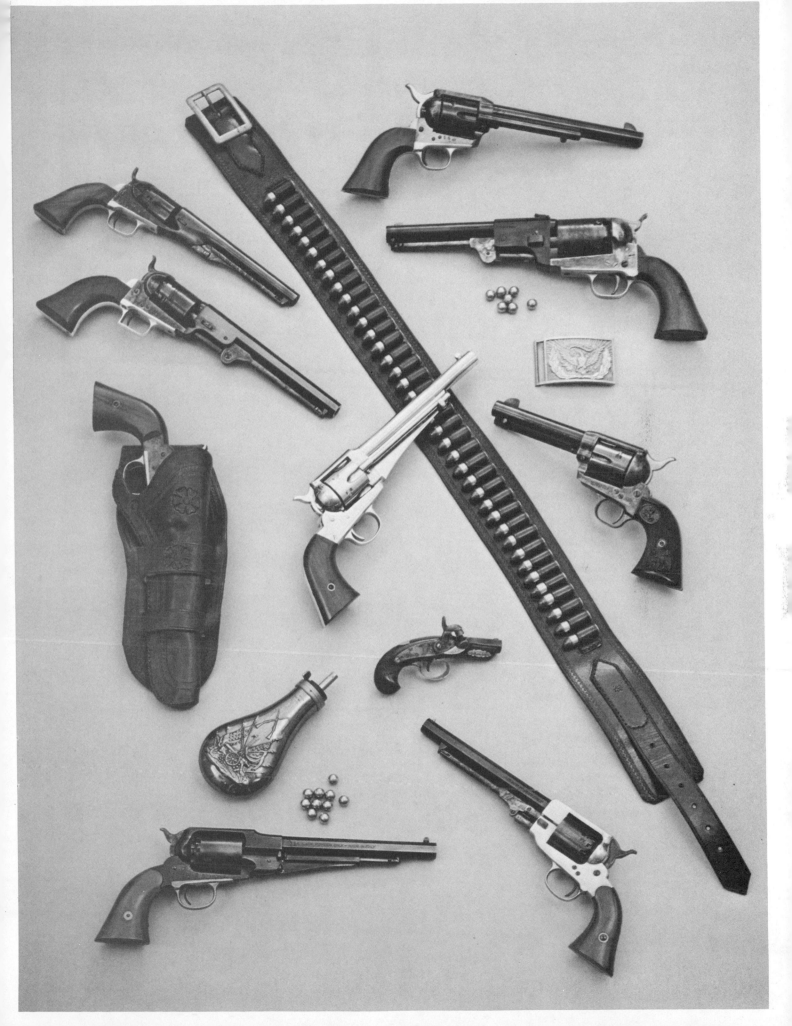

Doc Holliday

Dentist, Gambler, Gunfighter.
By E. Dixon Larson

Even through diligent research, little can be credited to Dr. John H. Holliday, dentist, but there are many facts to unmask concerning "Doc" Holliday's profligate life and his bar room behavior.

Holliday was born in Virginia in 1852, the son of a family of modest means. As he was passing from boyhood to manhood, his father, an officer in the Confederate Army, was killed in the late stages of the Civil War. Many believe this was the beginning of Doc's bitterness. Some five years after the Civil War, his family scraped together enough of their assets to send John to the Baltimore College of Dentistry.

Almost immediately after his graduation and upon his returning home, he became provoked at seeing four negroes in his childhood swimming hole, and took up his father's shotgun and killed two and wounded the others. This was one of the first signs of his uncontrollable temper.

Suffering no degree of remorse, but realizing that since the Civil War, which freed the slaves, such an act could result in severe consequences, he fled to Dallas, Texas.

After a few months had passed, he hung out his shingle which read, "J. H. Holliday-Dentist." Although a graduate dentist, he really had no talent for the profession and it soon

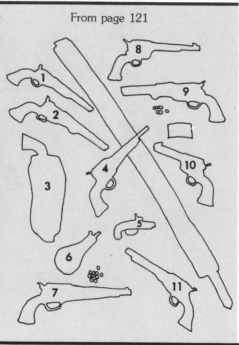

From page 121

With the boom in gun collecting, the Old West enthusiast who wants to shoot his firearms has suddenly discovered that they are just too expensive to take a chance with. A wide selection of accurate replicas now fills the gap and allows the aficionado to use old-style guns without hurting their value. This group of quality replica handguns, represents a good cross section of the types currently available. 1. Navy Arms .36 percussion Police Model; 2. Colt .36 percussion M-1851 Navy; 3&4. Navy Arms M-1875 Remington in Blued .45 and nickeled .44-40 versions; 5. Dixie Gun Works .41 Lincoln derringer; 6. Dixie Gun Works Colt-style pistol powder flask; 7. Lyman .44 percussion Remington New Model Army; 8. Iver Johnson .45 Cattleman; 9. Navy Arms .44 percussion Third Model Dragoon; 10. Colt .45 Single Action Army; 11. Dixie Gun Works .36 percussion Spiller & Burr. Belt and holster from Red River, Model 1851 U.S. Army buckle by F. Burgess. Photo by Larry Griffin.

The era of the gunfighter began during the reign of the percussion-lock system. Some of the first truly practical fighting handguns were Colt's 2nd Model Dragoon in .44 caliber (1); and their .36 caliber 1851 Model Navy Revolver (2). The somewhat smaller Colt Model of 1855 Pocket Pistol of Root's patent in caliber .28 (3), the .41 caliber Philadelphia Deringer (4) and the Colt Model 1849 Pocket Revolver in .31 caliber (5) were much preferred by gamblers and other shady characters who found the need for more concealable arms. The big 1861 Remington .44 (6), like the earlier Colts, were much preferred for serious shootouts and were greatly improved over the earlier configurations in handguns such

as the English-made .36 caliber "Pepperbox" pistol (7).

Accoutrements of the period are a skeleton-rigged Texican saddle circa 1850s (8), California-style, dogs-head design, silver-inlaid spurs (9), a tin of percussion caps (10), an 1860s-style civilian flap holster (11), a Colt .31 caliber bullet mold (12), balls and pistol powder flask (13).

Pistols Nos. 1, 3, 4, and 7, courtesy Sotheby Parke Bernet, Los Angeles. Pistols Nos. 2, 5, 6, and items 9, 10, 12 and 13 courtesy Erich Baumann. Items Nos. 8 and 11, from Phil Spangenberger. Photo by Mike Parris

From page 120

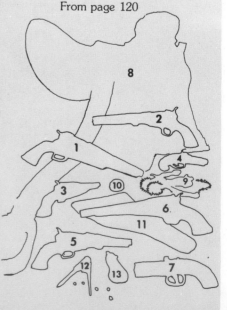

keeper of the Glenwood Hotel where he cashed in his "chips." It was probably one of his first acquisitions after his flight from Virginia to Texas. It now resides in The William S. Wells Collection.

The Pinkerton records reflect Doc as a frail, small man, 5 feet, 2 inches tall and just weighing slightly over 115 pounds. Regardless of the ambient temperature, he always wore a long black overcoat and was constantly coughing blood into a blue handkerchief. His dossier also states he had a wispy mustache and pale blue eyes, even though his eyes appear brown in all known photos.

Also in the Wells collection is an 1880 Remington, .41 RF double derringer, silver and gold plated with pearl grips, SN 474, bearing the engraved inscription on the back strap, "To Doc from Kate" The chemical composition of the silver and gold, when analyzed on the

John H. "Doc" Holliday was a graduate dentist who favored gambling, drinking and gunfighting to performing oral surgery. Despite several shooting scrapes, Holliday died in bed of tuberculosis. This photo was taken in Tombstone, Arizona around 1880.

Doc's trusty "street howitzer" was his favorite 10-gauge Meteor double shotgun with sawed off barrels and a cropped stock. It was worn on a shoulder strap attached to a brass swivel ring. This style was copied from a gun owned by the Mormon "Avenger" Porter Rockwell.

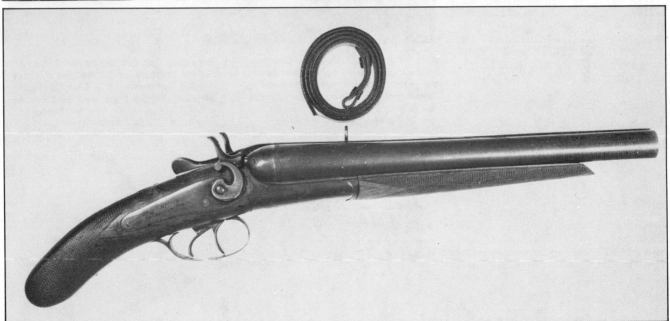

became apparent that his real talents and enjoyment were derived from the gaming tables of saloons. He also had an unquenchable thirst.

Doc probably owned more guns in his short life span of 35 years than he ever pulled teeth. Doubtless, he must have had a great appreciation for what is believed to be among or perhaps his first, a Colt 1851 Navy factory conversion to 38CF, nickel with ivory. This arm, with three others, was found neatly wrapped in a chamois cloth in his personal belongings and keepsakes at the time of his death by the inn

Mass Spectrometer, is that of the 1870 period with some slight retouch of the 1900s. Papers with the derringer show it changed hands after Doc's death in Glenwood, Colorado, from the innkeeper, to hotel manager, to the undertaker, to the proprietor of the "Springs Saloon,"

Doc Holliday

Bill Wells. It seems as though Doc left some unfinished financial obligations behind when he departed November 8, 1887.

Three other guns, including a 10-gauge cropped shotgun, believed to be in the McTague Collection, were given to Father Downey, chaplain for the U.S. Cavalry stationed at Leadville. Hearsay establishes the other two as Colt Single Action Army Models. Doc favored a cropped-shotgun suspended by a bandello type strap over the shoulder, which replaced his original Bowie knife arrangement.

Doc, however, never gave up the knife, but merely relocated it under one arm.

The shotgun was attached from a brass ring that had been installed in the barrel in such fashion that the gun would be perfectly balanced when loaded. Thus, when Doc pulled back his long coat, the gun barrels would raise automatically into their business position. Some say he patterned this arrangement after that worn by Brigham Young's bodyguard, Porter Rockwell, who is believed to be the originator of the 20-to-1 "street howitzer" which was to later gain Al Capone's favor.

Holliday's meager efforts to establish a dental practice in Dallas soon failed when a rancher accused him of cheating. The cattleman met his demise from shots delivered from under the table, another little technique Doc favored. The rancher was well-liked and had many friends. Considering this, Doc hastily left Dallas and fled to Jacksboro, Texas. Jacksboro was on the outskirts of a military post which naturally fostered all types of gambling and offered Doc some interesting opportunities for sudden wealth.

A few months later, Doc became incensed over a game of chance and killed a soldier. Most records do not depict John H. "Doc" Holliday as a "pistol prince," a quick-draw artists, or even give him honorable mention as a man who would stand up and offer a fair fight. Most accounts, periodicals and

Kate "Big Nose" Fisher was Doc's mistress and rowdy companion during the years he was in Fort Griffin and Tombstone. On one occasion she set fire to a hotel to provide cover for her and Doc's escape after a knifing.

Kate gave Doc this .41 Remington o/u Double Derringer about the time the pair lived in Tombstone. It is silver and gold plated with pearl grips, and its SN 474 dates it in the 1870s. The backstrap is engraved "To Doc from Kate."

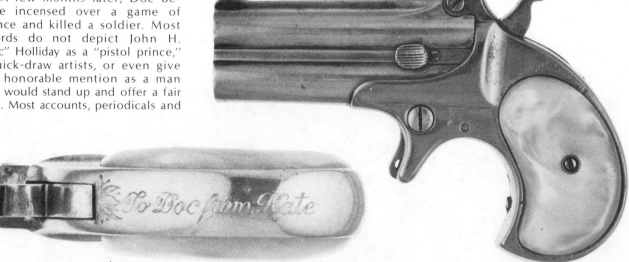

old newspapers lead one to conclude that Doc Holliday was a complex Jekyll and Hyde; a profligate little man with a goal of self-destruction. Perhaps this was due to the fact that he had tuberculosis, and had been told by doctors at the age of 16 that he could only live about four more years and probably felt he was continually living on borrowed time. After killing the soldier, Doc rode some 800 miles across the Texas Panhandle to Denver, Colorado. Here he hid out quietly for three weeks, then, according to records, carved up Bud Ryan in a gaming argument. In later years, Ryan was proud of his jagged scar across his cheek and exhibited it freely as hav-

comment made by Ed Bailey concerning the size of Kate's nose and knifed Ed in his chair at the gaming table. Kate had a flare for arson, as she set fire to the hotel to provide Doc and herself a means of escaping town. Because of the period of Doc's Remington Double Derringer, it was probably given to him by Kate between their stay in Dodge City and their period of getting

Wyatt Earp and Doc Holliday became fast friends because Doc once saved Wyatt's life by shotgunning down a "backshooter" who had his eyes focused on Earp. The lawman was also drawn to gambling and the saloon business and this helped to cement their friendship.

Doc some of the action in his saloon. Earp, although a lawman, always had a keen eye for the gaming and saloon business which may have helped foster their friendship. Through his respect for Wyatt, Doc, along with Big Nose Kate, migrated from Dodge City to help the Earps tame Tombstone, Arizona. In reality, the Earp brothers did not like Doc but merely tolerated him because of their brother Wyatt's fondness for him. On the way to Arizona, Doc killed three more men in Santa Fe when they questioned his honesty with cards. This deed was done with his double derringer and a six-shooter, presumably a Colt. Doc and Kate had a falling out in Tombstone. Kate, who was known to have trouble holding her liquor, got drunk and started a vicious rumor around town that Doc had committed an unsolved robbery of the stage of some $80,000. (It should be noted that such an accusation, in reality, touched off the Tombstone showdown at the O.K. Corral.) Doc became so enraged by one of the accusers, Bud Philpot, that he gunned him down in the street with his 10-gauge. Philpot was a McLowery-Clanton supporter. Tombstone was divided into two factions, anti-Earps, which included a newly elected Sheriff Behan, the McLowerys and the Clantons. Although Earp and Doc appeared on the scene in many western frontier towns, it was in Tombstone that both made their reputations.

It may not be known to many, but at the time of "Big Nose Kate's" yarn about Doc robbing the stage, Tombstone was saturated with law officers. Wyatt Earp had an appointment as deputy U.S. Marshal backed up by his brothers, James, Warren, and Doc, Virgil Earp, who was town marshal, with the fifth brother, Morgan, as Virgil's deputy. Wyatt had hoped to gain the position of sheriff, which would have netted him some $40,000 per year while also acting as the county assessor and tax collector for Chochise County. Under the law, the sheriff was permitted to keep 10 percent of the collections for his efforts. Therefore, Wyatt could readily foresee that with a little ambition and some professional tax collectors, this could be a very enviable position. As tension grew over Doc's killing of Philpot, and Kate's rumor, James and Warren Earp left Tombstone. Kate finally sobered up and told the judge that she had lied. But this was the "last straw" for Doc, as he gave her some money and told her if she ever came back "he'd do her in with the gun she gave him." She knew he meant it and never returned to his

ing been made by the ill-tempered Doc Holliday. At the time, however, Doc feared retaliation and fled from Denver to Fort Griffin where he met Kate Fisher, later known as "Big Nose Kate," because of the size of her proboscis. After a few months of living a vulgar life with his mistress "Big Nose Kate," and playing at the gaming palaces, it was inevitable—he became enraged over a derogatory

along prior to their final parting in Tombstone with the Earps.

After their escape from the fire, they settled in Dodge City. It was here that Doc saved Wyatt Earp's life by shotgunning a "backshooter" who had his eyes focused on Earp. Earp, who had a feel for psychology, recognized Holliday's emotional problems and almost from the start, they became fast friends. Wyatt gave

Doc Holliday

93365

This photo of the O.K. Corral was taken years after the famous fight between the Earp brothers, Holliday and Sheriff Behan, the Clantons and the McLowery faction. The famed meeting lasted less than 30 minutes in which some 30 shots were fired. (Bettmann Archives)

side. Although Holliday was cleared of the crime, it was evident that this had brought the feelings of both groups to a boil. James Earp reported in his memoirs that Doc was never a "sloppy drunk," but did drink four quarts of whiskey during a 24-hour period, usually starting with a pint before breakfast. He gave Doc's ways as the main reason he and his brother, Warren, left

sults were: Dead; Billy Clanton shot by Morgan Earp, and Frank McLowery dropped by Wyatt. Ike Clanton fled the scene on foot. Wounded; Morgan Earp and Doc Holliday.

The Earps and Doc were charged with murder, but were acquitted after a 2-month trial. It is interesting to review the diametrically opposed reviews in the town's two leading newspapers of that time;

modus operandi, when he put two shots from the double derringer into a player from under the table, who questioned his honesty with the deal. Doc arrived in Glenwood, Colorado on the Carson Stage in May 1887. Doc was now well into the advanced stages of tuberculosis and seemed almost too weak for violence. He took up residency in the newly-furnished Hotel Glenwood, on the corner of 8th and Grand Street, where Bullock's store now stands. (The Hotel Glenwood was destroyed by fire in 1945.) Doc mellowed some and was even friendly in his work at the faro table of Bill Well's "Springs Saloon." His last 57 days in the Glenwood Hotel were not pleasant, as he was bedfast. On the eve of November 8, 1887, Doc probably was disturbed by the frivolity downstairs of the celebration of the completion of the Denver and Rio Grande Railroad through the narrow canyon, an almost impossible task from Glenwood to Denver. Doc had been in a coma, but the noise level awakened him. Doc asked for a drink of whiskey, which he quickly downed. He looked at his bare feet and said, "I'll be

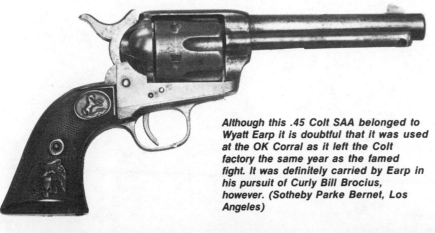

Although this .45 Colt SAA belonged to Wyatt Earp it is doubtful that it was used at the OK Corral as it left the Colt factory the same year as the famed fight. It was definitely carried by Earp in his pursuit of Curly Bill Brocius, however. (Sotheby Parke Bernet, Los Angeles)

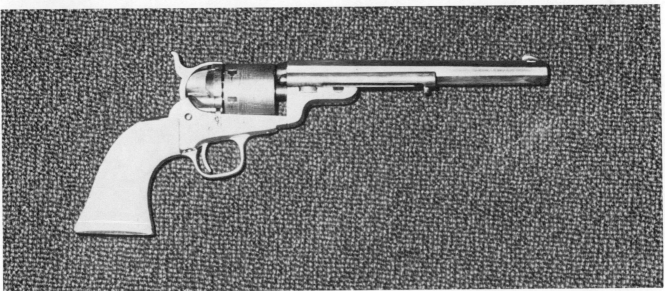

Tombstone before the accounted and fablized "Battle of the O.K. Corral," October 26, 1881.

In a summary, the gun battle was between two groups; one being Sheriff Behan, Ike and Billy Clanton, Tom and Frank McLowery. On the other, the Earps; Wyatt, Virgil, Morgan and Doc. Most detailed accounts will conclude the fight was provoked by the Earps and Doc. Doc, being a man of little conversation and impatience, fired a blast from his cropped-off 10-gauge into Tom McLowery, who was in the corral preparing to mount and leave town. In less than 30 minutes, some 30 shots were exchanged. The re-

Doc's early Colt Navy factory conversion was one of the first cartridge Colts and was never a percussion arm. It was manufactured as a .38 CF using Model 1851 parts. This specimen exhibits fine one-piece ivory grips and most of its original nickel finish indicating that it enjoyed excellent care.

"THE NUGGET" and "THE EPITAPH", of the trial. Shortly after Morgan died, as a result of being back-shot while playing pool in Wyatt's and Doc's famed "Oriental Saloon," Wyatt and Doc parted company. Doc went from Tombstone to Deadwood, then back to Denver, and from Denver to Leadville, Colorado. In Leadville, he followed the same

damned," and dropped his head in death. Doc had always said he would die with his boots on. Thus, Doc died after putting some ten accountable and five unverified persons in "Boothill." His Colt 38 Navy conversion, a Remington Double Derringer, a cropped 10-gauge shotgun and two Colt Single Action revolvers, almost all that composed his estate, was used as payment for his over-due hotel bill and burial expenses. Strangely enough, the folks of Glenwood had become fond of the mellowed Doc Holliday and his memories, and later donated the headstone that marks his resting place in Glenwood, Colorado.

Six Gun Trickery

Speed Wasn't the Only Skill Used By Gunfighters of the Old West.

By Jim Dunham

There is something about the American West that has always captured the imagination of both young and old. Jesse James is the American Robin Hood, and "Bat" Masterson is the Old West's knight in armor.

Even during the years of the Western movement, the characters themselves were caught up in the belief that there was a glamor and excitement to the Western adventure that was unique. The drovers that came up the Texas trails to the rail heads in Kansas were sensitive to what the writers of "dime novels" were saying about them. If Ned Buntline said that the cowboy was wearing a red bandana and Mexican spurs, many a young puncher would swap half a months wages for a piece of cloth and a pair of silver dollar sized rowels.

Without a doubt the cowboy was influenced by contemporary literature as well as his own peers when it came to choosing a defense pistol. The Colt revolver was not the only gun made in America after the Civil War, yet some books and almost all Western movies would have us believe that the "Wild West" was tamed by the .45 caliber Peacemaker alone.

Colt's contract to supply the frontier army with single action revolvers in 1873 played no small part in bringing the qualities of the six-shooter to the civilian population. Ultimately, this meant a greater familiarity with the Colt "Peacemaker," and a greater availability of parts over other guns manufactured at the same time. Also, there was a particular feel about Colt's new revolver that can only be described by one word—balance. The 1873 "Peacemaker" had the best of what was called the "plow handle" type grips.

century that there were three things that made the gunfighters of the Old West dangerous. The least important of the three things was speed with a gun. Second in importance was accuracy with a gun. And what he considered to be the most important was what he called "deliberation" or the ability to remain calm and make decisions under stress. You obviously don't get much more stress then when someone is shooting at you.

In order to put a gun into action more rapidly, the cowboy and gunman made changes in the common military flap holster. The open

Wearing the revolver in the military fashion of butt forward was common throughout the frontier. Left: To draw, the hand is turned palm-out, the gun is grasped and withdrawn; Middle: The piece is then cocked while turning to the target; Right: It is then leveled and ready to fire.

Four shots fired and one saved for emergency was a technique that was sometimes used for rapid-fire shooting from a Colt Single Action Army revolver. This was accomplished by "fanning" the hammer with the palm of the hand, as demonstrated by six-gun aficionado Jim Dunham before the quick eye of the camera. (Above) The gunfighter of the Old West tested his speed by dropping an object from the back of his hand, drawing, cocking and firing his revolver before that object hit the ground. Dunham's Colt .45 has "cleared leather" and fired while the falling cylinder is still inches from the ground.

Photos by Larry Griffin and Pat Brollier.

When it comes to gun dexterity, it would be foolish of us to assume that spinning and twirling tricks would be employed in a life and death shooting situation. However, it is very important that a gunman know his firearm when it comes to a fight. Surely the cowboy and gunman alike spent time becoming accustomed to his revolver. Fast draw did not mean the same thing to Masterson and Earp as it does to "fast draw" sportsmen today. Wyatt Earp once said that the most important thing to do in a gunfight, is to take your time—in a hurry. "Bat" Masterson wrote in *Human Life* magazine around the turn of the

top holster was popular in the west, but it never looked like the steel lined fast draw holsters used today in competitions and by the film industry. The old time holster had to be worn sitting, standing, and on horseback, and it had to protect the gun from dust and inclement weather. The tie-down used on modern rigs would have been a real problem in a fight, therefore the old timer's gun sat snugly in it's holster until it was needed.

In addition to holsters worn high on the hips, some gunmen such as John Wesley Hardin used a shoulder holster of some sort. Hardin is credited with inventing a vest

Six-Gun Trickery

with leather pockets allowing for two guns to ride under the arms with the butts forward making them excessible for the cross draw. Hardin may not have been the fastest gun in the west, but he was definitely a dangerous man who would kill without compunction.

There are several stories that link Wes Hardin with fancy gun handling. One such story says that after his arrest, Hardin's captors were curious to know just how good he was with a gun. Wes was handed a couple of handguns that had been carefully checked to make sure they were unloaded; whereupon he proceeded to amaze his audience by a series of spins, twirls, flips, and fast draws.

In his autobiography, *The Life of John Wesley Hardin,* Wes tells another story that is a bit too much to swallow. He claims that while in Abline, Kansas, during the summer of 1871; he sucessfully backed down Marshal Wild Bill Hickok by pulling the road agent spin. This is how Hardin says it.

"He [Wild Bill] pulled his pistol and said, 'Take, these pistols off.

I arrest you.

I said, 'all right' and pulled them out of the scabbard, but while he was reaching for them, I reversed them and whirled them over on him with the muzzles in his face, springing back at the same time! I told him to put his pistols up, which he did."

Hardin makes no mention how it was possible for Wild Bill to reach for Wes's pistols while holding his own. Even more important is the fact that there is no record of this

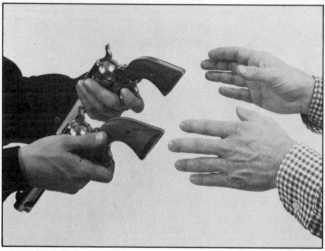 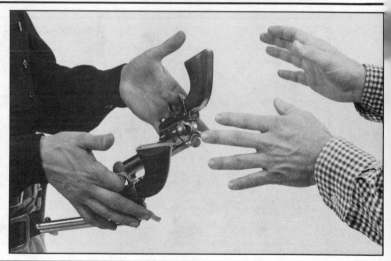

event taking place outside of Hardin's own book which was published after Hickok was safely in his grave.

The trick known as the "Road Agent Spin," was used, however, on October 27, 1880, by an Arizona gunman William B. Graham better known as Curly Bill Brocius.

Fred White, who had been town marshal of Tombstone for about ten months found Curly Bill drunk and disorderly in the streets of Tombstone, and with the assistance of Virgil Earp placed Brocius under arrest and ordered him to

←

The cross draw was quite popular in the Old West and was executed by: Left Reaching across the body; Middle: Drawing the gun and Right: cocking and leveling it on target.

On October 22, 1880, "Curly Bill" Brocius was told by Marshal Fred White to turn over his guns. Left to right: Brocius handed them both to the marshal butt first. As the lawman reached for the Colts, "Curly Bill" spun them around and cocked back the hammers. The marshal foolishly grabbed the two revolvers by the barrels and attempted to pull them from Brocius' hands. The guns went off, fatally wounding the marshal.

hand over his pistols. It is believed that Brocius was carrying two Colt single action .45s, probably with either 4¾ or 5½-inch barrels.

Curly Bill was not being arrested for a dangerous crime, and the marshal, who knew Brocius, had no reason to expect resistance to his demands. Perhaps because he was not completely sober, Curly Bill reversed the guns at the moment that Marshal White reached out to take them. Marshal White grabbed hold of the barrels of the guns as they were pointed at him fully cocked. Then either deputy Earp grabbed Curly Bill from behind or perhaps Fred White pulled on the guns. The result, however, was two serious wounds in the marshal's abdomen. Marshal White died from his wounds, but claimed from his death bed that the shooting was an accident and that Curly Bill had not intended to shoot him.

Today it would be a very serious crime to kill an officer of the law while resisting arrest. But, the nature of the times allowed Curly Bill to go free. Curly Bill Brocius would die a violent death, however, for if we can believe Wyatt Earp's biographer, Stuart Lake, Wyatt would soon kill Curly Bill in a

shootout with shotguns at Iron Springs, Arizona.

Even more famous than the Road Agent or "Curly Bill" Spin was a gun trick known as the border shift, and there were several historical gun fights where it was used. The border shift was a trick where a handgun was moved from one hand to the other. The need to do this could be either the inability to shoot effectively with the gun hand or the need to change rapidly from an empty gun in the shooting hand to a second loaded gun.

Some writers of Western history think that Billy Clanton shifted his gun during the so called O.K. Corral gunfight. If this is true, then the reason was due to the fact that he had been wounded by fire from the Earp faction and he could not continue to fire with his right hand.

The border shift was attempted in 1887 by long-haired Jim Courtright in Fort Worth, Texas. Courtright was involved with a protection racket and had been pressuring gunman/gambler Luke Short. On the evening of Feb. 8, 1887, Courtright sent notice to Short at his White Elephant Saloon that he wanted to see him in the street. Luke Short stepped out into the street and in-

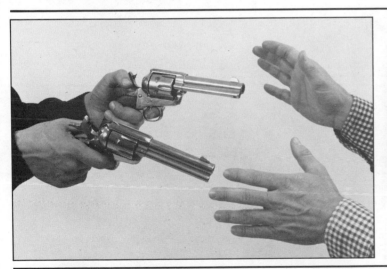

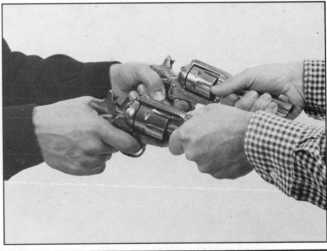

Author Dunham demonstrates the "border shift," a tactic that was actually used to change shooting hands or shift an unloaded gun from the firing hand with a minimum loss of time. Left to right: The pistol in the right hand has theoretically fired its last shot. By lowering the gun in the right hand, then flipping it into the left hand, at the same time passing the revolver in the left hand to the right and cocking it, a gunman could continue a fight with very little time lost.

Six-Gun Trickery

The "Curly Bill" or "Road Agent" spin is accomplished; Left to right: By holding the revolver by the frame, butt forward and hooking the trigger finger into the trigger guard, let the gun fall, using the trigger finger as a pivot; a quick forward flip of the wrist will throw the pistol in motion causing it to spin, butt upward and into the hand in a normal grasping position. When the piece is caught in the proper position the thumb will be at the rear of the frame just in front of the hammer; by pulling the thumb rearward the gun is then cocked and ready to fire.

formed Courtright that he was not heeled, but when Short began to open his coat to prove his point Courtright pulled his gun. Short had not been telling the truth about being unarmed and quickly brought his gun into action.

One of Short's shots tore off the thumb on Courtright's gun hand as he was trying to cock his revolver. Courtright vainly executed the border shift in order to fire with his left hand, but he was too late. Luke Short was of the gunman class and used the extra time to steady his gun and place an accurate and deadly shot.

If it is possible to make any conclusions concerning the use of tricks by the Old West gunman, it would be to say that anything that helped in producing better firepower without the loss of accuracy

might be used. Fanning was a way of getting off many shots in a short time, but except for modern shooting expert Ed McGivern, no one has been successful in demonstrating much accuracy when it comes to placing five or six large caliber slugs in a small target. Witnesses to a Dodge City gunfight on April 5, 1879 were amazed that the victor of the fight, "Cock-eyed" Frank Loving, with his .44 Remington was able to out-shoot and kill Levi Richardson. Richardson had a reputation as a dangerous fighter. The reason given for this gunfight upset is that Levi in anger had chased after Loving, fanning his gun. Richardson's gun contained five empty shells and not one of his shots hit his enemy.

Sometimes deception would be used by a gunman. If you could get the drop on your opponent by using

your hat or coat for cover, it might be done.

In spite of our image of wide open Western towns free from rules and regulations, many of the frontier towns had laws against carrying firearms within the city limits and especially inside business establishments. This led to a high use of concealed pistols and hidden holsters. Also many of our most famous western personalities were city folk and dressed in the best fashions of the day.

James Butler Hickok more often then not dressed in high style and wore his Navy Colts butts forward in a scarlet colored sash. He could therefore pull either gun with either hand.

Wyatt Earp who enjoyed being well dressed, went into the O.K. Corral gunfight wearing a brand new overcoat that had been fitted with a custom made canvas-lined, wax rubbed pocket designed for a fast draw.

Some of the famous frontiersmen would sit and spin tall tales on lazy Sunday afternoons. Exhibition shooting would often be a way to liven up the afternoon, and for some, a display of revolver skills might help to avoid a challenge later in the evening. Most of this shooting was the conventional type of shooting at a mark, but one fast draw trick is alleged to have been practiced. The trick was to hold an object, like a poker chip or a silver dollar on the back of the gun hand, and then dropping the hand out from under the object pull your gun and fire before the object hits the ground.

The drop trick is popular among fast draw gun handlers today, and using a modern steel lined holster that is tied to the leg, the trick can be done so fast that the object falls merely a few inches. Trying to get that kind of speed from the old time holsters is another thing, and just being able to equal the speed of the old timers is pretty satisfying.

Many an oldtime cowhand must have twirled his gun into his holster and a few must have developed dexterity equal to gun handling artists today. The difference was, both then and now, only a few people who have skills with firearms are able to face a life and death gunfight free from the kind of fears and concerns that tend to slow one down when it comes to pulling a trigger.

The gunmen of the American West will therefore always be surrounded with a special kind of magic and romance that can be really understood only by those who know that special pleasure of shooting guns. ♔

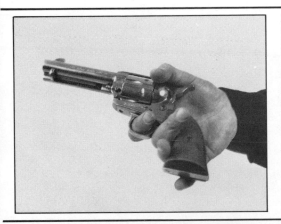

The hat trick was employed to relax or catch an opponent off guard. When the hat is tipped or taken off, it is brought down to cover the gun and holster while the gunman draws, cocks and levels his pistol. This ruse worked well with the broad-brimmed hats that were common on the Frontier.

Arizona Rangers

"The Fearless Twenty-Six."

By Burt Miller

Formed February 24, 1862, the Arizona Territory offered the only haven for those who escaped jail or death from the lawman's gun.

The few law enforcement officers were isolated in small towns. Cattle rustling and horse stealing went on on a wholesale basis. Stage holdups, burned ranch houses and murder were everyday occurrences.

Various groups of "rangers" and home militia were formed in the larger towns but proved ineffective due to lack of pay and any form of discipline and organization.

It was still ten years before

This photo of the Arizona Rangers was taken in 1903, just two years after the force was formed. The majority of the men are armed with Model 1895 Winchesters in .30-40 Krag. (Arizona Historical Society)

own law. Most were stockmen or cow punchers enured to the hardships and dangers inherent in the land and their way of life. Some were former peace officers and the fact that they were still alive was adequate qualification for the job.

Burton C. Mossman, a highly respected cattleman and then foreman of the 2 million-acre Hash Knife Ranch, was appointed as the first ranger captain responsible for the selection of the balance of the men that formed the company.

Operating under the military code of Arizona, each Ranger had to provide his own horse, firearms and other equipment. The privates recieved $55 a month; the sergeant, $75 and Capt. Mossman $120. One dollar a day subsistence and 50 cents for horse feed was drawn when in the field. Actually this was considered high pay for a dangerous job when a regular soldier drew $21 a month and "found."

These men were to establish a reputation not to be surpassed by even their counterparts in Texas. They made an immediate impact on the local outlaws but their major problems were the raids on cattle made from across the Mexican border. The sudden demise of foreign nationals, although caught armed and moving branded cattle other

statehood, in 1901, when Governor Oakes Murphy established the Arizona Rangers to bring the growing number of desperados under control. The organization was manned by 14 men; a captain, a sergeant and 12 privates.

Unlike previous efforts, these officers were selected by proven reputation established in a rough land where every man made his

Ex-rangers (l-r) William O. Parmer, Jack McRedmond, Clarence Beatty and Joseph H. Pearce, were photographed in Patagonia, Ariz. in 1952. Parmer carries his SAA Colt and Model '95 Winchester, while the others discuss the merits of the Winchester 10-ga. Model 1887 lever-action shotgun. Beatty claimed that the '87 could be shot from the hip like an automatic. (Arizona Historical Society)

134

than their own, still created a problem affecting diplomatic relations. Results of many of these encounters were never fully publicized but enough of the word got out to give the ranger force the nickname of the "Fearless Thirteen."

These men were highly skilled with firearms and many had learned their trade trailing Indians while in the Army. In a tough country they were simply the toughest and in spite of notorious reputations, few men would attempt to try a stand against them.

As all individuals of the time who depended upon their arms and their horse to keep alive, they had only the very best. The newest and most powerful rifles rode in their saddle scabbards; almost always they were Model '95 Winchesters, made famous by Teddy Roosevelt.

Gunplay was the rule in settling arguments or making an arrest. Typically, many aspiring bad men hoped to establish a reputation, but only shortened their lives as they faced the Rangers' favorite arm, the .45 Single Action Army Colt.

Augustine Chacon, whose group of murderous outlaws raided on

Rangers and had captured 74 criminals, having to kill only one in the process.

He continued his career in law enforcement and the cattle business. Highly respected for his major contribution to the history of Arizona he died at the age of 84.

Like most of his men, his favorite arm was a .45 caliber Colt Single Action Army revolver. His gun sported pearl grips and was fully engraved, including the 5½-inch barrel.

It was only when the force was

increased in 1903, that 25 badges were made. By now the small group had no doubt long since established their true identities throughout the territory. When a ranger left the force he was required to turn in his

This .45 Colt Peacemaker was used as a hideout gun by Ranger "Chape" Beatty. The shortened (2") barrel permitted the gun to be worn in the belt with the shirt pulled out enough to hide the butt, and allowed it to be easily drawn either sitting or standing. (Colt Industries)

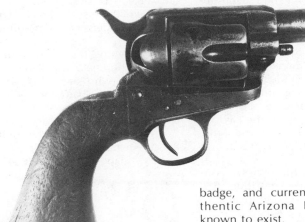

badge, and currently only one authentic Arizona Ranger badge is known to exist.

Rynning made his headquarters in the mining town of Douglas. Close to Mexico, it was the most lawless town in Arizona and a meeting place for outlaws from both sides of the border. Rynning had been a cowboy in his younger days, riding in the cattle drives to Dodge City from Texas. When he was 19 he joined the Cavalry and fought the Apaches. He made sergeant in the regular army and had served as a

John McRedmond was the last man to enlist in the Arizona Rangers. As with many other rangers, his favorite gun was the issue Model '95 Winchester. He served most of his time with the El Paso & Southwestern R.R. and the Southern Pacific R.R. during a private war between the two. (Arizona Historical Society)

both sides of the border, became the Rangers' priority target. Captain Mossman crossed the border 30 miles below Naco, Arizona to Carizzo Springs, captured Chacon, returned him to Arizona territory at Benson and turned the outlaw over to Sheriff Parks of Graham County. A few months later Chacon ended his career at the end of a rope.

A new governor was appointed by Roosevelt, due to allegations made by Senator Eugene Ives against Murphy of malfeasance in office. Mossman, expecting to be replaced, resigned and turned over command to Thomas Rynning in September 1902.

Mossman, in the meantime, had been appointed a deputy U.S. marshal. He had served a year with the

Arizona Rangers

lieutenant with the Rough Riders in 1898.

He and his 25 rangers made a lasting reputation when called upon to assist the local peace officers in the town of Monument against a mob of 3000 strikers. They were able to control the tense situation, each Ranger facing 100 strikers until relieved by the militia and Army.

The Ranger force had been increased by the governor to 26 men, which added three sergeants and eight privates to the company. Subsistence was dropped but the monthly pay was increased to $175 for the captain; $130 for the lieutenants; $110 for the sergeants and $100 for the rank of private. This was good pay—if you liked the work—and the odds! A private in the Army still only drew $21 per month.

The Rangers were to further demonstrate their efficiency by controlling another strike at Globe, Arizona, bringing a troubled peace to the district.

Typical of the times, a major feud between the cattlemen and homesteaders enflamed the region of the Mule mountains. Peace was established by the Rangers, and Capt. Rynning shortly was called to Mexico to break up a dispute between miners and mine owners.

Upon the request of Governor Kibbey, Rynning resigned in 1907 to take over as warden of the Territorial Prison at Yuma.

With his departure, an era ended for the Rangers. He had been Captain for five years and convictions totaled 5000 for the period.

Harry C. Wheeler followed Rynning as captain. He was the first to work his way up through all ranks after enlisting as a private in 1903.

Capt. Wheeler was to gain the reputation as one of the Ranger's finest shots. He was once able to enter international competition in Aldershot, England, where his marksmanship ability took high awards.

His past experiences provided an ideal ranger background. He had been a cowpuncher, had served in Cuba and had learned tracking from the Chiricahua Apaches while serving as a government scout.

The story is told that he was so fast with a rifle that he could throw five empty rifle cases in the air and hit all of them before they reached the ground with his .30-40 Krag. That is mighty fast bolt work!

His sidearm was the usual .45 Army Colt and he bragged that he had never fired first during any of his several shootouts.

It was under his command that peace and quiet finally came to the Arizona Territory.

He served as sheriff of Cochise County, Arizona from 1913 to 1917, and as a captain in the Aviation Service in World War I. He died in 1925.

The Arizona Rangers probably did more than any other group to build the image of the quick-draw specialist. The .45 single-action Army Colt was the choice of the professionals, both peace officer and outlaw alike. The shorter 5½-inch barrels were the usual choice. Longer barrelled models were not suited for their work!

Typical of the stories passed down, is the one about Ranger William Webb who drew his .45 and killed Lou Bass, bartender who was holding his gun on Webb at the time. Webb shot him twice.

The guns of the individual Rangers remain an intriguing part of history. Chape Beatty's Colt .45 was

Burton C. Mossman was the first captain of the Arizona Rangers, and was responsible for the selection of the balance of the company. Mossman turned command over to Thomas Rynning in September of 1902. (Colt Industries)

the usual single-action Army Colt with walnut one-piece grips but the barrel was cut off to 2 inches. Naturally it had no ejector and there was no need for a front sight for his "close up" gun.

One of the first to join the Rangers in 1902, Beatty made sergeant and retired after four years service. He was also quite partial to a sawed-off shotgun, a Winchester

10-gauge lever-action Model, 1887 for use in town or for breaking up an ambush.

One of the existing arms of the Rangers is the silver-plated, engraved, 5½-inch barreled .45 Colt Peacemaker that belonged to Jeff Kidder. His name is engraved on the back strap and the gun sports pearl grips. The Colt company records are complete on the gun, indicating it was ordered from the Aguirre Mercantile Store which had received the arm from Baker and Hamilton Co., of San Francisco, who in turn obtained the gun from Colt's Patent Fire Arms Manufacturing Co., of Hartford, Connecticut. The records show the gun was shipped on December 29, 1904.

Further information indicates that the Colt was sent to the factory for replating and repairs in late 1907 and returned on January 16, 1908.

The arm is now in the possession of Kidder's nephew, Dr. Burdette J. Goff of San Diego, California.

Kidder carried another .45 Colt single-action with a 4¾-inch barrel. This arm was a conventional undecorated "working" gun.

It is of interest that pearl grips were used extensively during this period when all features were a critical factor, quite possibly making the difference between life and death.

Today the fast-draw practitioner would frown upon use of the slippery mother-of-pearl. In spite of modern techniques in quick-draw, one is prone to believe the Rangers could have held their own with any of our modern quick-draw experts. One fact is certain—they played for keeps! Further, they had one attribute that made the difference, nerves as cold and unshakable as those of a rattlesnake. As relentless and implacable as the rattler, the Rangers had the same effect on the outlaw that dared to face him.

How else could this small group face down 3000 rioters? Or, as when Capt. Rynning, Webb and another Ranger named Foster walked up 10th Street in Douglas in the face of a gang threatening to get Webb after he had killed the saloon owner, Lou Bass. Armed with rifles and shotguns, the gang fled when the three Rangers turned and walked to face them. It is an understatement to say that these were an unusual breed of men.

As typical of the time with men that depended on their arms for survival, they owned the best that money could buy, tempered only perhaps by the long familiarity with a cherished arm that had proven adequate under all conditions.

During the short eight years the Rangers served the territory of Arizona, there was a wide variety of repeating arms available, including the .30-40 Krag that had superseded the .45-70 Trapdoor Springfield. The Springfield remained a favorite of farmers and ranchers of the day but was far outdated for the Ranger, who had to face the professional gunslinger who could be expected to have the best abailable arm around. He probably had a '95 Winchester in the same .30-40 caliber,

the '95 Winchester with the Ranger force.

Bear in mind that this was still the day of black powder, although the Model '94 Winchester was the first of the calibers to use smokeless powder. It took some time for these new arms and ammunition to spread through the west.

The 10-gauge had its own peculiar standing in the lever-action 1887 and 1901 models, although the 1887

The Remington 10-gauge Models 1882 and 1889 double barrels with their mule-ear hammers were popular—usually cut off to about 18 inches. The fact remained, the shotgun loaded with 00 Buckshot was deadly at close quarters and for breaking up an ambush, but a rifle was essential for shooting in the open spaces,

Sergeant Jeff Kidder had the reputation of being the fastest and most accurate with a side arm of all the Rangers.

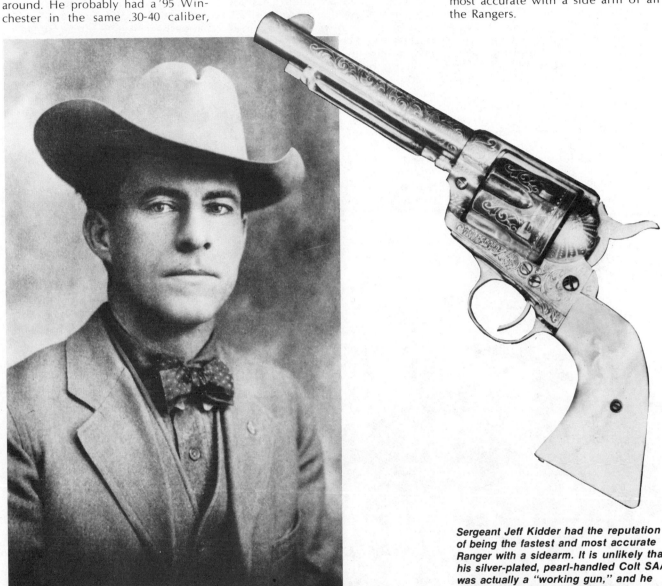

Harry Wheeler was the last captain of the Arizona Rangers. He took over from Rynning in 1907, and was later appointed sheriff of Cochise County. (Colt Industries)

Sergeant Jeff Kidder had the reputation of being the fastest and most accurate Ranger with a sidearm. It is unlikely that his silver-plated, pearl-handled Colt SAA was actually a "working gun," and he probably had plainer .45 Colts for everyday use. (Colt Industries)

or, a slower-handling Krag, but a few .44-40 slide-action Colt Lightenings were still in use by the rancher and bandit along with the Marlin 1894 and Winchester Models 1886 and 1892 in that same caliber. The group picture taken at the Morenci strike well proves the popularity of

was also made in 12-gauge. The lever actions quickly gave way to the 12-gauge slide-action Model '97 with its external hammer. The 12-gauge proved adequate with a load of 00 Buck and the 7¾ lbs., compared to the 9-pound Model '87, was a decided advantage for the man who lived in the saddle. The '87s had either 30 or 32-inch barrels. The Model '97 was available in a 26-inch version, takedown or solid frame. Many '87s were cut off for saddle use but lost the advantage of choke boring.

He had been rejected when he first tried to join the Rangers, due to the lack of a suitable background and experience. Anxious to gain entry to the force, he became a hard-riding cowboy who spent all his money for ammunition.

Capt. Rynning had heard of his dedication and enlisted him in April 1903. He was to serve for five years, making an outstanding reputation during the period.

He died of wounds on April 9, 1908, suffered during a shootout

Arizona Rangers

with a band of outlaws in Sonora, Mexico. Armed with only his .45 Colt, he killed four of his ambushers with the five rounds in the gun. Common practice was to load the single-action arms with five rounds, so the hammer could be let down on an empty chamber for safety; a practice that continued for a long time by the old timers, who weren't convinced the built-in safety features of the double-action arms were truly dependable. They *knew* the arm couldn't possibly go off if dropped, if no primer was under the firing pin!

An interesting sidelight on the history of the Arizona Rangers is an incident that occurred in more recent times. It pertains to the now well-known picture of the Arizona Rangers taken during the strike in Morenci in 1903.

A copy of the old photo was sent to the Winchester Arms Co., by a Texan, as each man appeared to be armed with a Winchester Rifle.

assuring themselves that these *were* Texas Rangers, the photo brought immediate response from many old timers, including writer Roscoe G. Wilson of Phoenix, Arizona, who recognized the photo as it really was. He knew some of the Rangers personally and had published an article on the picture in the *Arizona Republic* on September 2, 1962, appearing about the same time as Winchester's publicity effort did.

Wilson had provided a list of the personnel in the photo he used. Winchester's copy, due to poor quality, had been but off at each end, deleting five Rangers!

Only one of the group, C. L. Beatty, was living in 1962 when the story broke. He died in 1964. The only other living ranger was John M. Redmond, born on February 2, 1884 at Ballston Spa, New York, who came to Wilcox, Arizona with his grandmother in 1889. Here he learned the ranching business and later met Harry Wheeler who was to be the last of the Ranger captains.

Capt. Wheeler persuaded Redmond to join the Rangers on February 2, 1908. He served just over a

year and devoted much of his time to detective-type work. He later served as a guard at the Territorial prison at Florence (which had been moved from Yuma) and for two years was also the town marshal of Florence.

Redmond served in the Army during World War I. He had enlisted as a private and advanced in rank to captain. Active all his life, he was assistant secretary of state from 1921 to 1923 and was acting governor for part of that period. He retired at 70, having been supply officer at Davis, Mavana, Williams and Luke Air Force Bases in Arizona.

The coming of law and order through the efforts of this legendary force led to the demise of their own organization. With the danger gone, the voices of the politicians and the small-town peace officers, always resentful of the authority and reputation of the Rangers, were raised to discredit the force.

In spite of the efforts of Governor Kibbey to save the Ranger organization, the 25th Territorial Legislature, in February 1909, repealed the act that had created the Rang-

As no information was provided and the sending address unknown, the natural assumption was that the picture was of a group of *Texas* Rangers—some even being "identified" as such.

Publicized by Winchester, after

This group of Rangers exhibits the typical working garb of the force. Each man sports a wide cartridge belt for his .30-40 ammo. The third Ranger from the left is wearing a pair of issue cavalry gauntlets and his horse has a military bridle, indicating that he may have been in the Army at one time. (Colt Industries)

ers. The politicians could not, however, rob the Arizona Rangers of their contribution to the history of Arizona attained during a period of only eight years. A short-lived existence that brought peace to the last frontier of the 48 states.

THE WINCHESTER '95

The Saddle Lever Gun Goes Modern.

By Jim Woods

The first Winchester Model '95s were chambered for the .30-40 Krag (.30 Army) and later issues could be had in .38-72, .40-72, .303 British .35 Winchester, .405 Winchester .30 Government M/03 and .30 Government M/06 (.30-03, .30-06). This John Browning-designed gun was offered in carbine, rifle and musket versions in various styles, barrel lengths and other factory options. Our test gun, a 22-inch barrelled carbine, had to be one of the late ones since it was chambered for the .30-06. The '95, designed in 1895, first sold in 1896, was discontinued in 1938 at which time approximately 426,000 had been produced.

The first impression of the '95 is visual; it departs so greatly from the clean lines indicative of the Winchesters through Model 1894, that it appears ungainly. Primary reason for its awkward appearance is

The boxcar-coupling-like mechanism becomes disjointed in all directions as the action is levered open and closed. Like other lever actions, ejection is accomplished on the down stroke, and the bolt peels a round from the box magazine and into battery on the up stroke.

The Model 1895 was the first of the Winchester lever guns to abandon the tube magazine in favor of the box type that permits use of more modern, pointed nose ammo. This 22-inch barrelled carbine was a popular style but many variations were available.

The Winchester '95, using factory-loaded .30-06s produced a 4-shot, 3-inch group at 70 yards, firing offhand, and using open sights.

the built-in box magazine extending down from the stock just forward of the lever and trigger assembly. The action has enough elbows, linkages and extensions to satisfy the most ardent mechanical buff. The succession of solid clanks and clunks as the action is levered open and closed brings to mind the decoupling and coupling of a string of easy moving freight cars. The ungainly or awkward first impression is not a true one. The gun functions with beefy precision.

The carbine was fired at various long ranges—several hundred yards at times—just to kick up dirt or bust rocks. Our test facility is the Angeles Range in San Fernando, California.

I must report that the gun seemed eager to please its operator and always placed its rounds sufficiently close to intended targets to satisfy the shooter's ego. One paper target was recorded at 70 yards, offhand, that produced a 4-shot, 3-inch group. Most satisfying.

The Winchester organization can be proud of the Model '95, and if they only would bring it out again, I would be the proud owner of one—or more.

Belle Starr

Queen of the Bandits.

By Mary Elizabeth Good

Her black skirt was longer than a gossip's tongue. She was riding her favorite horse, a black mare she called Venus, as she headed back from San Bois toward her cabin at Younger's Bend on the South Canadian River, Cherokee Nation, Indian Territory. She rode easily and well, sidesaddle as was traditional among women of her day. Only this was a woman who had flagrantly flaunted tradition for most of 40 years.

In the afternoon, Milo Hoyt and another man at the ferry landing on the south side of the Canadian River heard the sound of gunfire. Moments later, the horse swam the river, the saddle empty. They followed the trail a short distance, until they saw a woman laying face down in the mud, a charge of buckshot in her back. When they rolled her over, they saw that her face and neck were generously peppered with turkey-shot.

Belle Starr, the most notorious female in the Indian Territory, was dead.

They buried her in what she called her "fancy clothes," with a Smith & Wesson Frontier .44-40 revolver in her hands,—a gun that Cole Younger had supposedly given her.

Myra Belle Shirley was born into the proper way of life on February 5, 1848. Her parents moved from

their Missouri farmstead into Carthage when she was eight. Along the busy trail from Independence to Fort Smith, John Shirley opened a livery stable, blacksmith shop and inn, which catered principally to folks traveling in caravans of white-topped wagons bound for Texas and points west, traders headed for Santa Fe and goldseekers hell-bent for California. Cattle drovers came north along this route and often stopped at the Shirleys.

Myra Belle was sent to the Female Academy to learn to spell and speak correctly, play the piano and to be a lady. She mastered Latin and

Belle Starr is dressed in her velvet gown, with an ivory handled Colt SAA revolver at her waist. She holds a Lightning Model Colt. Belle went to the Female Academy, where she studied Greek, Latin and algebra, as well as learning to be a lady. (Western Historical Collection, University of Oklahoma)

Greek and algebra easily, but fast-running horses and guns remained far more of a challenge than the schoolroom. She preferred a quirt in in her hand rather than a pencil, and gunfire to the sound of Mozart's melodies.

As slavery became an issue that

turned into a war, Missouri was divided. John Shirley was an enthusiastic Southerner. Guerrilla bands on both sides flourished in the border states; one was headed by Myra Belle's brother, Ed. Belle took to the guerrilla idea with a relish, playing spy and providing her brother's men with information on federal activities. This was the best excitement to come along yet and she idolized Quantrill's raiders, especially Cole Younger and Frank and Jesse James. To her, they were "heroes of a lost cause."

But when Ed was killed and Carthage razed by federal troops in the stifling summer when she was 15, Myra Belle turned serious and furious. Armed, with two percussion

removed and there seemed to be no other course for John Shirley than to take his family and move away.

They packed what was left of their belongings and started towards Fort Smith to intersect with the trail southwest that had been made famous by the Butterfield Overland Mail, until the war brought company activities to a halt. At North Fork Town, they turned south on the Texas Road, went on to Boggy Depot, and crossed Red River at Colbert's Ferry, continuing until they reached a rich farming area east of Dallas. John Shirley settled between Mesquite and Scyene; his neighbors' sympathies were as southern as his own. He returned to the plow and began raising horses.

Pearl Younger, then left the child in her parents' care and went off to join the lusty "saloon life of Dallas." Dressing in fancy clothes, she sang at the dance halls, dealt monte, poker, and faro at the gambling houses, finally gambling herself on a young horse thief named Jim Reed.

Her parents were horrified. In spite of her father's "violent opposition," Reed married Myra Belle. They took little Pearl and moved back to Missouri, to his home at Rich Hill.

Led by Texas outlaw John Fischer, the large outfit Reed had joined made a practice of cutting horses out of Texas herds and driving them north to sell. Belle eagerly approved and aided and abetted her husband's occupation.

revolvers strapped around her waist, she joined the guerrilla gang in earnest. The game became deadly pursuit of the men in blue she despised. She was clever and whatever tricks it took to gain information, she used them. She was successful. The guerrillas put to good use that information and it is speculated that Myra Belle took toll of the Union soldiers who died as a result.

Months passed, things grew worse and January of 1864 sent its moaning winds to wail the requiem of the past and prophesy the future. That year, guerrillas burned the courthouse in Carthage, the business section, and most of the houses, including the home of the Shirley's. This left a blackened and desolate town with fire-scarred chimneys pointing with skeleton fingers to heaven for vengance.

By then vengance seemed far

Belle Starr's home at Younger's Bend, I.T., as it appeared in 1888. The house was virtually inaccessible, except for one narrow canyon road, which made it a good hideout. (Oklahoma Historical Society)

Shirley put Myra Belle back into school, hoping, still almost afraid to believe, that her wild ways would be put aside. But for Myra Belle, things were very dull—until 1866.

Cole Younger, his brothers, and a couple of his other guerilla compatriots rode into the Shirley place after one of their post-war escapades, needing to keep out of sight for awhile. Myra Belle fell in love with Cole, and became pregnant with the outlaw's child. After he left Texas a few months later, she never saw him again.

Myra Belle's situation was the scandal of the countryside. When her baby was born, Belle named her

A case of mistaken identity resulted in the killing of Jim's brother by the Shannons, members of a competitive gang. Jim, in turn, strapped on his two Colt six-shooters, went after and shot the two outlaws, then found there were two warrants out for his arrest for murder. Reed went to California, then sent for Belle and the baby. While they were there, Belle gave birth to her second child, and she and Jim named him Ed, for the brother she had idolized.

Los Angeles did not remain a haven for long. Officials learned there was a reward offered for Reed. Then the robbery of a stage coach near San Diego made it imperative that he leave the area. Reed went into hiding on old Tom Starr's land in the Cherokee Nation near the Creek boundary. The Starr clan, and they were numerous—Tom had eight

Belle Starr

sons and two daughters, and lots of inlaws—were settled between Briartown and Eufaula along the sprawling, sluggish South Canadian River. Tom Starr had once led an epidemic of political murder and outrage in the Cherokee Nation for a period of almost eight years. In 1846, after 33 murders were recorded in ten months, the bulk of them attributed directly to the Starrs, the Cherokee Council, unable to capture Tom or kill him, made a treaty with Tom, granting him amnesty and giving him a $100,000 of tribal funds in return for his good behavior.

Belle was there in November of 1873, and learning that her husband and Daniel Evans were planning a robbery, rounded up some men's clothing to wear and joined them. They rode into the Creek Nation west of Eufaula and tortured Watt Grayson and his wife until Grayson told them where he had hidden better than $30,000 in gold coins.

The following spring, Jim came to Texas to visit Belle and could not resist joining a couple of his old Missouri cronies in holding up the Austin-San Antonio stage. Dallas and Austin newspapers told their readers how the robbers relieved the passengers of $2500 and four gold watches, then left their tired horses and "took the spirited animals belonging to the S.T. Scott & Co. stages." The Missouri pair were arrested later in April. It took lawmen until August to track down Jim Reed. On the 6th, a deputy's bullet felled him for good at a cabin near Paris, Texas. The reward money was never paid however, as Belle, spiteful, dry-eyed and emotionless when she viewed the body, denied it was her husband and refused to claim it.

Belle then sized things up, and took up where her husband left off. She packed up her children and delivered them to other relatives, then went to join Reed's gang in the Indian Territory where there were no "white man's courts." The Five Civilized Tribes had courts of their own, but tribal law did not apply to white offenders. This created an ideal haven for outlaws, and they took full advantage of it, not only as a refuge but a place to further blatantly practice their wanton professions.

The Federal Court of Western Arkansas had been responsible for law and order in the Territory, but its efforts were a farce, an incompentency that had degenerated into corruptness and scandal. It was not until 1875, when Judge Isaac C. Parker volunteered for the job at Fort

Smith and deputized 200 U.S. marshals to patrol the nearly 74,000 square miles to the west, that renegade bands from the States felt in much danger of the law. So thorough were the deputies—bounty was their only pay—and so iron-willed was Parker, that the threat of the gallows now cast a shadow across the criminals' paradise.

Belle rode in with a Model 73 Winchester across the saddle and a Smith & Wesson .44 American strapped to her waist. "Faster than seven devils can skin a catfish," Belle took control of the band she'd

Belle Starr, with a .44 S&W American at her waist and a quirt in hand, rides side-saddle on her horse Venus. (Oklahoma Historical Society)

joined. Using her caustic tongue, "superior intelligence, and sex appeal" to dominate her cohorts, she became the mastermind of their lawless escapades. For better than five rampaging years, they stole horses, peddled corn whiskey to the Indians, looted stores and robbed tribal payrolls and travelers. Belle was smart enough not to join them in these forays, for if she had, it would have been far easier to trace the crimes to her gang. But she made contact with "fences" who got rid of their contraband, joined them in whooping it up and carousing, and made love to those of her choice. Imaginative writers over the years have put Belle in more beds than George Washington ever slept in.

Still, somehow there was a way about her and the money she spent freely that promptly bought the freedom of her men, should they be captured by deputies. And her illiterate renegades found it somewhat wonderous that she could read war-

rants and wanted posters to them, and she actually understood what was involved in "arranging *nolle prosequi* paroles, releases, pardons, and suspended or light sentences."

But Belle Reed decided she'd like a change. And in Cherokee Volume 1-B, page 297, Record of Marriages and Licenses, is found the notice that she had accomplished it: *Starr & Reed On the 5th day of June, 1880, by Abe Woodall, District Judge for the Canadian District, C.N., Samuel Starr, a citizen of the Cherokee Nation, age 23 years and Mrs. Belle Reed, a citizen of the*

United States, age 27 years. H.J. Vann, Clerk.

Only Belle actually was 32.

Belle's marriage to Sam Starr, one of the sons of old Tom Starr, gave her the name by which she is known in history.

They went home to Sam's 62-acre tribal claim in the southwest corner of the Cherokee country. Sheltered by Hi-Early Mountain, Sam's cabin was almost inaccessible. The Canadian River, treacherous with deceiving quicksands and unpredictable channel, wound to the south and west, widening in a curve that Belle named Younger's Bend in memory of her first love. There was only one trail in, taking the course of a narrow canyon for three miles. Bluffs on both sides of the river valley made that land easy to guard from intruders. A spring-fed creek just east of the house, Belle named for herself. Belle and Sam Starr's place became a new hideout for fugitives. Hi-Early Mountain was pocked with cave-shelters, ideal for outlaw encampments.

Judge Parker's deputies got wind of this; still the inaccessibility of the terrain made it hard for any of them to drop in unexpectedly. It wasn't long until Younger's Bend became known by the exaggerated title as "headquarters for all the bad men operating in Indian Territory," and Belle's good intentions diminished rapidly.

She and Sam made their new

Newspaper reporters seized upon the opportunity to make Belle a national sensation. "Queen of the Bandits" they called her . . . "The Petticoat Terror of the Plains" the headlines announced . . . "Wild Woman of the Wild West . . . "The Lady Desperado."

And Belle did not disappoint her audience or the press. For the four days the trial lasted, she refused to take the stand. She frequently dashed off notes to her attorneys and "it was a subject of remark that they paid strict attention to the contents." At one point "when allusion

"Belle Starr and Sam Starr, larceny; sentenced one year each at Detroit."

In nine months, they were back at Younger's Bend, and at it again with another member added to the marauding gang.

John Middleton got around. In Arkansas warrants were out for his arrest for arson and larceny; in Texas he was wanted for murder. He'd called a sheriff to the door of his house and shot him in cold blood—his Colt .45 spurting deadly fire. A few night's before he came to Younger's Bend. He was a cousin of Jim Reed; and Belle, who was now

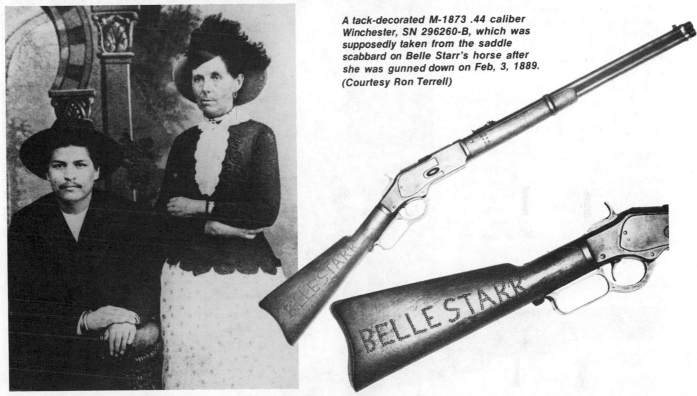

A tack-decorated M-1873 .44 caliber Winchester, SN 296260-B, which was supposedly taken from the saddle scabbard on Belle Starr's horse after she was gunned down on Feb. 3, 1889. (Courtesy Ron Terrell)

Belle Starr with her handcuffed lover, Blue Duck. She hired the best lawyers for him after he was sentenced to hang for murder by Judge Parker. His lawyers succeeded in getting his sentence commuted by Pres. Grover Cleveland. (Oklahoma Historical Society)

start by stealing horses again. And they successfully stole a lot of them. But in 1882, they were arrested at the home of an old negro couple early one morning near the Osage line, for stealing a neighbor's horses they intended to sell at McAlester. They had been practicing their skills too close to home. When captured, Belle, still in her night clothes, had a Colt .45 at her waist, and a .41 caliber over and under Remington derringer in her blouse.

Their trial came up before Judge Parker at Fort Smith on February 15, 1883. Parker's courtroom was jammed. This was the first time a woman had been tried in that federal court for being a horse thief.

was made to Jim Reed, her former husband and father of her child, tears welled up in her eyes and trickled down her cheeks, but they were quickly wiped away and the countenance assumed its wonted appearance."

The prosecuting attorney made a reference to Sam Starr's illiteracy. Belle turned furious. "If looks had been killing, the prosecutor would have dropped in his tracks." Belle listened with a "devil-may-care" expression to the volume of testimony against her. One observer noted, however, that "she lacked grace of carriage and looked much older than she was." No doubt, Belle did not overhear that comment.

When they appeared before Judge Parker on March 8 for sentencing, Sam was "sullen and defiant." Belle looked at the judge with a "bold and fearless glance." Judge Parker was lenient. On March 16, the *Fort Smith Elevator* reported:

bored with Sam, had an amorous eye for him.

Sam, at the moment, had his mind on other things. He and Felix Griffin had held up the Creek Nation treasury. Griffin had been captured by the Indian police, and now they were combing the area for Sam, who had gone into hiding elsewhere. Marshals, posses, and police were so thick in the canyon leading into Younger's Bend, Middleton decided he'd be safer in Arkansas. Belle made plans to go too. She and John rode together as far as Keota. So as not to attract suspicion, they separated there and took different trails towards Dardanelle. Belle waited at their meeting place for several days and growing angrier by the day, started home.

Middleton had gotten no farther than the mud banks of the ford at Poteau River in the Choctaw Nation. He was found with his face half blown away; Sam Starr "had trailed

Belle Starr

him silently." One Colt .45 was with his empty saddlebags, two were holstered in the cartridge belt found around the dead man's waist. Belle's attention turned to Blue Duck, who, on a drunken spree over in Flint District, had rode into a field and shot a young farmer named Wyrick. He'd even bragged about it before he was arrested by Deputy Marshal Frank Cochran. On April 30 he was sentenced by Judge Parker to hang on the gallows July 23. Belle hired the best lawyers in the country for her lover, and succeeded in getting the sentence commuted by President Grover Cleveland. But Blue Duck was still behind bars and Belle was lonely.

Occasionally, Sam would sneak back to Younger's Bend; one time to find the Cherokee police waiting for him. Sam escaped by jumping his horse off a 20-foot bluff and swimming the river.

On May 28, 1886, Belle was arrested again. This time it was claimed that Belle, dressed in men's clothes, led a party of outlaws to rob old N.H. Farrell and his three sons down in the Choctaw Nation. The woman had a six-shooter in each hand, Farrell said, and two of the other robbers carried Winchesters rifles.

Belle's .36 caliber percussion Manhattan pistol, SN 65104, now on display at the Sanders Museum, Berryville, Ark.

The *Dallas News*, June 7, 1886, with Fort Smith dateline of May 30, relayed:

"For the past week the noted Belle Starr has been quite an attraction on the streets of this city. She came to answer two indictments in the Federal Court and expected to have been tried in the present term. Court adjourned on Monday last, and her case went over until August next.

"Monday night Belle swung her Winchester to her saddle, buckled her revolver around her, and, mounting her horse, set out for her home on the Canadian. Before leaving, she purchased a fine pair of 45-caliber revolvers, latest pattern, with black rubber handles and short barrel, for which she paid $29. She showed them to your correspondent, with the remark: 'Next to a fine

horse, I admire a fine pistol. Don't you think these are beauties?'...

..."When at home her companions are her daughter, Pearl, whom she calls the "Canadian Lily," her horse and her two trusty revolvers which she calls her "babies." The horse she rides...is a beautiful animal, but looked rather the worse for hard riding when here last week.

Pearl Younger buried her mother out behind the cabins at Younger's Bend. Belle was laid out with a S&W Frontier .44-40 in her hands, which was given to her by Cole Younger. This gun was removed years later when the grave was robbed. (Oklahoma Historical Society)

Belle is a crack shot, and handles her pistols with as much dexterity as any frontiersman. No man enters Younger's Bend without giving a thorough account of himself before he gets out..."

The evidence against Belle this time was purely circumstantial, and at the hearing neither the old man or his sons could identify anyone involved. Belle was released, only to be arrested a few weeks later on a horse stealing charge. The jury said "not guilty," and Belle went home again.

Late in September Sam Starr was riding across a corn field, and was spotted by the Indian police. The call to surrender brought gunfire for

his answer. Bill Vann's shots from his heavy revolver wounded Sam and killed his horse. Taking the outlaw to a farmhouse, they had started to dress his injuries so they could make the long trek to Okmulgee, the Creek capital, when the Starr gang rode up, overpowered Sam's captors and took him with them. But the Indian police had come too close to quit now. The move was underway to organize a large posse "to wipe out Younger's Bend." Belle got wind of this and went to Tom's hiding place with an idea that appealed to him.

Sam did not relish the manner in which tribal courts dealt with offenders nor the type of punishment that would be meted out. To make matters worse, the chiefs had hated old Tom Starr for years, and his family with him. If Sam surrendered to the United States marshals, the Indian police couldn't touch him. Belle reasoned that Sam stood a far better chance on a robbery charge in federal court, and if he was convicted, at least there, there was an opportunity to appeal the sentance. Deputy Marshal Tyner Hughs and the citizens of Fort Smith were surprised on the morning of October 11, 1886, to see Sam Starr, unarmed, riding down the town streets, headed for the federal jail.

Continued on page 218

Model 1875 Remington Revolver

By Garry James

The single action revolver was one of the staples of the gunfighter. As can be seen in other articles in this book, the ubiquitous Colt Peacemaker figured into the majority of gunfights, shootouts, captures, etc., and was a favorite handgun of desperados and lawmen alike.

In 1875 another single action entered the scene, however. The Remington Army Model in .45 was submitted to the U.S. Army for testing along with the Colt, Smith & Wesson and the Forehand and Wadsworth revolvers. The Colt came out on top and was eventually adopted, although the Remington acquitted itself well.

The Model 1875 Remington followed the silhouette of the earlier Remington percussion New Model Army. It featured a loading gate and ejector rod similar to that of the Colt, but Remington decided to include a long under-barrel web, similar in looks to the loading lever of the older model. The web provided a housing for an extremely long cylinder pin, and acted as a holster guide of a sort. The angle of the grip was a bit different than that of the Colt, although in the hand the two guns feel quite a bit alike.

Because they were not as popular as the Colt when they were made, the Remingtons are scarcer

The Navy Arms replica M-1875 Remington proved to be an accurate and reliable pistol. Its balance is somewhat different than that of the Colt Single Action, but sighting characteristics are similar.

The Navy Arms M-1875 is offered in blued/casehardened and nickeled versions, as were the originals. The test gun was in .45, although .44-40 and .357 Magnum chamberings are also available.

today and command premium prices. They were originally offered in blued and nickeled versions, and ivory-gripped, engraved models are also fairly common.

Navy Arms of 689 Bergen Blvd., Ridgefield, NJ 07657, has recently brought out a replica of the Remington M-1875. It is chambered .45 Colt, .44-40, and the modern .357 Magnum. Blued and nickeled guns in each caliber are available. Rather than shoot a costly original, we de-

cided that a .45 version of the Navy Arms replica would give us a good feel for the Model '75 as quality was certainly on a par with the original. A notch cut into the full-length groove on the top strap (this feature was copied by Colt from the percussion Remingtons) acts as the rear sight. The front sight is a small blued blade.

Using both smokeless and black powder loads, we fired at a 20-yard target. Accuracy with both was about the same, 4-inch groups which patterned about 8 inches

above point of aim. The smokeless rounds were sharper in report and recoil than the black powder loads, and the black powder cartridges produced the heavy, sooty fouling inherent with that propellant.

General handling characteristics of the Remington are good, although the gun does not have the balance of the Colt. Functioning of the Navy Arms Co. replica and other original Model '75, we have handled is excellent. A wide trigger allows for a bit more controllability than with the SAA, though the lock time is somewhat slower.

All in all, one would have been very well armed with a Remington in the Old West. It was certainly as reliable as the Colt, and was as accurate. Looks are a matter of opinion, but personally I have always preferred the lines of the Remington. The Navy Arms replica reproduces them perfectly and is highly recommended for those enthusiasts who don't feel like shelling out $600-plus for an original they can't shoot. The replica version sells for about $175 in either blued or nickeled versions.

The Dalton-Doolin Gang

"Crime Does Not Pay"

By Ron Terrell

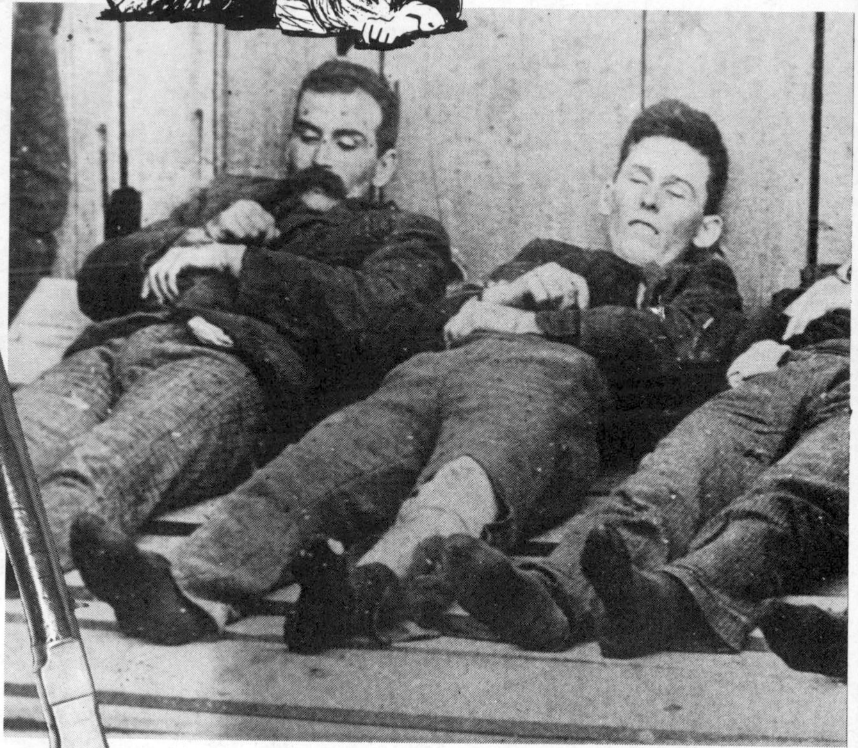

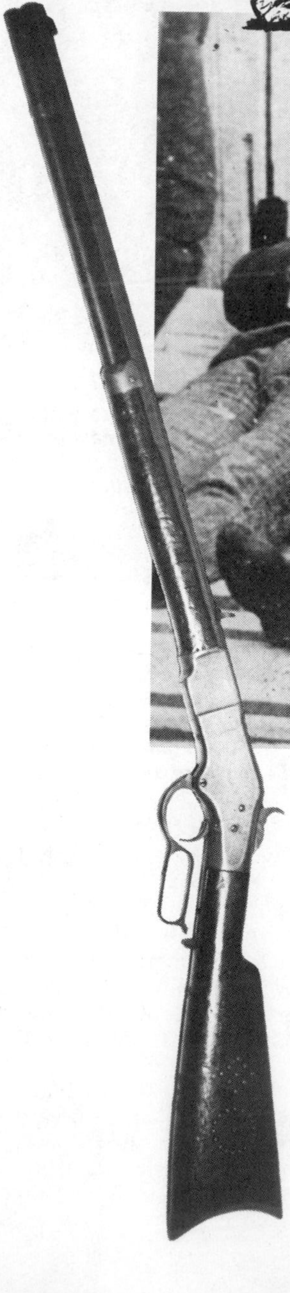

Emmett Dalton, sole survivor of the outlaw Dalton gang that attempted the daring double bank robbery of Coffeyville, Kansas, banks October 5, 1892, revisited the town in 1931. He and his wife Julia took a "second honeymoon" to visit the scene of his last criminal act. During a trip to the cemetery where his brothers (Frank in a place of honor after a highly respected career as Deputy U.S. Marshal and Grat and Bob, the outlaws) were buried, he commented: "I challenge the world to produce the history of an outlaw who ever got anything out of it but that", pointing to the grave of Grat and Bob, "or else to be huddled in a prison cell. And that goes for the modern bandit of the skyscraper frontier of our big cities, too. The biggest fool on earth is the one who thinks he can beat the law, that crime can be made to pay. It never paid and it never will and that was the one big lesson of the Coffeyville raid."

No one has ever been able to give a satisfactory answer to the questions asked when some members of a respected family turn to a life of crime. The Dalton family is an example of this perplexing question. Louis and Adeline Younger Dalton raised a family of 13 children—nine sons and four daughters. The older sons became respect-

Bill Doolin was carrying this M-1866 .44 Winchester the night he was killed by Deputy U.S. Marshal Heck Thomas. (Museum of the Great Plains)

ed farmers, two of the daughters married farmers and Frank became a Deputy U.S. Marshal. Grat, Bob and Bill were killed by lawmen and Emmett spent many years in prison.

For a brief period of time, it appeared that *all* the Daltons would be law abiding citizens. Most of the Dalton children grew up around Coffeyville where their father made an attempt at farming. His last real effort at settling down was in 1882 when he leased some land from an Indian living just across the Kansas border in Indian Territory. This Indian was partly responsible for Frank Dalton being commissioned a lawman out of Judge Isaac Parker's Fort Smith, Arkansas, court. When Frank was killed in 1887, Louis Dalton's disposition turned sour and he returned to Coffeyville where he worked at odd jobs after his wife divorced him. He died at the home of a friend in 1889.

The male Daltons had spread out over the West during the 1880s but, at their father's death, they moved back and settled their mother and themselves near Vinita, Oklahoma. Grat and Bob had followed Frank into law enforcement and were respected lawmen for a while. Bob had served as a deputy marshal out of the Wichita court for over a year. During that time, he often

Four of the outlaw Dalton gang that attempted the double bank robbery at Coffeyville, Kansas in August of 1892. All were killed in an exchange of gunfire with citizens who armed themselves at the local hardware store. (Oklahoma Historical Society)

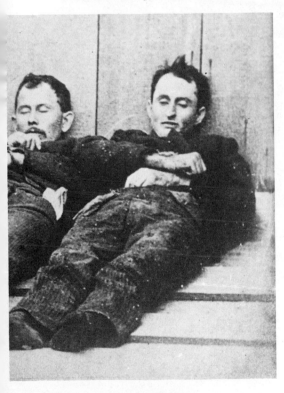

This Colt .45 Single Action saw considerable action in the hands of several owners. They included lawman Lafe Shadley, Bill Doolin, Bill Tilghman and Fred Sutton. The gun was carried by Tilghman the night he was killed. (Museum of the Great Plains)

rode as a posseman for Grat. Grat had been living in California when Frank was killed and returned to the Indian Territory "to fill Frank's boots." Heck Thomas, a noted deputy U.S. marshal had recommended Grat to U.S. Marshal John Carroll in Fort Smith and, partly on Thomas' recommendation, Grat was given a deputy's commission.

Frank Dalton was well liked by most people he met and this included Heck Thomas. The two lawmen rode on posses together after some of the wanted men hiding out in the Indian Territory. Thomas had been in the Dalton home on several occasions and it was this knowledge of the family that enabled Thomas to hasten the end of their outlaw careers. His efforts in avenging Frank's death brought him the gratitude and friendship of all the Daltons and this friendship led him to believe he could talk Grat, Bob and Emmett into giving themselves up without a fight if he could face them.

As a deputy marshal, Grat was probably more like Frank than either Bob or Emmett. According to Heck Thomas' memories of him, Grat was "a pugnacious fellow, but cautious. More like Frank than the others." He "wasn't much" on detecting criminals but he made up for his lack of brilliance by careful and consistent performance. He arrested a number of criminals during his early months as a lawman and his commission was renewed. He was unpredictable, though, and, late in 1889, he was fired. The incident that caused it also gives modern pistoleros an insight into his proficiency with a Colt .45. "Some men were standing in front of a store in Tulsa when Grat walked up. He had been drinking. He was talking to the men when he spied a negro boy walking down the other side of the street, eating an apple. 'Watch me scare hell outa him,' Dalton said. He called to the negro to halt, which the boy did, quickly. 'Put that apple on your head,' commanded Dalton, 'an' I'll show you some fancy shootin.'

The negro hesitated, trembling until his teeth chattered. 'Mistah Grat,' he stammered, 'I'se afraid yuh'll miss de apple an' hit me.' 'Then, by God, nigger, I'll kill you anyhow!' Grat called thickly. By now the boy was shaking so badly he hardly could hold the apple in place. There was a prayer on his lips as he awaited execution.

Dalton raised his pistol and fired. The bullet split the apple, knocking the halves in opposite directions. A William Tell trick, although Grat had never heard of the

original incident. When the report reached Fort Smith, Marshal Yoes dismissed him. As Grat himself put it, 'Old Jake gave me the ax.'"

The Daltons, as well as most of the others who later joined them in a life of crime, preferred Colt single action revolvers over all other pistols. Also, Bob was considered one of the best shots in the country with a Winchester. Even professional gunmen like Heck Thomas respected Bob's capabilities with a rifle. After a horse rustling trip aroused local farmers to form a posse, the Daltons were engaged in a gun battle. The posse leader was killed in the first exchange of slugs and the others quickly retreated. When Marshal Needles related the news of the Daltons' activities to Heck Thomas, he added: "The posseman was killed with bullets from a Winchester. He was hit by three bullets so close together the space could be covered with one hand. Nobody in the Territory can shoot like that except Bob Dalton."

According to the written record of the Coffeyville battle, Bob and Emmett did the shooting that caused the deaths of three of the four citizens. Two others were wounded and Grat killed Marshal Connelly at a distance of 20 feet by firing from the hip, while he was badly wounded himself.

The accounts of the Coffeyville raid are too well known to detail here. Briefly, however, a look at the twelve minutes during which the shooting took place might be of interest to modern gun enthusiasts. When the alarm went up, there wasn't an armed citizen in the vicinity of the banks. They quickly rallied to the hardware stores where stocks of arms and ammunition were broken out. This should say something to today's anti-gun supporter who feels private citizens should leave all defense against the outlaw to the local policeman.

Bob and Emmett had gone into the First National Bank while Grat, Bill Powers and Dick Broadwell went into the Condon and Company Bank. When the firing broke out and the gang members realized this would be no easy in and out robbery, Bob's accuracy with a Winchester took its toll. His first shot, from inside the bank, resulted in Charles Gump's having a double barrel shotgun smashed from his hands and a bullet torn hand. Apparently, however, a more serious wound was prevented by the bullet hitting the shotgun.

Bob and Emmett pushed the bank teller out the back door of the bank—just in time to meet young Lucius Baldwin. He apparently

The Dalton-Doolin Gang

thought they were citizens and either didn't hear or understand their command to stop. Bob shot him in the left chest, just missing the heart—from a distance of 50 feet. Baldwin died three hours later.

The next victim of Dalton bullets was George Cubine who was standing in a doorway across from the bank and armed with a Winchester. His back was to the Daltons and both Bob and Emmett raised their rifles and fired two fast shots each. Cubine fell with three bullets in his body: left thigh, ankle and heart. It is believed that one of Bob's bullets was the fatal shot.

Charles Brown, an old man who was close to Cubine, grabbed up the fallen Winchester, four more shots rang out and Brown fell two feet from Cubine's body—he also died after three agonizing hours. Both men were about 40 to 50 yards from the Daltons.

Thomas G. Ayres was the next citizen hit by a Dalton bullet. He too had grabbed a Winchester and faced the bank, expecting the Daltons to come out the front door. From a distance of 75 yards, Bob took deliberate aim and fired. The bullet entered below Ayres' left eye and exited near the base of his skull.

As soon as Grat and his two partners left the Condon and Company Bank, they were greeted with a hail of lead. Grat and Bill Powers were both hit hard but stayed on their feet. Powers was hit again as he tried to mount his horse and died almost instantly. Grat took refuge by a barn which hid him from view of the citizen's weapons. While he was resting there, City Marshal Connelly climbed through a board fence about 20 feet from him. He was facing away from Grat, looking towards where the horses were hitched in the alley. Grat shot him in the back, firing his Winchester .44-40 one-handed from the hip.

Broadwell had been wounded in the back but, during a lull in the firing, had climbed into the saddle and spurred his horse into a run. John Kloehr hit him with a bullet from his borrowed Winchester and Carey Seamen hit him with a load of shot. He was later found dead by the road a half-mile from town where he had fallen from his saddle.

Bob and Emmett were working their way to their horses during this time. So far, neither had been hit. Bob missed a snap shot at F.D. Ben-

The end of the outlaw trail for the two Dalton brothers. Bob (left) was shot in the chest and died shortly thereafter. Grat was shot through the chest but was killed by a bullet in the throat.
(Oklahoma Historical Society)

son as that man was climbing out a rear window to intercept the Daltons' return to their horses. Almost immediately afterward, Bob was hit by a bullet from someone in Isham's Hardware store. He staggered to a pile of stones and sat down, keeping his Winchester and firing several shots even though badly wounded. He missed a shot at John Kloehr, got to his feet and made it to the side of a barn—not far from where Grat had been resting a few minutes earlier. He exchanged shots with Kloehr but his aim was unsteady. He missed but Kloehr didn't. Bob fell with a bullet in his chest.

Meanwhile, Grat was making another try for his horse. When Kloehr shot Bob, Grat turned and tried to bring his rifle up but was unable to do so. Kloehr fired and Grat died

with a bullet through the throat, breaking his neck. He fell within a few feet of Marshal Connelly's body.

Emmett was the only Dalton on his feet, miraculously still untouched by lead from the defenders' firearms. He made it to his horse, still carrying the grain sack with the money. A half-dozen rifles were fired as he tried to mount and he was hit in the right arm, left hip and groin but still managed to get into his saddle.

Once mounted, Emmett stood a good chance of escaping but, instead of attempting it, he rode to where Bob lay and made an effort to get him up behind him. Bob weakly said "It's no use" just as Carey Seamen emptied both barrels of his shotgun into Emmett. He fell beside Bob, who died within a few moments.

The same coolness of mind and fast action that mobilized Coffeyville's citizens into "defenders" prevailed during the confusion surrounding the conclusion of the gun battle. The talk of lynching the wounded Emmett was quickly squelched and the bodies of the dead outlaws were taken to the jail where they were placed under guard while Emmett was taken to the doctor's office for treatment of his wounds.

Along with the bodies of the dead outlaws, the firearms they had used were collected and put under guard. Gun buffs are interested in types and calibers of firearms chosen by professional gunmen of all ages and, in this instance, we have accurate records. Each outlaw carried a Winchester and two revolvers. None of the pistols had been fired, though. Grat's .44-40 Winchester had been fired several times but was not empty (although he may have reloaded while resting by the barn) and the same was true of Emmett's rifle. Both Bob and Bill Powers had empty Winchesters.

There is a story that Bob had bought 10 new Colt .45 revolvers for this "last" raid and their older guns were left behind with other personal belongings and identification. A Colt .44-40, serial number 83073, with a 5½-inch barrel, belonging to Emmett, is now in the Los Angeles County Museum, having been given to Charles Martin by Emmett in 1935. This is one of the older guns left at·the family home. However, if the story of the new .45s being bought is true, some of the other occasional gang members not along on this raid had them—or else the outlaws changed their minds and relied on their old favorite sidearms. For, among the arms carried by the outlaws on that fateful day, there is a Colt .32-20 Single Action in the J.M. Davis Gun Collection at Claremore, Oklahoma, that had been taken from Dick Broadwell; a Colt .38-40 taken from Emmett by John Kloehr and now in a private collection but on display at the Museum of the Great Plains, Lawton, Oklahoma, and a .38 Smith and Wesson carried by Bob Dalton. It appears that each outlaw carried a Colt .45 Single Action as one of his pistols but at least three of them carried these other revolvers.

An interesting sidelight to these guns and their use by the outlaws can be seen by looking at Bob Dalton's proficiency with his Winchester. This rifle, an 1886 model chambered for the .38-56, serial number 40302, is in the same collection with Emmett's .38-40. It was bought at a sheriff's auction by W.S. Upham of Coffeyville and passed on to his son who sold it in 1931 to a private collector. Shortly after obtaining the rifle, the new owner received a letter about it from a man who had engaged in a target match with Bob—

the stakes being a horse. Quoting from the letter, we'll use the same spelling used by its author. For continuity, however, punctuation has been added.

"I seen an artical in the paper that you had obtained Bob dalton Winchester from g.W. upham of coffeyville, Kansas. I was present and remember what transpired befor and after the roberry. george upham father did by the gun at sheriffs sale. I remember the gun for it won a good saddle hors from me. I lived at salleysaw, indian teritory, 80 miles dew west of fort smith, Arkansas, and was buying and selling horses. Bob rode up to the barn and wanted to buy the best saddle horse I had. I priced the horse at 175 dollars. he stade all knight with me. at the sale barn in the morning I proposed a riffle shooting mach. the turms wer if he beat me shooting 3 out of 5 shots he got the horse free and if I beat him he pade doble price for the horse. he took me up on those turms. the distance to shoot was 200 yards and we wer to shoot of hand and boath of us wer to use his gun. in them days I wasn an extry good shot and to win in a shooting mach one had to get in senter. in the 5 shots none of the bullets mist senter over ½ inch. I won the first shot, Bob won the second by the width of the bullet. Bob won the third by a quarter of an

inch. I won the forth, Bob won the fifth. I was well aquanted with the dalton boys when they wer U.S. marshels and I must say that an officer of the law had a mity hard row to hoe in the indian teritory wher evry one carried a gun and was redy to shoot on the second. evry day the officer lived only by the quickness of his hand. he took all of the risk for 2 dollers a day and millege so you see it is not much wonder that the dalton boys turned into outlaws. with that small sallery and death waiting just around the corner would have turned you and me into outlaws.—Tom Rivington, gearing, nebraska."

Another witness to Bob's shooting skill came from an even more impressive source. Heck Thomas, in his written reminiscences of his years as a lawman, described Bob like this: "He was a smooth-faced, handsome youth, not more than 20-years-old when Frank was killed. He was a bit of a dandy, much given to fancy boots and guns and known to be utterly fearless. He was one of the most accurate shots I ever saw . . . shot his rifle mostly from his side or hip, very seldom

This .38-40 Colt Single Action with pearl grips was taken from Emmett Dalton by John Kloehr, the Coffeyville defender who killed Bob and Grat Dalton. (Museum of the Great Plains)

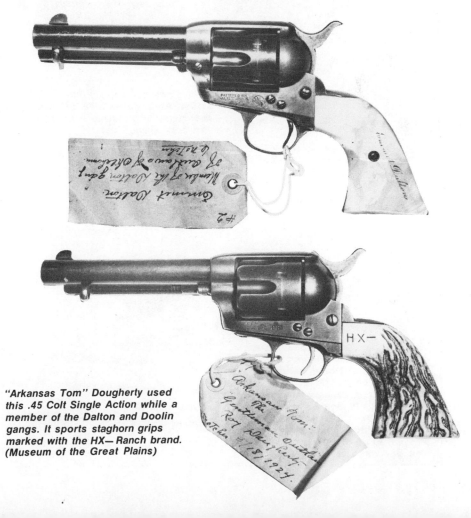

"Arkansas Tom" Dougherty used this .45 Colt Single Action while a member of the Dalton and Doolin gangs. It sports staghorn grips marked with the HX— Ranch brand. (Museum of the Great Plains)

The Dalton-Doolin Gang

bringing the gun to his shoulder." Willful, reckless and impetuous, always wanting to be the leader, he had boasted to Heck that there would have been a different outcome had he instead of Frank gone after the Smith-Dixon gang.

At one time or another, the Dalton gang was made up of nine or ten men. Emmett had spent some time cowboying on the HX—(HX Bar) Ranch where he was saddlemate to Bill Doolin, Dick Broadwell and Bill Powers. They were to join Emmett and his brothers on several of their forays. Adjoining this ranch was the Turkey Track ranch where "Black Face" Charlie Bryant, George "Bitter Creek" Newcomb and Charlie Pierce worked as cowboys. They, too, became members of the Dalton gang. Newcomb and Brant were among the first to join the Daltons after they chose to "ride the outlaw trail."

By the end of the summer of 1891, Doolin, Powers and Broadwell had joined the Daltons. Heck Thomas, who had been on the trail of the gang since their first train robbery,

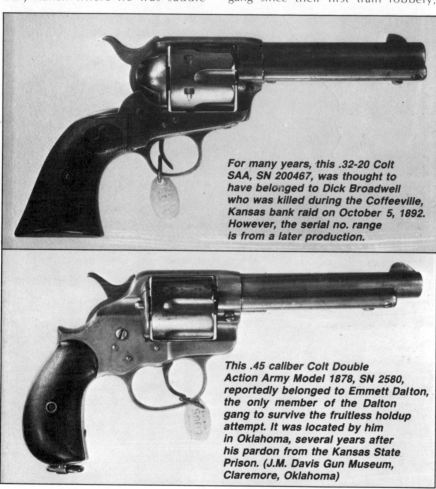

For many years, this .32-20 Colt SAA, SN 200467, was thought to have belonged to Dick Broadwell who was killed during the Coffeeville, Kansas bank raid on October 5, 1892. However, the serial no. range is from a later production.

This .45 caliber Colt Double Action Army Model 1878, SN 2580, reportedly belonged to Emmett Dalton, the only member of the Dalton gang to survive the fruitless holdup attempt. It was located by him in Oklahoma, several years after his pardon from the Kansas State Prison. (J.M. Davis Gun Museum, Claremore, Oklahoma)

Little Bill Raidler was considered one of the fastest gunmen to ride with the Dalton/Doolin gangs. He preferred Colt pistols in .38-40 caliber. For years, this 4¾-inch barreled SAA, serial number 202413, was believed to have been the one taken from Raidler's body by lawman Bill Tilghman. However serious research proved this gun to be of later production. (J.M. Davis Gun Museum, Claremore, OK).

added the information he had on these new gang members to what he already knew about the Daltons.

Bill Doolin, who emerged as leader of the surviving gang members after the Coffeyville raid, was the son of Mack Doolin, an Arkansas cotton farmer. He had no education but later learned to read and write. He drifted to Indian Territory as a young man where he got a job on Oscar Halsell's HX—Ranch because of his ability with an axe—Halsell was building corrals and none of the cowboys could split rails like Doolin.

Another HX—cowboy was "Little Dick" West, a small, wiry youth picked up by Halsell when he was 13 and wandering the streets. He was an orphan who acted more animal than human. Halsell felt sorry for him and took him home with him. West finally outgrew many of his attitudes but one thing he never got over was a fear of sleeping indoors. Regardless of the weather, he slept outside. This came in handy for Doolin since West could hear anyone who might be approaching the outlaw's camp at night.

When Little Dick met Doolin on the Halsell ranch, he was already quite proficient with a cowboy's tools, especially firearms. He was considered a fast draw and deadly shot with pistol and rifle both.

Another cowboy on the HX—Ranch, Bill Raidler, was a well-educated young Dutchman from Pennsylvania. He was fascinated by the West and drifted to Oklahoma where he started working as a cowboy for Halsell. He became adept with the sixgun and, in fact, was the fastest and deadliest pistol shot of the outlaw gangs he rode with. He was one of the few gunfighters who was good enough—and chose—to use a simultaneous draw of both his revolvers.

On May 20, 1894, Doolin and his henchman robbed the Southwest City, Missouri, bank of $4000. Citizens became aware of the robbery and opened up on the outlaws as they left the bank and continued exchanging shots with them as they rode out of town. Little Bill Raidler rode out with both revolvers in his hands and blazing away. One of his bullets passed through Oscar Seaborn's body, wounding him slightly, and then hitting Oscar's brother, Joe, killing him instantly.

Except for Bill Doolin's .44 Winchester, the only guns pinpointed to specific members of this outlaw gang belonged to Little Bill Raidler, Roy "Arkansas Tom" Daugherty and George "Bitter Creek" Newcomb. In U.S. Marshal Ed D. Nix's book "Oklahombres", he states that Little Bill and Bitter Creek took some of the proceeds of one of their robberies and traveled by train to the Chicago World's Fair in 1893. While there, each bought a pair of Colts.

The Colts purchased by Little Bill Raidler were taken from him by Deputy U.S. Marshal Bill Tilghman on Sept. 6, 1895. Tilghman had learned that Raidler was staying on the Sam Moore ranch, 18 miles south of Elgin, Kansas, and he went there to take him. He carried a double-barrel shotgun (the same one Heck Thomas later used to kill Doolin) in addition to his own Colt .45. About sunset, Raidler rode in, unsaddled in the corral and started walking to the house. As he passed Tilghman, concealed just inside a shed, Tilghman said: "Raidler! This is Tilghman! Throw up your hands!" Instead, Raidler drew, whirling as he did, and snapped off a fast shot. The bullet grazed Tilghman's head, knocking his hat off. The marshal fired one barrel of his shotgun and knocked the outlaw down but Raidler kept firing wildly until his Colts were empty.

Tilghman rushed the barely living outlaw to a doctor and kept him alive. Six years later, he even appeared before the pardon board on Raidler's behalf when it was learned he just had a short while to live. He also helped set him up in a small business on his release from prison.

It appears that Raidler had a preference for the .38-40 caliber, for there is a Colt Single Action in that

Bob Dalton's .38-56 M-1886 Winchester was carried by him and used in the Coffeyville, Kansas raid. (Museum of the Great Plains)

chambering that belonged to the little outlaw in the J.M. Davis Gun Collection, Claremore, Oklahoma. That pistol was given to the museum (or, rather, Mr. Davis before the museum as such was in existence) by Bill Tilghman. Tilghman also liked the .38-40, for one of his own pistols in that caliber is in the Davis Museum.

The Raidler Colts were given by Tilghman to Fred Sutton who sold them in 1929 to a private collector. They still belong to that family and are on display in the Museum of the Great Plains, Lawton, Oklahoma. In the same display is the shotgun Tilghman used against Raidler, and Thomas used on Doolin.

The two Colt .45s Bitter Creek purchased in Chicago were described by Fred Sutton: "Bitter Creek bought a beautiful pair of Colt .45s; however, they were not silver mounted [as described by Ed Nix in his book] as men of his kind always preferred a blue or black barreled gun. The guns did not have ivory handles, but had pearl handles. On one was carved a beautiful American Eagle, on the other was carved the head of a long horn steer."

Bitter Creek and Charlie Pierce were killed by Heck Thomas, Bee and Cal Dunn as they rode in to the

Continued on page 219

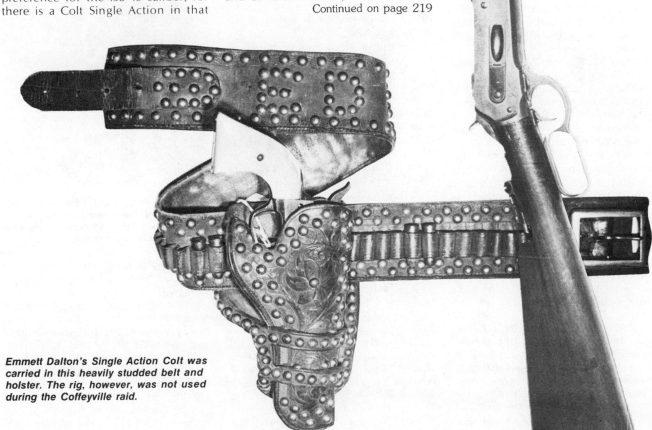

Emmett Dalton's Single Action Colt was carried in this heavily studded belt and holster. The rig, however, was not used during the Coffeyville raid.

A TRIO OF .44-

Two Winchesters That Helped in Winning The West—And One That Arrived 100 Years Too Late for the Fight.

By Jim Woods

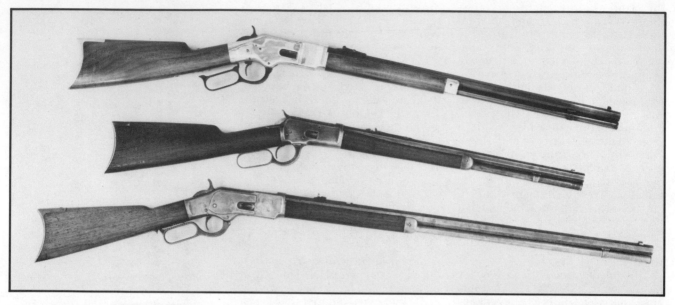

Hardly any gun commands more respect from the student and collector of Western Americana than the Winchester lever action rifles. The only other gun with such a following is the Colt in its many variations. However, the Winchester has an equally colorful history, along with a multitude of models to whet the collector's appetite.

Most Winchester fans are aware of the Henries, Volcanics and a couple of other rare and obscure predecessors to the lever guns that carry the Winchester label. The first of the breed to carry the proud name of the Winchester Repeating Arms Company was the Model 1866. The gun proved to be immediately popular and more than 170,000 were produced in carbine, rifle and musket configurations up through the year 1898. All models were chambered for the .44, as were the earlier Henry rifles.

No recreation of shooting the famed Winchesters could be complete without firing the 66. Unfortunately, none were available for shooting, so we went to an excellent alternate—the Navy Arms Company's replica 66 in caliber .44-40. This replica has the look and feel of the original. More importantly, it functions as the original and proved to be an excellent shooting gun. With a model so true to the original in most areas, one easily can ignore the strange legend stamped on the

Three .44-40 lever guns selected for test includes two Winchesters, a Model 1873 long barrel rifle (bottom) and a 1892 carbine (center). The almost-a-Winchester at top is the Navy Arms Model 1866 replica.

barrel that gives the origin of the rifle as somewhere other than Connecticut, U.S.A.

Perhaps even more popular, with current victims of the Winchester mystique, than the hard-to-find 66s is the Model 1873. Originals certainly were popular with the buying public from the year of its introduction until it was dropped from production in the 1920s. Altogether, nearly ¾ million of the Model '73s were manufactured—in calibers .44-40, .38-40, .32-20 and .22 Rimfire.

The 73 was offered in standard carbine, rifle and musket versions, but a number of factory options were available. Our test gun was factory-fitted with an optional 30-inch barrel, taking the rifle out of the saddle-gun category. The gun was in extremely fine condition and functioned perfectly with the modern smokeless equivalent factory loads.

With the long barrel, the gun was just a bit unwieldly to fire from the offhand position—the muzzle tended to wander a bit. Accuracy out to 200 yards was no better, no worse, than another shorter barrelled gun tested at the same time. No doubt, if a rest were used with

Author test fired an old 73 in near new condition and a new version of an old gun, the Navy Arms '66 replica. Old and new both were good shooters.

that long barrel, that extra ten inches of sight radius would prove effective.

The short barrel model just referred to was a Model 1892, a scaled down version of the Model 1886 that followed the Model 1876, that, in turn, followed the 73.

Model '92s were produced in the same calibers as the 73—.44-40, .38-40 and .32-20—but also were factory-chambered for the .25-20 and even the .218 Bee for a short while. More than a million Model '92s

40 LEVER GUNS

The '73 Winchester with 30-inch barrel was noticeably more difficult to handle—swing and hold—than the shorter, 20-inch barrel 92. Performance results—accuracies—were close to identical with both long and short guns. There's a tendency to lean backward with the long gun; lean into the carbine.

were made from the year of its introduction through 1941 when production was finally halted.

Which one of those one million guns was our test Model '92? No one without elaborate equipment to recover the obliterated serial number will know. It was just one of the many that were working guns somewhere in the Western U.S. or Mexico. Its condition reflected a rather hard life and long service—but it was still operable and seemingly still accurate. Its 20-inch barrel contrasted greatly with the 30-inch 73; and the shorter 92 was much easier to bring to target than the longer gun.

Thus, our test guns ran to the extremes of a well-worn but still serviceable Model 1892; a near perfect Model 1873; and a brand new European copy of the Model 1866. All were fired with currently manufactured smokeless loads designed to duplicate the black powder .44-40s for which they were all chambered.

And what of the performance of these .44-40 loads? Naturally, comparison must be made to the more modern high velocity and high power magnum loads. The new loads would easily win the race to the target; at 200 yards the lag from trigger to target with the .44-40 was definitely perceptible. Recoil was practically non-existent. Nonetheless, the old lever guns placed the heavy bullets on target every time; and 200 grains of lead at the computed 200-yard velocities for the .44-40 is still close to 1000 fps—a force to be reckoned with.

There's something about lever actions that lets the shooter know that he is in command of the gun

The Navy Arms replica 66 is accurate out to several hundred yards and is a real boon for Winchester fans who need a shooter in order to preserve the collectibles. Navy Arms also produces fine replicas of the 73 in both rifle and carbine versions.

and the situation that calls for use of the gun. Its *clank-clunk* ejection-reload cycle is more satisfying than any artillery piece bolt action rifle, and it puts the shooter in charge more than the auto loaders. Small wonder, the following the Winchester lever guns enjoy—they are truly the "Guns That Won The West."

Texas Rangers

"The Texas Devils"
By Burt Miller

Winchesters of varying models and calibers were extremely popular with Rangers. Bob Speaker (far left) favored the .45-75 Model '76 carbine, While (l-r) Jim Putman, Lon Odam and Sgt. John R. Hughes carried Model '92s. The grips on Speaker's Peacemaker look pretty worn, indicating hard Ranger useage.

The feeling of the day and time at the turn of the century may well be gained from Texas Ranger Captain J. C. Brook's terse statement, "My men are crack shots and I'm not afraid of them getting the worst of anything." His comment sums up the attitude and self-reliance typical of each and every Texas Ranger.

Not only did the Rangers believe their own capabilities, but so did those they came up against during those turbulent times. One factor that stands out all through the history of the Texas Rangers is that a high percentage of these men entered law enforcement at very young ages.

James C. 'Doc' White enlisted before he was 21 years old. Among the youngest was Gus T. 'Buster' Jones, who fought in the Spanish-American War at the age of 16, and was city marshal of San Angelo when he was only 21. He went on to serve six years in the Rangers, then as a customs agent, border patrolman and finally worked for the FBI. Both of these men were involved in the capture of the infamous Machine Gun Kelly.

During this same period, Dogie Wright, son of Ranger Captain William Lee Wright, joined the Rangers at the age of 17. By 1968 he had completed over 50 years in law enforcement.

Captain Charles Schreiner was the youngest Ranger of all, joining at 16 years of age. He resigned at 19 to raise cattle, and later gained his title of captain in the Home Guard, organized to keep down the Indians plaguing the ranchers of Kerr County.

It is hard today to conceive that these young men could make such an impact on the Texas frontier. Responsibility came at an early age at that time, and the use of the rifle and revolver started at eight to ten years of age.

Each prospective Ranger was selected by qualifications based on the essential skills that meant not only his own survival but that he could also protect his comrades in a shoot-out as well as the property and lives of the citizens that paid his meager salary.

Capability as a tracker, skill with arms and horses, and proficiency in living off the land for prolonged periods went arm-in-arm with those mandatory but unidentifiable traits of character that are usually lumped together under one term—bravery.

These were the inherent characteristics evident in only those few men that were to build the mantle of invincibility that rode on the shoulders of every Texas Ranger; the reputation that earned them the title of "Los Diablos Tejanas," (The Texas Devils).

This is the mystic capability that permitted a lone man, unassisted, to put down a riot.

We must assume, or more appropriately, accept the fact that those young men, living at a time when a life span could be ended in

moments, more often than not over a trivial matter, learned the art of survival in their early teens. In doing so they had to develop their skills to a level surpassing those of many men who had survived over 50 or 60 years as outlaws and murderers with a price on their heads.

One can only conjecture that the limited earnings of these youngsters were devoted to attaining a fast horse, the best possible firearms and ammunition, for these things helped qualify them for a place among this elite group. Some were undoubtedly assisted by well-to-do parents but most of them made it on their own.

It has been just over 150 years since Stephen F. Austin obtained permission from the Mexican government to establish, in 1821, the town that now bears his name and later became the Texas state capital.

The 300 families that Austin settled on the rich farm and pasture land along the banks of the Colorado River, soon learned that they were not to live in peace. Marauding Commanches, resenting the settler's invasion, raided from the hill country only 50 miles to the west.

By 1823, Austin had decided that they would have to provide a means of protection for the outlying homes and ranches. He established a group of ten volunteers, selected by their tracking and marksmanship capabilities.

Describing their duties, which were "to range over the area between the oak covered hills to the west and the settlement on the Colorado River," provided the name for the small group of men that was to become the most renown and the oldest state police organization on the North American continent. The term "Ranger" became official when the Texas Ranger Force was established in 1835 by the state's general assembly.

The trouble with the Indians was to continue even after the Mexican War of 1846 and the War Between the States that was to follow in 1861.

Such notorious men as John Wesley Hardin, Sam Bass, King Fisher and Juan Cortinas indicate the cold-blooded caliber of desperados the young Ranger of the time could expect to face. Some failed to survive, but not one was ever faced down or turned away from trouble regardless of the numbers he encountered.

Ranger history abounds with names and places that mark the turmoil and violence of the times. Captain Jack Hays and his men battled the Commanches at Enchanted Rock, Bandera Pass, Plum Creek and at the Battle of Salado. Later he was to fight at Monterey and Mexico City as colonel of the First Regiment, Texas Mounted Volunteers.

Ben McCulloch carried a Colt First Model Dragoon while commanding a company of Rangers under General Zachary Taylor. When Texas seceded from the Union he was to become a general in the Confederate Army.

Sam Houston stated that every soldier could be withdrawn from the borders of Texas if replaced by one regiment of Texas Rangers. How better could the respect of these men be expressed? That type of opinion contributed greatly to the reputation for tenacity and invincibility of the Rangers.

Specific details pertaining to the arms of Austin's early settlers are scarce but we are aware that their choice was limited. Undoubtedly those first ten Rangers depended upon the flintlock Jaeger rifle of .60 caliber, brought over from Germany and Switzerland and the lighter and smaller caliber "Kentucky" rifle from the gunsmiths in the hills of Northern Pennsylvania.

By 1825 these were followed by

Texas Rangers

the shorter percussion plains rifles such as the Hawken or Leman and the .69 caliber U.S. M-1842 musket. The flintlock Kentucky rifles were later modified to percussion and many were to be used by the Southerners during the Civil War.

Perhaps a few double-barrelled "fowling pieces" were used as well. Although cumbersome, the extra barrel was welcome against the Indians in particular, and was used as a most effective weapon during the period of 1820 through 1840.

Although percussion pistols had made their entry, such arms as the derringer were to be more popular with the riverboat gamblers and "fancy" women.

Dueling in frontier Texas was usually settled with rifle or Bowie knife, although the custom of formal duels continued to flourish until the 1850s in the "deep south."

It was with the advent of the Colt revolver that the sidearm became a permanent and practical part of the armament of bandit, outlaw, peace officer and rancher alike.

By 1836, there was a very direct

This 1900-period Ranger group supports the theory that Winchesters and Colt SAA revolvers were the most popular sidearms. The cartridge belts appear to have provisions for pistol and rifle cartridges.

association of the first Colts with the Rangers in relation to the Paterson Model, named after the factory established in 1836 at Paterson, New Jersey. As a matter of fact, Captain John Coffee Hays with Samuel H. Walker and 14 other Rangers in one exploit defeated 80 Commanches near the Nueces River using 9-inch barrelled, .36 caliber "Texas" Patersons. These arms were weak at best, but the surprising evidence of superior fire power probably had the

greatest effect on the astonished Indians, although the Rangers killed 35 in the battle! The well-known 1847 Walker Colt was the next arm and, again, Ranger history was directly involved. Colt had gone broke in 1842, but in 1846 Captain Samuel H. Walker, now with the Army, who considered the Paterson inadequate in design, worked out new specifications with Colt and persuaded the Army to order a quantity of 1000 with a promise of 2000 more. Thus, the powerful six-shot Walker .44 put Colt back in business.

Walker was carrying two Walker Colts when he was killed in battle with the Mexicans. One of these, serial number 1020, was returned to Samuel Colt after Walker's death. It was 1 of 100 over-production guns made for gifts to friends of Colt. This revolver is still in the possession of Colt Firearms of Hartford, Connecticut.

The Walker as well as the smaller Colt .44 Dragoon revolvers were favored early handguns of the Rangers. Colt turned out three smaller models in an attempt to reduce bulk and weight. Due to its size, the 4-pound Walker was too large, even for a mounted man, and Colt want-

ed a gun suitable for more general military use.

The fact remains that the Walker served well during the Mexican War and was far superior to anything the enemy possessed. Two Walker Colts were with each Ranger at the Battle of Vera Cruz.

One of the better known Texas Rangers of the period, Ben McCulloch, was born in Tennessee in 1811. At the age of 25 he was in the fight for Texas virtually from the day he joined Sam Houston at San Jacinto.

He commanded a group of Rangers at Plum Creek in 1840 and scouted for Captain John Coffee Hays in 1842. With his own company of Rangers he and his men

served as spies for General Zachary Taylor during the Mexican War. When Texas turned to the Confederacy he assisted in attaining the surrender of Federal Troops in Texas.

As a Brigadier General his men won the battle of Oak Hills in 1861. A few months later he was killed during the battle of Elkhorn Tavern. The gun he carried during the latter part of his career was the First Model Colt Dragoon revolver. Samuel J. Barker a former Ranger serving with the Texas Cavalry during the Civil War, used the same model Colt.

Samuel Colt also produced a series of smaller pistols including the Baby Dragoon and the M-1849 .31 caliber pocket pistol. These small arms suited those who had reason to carry a concealed weapon, but were not fitted to the needs of the average peace officer. The .36 caliber Navy revolver was produced in 1851 and the .44 Army revolver followed in 1860. Well-designed, both of these models were very popular and the Rangers were quick to adopt them. Information is sparce in most instances of specific arms carried by individual Rangers, but occasionally some records do make direct reference to a particular firearm.

Ranger John B. Dunn wrote a book about his life, "The Perilous Trails of Texas." Born in 1851 at Corpus Christi, he was later to defend that city from the Mexican raid in 1874. He was to be buried there in 1940. An Army cap-and-ball Colt of his, has a dozen notches on the left grip with brass tacks spelling out Texas at the base of the walnut grip.

There remains to this day, some mystique related to both the Colt and the Winchester, particularly during this phase of Ranger history. Up until very recently these two had little competition, although Remington produced both .36 and .44 caliber cap-and-ball models that were at least equal if not superior to Colts.

Smith & Wesson incorporated the idea of a metallic cartridge using Rollin White's procedure of boring the cylinder through to accept cartridges from the rear. These arms were placed on the market with the expiration of Colt's patents in 1857. Colt had laughed at the idea, although he had been offered the system earlier. He was soon to regret his decision. Smith & Wesson controlled the market for cartridge revolvers until 1869, when their patent expired. One must assume that the Rangers and desperados alike, at least once tried one of the new Smith & Wesson's. Smith & Wesson produced their Model 3 "American" in .44 caliber (.44-40). The six cartridges or empty cases could all be ejected at one time in this break-

Frank Hamer (standing, left) with other Rangers photographed in Del Rio, Texas. Hamer holds a Model 1894 Winchester while the kneeling Ranger has a Model 1873. The man in the center seems justly proud of his new Luger, although the Ranger at the far right keeps his Winchester hidden in its saddle scabbard.

open arm, and its popularity continued until the Smith & Wesson patents expired. It fired a centerfire cartridge loaded with 25 grains of black powder and a 218-grain bullet developing 316 ft-lbs of energy.

Smith & Wesson's Model 1 was popular in the East, but other than as a lady's firearm or for a hideout firearm, the 7-shot .22 caliber rimfire was too small to risk your life on. The Model 2 in .32 caliber, was a slight improvement, but fell in the same category. Needless to say, these failed to fulfill the needs of a Ranger but were purchased in considerable numbers by individual soldiers during the Civil War.

With the expiration of Smith & Wesson's patents, Colt came out with the 1871 Richards conversion, which provided a means to modify the old percussion models to fire metallic cartridges. His new cartridge model, in 1872, had an open top and was quickly replaced by the

1873 Single Action Army, commonly called the Peacemaker or the Frontier model. This arm, in .45 caliber, became undoubtedly the most popular revolver ever produced, and, to this day, remains the most prized arm in many a collection.

A name that is familiar to many of us is that of Charles Schriener, who in 1852, came to San Antonio from France as a youngster of 14. Two years later he joined the Rangers. He became a widely-known cattleman, driving longhorn cattle to Kansas during the period following the Civil War through the '80s. He died at the age of 80 but his name is carried on. The Schriener ranch, which he established, is the famous YO. The traditional Colt revolver was his sidearm, including the .36 caliber Navy model of 1851 and later the Single Action Army, no doubt in several calibers although I would venture to say these would include but two, the .44-40 and the .45 Colt.

One of the surviving arms of the Rangers is the ivory-handled Single Action Army Colt that belonged to Thomas C. Frost. Born in Alabama in 1833, he went to school in Tennessee and later studied law under Sam Houston while teaching Latin at Austin College. A highly educated man by standards of the time, he

moved to Commanche County to practice law but a year later, in 1857, he organized a Ranger company against marauding Indians. He fought with the Confederacy and ended the war as a lieutenant colonel. He died in 1903—his name is carried on today by the Frost National Bank of San Antonio.

By 1878 the Peacemaker, that could be used for such other mundane purposes as driving fence staples, tacking up reward notices on a tree or subduing an unruly drunk, was available in the popular .44-40 caliber. This was the caliber favored by all peace officers, as one belt load of cartridges could be used in either the Colt or the 1873, 1892 or 1894 Winchester.

Another model gained popularity with peace officers, including some Rangers. The double-action Colt Lightning in .38 caliber. Captain Neal Coldwelo, who had arrived in Texas just as the Civil War broke out, served with the Texas Cavalry and later commanded Company "F" of the Ranger Frontier Battalion in 1874. He served until 1883 and during this period after the taming of the border regions he carried a Colt Lightning and a single shot .41 caliber derringer. The .41 Thunderer in the same design was also produced in 1877. These arms have a relatively small frame compared to the Peacemaker and were convenient under certain circumstances, but they were soon superseded by the modern double-actions. Smith & Wesson's Model 1880 in .38 caliber provided considerable competition to the Colt Lightning. The "Thunderer" was

Rangers George Black (left) and J.M. Britton of Co. B were photographed with their Model '73 Winchesters and Colt Peacemakers. Both men also sport small "in-fighting" dirks on their cartridge belts and wear practical straw sombreros.

Texas Rangers

reportedly Billy the Kid's prized arm and helped him live for four short years after its arrival on the market.

It was not unusual for a turn-of-the-century Ranger expecting big trouble, to be armed with two Peacemakers, a Model '92 or '95 Winchester and a Model 1887 10 or 12-gauge lever-action Winchester shotgun. This required at least two belts of ammunition. Unlike the movies and television today, that portray the man in the white hat making unbelievable shots with a revolver, the real peace officer and outlaw that wanted to live, depended on the rifle at any distance much over 25 yards, unless a shotgun was convenient for "in town" use.

Both the 1887 and 1901 Winchester lever-action 10-gauge shotguns were popular with law enforcement officers as well as stagecoach guards who rode shotgun. A few 1887s were produced with 20-inch barrels as "riot" guns, although 30 and 32 inches were standard. Such lengths were obviously awkward and a cut-off barrel did a good job of sweeping a wide street! These guns usually had the barrel shortened for convenience in handling. The 12-gauge, 1897 Winchester pump gun appeared and quickly replaced the lever-action. By 1899, these were produced in a 20-inch barrel riot model—a gun that is still stored in police arsenals and carried in patrol cars across the nation. It was commonplace in the hands of the Rangers. Faster to handle than

The men of Co. A, Texas Rangers were photographed in their working gear in 1918. A number of the troopers can be seen wearing their distinctive badges, and all seem to favor Colt Single Actions. Many of the Rangers sport handguns on their hips and spares looped over the saddle horns.

the lever-action, it proved deadly in close combat during World War I trench warfare. Popularity of these shotguns was due in part to the exposed hammer. Marlin's Model 42A slide action is a near counterpart to the Winchester, but easily identified by the solid top, unlike the '97 that ejected from the top.

By 1905, the Browning Model 5 and it's look-alike the Remington Model 11 semi-automatic, appeared in the hands of the criminal and Remington produced their riot model in 12-gauge. Rangers, however, tended to favor the manually operated slide action as less subject to malfunction.

An era in firearms that was to see the development of the "Rifle That Won The West" was initiated with the Volcanic pistol and rifle. An investor in the company was Oliver Fisher Winchester who later bought out the company which, due to poor ammunition design, never attained any success.

In 1858, Winchester assigned Benjamin Tyler Henry the task of designing a suitable cartridge for the rifle which became a .44 rimfire with a 216-grain bullet and a velocity of 1200 feet per second. Holding 16 rounds, this lever-action rifle was available for sale by 1862. It could have made a major impact on the Civil War, but Army ordnance clung to the simple muzzle loader.

Although 1800 Henrys were purchased by the military, only a few saw combat in the war, but this repeater became popular with civilians and many were obtained by Rangers and other peace officers. Its competitor, the seven-shot Spencer rifle, of heavier caliber, attained a greater military success but was discontinued at the end of the war due to lack of civilian interest. However, the Spencer was used in limited numbers by the Rangers. Old records and photographs confirm this.

When Sgt. James B. Gillette enlisted in the Frontier Battalion in 1875, it was required that a .50—caliber Sharps and a .44 Army cap-and-ball Colt revolver be provided by the individual Ranger. This indicates a considerable time lag for the Rangers to acquire repeating rifles such as the 1866 and 1873 Winchesters and that the Sharps was still adequate for use on the frontier.

Sgt. Gillette's personal arms are on display in the Ft. Fisher Ranger Museum just out of Waco, Texas. Among other arms included are a sawed-off shotgun, a Spencer, a Sharps carbine, a cap-and-ball Colt revolver and his favorite rifle, a Model 1873 .44-40 Winchester.

The 1866 Winchester started the trend, along with several competitors including Marlin, in the lever-action design that retains its high popularity to this day. The inclination was towards smaller calibers of higher velocity and shorter and lighter arms. Such arms were acquired by the individual Rangers as quickly as they appeared, as did their outlaw competitors, who, through the wages of sin, were often in a better position with plentiful cash in hand, to keep up with the latest in arms development.

Soon, Winchester rifles were common in 20-inch saddle carbines, or 24 to 26-inch barrel lengths. The brass receiver of the 1866 was changed to iron and finally blued steel.

Changes to the Winchester series of lever-action rifles continued in caliber and some details. The famous Model 1873 incorporated an iron frame and was designed to handle the new caliber .44 Winchester, more commonly termed the ".44-40." Made popular by "Buffalo" Bill Cody as a hunting and show arm, it received wide acceptance. Winchester had made sure that a new model at the time would be a

superior arm, and wide publicity was given to selected rifles marked "1 of 1000" and "1 of 100." (This must have been the first of the "collector" models that now appear at regular intervals.) This was a widely used arm among the Rangers, as it was chambered for their essential interchangeable .44-40 cartridge as well as several others.

Like the 1873, the 1876 model had a sponsor. Teddy Roosevelt expounded on its virtues in the .45-75 caliber in his book, "Hunting Trips of a Ranchman." The 1876, chambered for the same .45-75 cartridge, was adopted by the Northwest Mounted Police, the Canadian counterpart to the Texas Rangers.

John Moses Browning joined Winchester in 1879, and patented what became the Winchester single-shot, followed by the rugged Model 1886 lever-action, designed and produced in 12 heavy loads of up to .50 caliber, including .45-70; a caliber that remained popular for years, as is common with all military cartridges. It found its way into some saddle scabbards of the Rangers, but the light-weight Model 1892, chambered in .44-40, .38-40, .32-20 and .25-20, quickly replaced it. The rifle magazine held 13 rounds and the 20-inch barrelled carbine, 11. The carbine weighed under six pounds. It was available in barrel lengths of 14, 15, 16 and 18 inches on special order. Due to the .44-40 caliber and the short barrels, the 1892 probably was the most popular of all the Rangers arms although the '95 superseded it, but only for a time.

The Winchester that has probably taken more deer than any other—as well as its share of men—is the Model '94. It later replaced all other models in popularity with the Rangers and other law enforcement agencies. This was primarily due to it being designed specifically for the new smokeless powder and higher velocity loads than the long popular .44-40. (Now the user need not scrub the bore each night with hot water to remove the black powder fouling and stop early rust!) Three million 94s have been produced and it is still in production. Along with the still popular and the first smokeless cartridge, the .30-30, the rifle was also chambered for the .32-40, .38-55, .25-38 and the .32 Special. The 20-inch barrelled carbine and the Trapper Model became favorites of the Rangers, and along with the 92, were probably the most convenient saddle arms ever produced. A departure from the usual tube magazine was the Model 1895, with its box magazine.

As late as 1921, Ranger C. L. "Blackie" Blackwell was photo-graphed near Presidio wearing two single action Colts on a belt with two rows of revolver ammunition and a second belt slung over his shoulder a la Pancho Villa, apparently filled with .30-06 ammunition for his Model '95 carbine. It is noted that his holsters are for right and left hand draw and not for a cross draw. In the photograph he also sports a sheath knife stuck in behind his pistol belt for show, probably normally worn to the rear of a holstered revolver. The Mexican sombrero he is wearing served to provide a bit of disguise from a distance while riding along the Rio Grande and is not necessarily his usual head gear.

A photograph of Captain Will Wright and his company of nine Rangers indicates the popularity of the 1895 Winchester. All but one man has either a 95 carbine or rifle, the one odd rifle is probably a 24-inch barrelled Model '94. Of the 95s, only one is a rifle and two of the carbines appear to have been cut off to 18 inches.

The Model '95 rifle was chambered in .30-40 Krag, .30-30, .303 British, .38-72, .40-72, .35 and .30-06 calibers. The barrel lengths available were 24, 26 and 28 inches. The carbine, with a 22-inch barrel, was chambered for the .30-40, .30-30, .30-06 and .303 only

It appears that almost every Ranger rushed out and obtained a Model '95. Most selected the .30-40 caliber but again when the Army changed to the .30-06 Springfield in 1906, it influenced many Rangers to switch to the new and more powerful cartridge with its long-range capability. Even a few .405 Winchesters were used, but these were the exception—if for no other reason than the need for a 28-inch barrel to keep the report within reasonable bounds; a clumsy arm on horseback, at best!

When the Colt M-1851 .36 Navy revolver was introduced it was rapidly adopted by the Rangers. This engraved, ivory handled version, with its original holster, is typical of the type used. The Navy was fast, reliable, accurate and easily the most popular handgun of its day. (Windy Drum)

The highly respected Ranger Dudley White served a long period with the Rangers, starting in 1905, under Captain John R. Hughes, broken by service as a Houston policeman and with the U. S. Border Patrol. His father was a peace officer before him and his son Dudley White, Jr., also served with the Rangers.

Trying to apprehend two Army deserters, Dudley Sr., was seriously wounded. His partner, Ranger Rowe, was also shot and Dudley bled to death before he was found. His weapons were typical of the period from 1905 through the WWII period. He carried a pearl-handled .45 Frontier Single Action with a heavily inlaid, blued finish. His rifle at the time was the typical favorite, the Model '95, but it had a 26-inch barrel in .30-06 caliber. Previously he had also used a .30-40 Model '95 carbine.

Numerous pictures of Captain John R. Hughes, who served from 1887 to 1915 and made a name for himself as "Boss of the Border," show him with a wide range of weapons. These include the Model 1886 Winchester carbine, a Model '95 and a lever-action; either a rifle with a pistol grip and curved lever or a lever-action shotgun. Only in one photograph is his ivory Colt Single Action Army clearly revealed due to the usual coat or vest; customary dress of the day and time. In this one instance the left-handed holster is stitched to an inch-wide shoulder strap suspended from the left shoulder. A flower-carved 1½-inch belt is worn outside of his trousers loops and between the gun butt and holster which has no loop. The trousers

Continued on page 220

Interview with a Texas Ranger

70 Years Later—A Texas Ranger Tells It Like It Was.

Interview conducted by Lee Silva

Editor's Note: The following interview took place during the summer of 1974. "Put" Putney is a native-born Texan who, from 1900 to 1906, was a Texas Ranger with several Ranger companies, working "on call" wherever and whenever he was needed.

He is 92-years-old now, and one of the last of a rapidly diminishing breed of men who is able to look back into his memories and give us a first hand glimpse at the West the way it really was

Q. When were you born?
A. 1883. I'm 92 now.
Q. You were a guide for the Texas Rangers?
A. I was at first. They wouldn't let me join, because I was too young. But I joined them in 1900.
Q. You actually were a Texas Ranger then, besides being a guide?
A. Yes, I was in the Spanish American War. I guided the Rangers for a while. I was a Ranger for six years. From 1900 to 1906.
Q. Why did the Texas Rangers need a guide?
A. To get across the bayous. I lived right near the Mexican border, south of Houston. The bayous and swamps was so bad, you sometimes could go 20 feet in a different direction and get in trouble. You had to know right where you were going all the time.
Q. How did you know that country so well?
A. I was born and raised there—in the Chocolate bayou. I was guide for the Rangers from the border to the bay. We were pretty far south.
Q. What bay is that?
A. Galveston Bay.
Q. You mention the border. What was the actual border?
A. The Rio Grande.
Q. The movies have always made

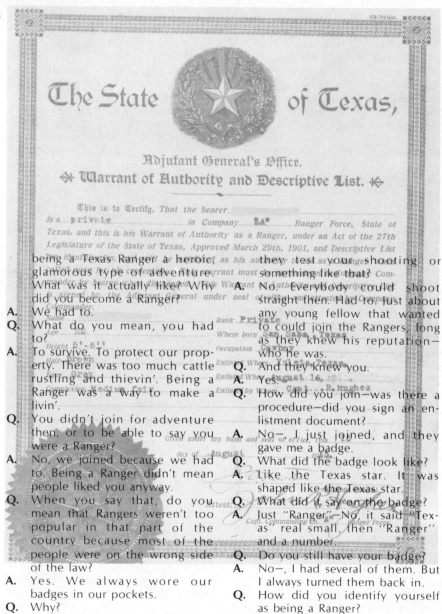

being a Texas Ranger a heroic glamorous type of adventure. What was it actually like? Why did you become a Ranger?
A. We had to.
Q. What do you mean, you had to?
A. To survive. To protect our property. There was too much cattle rustling and thievin'. Being a Ranger was a way to make a livin'.
Q. You didn't join for adventure then, or to be able to say you were a Ranger?
A. No, we joined because we had to. Being a Ranger didn't mean people liked you anyway.
Q. When you say that, do you mean that Rangers weren't too popular in that part of the country because most of the people were on the wrong side of the law?
A. Yes. We always wore our badges in our pockets.
Q. Why?
A. So we didn't get shot at so much. If we was in a shootout, we always liked to be shootin' first.
Q. In other words, the badge made you a target?
A. Yes. We didn't like people to know who we were until we had to.
Q. Did you have to qualify in any way to become a Ranger? Did

they test your shooting or something like that?
A. No. Everybody could shoot straight then. Had to. Just about any young fellow that wanted to could join the Rangers, long as they knew his reputation—who he was.
Q. And they knew you.
A. Yes.
Q. How did you join—was there a procedure—did you sign an enlistment document?
A. No—, I just joined, and they gave me a badge.
Q. What did the badge look like?
A. Like the Texas star. It was shaped like the Texas star.
Q. What did it say on the badge?
A. Just "Ranger"—No, it said "Texas" real small, then "Ranger" and a number.
Q. Do you still have your badge?
A. No—, I had several of them. But I always turned them back in.
Q. How did you identify yourself as being a Ranger?
A. With the badge.
Q. Was there a way of identifying you with the badge—, so that people knew it was your badge?
A. I don't understand what you mean.
Q. I mean, how did people know that you were really a Ranger—, that the badge really belonged to you? Did it have your name

on the back. or anything like that?

A. No—. We just showed them the badge. It was identification enough.

Q. Well what if someone wanted to shoot you and steal your badge and use it himself for illegal purposes?

A. A Ranger didn't get shot. We were careful not to get shot.

Q. Oh.

A. Besides—, nobody'd want to take a badge anyway.

Q. Because of what you said before?

A. Yes.

Q. Well, what if somebody tried to ambush you?

A. We always rode in two's.

Q. Always?

A. Yes.

Q. Do you remember any particular incident or person that stands out in your mind?

A. No—, it was pretty much all the same. It was a long time ago. Frank James, I guess— I worked with Frank James for about four years.

Q. You knew Frank James pretty well then? What did you think of him as a person? Did you think he was bad—, good?

A. He was real nice—, a prince of a fellow. His family had it pretty rough, you know. His sister was raped, his mother was raped. His father was beat to death by a gang. They had a lot of trouble. They started robbin' 'cause they had to.

Q. When you say "they," do you mean Jesse James too?

A. Yes.

Q. Obviously you never knew Jess. Do you remember when he was killed?

A. No—he was killed about the same year I was born, I think— around 1883. I don't know exactly.

Q. When you say you worked with Frank James, what do you mean?

A. He was a U.S. marshal—, deputy U.S. marshal. I was a Ranger.

Q. That must have been after he was out of jail?

A. He was never in jail. But he was pardoned. He never was in Jail. But Jesse James was. Frank just *took* Jesse out of jail once.

Q. *Took* him out?

A. Yep—, just took him out.

Q. I'd like to talk about that more next time but I'd like to ask you, did Frank James ever say anything about how Jesse James really died? I'm talking about what a lot of people have said, that Jesse James wasn't really shot in the back by Bob Ford

while hanging a picture, that they just set it up that way to get rid of the pressure from the law.

A. There wasn't any pressure from the law. Not much anyway. People liked Jesse. Jesse James was shot by one of his own men.

Q. Well, did Frank James ever talk to you about it? Did he say anything about how Jesse James really died?

A. No, he never said anything about it.

Q. Did you ever ask him about it?

A. No.

Q. Why not?

A. It wasn't my place to. Was none of my business.

Q. In other words, the old custom. You didn't ask questions—get nosey?

A. No. If people wanted you to know something, they'd tell you.

Q. What was your method of approaching someone you were after?

A. We always made them drop their gunbelts.

Q. Always?

A. Sure. Tried to, if we could. If we couldn't, we'd shoot first.

Q. What do you mean, you'd shoot first?

A. If he made any kind of a move, you shot. You didn't give him a chance to shoot you before you could shoot him.

Q. What do you mean, "any kind of a move?"

A. Anything that looked bad, like he might use his gun.

Q. In other words, in the movies, the good guy always lets the bad guy go for his gun first. You didn't do that?

A. No. You couldn't afford to. He might kill you. Everybody could shoot pretty straight.

Q. When you had to shoot at a man, did you try to wound him instead of kill him, like in the movies?

A. No! (emphathatically). You didn't give him a chance, a second chance to shoot you. You never gave anybody that chance. You never gave them the chance to shoot first, and you never gave them a second chance to get you. Couldn't afford to.

Q. So you always shot to kill?

A. Sure. Had to!

Q. So you always made them drop their gunbelts first, to get rid of their guns?

A. Yes, we watched their hands. If they made a move, we didn't wait.

Q. I've talked to other lawmen in

the past. They usually don't want to talk about how many people they've killed, or shot at. Were you actually in quite a few gunfights—?

A. I'd rather not say. Besides, I really can't remember.

Q. You don't know how many people you had to kill, or shoot?

A. People don't like to know you killed people.

Q. In the past, people just wanted to know the blood and guts— who got shot—and how. But people are different now. We want to know about the events more than the bloody part. We want to know *why* things happened, and what it was like. Too much of the West was only glorified. Now we want to make a biography of it. We want to document it—to record it. It was a very short era that needs to be recorded. We want to know how it really was—, not who got killed and how. If you understand that, you shouldn't be ashamed to talk about it. You shot people because it was your job, and you had to. Do you understand what I mean?

A. Yes.

Q. Do you want to talk about it?

A. I had to lead it out now and then.

Q. But you can't remember how many times?

A. No. Besides, you never knew who shot who anyway.

Q. What do you mean?

A. We always rode in two's. If a man made a move, we always tried to see who could hit him first.

Q. Like a contest?

A. No. I don't mean it that way. We just didn't wait. If we saw a move, we'd lead it out. That's how you survived.

Q. Like instinct?

A. Yes.

Q. What kind of pistol did you use?

A. My six-shooter.

Q. Was it a Colt?

A. Sure, there wasn't any other gun to use.

Q. You mean nobody liked anything else? You didn't use Remingtons or Smith and Wessons?

A. No. The Colt was proven. Nobody used anything but a Colt.

Q. What caliber was your Colt?

A. A .45. It had a 7½-inch barrel. It'd shoot almost as far as a rifle.

Q. Your Winchester is a .45-90. That's an awful big caliber too. I guess when you shot something, you wanted it to stay shot.

161

Interview with a Texas Ranger

A. Yep.

Q. It's loaded?

A. Sure. I keep it right under the bed. I've slept with that gun all my life. Bought it brand new.

Q. Do you remember what year you bought it?

A. No. About 1893 or 94, I think. I was just a kid.

Q. Your rifle is just a plain Winchester, nothing fancy. Was your Colt the same? Did it have black rubber or wood grips?

A. Wood. I liked the wood better.

Q. In the movies, the guns are always fancy—pearl grips and engraved. Did you and any other rangers like fancy guns, or just good old workhorses?

A. Nah, just a plain old blue gun.

Q. In other words, it was a working tool to use when you needed it.

A. That's right.

Q. Did you have any favorite type of horse that you preferred over others?

A. It had to be a big horse. Because of the rough country. And a light saddle. I had one, 16 hands.

Q. Did you prefer any particular breed of horse?

A. Quarter-horse. We always rode quarter-horses.

Q. Did you actually call them quarter-horses back then?

A. Sure. That's what they were.

Q. When you were buying a horse, was there anything in particular that you looked for that would indicate to you that it would be a good horse?

A. I knew all the horse-traders' tricks. No, just a big horse.

Q. Did you have a favorite horse?

A. I did for a while. But horses are only good for three or four years. I've dug more bullets out of horses than I have out of men. But we usually had two horses. Use one for pack, and switch off.

Q. How did you dress? What kind of clothes did you wear?

A. Like what?

Q. Pants?

A. Blue jeans, cheap blue jeans.

Q. Always?

A. Well, almost always. And chaps, leather chaps of course, for riding through the brush. Sometimes the brush was so bad, we had to walk our horses through it.

Q. What kind of shirt did you wear?

A. What kind?

Q. I've read that the usual shirt was a cotton shirt without a collar.

A. Nah, we wore shirts with collars and without. Whatever you could get.

Q. What about your hat? Did you wear just anything, or did you make sure you had a Stetson?

A. What do you mean?

Q. When you went to buy a hat did you buy any brand, or did you always buy a Stetson?

A. Oh, we wouldn't wear anything except a Stetson. A man's not a man without a Stetson. Boots and hat were the most expensive thing.

Q. Did you prefer any particular brand of boot?

A. No, they weren't like a Stetson. There was lots of local bootmakers everywhere, and we just got them wherever we could.

Q. How did you eat when you were on the trail? Did you pack pemmican, jerky, sourdough? What did you take to eat?

A. Coffee.

Q. Coffee?

A. Yeh. Arbuckle's coffee. Ever hear of it? Always took an old coffee pot and Arbuckle's coffee.

Q. But what about food?

A. Nah, we always killed our chuck.

Q. So you didn't make a point of taking along any meat or bread or staples?

A. Bread was too expensive. We killed our own meat. We lived pretty good. Meals were cheap in the towns. Everything was cheap.

Q. What if you weren't near any towns?

A. Sometimes we'd get a meal at a farmhouse. Otherwise we killed our own.

Q. What if you couldn't find any game?

A. Sometimes we went a day or two. But there was always something.

Q. How much did you get paid as a Ranger?

A. I don't remember.

Q. Was it a set amount, so much a month or something?

A. No, we just got paid for what we did. It wasn't much. You really didn't need much.

Q. You just got paid according to the particular assignment?

A. Yes. You could get a meal for 25 cents. Rooms were a dollar a day, and you got three meals with that. They just put the food on the table and said come and get it. There was plenty. You didn't need much pay.

Q. As a Ranger, what were your usual assignments, what kind of crime were you after?

A. Down there, it was all cattle rustling and robbin'.

Q. So what you did was to go after people?

A. Yes.

Q. When you were after someone, how did you know if you had the right person when you caught them, besides the obvious thing, like branded cattle?

A. If a man didn't look like he belonged where he was.

Q. What do you mean?

A. We tried to identify him, if he didn't look like he belonged on the land.

Q. How did you identify someone properly?

A. We'd usually take him back to the farm or the town and have him identified.

Q. By the people who saw the crime?

A, Yes.

Q. How did you know if you caught all of the people involved.

A. We always looked for the other fellow. Where there's one snake in the grass, there's usually another one too. We were always careful. When we went into a town we always looked up the local sheriff first, so he'd know who we were and what we were doing.

Q. I forgot to ask you before, did you carry a knife?

A. Sure, we always carried a knife. Only used it for dressing game and eating though.

Q. Why is that?

A. We never let anyone get close enough to have to use a knife. Tried not to anyway, although I got cut bad in the hand once.

Q. So you never used a knife for fighting?

A. No, we used our guns. I used my knife for eating. I still eat with a knife. Can't break a habit, I guess.

Q. Did you have a particular name for a knife? Did you call it a Bowie knife?

A. Nah, just a hunting knife. Usually a blade about 5 inches long.

Q. Can you remember any particular incident that you were involved in with Frank James?

A. No, but I can tell you a story about Frank James. It's second hand from him. One time they were riding across country and stopped at a farmhouse to put up for the night. The woman who had the place was a widow, with kids, and she was be-

Continued on page 214

Pat Garrett

The Man Who Shot Billy the Kid.

By Robert E. NcNellis

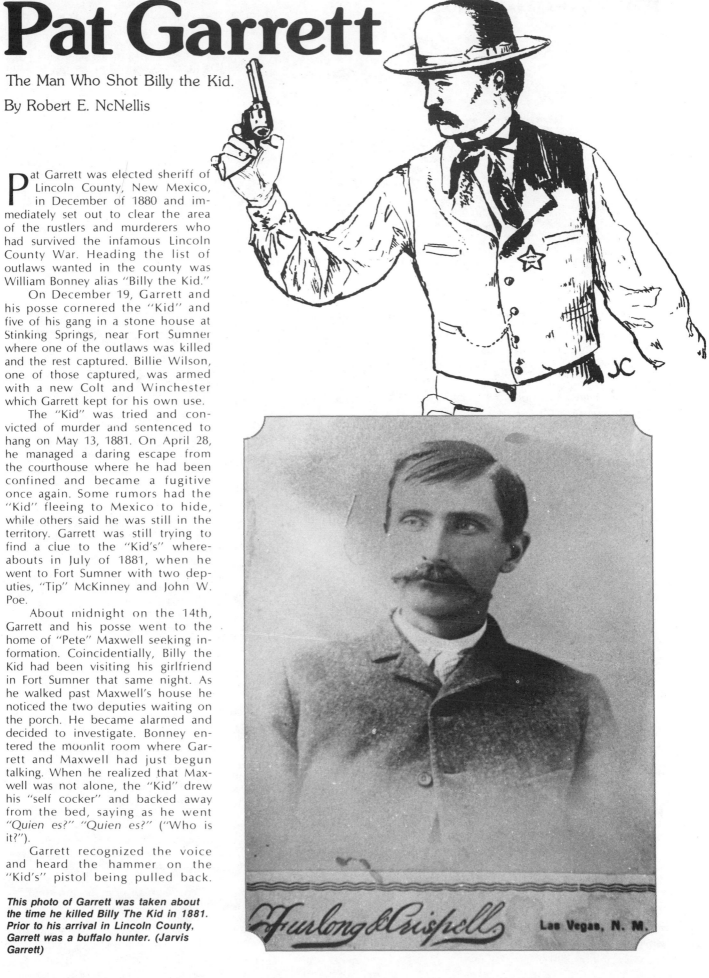

Pat Garrett was elected sheriff of Lincoln County, New Mexico, in December of 1880 and immediately set out to clear the area of the rustlers and murderers who had survived the infamous Lincoln County War. Heading the list of outlaws wanted in the county was William Bonney alias "Billy the Kid."

On December 19, Garrett and his posse cornered the "Kid" and five of his gang in a stone house at Stinking Springs, near Fort Sumner where one of the outlaws was killed and the rest captured. Billie Wilson, one of those captured, was armed with a new Colt and Winchester which Garrett kept for his own use.

The "Kid" was tried and convicted of murder and sentenced to hang on May 13, 1881. On April 28, he managed a daring escape from the courthouse where he had been confined and became a fugitive once again. Some rumors had the "Kid" fleeing to Mexico to hide, while others said he was still in the territory. Garrett was still trying to find a clue to the "Kid's" whereabouts in July of 1881, when he went to Fort Sumner with two deputies, "Tip" McKinney and John W. Poe.

About midnight on the 14th, Garrett and his posse went to the home of "Pete" Maxwell seeking information. Coincidentially, Billy the Kid had been visiting his girlfriend in Fort Sumner that same night. As he walked past Maxwell's house he noticed the two deputies waiting on the porch. He became alarmed and decided to investigate. Bonney entered the moonlit room where Garrett and Maxwell had just begun talking. When he realized that Maxwell was not alone, the "Kid" drew his "self cocker" and backed away from the bed, saying as he went *"Quien es?" "Quien es?"* ("Who is it?").

Garrett recognized the voice and heard the hammer on the "Kid's" pistol being pulled back.

This photo of Garrett was taken about the time he killed Billy The Kid in 1881. Prior to his arrival in Lincoln County, Garrett was a buffalo hunter. (Jarvis Garrett)

Furlong & Crispell   Las Vegas, N. M.

Pat Garrett

This collection of Garrett memorabilia includes a pair of presentation pocket watches and the .44-40 Colt Single Action, SN 55093, and holster used in the Billy The Kid shooting. (Jarvis Garrett).

Realizing that he was only a few feet away from an armed and dangerous murderer with a loaded gun in his hand, Garrett took the only rational course of action. He fired in the direction of the voice. The shot hit the "Kid" in the heart, killing him instantly.

The "Dime Novelists" got ahold of the story and profited greatly by lauding the "Kid" as a heroic victim and condeming Garrett's action as unfair! The true injustice, however, was their treatment of Garrett, since any lawman would have taken the same action were he confronted by an armed escaped killer.

That night in July of 1881, brought instant fame to Pat Garrett and he became the best known southwestener of his era. He was at times respected, at times hated, but always controversial. The people of Lincoln were grateful for his actions in ridding the Territory of William Bonney and showered Garrett with all types of gifts and monies. Two watches presented to him during this time were: An Elgin serial number 637135 inscribed, "FROM GRATEFUL CITIZENS OF LINCOLN COUNTY TO PAT GARRETT, SEPTEMBER 1881" and an American watch, serial number 646192 which is inscribed, "SHERIFF PAT GARRETT FROM 3 CITIZENS OF LINCOLN N.M.". It is obvious from these gifts and gratuities that Pat Garrett's actions were justified in the eyes of most citizen's of the New Mexico Territory.

The gun that Pat Garrett used to kill Billy the Kid is one of the most desirable pieces of Western Ameri-

Pat Garrett's youngest son, Jarvis, holds his father's .30-40 M-1895 Winchester. The lawman used this rifle during hunting trips into the mountains near his Las Cruces, New Mexico, ranch.

cana in existence, so it is not surprising that many guns have claimed to be the one used on July 14, 1881. One Colt .45, Single Action Army bearing the serial number 139345 has been reputed to be the gun Garrett used on the "Kid." An old-timer named Fred Sutton claimed that Garrett had sent him the gun on January 12, 1902 from Las Cruces, New Mexico. There are many holes in this story. Colt did not make this gun until 1891, ten years after the "Kid's" death, and papers still in the Garrett family show that Pat was in El Paso, Texas (not Las Cruces) on

January 12, 1902. By any stretch of the imagination this could not have possibly been the gun that killed "Billy the Kid."

The gun that actually killed the outlaw reposes in a bank vault along with other guns and personal possessions of Pat Garrett and belongs to his youngest son Jarvis. This was the Colt that Pat Garrett took along with the 1873 Winchester from Billie Wilson in December of 1880 when he was captured by Garrett's posse. It is ironic that the "Kid" was killed with the same gun that had belonged to his outlaw companion. Garrett had liked the guns that Wilson surrendered because they fired the same ammunition, .44-40 and they were new. The Colt that Billie Wilson turned over bears the serial number 55093 and the Winchester has the serial number 4762. Pat Garrett used them until about 1900.

In 1906, Garrett left three guns with his friend Tom Powers, the owner of the Coney Island Saloon in El Paso. These were to be included in a display there along with other guns of historic interest. When Powers died in 1930, Garrett's widow sued his estate for possession of these guns. Those in question were the Colt, serial number 55093, the 1873 Winchester, serial number 47629, and a Colt "Thunderer" bearing the serial number 138671.

It was not known with any certainty whether Pat Garrett had sold the guns to Powers or simply loaned them for exhibition. Based on the testimony of Ed Warren, an old Powers employee, the Colt single action, serial number 55093, was awarded personally to Mrs. Pat Garrett in 1933. The gun that killed the "Kid" was therefore returned to it's rightful place in the Garrett family. The balance of Power's collection, including the Winchester and the "Thunderer", was sold in 1936 to J. W. Johnson for the token sum of $200. The facts concerning the three guns are outlined in a letter written by Pat Garrett in 1906 which is in the probate file of Tom Powers located in the records of El Paso County, Texas.

Another sidelight into the guns of Pat Garrett occured early in the 1900s when Billie Wilson, who was by then a respected Texas sheriff, came to El Paso and identified his former guns for Garrett and Powers. Garrett and Wilson went to the Coney Island where the guns were taken down, examined, and then returned in their honored place over the bar.

The Colt that killed "Billy the Kid" is in good shape today, although no original finish remains and scattered pitting is visible. It was shipped from the Colt factory on April 22, 1880 to B. Kittridge and Company of Cincinnati, Ohio. The Winchester 1873 carbine was shipped from the factory on March 15, 1880, but no records remain as to where it was sent. The Winchester is in about the same condition as the Colt, showing the same light pitting. The forearm is worn from having been carried for many years in a saddle scabbard. Both guns show heavy use and testify to Pat Garrett's reliance on them during many years as a lawman. It is not known where Billie Wilson got the guns, but since Kittridge did business all over the West, it might be assumed that they were acquired in New Mexico or Texas.

Before his arrival in Lincoln

is very worn. It remains with his descendants.

After the death of the "Kid," Garrett remained in the sheriff's office just a little over a year. He chose not to run again in 1882 and retired to his ranch in Lincoln County. His life as a rancher was short-lived; however, as he was needed in Texas. On March 10, 1884, Garrett was appointed a lieutenant in the Texas Rangers by Governor John Ireland. The governor felt that Garrett could clear the Texas Panhandle of the outlaws operating there and make the area safe for the homesteaders who were beginning to arrive. Garrett's commission as a Ranger is very curious in that the rank of major was originally placed on the document, then crossed out and the rank of lieutenant substituted.

acre ranch near Roswell. His visions of irrigating the Pecos Valley soon led to the formation of a company dedicated to building canals for carrying water to the farms in the area. But lack of capital caused the company to fail. Besides his ranching and irrigation interests, Garrett owned a livery stable and a stage line in Eddy (now Carlsbad), New Mexico. It was about this time that Garrett recieved a Hopkins and Allen .32 rimfire pistol bearing the serial number 3164, with "PATRICK FLOYD GARRETT" engraved on the barrel. This pistol is also a family keepsake.

Pat Garrett wanted very much to be the first sheriff of the newly-formed County of Chaves, New Mexico, but when he ran for that office in 1890 he was defeated. Gar-

Garret used these arms during various time in his career, (t-b); 73 Winchester taken from outlaw Billie Wilson in 1880; Colt .41 M-1892 revolver presented to Garrett by friends in Dona Ana County; .32 RF Hopkins & Allen engraved "PATRICK FLOYD GARRETT" on barrel; Smith & Wesson .38 New Departure revolver. (Jarvis Garrett)

County in 1878, Pat Garrett was a buffalo hunter and operated out of Fort Griffin, Texas. The whereabouts of the gun that he used in this business is not known today, but Garrett always selected a Winchester over the more popular single-shot Sharps because of its rapidity of fire. It is known that he purchased a Winchester from Frank Conrad's store in Fort Griffin and used it on the buffalo range. It was probably a Model 1876 Winchester since many of them were chambered for the powerful .45-75 cartridge. An 1873 Model Winchester, in a .44-40 caliber, would have been a bit light for the big buffalo at long range. Another gun that he owned and probably carried during the buffalo days is a Smith & Wesson 3rd Model .44 caliber Russian, having the serial number 1096. This old Smith and Wesson was made in 1874 and its condition

Since the commander of the Frontier Battalion is the only major in the Rangers, was the slip of the pen just a mistake, or perhaps did the governor have bigger plans for Garrett? As a Ranger, Garrett cleared out most of the rustlers and outlaws that operated in the Panhandle area. It is thought that during this period, he was given a .41 Forehand and Wadsworth revolver bearing the serial number 4318. This gun is inscribed "Pat F. Garrett" on the backstrap and also remains in family hands.

In 1885, Garrett returned to New Mexico, settling on an 1800

rett subsequently moved to Uvalde, Texas.

These years in Uvalde were the happiest of his life. The family was content, and he devoted himself to raising horses. Garrett became a well-known figure at race tracks throughout the Southwest and Louisana. His horses were among the best in the country. It was about this time that Garrett was given a cased Merwin and Hulbert revolver bearing the serial number 16648. The gun is .38 caliber, silver-plated, with the ivory grips and the lid of the case marked "PAT F. GARRETT." Another momento of his Uvalde

Pat Garrett

days is an Illinois watch, serial number 330804 and inscribed "CAPTAIN PAT GARRETT-UVALDE, TEXAS."

In February of 1896 an event occured that was to have a profound effect on the life of Pat Garrett. This was the murder of Albert Fountain and his son, Henry, in the White Sands of southern New Mexico. Immediately, Governor Thornton requested that Garrett return to the Territory and aid in solving the murder. Garrett agreed and worked on the Fountain case, first as a de-

Garrett's cased .44 Merwin & Hulbert Pocket Army revolver, SN 16648, is silver plated and has ivory grips. The grips and case are marked with the owner's name. The gun was presented to the lawman around 1891.

tective and later as the sheriff of Dona Ana County.

His friends in the county presented him with a pistol, a Colt D.A. .41 bearing the serial number 71517. The pistol is nickel-plated, has checkered wooden stocks and the backstrap is inscribed, "FOR SHERIFF PAT GARRETT-APRIL 29th, 1896". The gun was shipped from the factory on January 29, 1896 to E.C. Meacham Arms Company of St. Louis, Missouri. Another gun that Garrett acquired at this time was an American Arms D.A. .38, serial number 3419, finished in nickel and having "P.F.G." engraved on its butt. At the outset of the Fountain murder investigation, Fountain's Army National Guard unit presented Garrett with an Elgin watch, serial number 2659472 inscribed, "PAT GARRETT FROM THE MESILLA SCOUTS."

After three years Garrett was fi-

nally able to accumulate enough evidence to bring the suspected murderers to trial. But when they were aquitted, Garrett resigned in frustration.

Upon his resignation Pat Garrett again became a private citizen and retired to a ranch he had purchased near Las Cruces, New Mexico. There he raised horses and cattle and engaged in mining ventures in the area. On April 24, 1900 the Winchester Company shipped a rifle that was to become the property of Pat Garrett. The gun is a model 1895 lever action in .30-40 caliber, which carries the serial number 25530. A small golden oval is attached to the right side of the stock and is inscribed, "PAT GARRETT-LAS CRUCES." Garrett used this gun during hunting trips into the mountains near his ranch. This gun retains 80 percent of its original blue, attesting to the fact that it was hardly used.

Pat Garrett had enemies in Dona

Ana County and for self-protection he was always armed. One gun that he carried in a "hip pocket" holster is a Smith & Wesson Safety Hammerless serial number 140122. The gun is blue and has black rubber stocks. The trigger-guard is engraved "P.F.G." It was shipped from the factory on May 14, 1901, and since it was small and lightweight, Garrett kept it with him for many years.

On December 20, 1901, President Theodore Roosevelt appointed Pat Garrett to the post of Collector of Customs at El Paso, Texas. Garrett served in that post for three stormy years. His firm and honest handling of the Customs House and his refusal to lower the duties on cattle imported from Mexico made him numerous enemies. These adversaries vainly attempted to have him removed from office. On the other hand, these same qualities earned him many loyal friends. As a token of their respect, several of them ordered a pistol for him in 1903. It was a Colt "Thunderer" .41 caliber, double-action with the serial number 138671. The gun is engraved, silver-and-gold plated, and the stocks are made from solid silver. The backstrap is engraved, "PAT F. GARRETT FROM HIS EL PASO FRIENDS." The right grip is inscribed, "CUSTOMS COLLECTOR," and the left grip is marked to commemorate his areas of public service, "LINCOLN, DONA ANA, EL PASO." The gun was originally shipped to M. Hartley and Company on Oc-

This .41 Colt "Thunderer," SN 138671, was presented to Garrett when he was a customs collector in 1903. The silver grips are engraved "CUSTOMS COLLECTOR" and "LINCOLN, DONA ANA, EL PASO" is inscribed "PAT. F. GARRETT FROM HIS EL PASO FRIENDS." (Jarvis Garrett)

Garrett posed for this portrait in 1903 while he was a customs collector at El Paso, Texas. (Jarvis Garrett)

This Smith & Wesson .44 Russian, SN 1096, was used by Garrett while he was a buffalo hunter. It surmounts his commission as a lieutenant in the Texas Rangers. (Jarvis Garrett).

tober 29, 1902 and it is believed that the engraving, plating, and stocks were added by this firm on special order.

In 1906 Pat Garrett again retired to his ranch near Las Cruces. On February 29, 1908, while he was driving his wagon to town, Pat Garrett was fatally shot in the back of the head. A cowboy named Wayne Brazel, who had been quarreling with Garrett over a land lease, confessed to the murder but was later acquitted. Brazel claimed that Garrett was reaching for his folding Burgess shotgun and that he had shot in self-defense. Many people feel that Brazel was not the murderer and only took the blame for someone else.

At least one historian has made a good case for the theory that a hired killer was brought in to assasinate Garrett because he was very close to solving the still unresolved Fountain murder case. Pat Garrett's son Jarvis, however, believes that a man named Carl Adamson, a passenger in the buckboard that day, actually was the murderer. As for the shotgun that was found still in its case next to Garrett's body that day, it was the folding Burgess that Brazel described.

The weapons herein described are but a token of the total once owned and used by this famous lawman. Even so, one is able to grasp the importance of these weapons in the hands of Garrett. Working together they earned an acknowledged share in the settling of the West.

The author wishes to thank Jarvis P. Garrett for the opportunity to photograph and examine the possessions of his father, Pat F. Garrett.

1874 Sharps Buffalo Gun

By Phil Spangenberger

The big single-shot Sharps rifles were among the most accurate arms ever produced. This .45 cal. 1874 Sporting Rifle was made between 1876 and 1881 and is of the type shipped to Meacham Arms Co., of St. Louis, Mo., suppliers to the buffalo hunting industry. (Author's collection)

Using the double-set triggers, the Sharps is capable of pinpoint accuracy at several hundred yards. It is an easy gun to operate, enjoyable to shoot, and was a favorite on the frontier.

The Sharps "Old Reliable" was a favorite of buffalo hunters and gunfighters alike due to its long-range capabilities. Revolver is the .44 S&W Russian model.

Probably no gun ever made can equal the record that the big "Buffalo" Sharps rifles have. They account for more one-shot kills than any other arm known. In the old days, they were put to use as manhunting guns as well as for big game animals. Billy Dixon made his famous 1500-yard shot which dropped an Indian at the battle of Adobe Walls, using a .50 caliber Sharps. There are many recorded accounts of the old hide hunters killing 54 buffalo with 54 cartridges, 59 buffalo while only using 62 cartridges, and of killing 100 or more of the shaggy brutes in a single day, all using Sharps rifles. Many gunfighters, having been buffalo hunters at one time, had Sharps rifles in their arsenal. They knew they could rely on this big rifle for any long-range shooting that might be necessary.

The Sharps rifles were so highly thought of by hunters and fighting men alike that they were referred to as "Old Reliable." Sometime around 1876, the company itself began stamping the barrels of their rifles with this popular nickname.

The "Buffalo" Sharps were most popular in .40-bottleneck, .44, .45 and .50 caliber. The 1874 Sporting Rifle in .45 caliber was one of the more popular of the big Sharps rifles, and accounted for a fair portion of the famous rifle company's enviable record.

The '74 Sporter was generally ordered with double set-triggers, which aided the hunters greatly when using the cross-sticks method of shooting. It used a variety of loads ranging from 90 to 120 grains of black powder along with a choice of slugs from 350-grain "Express" to a 550-grain bullet. The rifle sold for under $50 in the late '70s and early '80s.

I used my own 1874 "Old Reliable" Sharps for this shooting impression. The 2⅞-inch casings came from RCBS, Inc., in a 3¼-inch length and were trimmed down to the proper size. Using the 100-grain charge of FFg black powder with a 430-grain bullet produced some very pleasurable shooting. Accuracy is almost taken for granted with one of these big guns; 3-inch groups are not difficult at 200 yards from a rest and off-hand shooting gives very satisfactory results. Loading is simply accomplished by dropping the block and pushing the mammoth cartridge along the wide groove at the breech. When the breech is opened after firing, the expended casing is ejected quickly and away from the working area. The double set-trigger can be set for just the thought of a touch if need be, and when used, the utmost care must be taken to avoid a premature discharge from an itchy finger. Recoil is as would be expected in any large calibered black powder rifle. A comfortable pushing sensation that lets you know that you are handling a powerful firearm.

The Sharps rifle is one of the most pleasurable guns that I know of to shoot. It is too bad that nobody has come out with a replica of these old "Buffalo" guns.

Henry Starr

"Thumbs Up and Stand Ready!"

By Lee Adelsbach

Starr's career as an outlaw spanned a period of 27 years. This portrait is from his early days of banditry. (Oklahoma Historical Society)

The bank, train and store robbery career of Henry Starr came to its end on February 18, 1921. Starr's career was the longest of any of the outlaws of his or his parent's generation. It spanned a period of 27 years, although 15 of those years were spent in prisons. He was pardoned or paroled by three governors and was even given a pardon by a president.

Henry was born near Fort Gibson in the Indian Territory on December 2, 1873. His mother was the highly respected half-Irish daughter of a white man, Sterling Scott. By his own statement, his mother worked to bring him up well.

His father was George "Hop" Starr, son of a notorious Cherokee outlaw.

Starr was a well-educated man for his time although he only attended formal school for about 2 ½ years starting at the age of 8, and leaving the Indian School at the age of 11 when, according to his judgment, he was in the sixth grade. He left school due to his father's illness, and continued his education while on the scout. He read the classics even then, as he carried Shakespeare and others in his saddlebags.

In 1888 Henry went to work on the Half-Circle Box Ranch and stayed there until he got into a spat with another man who was working for the same boss, James S. Todd.

This problem came about when Henry used the man's horse and rode him hard to turn back some stock that was straying. The man caught Starr with his sweaty horse and was furious. After this episode, Henry went to work for the Open A Ranch herding steers.

In the fall of 1890, the Open A had shipped all of their steers and Starr went to work for the Roberts Brothers on their small spread near the Open A. He, along with Bill Doolin and his boys, were some of the few badmen of the times who were actually working cowboys, while others were mainly just drifters. While working on the Roberts spread, Starr was again arrested, this time for horse stealing. He had picked up a stray and the horse's owner, Charles Eaton, had even offered to pay Henry for taking care of the horse when he came after the animal in October of '91. In December Henry was arrested on a warrant sworn by Eaton, and was taken to the Fort Smith jail. Later Eaton admitted that Starr had not stolen the horse and Starr was freed.

Henry had bad feelings from this episode and decided to go on the scout. In the *Wichita Eagle* series, Starr said, "My resolve being taken, I lost no time, for in my chosen path, as in all others, delays are dangerous. I was accompanied by but two companions when I last turned my first trick and faced the wilderness—a pariah of civilization." The companions were known as Ed Newcome and Jesse Jackson.

This threesome, in late July of 1892 when Starr was 19 years old, hit the Missouri-Pacific Station at Nowata. There was a small group in the station, including the railroad's auditor. Starr and his companions walked in and put their guns on the men in the station and there came the words that were to be Henry Starr's trademark for the rest of his outlaw career, "Thumbs up and

Henry Starr

Starr posed for this picture outside the Chandler Jail in 1915, shortly after the unsuccessful double bank job at Stroud, Oklahoma. At the time he was still recovering from his leg wound received from 17-year-old Paul Curry's .30-30 "hog gun." (Oklahoma Historical Society)

stand ready." This job brought $1700 to the bandits' pockets.

During his escape attempt Henry's horse ran into a barbwire fence. He left the horse and continued on foot. The next morning he went back to look for the horse which had gone to a nearby house. The horse was cut badly and the farmer had taken the saddle to Nowata. Not long after this Starr was arrested and taken to Fort Smith.

He pleaded not guilty when arraigned. Chief Harris of the Cherokee nation, E. E. Starr who was treasurer of the tribe and Ridge Paschal, an attorney of Cherokee blood, stood bail for Henry. Again, to quote from Starr's own statement of his feelings, "and with but a few days loss I was back again on my

own prairies, chuckling at the ease of my release."

By the time of his trial date, Henry Starr had been joined by a "catch pole" deputy marshal named Milo Creekmoore who had decided it was easier to join Starr than to trap him. Together they turned a couple of tricks. There was an "old-timer" who said that "all Indians

Starr's Model 8 .35 caliber Remington that he used in the Stroud robbery. There are four notches in the stock. A note on the picture says four men were killed with this gun; however, it is known that Starr actually killed only one man. (Courtesy Mr. Glenn Shirley)

Colt Officer's Model .38 Special given by Starr to H. S. Holliday, special officer with the Kansas City Southern Railroad after Holliday arrested and released Starr at Lake Charles, Louisiana. (Courtesy J. M. Davis Gun Museum, Claremore, Oklahoma)

were natural born thieves". They relieved him of two of his best horses and his only saddle—farther down the road they stole another saddle.

They stayed all night at a friend's house and the friend told Henry that he had put $300 in a store at Lenapah, a small railroad town. They only had an "old white-handled .45 and three cartridges" between them. It is probably safe to assume that this old .45 was an ivory stocked Colt single action Army. With this armament they relieved the store of the farmer's hog money.

After this job they rode about 60 miles into the Osage Country. Here they got one of Starr's friends to buy them a Winchester Model 86 in .38-56 and a new revolver each

and plenty of ammunition. Starr bought a new Cheyenne saddle from a cowboy. They turned the stolen horses loose and bought new ones. A few days after Starr's trial date, he and Creekmore hit Carter's Store at Sequoyah, Cherokee Nation for $180. While on the move they stopped at the home of Frank Cheney, whom Starr had not met before. Cheney later became one of Starr's men and made a fair reputation for himself.

With Starr's failure to appear at Fort Smith for his trial, and the forfeiting of their $2000 bond, his benefactors offered a reward for his capture. At the same time the U. S. Commissioner issued a warrant. It was this warrant that almost cost Starr a trip up the gallows stairs. An express company detective, Henry C. Dickey and a former deputy marshal, Floyd Wilson, set out after Starr. Wilson, as a marshal, had a reputation for being a "tough, dogged manhunter," he was also ill-tempered and quick to shoot. At one time he had often used Bob Dalton as his posse, before Dalton's turn to outlawry.

Wilson got jerky and didn't wait for Dickey when Starr was located. He rode after Starr in an opening on Wolf Creek. Starr got off his horse with his rifle in his hand upon seeing Wilson. The lawman stopped, facing Starr with about 30 yards separating them. He ordered Starr to surrender and the wanted man tried to "work away." Wilson rode up to

within 25 or 30 feet of Starr saying, "Hold up! I have a warrant for you." "You hold up!" was Starr's reply as he made no move to get away.

Wilson jumped from his horse and fired, missing Starr. Henry, who had been standing holding his rifle with the muzzle pointed down, returned the fire. He continued to fire rapidly, and Wilson, wounded, went down. His rifle jammed, and he dropped it and reached for his revolver. Starr fired two more shots as Wilson sank to the ground. The outlaw had been advancing during this entire shoot-out, and he fired a final bullet into Wilson's heart from so close that the muzzle flash actually scorched Wilson's clothing. Both horses had been frightened by the shooting but Starr caught Wilson's horse and left the scene on the fly.

Starr was able to stay out of the law's grasp by having a thorough knowledge of the country and many friends who put him up and shielded him from the law. Starr remained loyal and faithful to such friends as these. Starr was not a killer although he was a bandit,

Frank Cheney re-entered Henry's life as the first member of the new gang. Just to "keep in shape," while waiting for the gang to fill out, they hit the little town of Choteau in late January. They rode in to rob the 8 o'clock northbound, but arrived as the train was leaving the station. Alternately they held up the agent and four passengers that

had gotten off the train and picked up $180 here. The group then hit Haden's Store which did most of the banking for the cattlemen and usually had $5000 or $6000 on hand. Unfortunately for the bandits, the clerk had taken the money to the bank in Vanita the previous day. Starr smashed out the window, cussed the clerk and they left with $390. Their next job was the town of Inola on the Missouri-Pacific line where they picked up $220 and a watch. Cheney then returned home and resumed his farmer's role, and Starr, who did not intend to be seen around Cheney's, moved north through the Verdigris bottoms.

Starr became more contemptuous of the marshals with his increasing experience. Stories began to spread that he wore a steel breast plate and some person claimed that he had seen the breast plate with bullet marks on it. This kind of talk along with Starr's extreme accuracy with any type of arm tended to dissuade many a marshal and detective. It was claimed by one man that he had seen Starr kill a coyote on the run at 685 yards with a rifle. Starr claimed this demonstration took place at a friend's home with several other witnesses present. He also claimed that at this same show he "shot a rabbit dead at 150 yards on the run."

In March of '93, he and Cheney started to plan a bank job—Henry's

first true bank robbery. On March 27th, they hit the Caney Valley Bank in Caney, Kansas. Although they both had fine horses they bought two common cow ponies, and they hid good horses about 20 miles below the Kansas border and took the ponies to make their first run after the holdup. They each had two rifles (Winchesters by Starr's account) and two revolvers. They hid their rifles about two miles from town and pulled the job with revolvers.

During the robbery they found a hidden Winchester belonging to the bank and took two revolvers from the clerk who had them hanging under the counter. The robbery went smoothly and after the money was sacked up, they left, using the bank's rifle to cover three men coming from the livery stable after stopping them with the familiar Starr "Hold up your thumbs." They got on their horses and rode to where their rifles were hidden and bent the barrel of the bank's rifle over a fence post, picked up their own rifles and were on their way to pick up their good horses. The robbery was completed with no one killed or even wounded. They had scooped up a lot of bills, but were disappointed with their take when they counted only $4900. The clerk had hidden the large bills behind a pile of ledgers and the hidden monies that the robbers missed amounted to $16,000.

The success of the Caney job led to the organization of a full-fledged bandit gang. The gang consisted of Starr, with Frank Cheney, 35, as his lieutenant, and Bud Tyler, age 30, Hank Watt, 35, Link Cumplin, 30, Happy Jack, 27, and Kid Wilson, 19. This bandit gang set off for their first job well equipped. "To show our contempt for the dinky deputy marshals, we fitted out a chuck and ammunition wagon, and as Tyler was the weakest at arms, we made him a teamster."

The gang's first job was the robbery of a southbound passenger train of the Missouri, Kansas and Texas Railroad. They hit this train at Pryor Creek and they made no attempt at hiding their identity by wearing masks. They took $6000 and a consignment of unset diamonds from the express car and the passengers. "No one was hurt, although we did a lot of firing as a means of intimidation." was Starr's statement in his own story.

The crew rode back to the area of Nowata. Here they put on a show of nerve for their "farmer friends." "We all were superbly mounted on well-bred horses and cowboy saddles. We wore spurs and each man carried a Winchester Model 86 of large caliber and two Colts in fine wide leather belts. Instead of form-

This Colt Single Action Army revolver in .41 cal. belonged to Henry Starr. It has a 4¾-inch barrel and is Serial No. 148049. It was originally shipped from the Colt factory in 1892 to E. C. Meacham Arms Company in St. Louis Mo., a large gun wholesaler of the period. (Courtesy Greenleaf's Opals and Antiques, Rosamond, Calif.)

ing a line like the cavalry, we formed a fan shape; each man on the outside was to begin shooting always at the extreme right or left, and the center to center; this was done to keep two or more from firing at the same target, if attacked. We were shooting at least a hundred bullets a day each, to keep in trim." The large caliber Model '86s

Henry Starr

were undoubtedly Winchesters, either .45-70 or .45-90. These were the more common large calibers in the Model '86, although Winchester did make a .50-110 Express model.

The next job was Bentonville, Arkansas. Starr's target was the People's Bank, one of the richest banks in the area. They "hired a buggy in Bentonville the night before the robbery to transport our rifles across this farming district without attracting attention." The date of this robbery was June 5, 1893.

The bank was hit at 2:30 p.m., the currency and gold amounting to $11,000 was put into one bag and the silver into another. The towns-

der his pillow but offered no resistance. At the hotel after awakening Mrs. Jackson, the police found $1600 in currency, $500 in gold and

Henry Starr lived and died by the gun. Bottom: One of his favorite arms was the Model 1886 Winchester in .38-56 caliber. Top: His end was brought about by a 60-year-old bank clerk using a .38-40 caliber Model 1873 Winchester. (Sotheby Parke-Bernet, Los Angeles, Calif.)

defense. Claiming that he did not know Wilson had a warrant for his arrest and that he did not fire until fired upon. This defense did not work in Judge Isaac Parker's Court, and the "hanging judge" of Fort Smith sentenced him to hang "on Tuesday, February 20, A.D. 1894, between the hours of 9 o'clock in the forenoon and 5 o'clock in the afternoon of the same day."

The sentence was appealed and

people realized their bank was being robbed and the alarm spread. The sack containing the silver was given to the bank clerk to carry—he was to be used as a hostage, but the clerk got away in the melee after they left the bank and the silver was lost. Several citizens were wounded and gang member Link Cumplin was wounded several times and had to be helped to mount. The official take, according to the bank's figures, was $11,011.53. The gang broke up after getting away, but the Bentonville job was to haunt Henry Starr to his dying day, as the State of Arizona kept the warrant out for him until after his death.

Starr and Kid Wilson were both arrested in Colorado Springs after Starr was recognized by a Fort Smith storekeeper who was in Colorado Springs on business and was staying at the same hotel. Starr had 17-year-old May Morrison with him and they had registered as Frank and Mary Jackson of Joplin, Missouri. Feuerstine, the storekeeper, reported the presence of Starr to Police Chief Dana who later, along with a Captain J.W. Gathright, took Starr by surprise and pinioned his arms. Detective Atkinson and some others came in and Starr was relieved of a ".45 Colt revolver concealed under his coat."

Kid Wilson was arrested in a bawdy house in Colorado City. He was lying in bed with a revolver un-

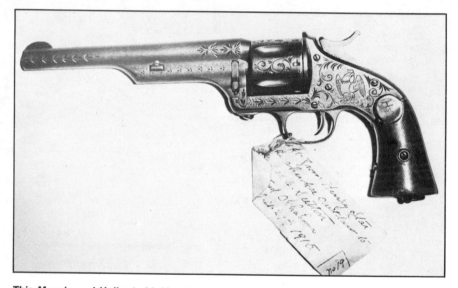

This Merwin and Hulbert .44-40 cal. revolver, Serial No. 8686, was reportedly owned by Henry Starr. It is engraved with the Mexican crest and bears the letter H and a star design on the hard rubber grips. (Courtesy Ron Terrell)

a pearl-handled .38 revolver. After these arrests, while Starr and Wilson were being transported to Fort Smith, many sensational stories came out about them in the papers.

Starr was indicted for the train robbery at Pryor Creek, the robbery of the Carter Store at Sequoyah and Shufeldt's Store in Lenapah. On August 10, he was arraigned for the murder of Floyd Wilson and his trial set for October 16. Starr and Wilson took part in an abortive jailbreak while in the Fort Smith lockup.

Starr didn't deny killing Wilson, but put his faith in a plea of self-

a stay of execution was granted by the Supreme Court. The sentence was reversed by the Supreme Court on June 7, 1894 and a new trial ordered. Starr was held and retried starting on September 15, 1895 and was again convicted of murder and sentenced to the gallows. The case was appealed and for the second time the conviction was reversed.

Congress took jurisdiction over the Indian Territory and removed the Territory from Parker's control. The Honorable John R. Rogers, a former member of congress, was appointed to fill the place of Judge Parker. He allowed Starr to plead guilty to a charge of manslaughter on October 6, 1897 and in January he was sentenced to three years in the penitentiary at Columbus, Ohio. He drew seven years and seven days

Continued on page 221

John Slaughter

Little Giant with a Sixgun.
By Allen Erwin

John Slaughter never was out of reach of a gun. He was a typical product of a wild turbulent frontier, nurtured by the environment which tests the mettle of the strong and frail, and coddles the brave.

A man of unusual prowess, fitted to the frame of his well formed, but diminutive stature, his life's style was balanced with his keen ability in the handling of firearms. This augmented his power, and made him a man to be reckoned with. These fine and necessary attributes, coupled with good judgement, and an exceedingly cool mind during times of great odds, seemed to spur fate to provide him a long life. For certainly he died with his boots off.

Few men who grew up with the dangers of a wild frontier, had so many close encounters with death, and survived, hardly unscathed. On many occasions while he was sheriff of Cochise County, Arizona, he would take along his wife Viola, in a horse drawn phaeton. As a respected rancher, as well as lawman, it was proper for Mrs. Slaughter to be along, as they often stayed overnight, when the sheriff had lesser duties to perform. It too, was appropriate in keeping up a social rapport, and thus giving the electorate a good feeling of the man they put into office.

Now, even though the mode of transportation may have appeared as somewhat of a display of wealth, Slaughter made certain to off-set such illusions, by bringing along a fine saddle horse, which he kept tied to the rear of the vehicle. The horse remained bridled and saddled, bristling

Slaughter was a man of unusual prowess, with a well-formed but diminutive stature. His life style was balanced with his keen ability in the handling of firearms. Here he is at age 46, while serving as sheriff of Cochise County, Arizona. (Arizona Historical Society)

Slaughter's saddle was always bristling with guns. This photo of him, taken in his later years, reveals a long arm in the scabbard and his pearl-handled single action Colt .45 strapped to the pommel in the same manner as used years before in the fight with cattle rustler Barney Gallagher. (Author's collection)

with guns that protruded from scabbards. He also carried with him a powerful set of binoculars, and should outlaws appear, Slaughter was ready to ride, leaving Viola to push on with the phaeton to a given location.

The movies have created many terms and characters the old west never experienced. Gunslingers, gun-fanners, hired guns and fast-draw artists were not a part of the old west. Fisticuffs were something that mining and lumber camps, or army barracks excelled in, whereas the six-shooter, later refered to as the handgun, firmly

John Slaughter

settled grievances between one another. Often the vigilantes took the law into their own hands to dispatch a horse thief awaiting trail. One's survival became so much in jeopardy, that this was a time when firearms were the main protector of one's family and chattels. But as the west became more and more settled, the role of such peace makers as John Slaughter became an established entity in law enforcement.

When John Slaughter left Texas to settle in Arizona, he was not to receive a pleasant going-away party—Barney Gallagher was to see to that, and it proved to be the gravest mistake of his life. One historian described Gallagher, as a native of Dimmit County, Texas, and a typical oldtime cowboy-type of character. For a time he was revered as a cattleman of high esteem, until he entered the rustling profession. A band of highwaymen known as the Fort Stockton Rustlers had a corner on what seemed to be a lucrative business. The trail drivers were selected as the victims, while the Indians were used as scapegoats. Barney Gallagher was appointed chief of the Fort Stockton Rustlers.

Horsehead's Crossing on the Pecos River was the main focal point of activity. For it was here that the trail

This unique composite illustrates Slaughter's intense interest in firearms. While he is obviously posing as a duck hunter with his M-1887 Winchester lever action 12-gauge shotgun, he is nonetheless prepared for any emergency with his Colt .45 "Peacemaker" worn in cross draw fashion. (Arizona Historical Society)

While Slaughter was deadly with his guns and commanded the respect of good and bad men alike, he was a peaceful family man at heart as evidenced by this frolicking with his grandchildren on a Sunday at his ranch. (Author's collection)

drovers from Texas usually crossed the river with their herds, enroute to New Mexico, Arizona and Colorado. John Slaughter was to use it in the fall of 1876. Gallagher and his gang of rustlers had certain plans about Slaughter and his herd.

The first inkling of Gallagher and John Slaughter ever becoming loggerheads with one another, took place at Jack Harris' saloon in San Antonio, over a poker game. Slaughter came out the winner and Gallagher vowed he would someday even the score. The fact that Slaughter had a herd enroute to John Chisum's South Springs Ranch from the Devil River country in south Texas pleased Gallagher. Slaughter

had already, crossed the river at Horseheads and was well on the way to Chisum's Jingle-bob outfit, before Barney Gallagher and his men tracked him down.

What pursued in the next few days and the final result of the meeting rested upon an ingenious plan of Slaughters in the way of presenting arms.

Barney Gallagher was by no means a coward. Yet it would have been thought he would have given some credence to a man of Slaughter's stamp. It may have been that as chief of the Fort Stockton Rustlers, it would look good if he challenged the likes of John Slaughter. He had men in his crowd who knew of Slaughter's reputation, and in the true traditions of cowboy humor were conducting side-bets as to who would be the victor. Such a grand occasion called for the mob to be whiskied up and feeling in high spirits. By the time they reached the tail end of Slaughters drive, the latter's herd was just ready to leave Chisum's New Mexico headquarters.

As liquor got the best of them, Barney Gallagher was not only boasting of killing Slaughter, but with the help of his men was going to make-off with all of the Slaughter herd. The many Army forts across the southwest, along with Indian reservations were crying out for beef, so a ready market for such a herd would be a most welcome commodity. It was a case of immediate money on the barrelhead. There was no doubt in Barney Gallagher's mind his mission would be a success. To do the necessary negotiations, he had with him a short, sawed-off, double-barrel shotgun, concealed under a three-quarter length coat. He was positive that he would make

mighty short work of his adversary.

Now the time had come for the show-down. The rustlers grouped together and confabbed with their chief. One of them was so brash that he told the rest of them, in front of Gallagher, that if John Slaughter would emerge as the winner, that he (the rustler) would become the proud owner of Barney Gallagher's fine silver-mounted Mexican hat. Gallagher immediately bequeathed it to him. Letting his subordinate know, however, that his boss would be wearing the fine headpiece for a long time to come.

Gallagher ordered one of Slaughter's trail waddies to go fetch Slaughter at the pilot end up front. "Go tell your boss, I'm here to kill the little ratheaded S.O.B.!" Gallagher bellowed, ferociously. The waddie instantly responded. John Slaughter had with him some of the most dangerous desperados in Texas. He was not concerned with their past. He knew they were excellent men with a trail herd, and that in the event of just such an occasion, they would stand by him. So if Gallaghers men had any ideas that a picnic was in store for them, they were badly mistaken. In fact, some of the Fort Stockton Rustlers recognized Slaughter's trail herders immediately.

As soon as Slaughter got the runner's message, he put the spurs to his horse. The animal responded into a steady lope towards Gallagher's band of rustlers. Slaughter grasped the reins in his left hand. His open coat floated rhythmically over the high cantle of his Texas-made stock saddle. The yellow dust of the Pecos sands billowed out behind his cowpony as the distance between the two men shortened. The Fort Stockton Rustlers remained grouped and looked on. Gallagher walked his horse toward Slaughter keeping his shotgun concealed. He awaited Slaughter to get in close range, so he could give him the full brunt of both barrels of buckshot.

Something went wrong with the Gallagher ruse. Slaughter suddenly reined his horse sharply and at the same time his right hand grasped a .45 Colt's pistol. It was discharged the same time as it was pointed. Gallagher's body hit the ground with a thud as his men looked on in disbelief. Only one shot was fired from Slaughter's Peacemaker. The bullet went right through Gallagher's heart.

By this time some of Slaughter's trail-hands had joined in. They rode up to the Gallagher mob and told them to bury Gallagher. Slaughter cussed them out and gave them some good advice, which they took without a murmur. But as soon as Slaughter and his men had returned to the herd, Gallagher's men celebrated by passing the bottle around. The fellow who was bequeathed the fine sombrero was allowed to wear it. He put his own on the dead man's head before they rolled him up in a saddle blanket and buried him. The unmarked grave where Gallagher was laid to rest, almost a century ago, still remains.

Where did John Slaughter come up with the pistol so suddenly? He did not reach for the gun at his side. The holster bearing a pistol could easily be seen as he approached Gallagher. But the gun he used, was strapped to the pommel of the saddle, inches from his right hand. The idea which Slaughter had come up with caught his opponent off-guard. The ingenuity of this very incident was indicative of Slaughter's uncanny character. Never did he take the same trail twice. He was up and dressed at four every morning. By the time the sun was up, Slaughter and his cowboys were busy with the work of the ranch. It was a precaution of not being waylaid. He had many enemies out to get him, but he never gave them an opportunity.

During his lifetime Slaughter accumulated many guns of various caliber rifles, shotguns, and handguns. He had received many of them in the form of gifts from his admirers and close friends. He gave away just as many. He had his favorite weapons and, like his horses and saddles, they were his companions. He kept an abundant supply of cartridges on hand, for he lived in the very heart of Geronimo country. For bird hunting he had shotguns of

John Slaughter

John H. Slaughter in 1907, during the time he was in the Arizona Territorial legislature. (Author's collection)

various gauges. The Henry rifle was probably his favorite gun for long-range firing. The revolver was forever on his person.

Even after he had served his two terms as sheriff of Cochise County, he was commissioned as an officer of the law in one form or other. This gave him the right to make arrests and bear firearms almost anywhere.

John Slaughter had the jail cells well-filled when he was the sheriff of Cochise County. The courthouse was nicknamed, "The Slaughter House" while he held office.

Tombstone had its first breathing spell of violence. A desperado by the

Slaughter served as sheriff of Cochise County, Arizona from 1887 to 1890. During this time he relied heavily on his pearl-handled, engraved Colt Single Action .45 with 5½-inch barrel and a 12-gauge Remington sawed-off shotgun. They are both shown flanking the handcuffs he also used. (Photo from author's collection)

name of "Buckskin" Frank Leslie, surrendered to Slaughter as meek as a lamb after he had committed a couple of murders. He was taken to the Yuma Prison to serve out his time. While Tombstone quieted down, the far reaches of the county experienced depredations and crime, which often took Slaughter to New Mexico to pick up law breakers who had fled Arizona, who were arrested and held to stand trial in Cochise County.

Once a cowman, always a cowman though, and this was uppermost in John Slaughter's way of life. In 1884, he bought the San Bernardino Ranch which straddled both sides of the U.S. and Mexican border. Just south of the Slaughter ranch headquarters, small border markers were erected. There were no fences, and Slaughter enjoyed the freedom of running his livestock in both countries, without any interference. He could speak Spanish as well as English, and many of his helpers were Mexicans.

Augustine Chacon was a Mexican bandit that openly bragged he would kill Slaughter on sight. He would even come to Tombstone and pay him a visit. He was as brash as Barney Gallagher, but twice as dangerous. He once rode with the famous Mexican Border Rurales, so he knew what it was like to serve on both sides of the law. He had murdered and plundered in Arizona and was provided protection by friends across the border. He had laid traps to get Slaughter, but always

Slaughter was very active in community affairs. He is seen second from left at this gathering of cattlemen in Douglas in 1903. His white horse, "Pochie" carries the ever-present armament, probably the M-1887 Winchester shotgun. (Author's collection)

Although Slaughter was an excellent lawman, his real life's pleasure was ranching. In the top photo he (center) inspects a yearling during branding time on his ranch. In the bottom picture he is seen checking out an artesian well on the Slaughter property. (Author's collection)

his ruse had been unsuccessful.

One night while John Slaughter was sheriff, and was at the courthouse in Tombstone, word came that Chacon was only yards away in an arroyo, in a tent. Slaughter had his deputy go to the back of the tent and cause a commotion, while he stood along side the front entrance and waited for Chacon to emerge through the exit. The inside of the tent was visibly lit by a dim-burning kerosene lantern. Slaughter yelled for Chacon to come out with his hands up. Chacon dove out and tripped over a guy wire of the tent. At that moment Slaughter opened up with his shotgun. Chacon was saved from receiving the buckshot by his fall. Slaughter ran in and grabbed the lantern and ran down the arroyo. Chacon had his horse saddled and ready to mount. The late night was

Continued on page 223

Slaughter lived hard, but was also a successful rancher and enjoyed the good outdoor life of the West. Here he sits in the rear seat of his chauffered automobile on the San Bernardino ranch shortly before his death in 1922. (Author's collection)

Melvin Purvis

Flamboyant FBI Gunfighter

By Rick Fines

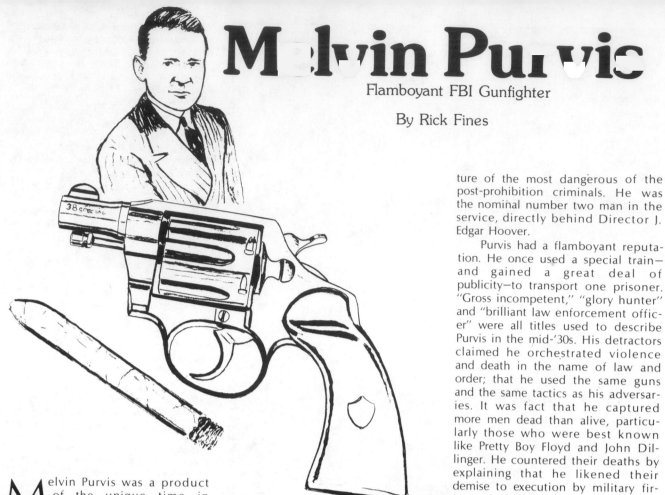

Colt .38 Special Police Positive. As long as they were stock items in police arsenals, they were chosen first along with automatics by Purvis as well as his enemies.

Melvin Purvis was a product of the unique time in which he lived and worked. He was born in Timmonsville, South Carolina, attended school there and went on to the University of South Carolina where he earned a degree in law. For some 20 months, he rather unsuccessfully practiced criminal law in Florence, South Carolina. Purvis became bored with his practice by early 1927 and decided to enter the diplomatic service. He journeyed to Washington and was turned down at the State Department, and subsequently applied for work at the Department of Justice. He was hired as a special agent and progressed rapidly. By the time Melvin Purvis had assumed a post of responsibility, both the F.B.I. and the nation had changed considerably from what they had been in January of 1927, when he took the oath of office.

All during the '20s, when alcohol was not available, the average American subsidized the criminal by buying his liquor and gave tacit approval to the activities of organized crime. The '30s brought the repeal of prohibition and put most of the criminals out of work. The hoods, with no product to sell and no customers, turned to simple extortion, kidnap and general terrorism. The rest of the populace, sobered by the depression, was finally ready to support a real effort to put an end to

the criminals. Local and state agencies had long demonstrated an inability to deal with the problem, so the federal government stepped in. On June 18, 1934, President Roosevelt signed legislation passed by the 73rd Congress, which gave the special agents of the F.B.I. the power to carry a gun and the power to make arrests. The F.B.I. had previously been very limited in scope and had been required to turn prisoners over to the U.S. marshal. Guns had been issued only under dire circumstances. Now the Bureau was a force to be reckoned with.

For almost 2½ of the nearly nine years Melvin Purvis served the F.B.I., he was boss of the Chicago office. At a time when the F.B.I. numbered less than 700 men, Purvis commanded nearly a hundred of them and was directly responsible for the cap-

ture of the most dangerous of the post-prohibition criminals. He was the nominal number two man in the service, directly behind Director J. Edgar Hoover.

Purvis had a flamboyant reputation. He once used a special train—and gained a great deal of publicity—to transport one prisoner. "Gross incompetent," "glory hunter" and "brilliant law enforcement officer" were all titles used to describe Purvis in the mid-'30s. His detractors claimed he orchestrated violence and death in the name of law and order; that he used the same guns and the same tactics as his adversaries. It was fact that he captured more men dead than alive, particularly those who were best known like Pretty Boy Floyd and John Dillinger. He countered their deaths by explaining that he likened their demise to execution by military fir-

ing squad and that certainly the members of a firing squad would never have been considered murderers. The Purvis backers rightly asserted the fact that he got his men—at least eventually—and the detractors said he was little different from the men he hunted. He simply had more resources at his command.

The F.B.I., under Purvis, in Chicago began to use many modern tools of detection and record keeping, but the most often used weapon was still the gun. Radio and many of the gadgets which have been taken for granted for years, were then in very primitive stages and were used simply to aid Purvis in bringing criminals under the guns of his agents. The gun best known and most used by both sides was the Thompson submachine gun. The the '03 Springfields or the .351 Winchester autoloading rifles. The Thompson could certainly do a job on men at close range, but then so did the Winchester '97s with 00-buck. It simply came down to a matter of aesthetics. Once J. Edgar Hoover posed with the Thompson, every county in the country bought some for their sheriff's people to play with and any crook with the his agents or his enemies. The gun looked right, despite the extreme drop of the stock, the fine sight that was useless and the barrel fins that did little. The Thompson looked proper in the way that a full-rigged ship or a 1930 Cadillac V-16 looked proper. One other note of interest was price. By 1934, a new 1928 model with 50-round drum and Cutts Compensator sold for around $300.

The same amount of money would buy something in excess of six Colt 1911 .45 pistols. General Thompson was so succesful in his design of a classic metal sculpture that one of the fringe benefits was the first federal gun laws to control automatic weapons.

The .45 caliber Thompson submachine gun was a favorite of the FBI agents under Purvis. This Model 1921 used either the 20-round straight magazine, or 50 or 100-round drum. (Lisle Reedstrom)

Portrait of Melvin Purvis taken during the height of his career as an FBI agent. Purvis was responsible for the killing of John Dillinger.

Thompson was a curious weapon for the F.B.I. to use and also surprising for the criminal to have so universally adopted. The "Tommy gun" did have firepower, about 800 rounds per minute in the 1921 version; but the firepower was largely noise power. The .45 ACP slugs were not much for tearing through walls or shooting through automobile bodies. The Browning Automatic Rifles the agents hauled around were far better suited to those tasks, as were least amount of respect either bought or stole a Thompson from one of the many police departments who had them neatly racked. A man carrying a Thompson was not to be trifled with. He was either a bad man to be avoided, or he was the law chasing a bad man. There was no doubt about him being a bird hunter or even a no-count armed robber. Even the details on the Thompson were for looks and visual effect. The '21 and the '28 both carried fine Lyman adjustable sights that would have looked at home on a match rifle. It was doubtful that they were used or noticed by Purvis,

The abortive attempt to recapture Dillinger after his break from the Crown Point, Indiana jail was illustrative of the new methods and firepower that Purvis brought to bear on the organized criminal. The excuse Purvis needed to pursue Dillinger was that in the escape from Crown Point, an automobile had been stolen and moved from Crown Point to Wisconsin. A federal crime had been committed and the F.B.I. could act.

It was late afternoon of April 22, 1934 and Purvis was in one of three airplanes loaded with F.B.I. special agents converging on Rhinelander, Wisconsin. A Mr. Voss, via the local U.S. marshal, had been the informant who revealed that Dillinger and five of his associates were holed up at a resort called Little Bohemia. Purvis rounded up every available agent within minutes and obtained clearance for the raid from Washington. Automobile loads of agents started for Rhinelander from both Chicago and St. Paul. Two planes were chartered in Chicago and Purvis arranged for bullet-proof vests, Browning Automatic Rifles, teargas bombs and pistols to be

Melvin Purvis

loaded along with the agents. Additional agents who had flown from St. Paul were already on the ground at Rhinelander when Purvis and the Chicago men arrived. They were absorbed in trying to arrange for automobiles to cover the last 50 miles to Little Bohemia.

Mr. Voss, the original informant, met Purvis at the airport. Voss had been instructed to tuck a handkerchief in his collar so that he would be recognized. He repeated his story of the morning, adding that four women were accompanying the Dillinger gang. A man named Emil Wanatka, Voss' brother-in-law, was the proprietor of Little Bohemia and was being held along with his wife and children by the gang. At this point, the Rhinelander airport was covered with airplanes, serious looking men and many bundles containing Thompsons, BAR's and all manner of ammunition. Purvis, fearing that Dillinger might have lookouts at the airport, threw off the suspicion of the locals when he informed them that all the men, planes and cars were involved in a wedding party.

It was now 6:30pm and it was dark. Purvis had orchestrated an incredible move of men and equipment by the standards of 1934, but he still had one problem—getting the "wedding party" that last 50 miles to Little Bohemia. Voss' wife suddenly appeared and told Purvis that Dillinger was planning to leave right after dinner that night, rather than staying several days as originally planned. Purvis had to work fast. He commandeered the services of a young man named Isidor Tuchalsky to drive him to town. In Rhinelander, it was learned that the local Ford dealer had no cars available to rent for the raid.

Purvis identified himself to Tuchalsky and convinced him to rent his car to the F.B.I.. Four other cars were found, two of which broke down on the trip to the raid. Purvis had spaced the cars at discreet intervals so they would not attract attention. After the breakdowns, the eight agents from the two dead cars rode the remaining distance hanging on to the running boards; half frozen in the cold of the still wintery Wisconsin night. The weapons had been divided so that each car contained a Thompson, a BAR, a Model '97 Winchester trench gun and tear gas equipment.

Voss, who had ridden along to show the way, told Purvis the convoy was nearing Little Bohemia. Purvis halted the column, all lights were turned out and no one was permitted to smoke. The agents and their arsenal stumbled through the darkness and the bitter cold. Two borrowed F.B.I. cars crept, lights out, up the only driveway and pulled across in a V-shape to block sudden exits. The building which housed Dillinger and the gang was about 400 yards down the driveway. Flood-

The notorious John Dillinger's career was brought to an abrupt end by Melvin Purvis and his FBI agents. (FBI photo)

lights illuminated the front of the lodge as the agents stood quietly in the dark and cold making their weapons ready.

Despite the problem with the cars, all of Purvis' careful planning went on as intended. Purvis whispered orders to the agents. They responded at once, but so did a large dog who began to bark like fury. Five men appeared at the front door of the house. Three of them jumped into a coupe parked in front of the door. Purvis shouted, "federal officers!." The agents opened fire on the car at the same time. One of the men in the car jumped out and ran for the woods; the driver was killed instantly. The third man slumped on the running board badly wounded having taken four slugs. Purvis discovered that the three men were neither Dillinger nor members of the gang. They were frightened locals who had been drinking beer at the lodge and blundered into the trap.

From the lodge, a man opened up on Purvis with a machine gun. (the man was later determined to be Baby Face Nelson) Purvis returned the fire with his Thompson, but the

Two views of Purvis' Colt .38 caliber Detective Special that he carried when Dillinger was killed. Custom grips are of a marbleized Bakelite with a gold shield inlay. (Sotheby Parke Bernet, Los Angeles)

weapon jammed. The man ran out the door and headed for the woods. Purvis fired after him with a .45 auto and missed. All the agents were spraying away with BAR's, Thompsons, .351 Winchester autoloaders and 00-buck from the shotguns. Some of the gang were returning the fire. It seemed impossible that the gang could live through the barrage. They all escaped from a rear second story window and made their way through thick brush to a nearby lake and disappeared.

Two agents took Tuchalsky's car, and, in the company of a local constable named Carl Christenson drove to the telephone at the Koerner store, a short distance down the

Purvis ordered the agents to open fire. The front of the auto was hosed down with Thompson fire, but Pat Reilly, a minor member of the gang escaped unhurt with his girlfriend in the riddled car. The car did not get far, but Reilly did. He was out in the fields and made his way back to St. Paul. By morning, Purvis and the other special agents were still on the scene. A local posse wanted to join the fight, but the battle was over. Dillinger and his friends had all gotten away. Purvis had captured the women. J. Edgar Hoover was presented with a petition urging Purvis' ouster in the wake of the Little Bohemia fiasco. Purvis offered to resign, but Hoover

remember that law permitting the F.B.I. to go armed and to make arrests was signed on June 18, 1934. The raid took place on April 22, 1934.)

Purvis continued to employ his tactics of investigation followed by fire power through his career with the F.B.I. He orchestrated the capture and death of Pretty Boy Floyd, Dillinger, the "Terrible Touhys, and many other criminal celebrities of the '30s. After the lead of Purvis and Hoover became the stated policy of the F.B.I., bank robberies, kidnapping and other crimes, over which the bureau had jurisdiction, dropped dramatically.

After resigning from the F.B.I.,

THOMPSON SUBMACHINE GUN MODEL Nos. 28A and 28AC

Selective Action—Single Shots or Bursts of Automatic Firing

LIST PRICES

Each

MODEL 28A—Thompson Submachine Gun complete with Type XX 20-cartridge capacity box magazine.

$200.00

MODEL 28AC — Thompson Submachine Gun, Standard Model, (Vertical Foregrip), complete with one Type XX 20-cartridge capacity box magazine with Cutts Compensator.

$225.00

MODEL 28AC—Thompson Submachine Gun, U. S. Navy Model (Horizontal Foregrip and Sling Strap), complete with one Type XX 20-cartridge capacity box magazine and with Cutts Compensator attached. This model, is used by the U. S. Army and U. S. Navy.

$225.00

road. Baby Face Nelson was waiting for them. Nelson killed Agent Carter Baum and wounded Agent Jay Newman and Christenson. He stole the car in which they had arrived—which happened to be the fastest in the convoy—and took off. The wounded agent emptied a .45 at the moving car with no effect. Purvis ordered the lodge filled with tear gas. After the gas billowed, three women, who had been with Dillinger, offered to surrender if Purvis would stop shooting. He did and they came out. Later that night, a car approached the drive. The driver seemed to sense that something was wrong and began backing rapidly.

Thompson submachine guns were never inexpensive as indicated by this 1936 catalog price listing. (Author's collection)

declined to accept.

The men at Little Bohemia got away that night, but they did not get away for long. The following men of the group died by police gunfire: John Dillinger—tracked down and shot at the Biograph Theatre on July 22, 1934 by Purvis and his men. John Hamilton, an old friend of Dillinger from prison, was shot by police, as were Homer Van Meter and Tommy Carrol. Pat Reilly, the young man who escaped from Purvis, was the only one of the gang to see prison. (As a note of interest,

Purvis returned to the practice of law and prospered. By 1957, he was practicing civil law in Florence, South Carolina. He owned a local radio station, lived on a six acre estate and lived quietly. Movies subsequently made about his life were interesting, but not terribly accurate. Until his death in the late '50s, Purvis was haunted by the rumors that Dillinger was alive; that the man at the Biograph was an imposter. By now the question is academic. Melvin Purvis bridged the gap between the era of the shoot-out and the time of careful, quiet and scientific police work. He perfected the old way and pioneered the new.

Shooting Impression

Thompson Submachine Gun

When the Editorial Staff first began to assemble this book of gunfighters and the tools of their trade, it was agreed that we would be remiss in our duty to firearms collectors if we did not include some of the more modern personalities and guns. Hence, we have expanded the term "Gunfighter" to beyond just the Western era gunslinger, to include Dillinger, his nemisis Melvin Purvis, and the near legendary duo of Bonnie & Clyde.

One commonality in firearms of these gunmen (and gals) was the most devastating weapon of the day—the Thompson Machine Gun.

Since our format includes shooting impressions of various guns used by the gunfighters, a test of the Thompson was considered an absolute must. It's just not the kind of gun available to every gun buff due to the legal restrictions on their possession and use.

Our test "Tommy Gun" is a legal one, a Model of 1928 with vertical forestock and Cutts compensator. We were outfitted with 1000 rounds of .45 ACP reloads and two 30-round magazines, for the three Staff shooters.

The competition was lively to maintain custody of a magazine—the theory being that if the gun couldn't be fired without one, the holder of a magazine was next in line for the gun. Test shooting was conducted at a range which was closed to the public at the time. "Targets" were a dirt embankment and a dry creek bed; however, some clay birds of the skeet/trap variety were used for spot targets.

Firing the Thompson was such a unique experience that this shooting impression had to be one of the staff's highlights in preparing this book. All three writers of the GUNS & AMMO Books group give their particular feelings about it in the accompanying mini stories. **Editors.**

By Jim Woods

Exhilarating is the best one-word description of firing the "Tommy Gun." I sincerely believe that emptying those 30-round magazines, within a couple of seconds, into a dirt bank, or stitching the same load down a dry creek bed, could replace bourbon and branch water as *the* way for a man to unwind at the end of a hard day.

Those of us who earn our daily bread by association with firearms, generally let the job carry over into our leisure time—hunting, competition shooting or casual plinking. We shoot for recreation for the same reasons anyone else does. It's enjoyable, relaxing and satisfying.

But I have rediscovered a truism after shooting the Thompson for the first and only time in my life: The pleasure derived from casual shooting is directly proportional to the speed with which the rounds can be fired off. I say "rediscovered" this truth because my first lesson in this came when I traded my very first gun, a Marlin Model 80C bolt-action, eight-shot, box magazine .22 rifle for a Remington Model 121 pump gun with a long tube magazine. Fast? Why I could pump a chain of slugs out that barrel that must have looked like a solid string of lead to those Kentucky sparrows. Of course, I didn't hit a thing, throwing the slide that fast and hard—but it sure was fun—right up to the instant that I realized that I had shot away a whole afternoon's ration of .22s in but a few minutes.

But it was different with the Thompson. The ammo expense, thankfully, was not out of my pocket, and the opportunity to fire a fully automatic gun seldom comes along. I jumped at the chance, and let me tell you, that chopped-up dirt bank won't give anybody any trouble any more.

Author discovered that the Tommy Gun shootouts of the roaring '20s could have been just good clean fun if real people had not gotten in the way. Firing the Auto Ordinance Model 28 Thompson with Cutts compensator and vertical fore grip was an exciting, probably once-in-a-lifetime experience.

Burt Miller, Vice President of Armalite, Inc., tutors the GUNS & AMMO Books staff in the finer points of the Thompson chopper.

By Garry James

By the time I entered the Army the Thompson submachine gun was considered a military relic. My experience with fully automatic arms was limited to M-60s, M-14E2s and .50 Brownings, but having been brought up with the stories of my elders about how their favorite "Tommy Gun" saved their lives in France, Germany, Guadalcanal, etc., I felt that I had really missed something.

The Thompson is certainly one of America's most romantic firearms. It arrived on the scene just in time for the depression and was used by many different armies during the Second World War.

There are few gun enthusiasts who would not relish firing an original Thompson, but federal regulations have made them taboo items for the average shooter, and when we were offered the opportunity we eagerly accepted.

The Thompson is a comfortable little gun, which is a bit heavier than it looks. The cyclic rate of fire is so low that one can easily fire single shots without moving the selector to semi-automatic.

Naturally the first rounds were taken apprehensively. Having been raised on tales of how the "Tommy Gun" sprays lead all over the landscape, we expected it to handle more like the spastic 7.62 mm M-14E2. Not so. The .45 Thompson is very easy to control. It points naturally and after a couple of test magazines, from-the-hip bursts could be accurately directed.

One of Dillinger's favorite tricks was to remove the Thompson's buttstock to aid in concealability. Wondering how this would affect the feel of the gun, we fired a few bursts, minus the butt, and found that the gun still retains its easy-handling characteristics.

It was found that bursts from the shoulder had a tendency to rock the shooter backward—not because of heavy recoil, but from the repeated push of 30 rapid-fire shots. If one leans into the gun, this is practically eliminated.

The Thompson easily lived up to all expectations, and was, without a doubt, one of the most enjoyable guns I have ever fired. Return shooting invitations will be eagerly accepted. 🎥

The Tommy Gun was a delight to shoot, grimace on the author's face notwithstanding. It was easily controlled, and went through 1000 rounds without a misfire. Here the buttstock has been removed, á la Dillinger, without any handling difficulties.

By Phil Spangenberger

Normally, for recreational shooting, I prefer guns that are slow to load, have a rate of fire of one-shot-a-minute, and are hard to clean. But the Thompson submachine gun has blasted its way into my "shooters heart."

I guess I will have to make room for another "favorite thing to do" now that I've fired it. I had anticipated an enjoyable shooting session, but had no idea of the number of variant ways a "Tommy Gun" could be worked. I shot it single-fire, as well as fully automatic, with and without the stock in one or both hands. The gun is a real thrill to operate and an extremely easy one to handle.

My next statement will probably be fodder for any anti-gunners who accidently stumble across this page. Handling a gun like the Thompson submachine gun gives one a thrilling feeling. The Thompson is one of those guns that just seems to have that feel of excitement and adventure about it. It conjures up visions of the Dillinger gang, or an old George Raft movie. Like a Colt "Peacemaker," the "Tommy Gun" is a legend that you can put your hands on and actually work the mechanisms. It is real. Firing the gun into a dirt bank rather than a *city bank* is my idea of fun, but I certainly understand the feelings that some of the desperadoes of the '20s and '30s must have experienced when brandishing one of these weapons.

The rate of fire is certainly rapid, especially when compared to my muzzle loaders or six-shooters. However, the speed is such that controlled bursts of fire are easily obtainable. A short burst will really play havoc on a given target or target area.

Since the Thompson actually chambers a pistol cartridge, the recoil is slight. The majority of recoil comes from firing the gun on full automatic. It tends to climb, but even this is controllable once you get the hang of it.

We set some clay pigeons several yards apart against a dirt embankment about 30 yards to our front and proceeded to tear them up. I quickly found that you don't use a "Tommy gun" for target shooting. I don't think I hit one or two of those damned clays in several magazines full of ammo, but I certainly changed the terrain around them.

I was particularly impressed with the fact that in about an hour and a half, my compadres and I shot 1000 rounds of ammunition without one single instance of the weapon jamming on us. The only real trouble I experienced in the day's shooting was getting one of the two 30-shot magazines, that the four of us had to share, away from those other "greedy" guys. 🏰

Associate Editor Phil Spangenberger found the Thompson to be free of malfunctions in prolonged shooting, light in recoil and easy to handle; an impressive firearm with a good feel about it.

The Wild Bunch

Butch Cassidy & Co.

By Clair Rees

Led by Robert Leroy Parker, who left his Circleville, Utah home and staid, Mormon upbringing right after his 18th birthday and tackled his first bank just three years later, the Wild Bunch in the space of a dozen years rustled enough cattle, held up enough trains and robbed enough banks to insure them a permanent place in the outlaw hall of fame.

In its heyday, the Wild Bunch operated from a badlands hidaway in southeastern Utah known as "Robbers Roost" to raid victims in Wyoming, Nevada, Montana, Colorado and Utah—and inconvenienced the Union Pacific Railroad to the point that it finally retained the services of the Pinkerton Agency to put the too-successful train robbers out of business.

Parker, who adopted the alias of "Cassidy" after working as a sometimes cattle butcher (hence the name, "Butch") for a rustler named Mike Cassidy, began making a name for himself as a serious outlaw on June 24, 1889—the date he, Matt Warner and Warner's brother-in-law, Tom McCarty, robbed the San Miguel Valley Bank in Telluride, Colorado. (The amount of loot taken varies between $10,500 to $21,000, depending upon which historian you're listening to—and one authority sets the date for this first robbery some two years earlier in March, 1887, and refers to it as merely an unsuccessful attempt.) Whatever the actual outcome of that first bank holdup, "Butch Cassidy" was on his way to becoming a well-known outlaw.

Cassidy avoided banks for the next few years and worked as a cowhand in Wyoming,—supplementing his wages by rustling the odd cow or two. Finally, his reputation for swinging a wide loop caught up with him, and he was committed to the Laramie Penitentiary on July 15, 1894 to serve a two-year term for horse thievery.

He served all but the last few months of his sentence, and was released in January 1896. He never spent another day in prison.

One of his first acts as a free man was to rearm himself, and he purchased a .45 caliber Colt Single Action Army model from a hardware store in Vernal, Utah. The gun had a 4¾-inch barrel and, except for a blued frame and backstrap, wore a nickel finish. This well-documented

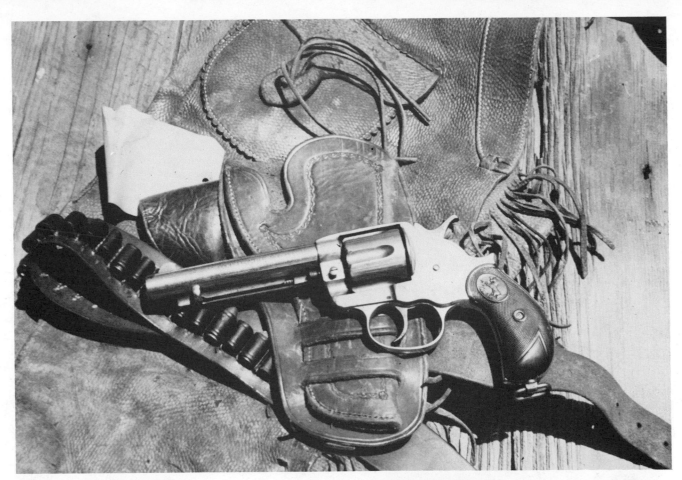

This Colt M-1878 .44-40 Frontier revolver, SN 30245, was owned by C.L. "Gunplay" Maxwell—a member of the Bunch who just couldn't do things right. (E. Dixon Larson Collection)

handgun was later surrendered by Cassidy to Juab County (Utah) Sheriff Parley P. Christensen (or Christison) when he sought a meeting in 1899 with Utah Governor Heber C. Wells in an unsuccessful attempt to obtain amnesty. This gun was apparently worn in an August Brill holster, usually concealed under a coat. The Cassidy Colt is now owned by Ron Lukas of Chicago.

Another gun also surrendered at that time—a model 1873 .44-40 Winchester carbine, serial number 64876—disappeared from the Juab County courthouse soon after Cassidy gave it up. It reappeared not too many years ago, and it is now in the Jim Earle collection in Texas.

According to some accounts, Cassidy also used a model 1875 Remington on some of his forays, and doubtless used other guns, as well, during his lucrative career. Unlike many gun-toting badmen, however, there is no record of Cassidy ever killing a man. He was a rustler, horse thief, bank robber and train robber—but apparently drew the line at murder.

The same can't be said, though, for some of his close associates. Over the years, several outlaws rode

The top Colt SAA was purchased by Cassidy in Vernal, Utah after he was released from Laramie Penitentiary in July of 1894. It was turned in to Sheriff Parley P. Christensen in 1899 when Butch sought a meeting with the Utah governor to ask for a pardon. The lower Colt was owned by William "Bill" Kick Darby, a lesser-known member of the Bunch. The Cassidy gun is in the Ron Lukas collection, while the Darby gun belongs to the Bianchi Leather collection.

with the Wild Bunch—including such notables as Flat Nose George, Elzy Lay, Harvey Longabaugh (The Sundance Kid), William Carver, Ben Kilpatrick and others, along with many lesser-known badmen.

The worst of this lot was easily Harvey Logan, alias Kid Curry. According to a wanted poster issued by Pinkerton's National Detective Agency, he was dark complexioned, stood 5 feet 7½ inches tall, weighed somewhere between 145 and 160 pounds. The Pinkerton dossier said Logan typically had a "reserved manner," and went on to note in classic western understatement that he "drinks heavy, and has bad habits"—these "bad habits" apparently

The Wild Bunch

included killing people at the drop of a hat, as the same dossier credits him with no less than nine deaths and a number of other shootings. The list of victims includes three sheriffs and a deputy, and is almost certainly far from complete, as it accounts for only seven years of Logan's action-filled career.

In addition to the nine killings, the above-named abbreviated account credits Logan with at least one known bank robbery (the Belle Bourche Bank in South Dakota), two train robberies and two escapes from jail. In addition, he is known to have participated in several other bank and train robberies as a member of Cassidy's Wild Bunch—including the robbery of a Union Pacific train near Tipton, Wyoming on August 29, 1900, and the holdup of a Great Northern train near Wagner, Montana in July 1901. The Wagner train robbery was the last holdup pulled by Cassidy and Longabaugh before the famous (or infamous) pair departed for what they hoped would be a far healthier climate in South America.

According to some accounts, Harvey Logan was later trapped after an attempted train robbery at Parachute, Colorado in June, 1904 and committed suicide with a Colt .45. Others say it was Logan, not Cassidy, who was killed in 1909 by Bolivian soldiers. Another version of Logan's death is that he did travel to Bolivia with Cassidy and Longabaugh, but was killed in an accident with a mule.

E. Dixon Larson, of Utah, has in his collection a gun that lends credence to the story that Logan indeed met his end after the ill-fated Parachute robbery. The gun is a single action Army Colt .45 bearing the serial number 147144. The factory-engraved handgun wears unusual grips that narrow toward the butt in a reverse taper. Mr. Larson has affidavits to show that this particular gun was taken from Logan's body by

Deputy Fred Carlson, at Parachute, Colorado.

While "Kid Curry" Logan had a justifiable reputation as a nerveless killer, there were others associated with the Cassidy gang who had considerably different reputations. One of these was a man who called himself "Gunplay" (C. L.) Maxwell.

While "Gunplay" Maxwell thought of himself in terms of a hardened criminal, he had a hard time living up to his self-image. He just couldn't get the hang of being a successful outlaw.

On one occasion he tried to intimidate a group of unarmed prospectors—and ended up being stripped of his guns and nearly beaten to death. Later, he and a saddle bum named Porter held up the bank at Springville, Utah—with a buckboard waiting outside for the getaway. The unweildy buckboard proved no match for the much faster, horse-mounted pursuit and the fleeing pair were soon cornered on foot in a brushy draw. Porter was killed during the shoot-out that ensued, and Maxwell was captured.

Like several other badmen of the day, Maxwell once tried to work the other side of the street by turning lawman. He applied to the Carbon County (Utah) commission to

fill the job of deputy sheriff in April, 1897. He was turned down.

While "Gunplay" evidently considered himself a member of the Wild Bunch, it's not clear whether he was ever actually accepted as such by the group. He kept trying to be a *good* badman, but he just didn't seem to have the knack. He was finally killed in a shootout several years after the Wild Bunch broke up.

One of Maxwell's guns—a double action model 1878 Colt Frontier .44-40 with a 5½-inch barrel—is now in the E. Dixon Larson collection. To complement "Gunplay's" self-styled flashiness, the gun wears nickle plating throughout.

During the relatively brief time Butch Cassidy's Wild Bunch was ac-

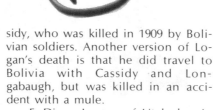

Harvey "Kid Curry" Logan's Colt .45 Single Action featured a 4 3/4-inch barrel, factory engraving and unusual "reverse taper" stag grips. The gun was reportedly taken from Logan's body after the Parachute, Colo. train holdup in 1904. (E. Dixon Larson Collection)

This Winchester M-1873 .44-40 carbine, SN 64876, belonged to Cassidy, and was turned into Sheriff Christensen along with the bandit's Colt SAA revolver.

A few of the more prominent members of the Wild Bunch posed for a Fort Worth photographer around the turn of the century. Seated, 1-r: Harry Longabaugh (the Sundance Kid); Ben Kilpatrick and Robert Leroy Parker (Butch Cassidy). Standing, from left, are William Carver and Harvey Logan (Kid Curry). According to one account, this picture was taken while the Bunch was celebrating the successful holdup of the Winnemucca, Nevada bank, and was sent along to the bank with a note of thanks for the "contributions."

tive, it took many thousands of dollars from banks and trains in a five-state operating area, and enjoyed (if that's the word) a fair amount of notoriety. And while Cassidy maintained leadership over the group, many other outlaws came to be associated with the organization as its numbers swelled and receded. It's likely we'll never know how many

men were actually members of the Bunch, but we do know that there were many who, at one time or another, rode with Butch Cassidy and his boys.

Similarly, we can't be certain as to how, or when, Butch Cassidy (or for that matter, Harry Longabaugh) finally met his end. The version most generally accepted is that Butch and Sundance were killed by Federales in San Vicente. However, *The Wyoming State Journal* on July 2, 1957 reported another version allegedly told to Ed Farlow by Cassidy himself several years after the shootout had occurred. According to this story, Cassidy was able to strip the uniform from a dead Bolivian soldier and escaped during the night with the help of this disguise. The dead soldier was left clothed in Cassidy's garments.

Still a third version exists in which neither Cassidy nor Longabaugh were killed—this account has the pair leaving town before the battle actually started, and two other American outlaws named Harry Nation and Dick Clifford getting it—quite literally-in the neck.

Which story is the true one? Take your pick—but there's one bit of evidence that you might want to weigh before deciding. The long-standing "dead or alive" rewards totalling some $50,000 on the two men were never paid.

And oh yes . . . several people who knew Cassidy well—including members of his family in Circleville—swear that he returned to the states and visited them. They report he became a resident of Salem, Oregon, and died there of pneumonia in 1937.

Eyewitness to Six-Gun Law

By Elmer Keith

Elmer Keith is one of the nation's most highly respected gun experts. From first-hand experience he knows all the factors that come into play in a gunfight, and he has been able to put this knowledge to good use in devising new techniques and designing new guns.

The early West developed a large number of trained and experienced gun fighters. The westward course of the Empire produced a breed of men unique in history. Life was cheap and killings commonplace. Outlaws preyed on the honest miners, citizens and early ranchers. About the only law was the town marshal and the early sheriffs. These men were hired or elected more for their ability with a gun than for their knowledge of the law. They had to try to control the toughest elements of society ever thrown together in one heterogenous mass of humanity.

Of these times and conditions the gunfighter was born. The menace of wild Indians and organized bands of outlaws preying on immigrants moving westward to the gold mines of California and the rich farm lands of Oregon was ever present. The law was confined to small communities backed by a gun fighting marshal, or was nonexistent. Over a goodly portion of this continent the law was a sixgun that was packed by each individual in six chapters. The age old law of nature, the survival of the fittest, ruled.

Many outlaws and peace officers became very fast and deadly with a gun; they had to in order to survive. There are only two classes of gun fighters—the quick and the dead. Those on the side of the law, backed by honest citizenry, gradually shot some semblance of decency and order into each community. Many a Western town had a dead man to bury every morning. I saw the last of that era as a very small boy in Montana before the coming of the automobile.

Sheep and cattle wars, the Lincoln County War in New Mexico, the vigilantes of Montana, the numerous Indian wars, the Mormon migration, all had gunfighters in important roles.

Many outlaws became professional killers and for a fee would dry gulch anyone, or if necessary, provoke a gunfight and murder their man as surely as if they had shot him in the back. The killing of many an honest citizen was thus arranged and carried out for a price. While many of these professional killers ran up long lists of victims, either dry gulched or killed in so-called fair fights, they sooner or later met a peace officer, equally good with a gun and wound up in the cemetery. Usually nothing was done about such gun fights. If the killer had witnesses to swear the victim had an even break, he got away with it. A horse thief was considered beyond the pale and, if caught, was left dancing on air at the end of a rope.

John Newman told me of the death of Soapy Smith at Skagway, Alaska. Soapy headed a gang that preyed on the returning miners and frequently relieved them of their pokes. A citizens' committee repaired to an old wharf storage house to deliberate on what was to be done with Soapy and his gang,

down his .38-40 single action shot Soapy through the heart. Smith's .45-70 slug hit Reed in the groin and he died shortly afterwards. Reed's gun snapped on a defective primer, or he might have saved his life. Soapy fired as Reed cocked his gun for a second try. The committee properly organized and cleaned up the rest of the gang, bringing law and order to Skagway.

Another time Newman entered a saloon looking for a man who had sworn to kill him. The man raised a double barreled sawed-off shotgun, but Newman proved the faster and killed him with his .45 S A Colt slip gun.

Newman told me how he and

hard enough to settle the outlaw's accounts.

I witnessed a gun fight in Helena, Montana, that proved the .38 Special standard load a very poor man stopper. I had just ridden to town from the ranch when a cop friend named Martin waved us over to the corner of Sixth Ave. and Main St. He talked a few minutes as I sat on my cow pony, then pulled out a new 6-inch barrel Smith & Wesson M & P target revolver. He passed it over asking what I thought of it for a police gun. I told him then it was too small and if he ever got in a gun fight he might have to shoot a criminal more than once to stop him, or he might have to kill him

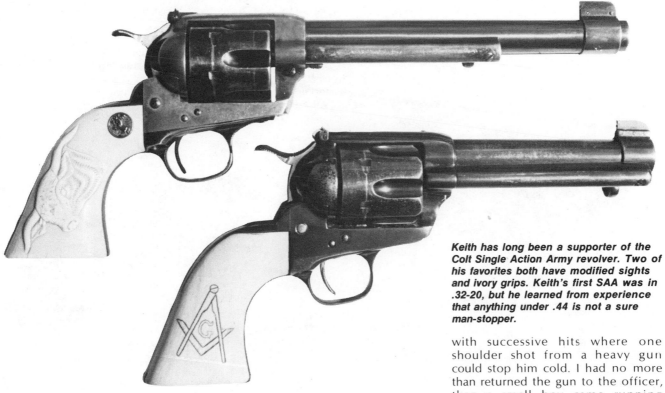

Keith has long been a supporter of the Colt Single Action Army revolver. Two of his favorites both have modified sights and ivory grips. Keith's first SAA was in .32-20, but he learned from experience that anything under .44 is not a sure man-stopper.

leaving a guard behind. The guard's name was Reed. He was armed with a .38-40 single action Colt. When Soapy Smith heard of this, he picked up a .45-70 Model '86 Winchester, and headed for the dock to break up the meeting. John Newman followed him but at some distance. Soapy turned around and yelled to get back or he would kill him. Newman had only his .45 Colt slip gun and the range was too great to risk starting a gunfight against a rifle. He continued to follow Soapy and was again cussed out and ordered to stop. Soapy again went on, Newman followed and was an eyewitness to his demise. Smith came up to Reed and ordered him out of the way, then struck at him with the gun barrel. Reed grabbed the barrel with one hand as Soapy turned the rifle on him and fired, but as he went

two boy friends were once captured by a gunman and forced to work for him for nothing. Only Newman had a gun, a .45 S A Colt. The outlaw had taken all of Newman's ammunition but left him his gun. One day the boys found a loaded .38-40 cartridge. They had become well fed up with working for nothing while the outlaw kept them under guard. They wrapped paper around the .38-40 hull, until it could just be driven into a chamber. It fitted tight enough so Newman knew it would stand the blow of the firing pin. At the first chance they jumped their boss and when he went for his gun, Newman let him have it at close range, the .38-40 bullet wobbling down the .45 caliber barrel. It did the business. They took a long chance but the 40 grains of black powder threw that 180-grain bullet

with successive hits where one shoulder shot from a heavy gun could stop him cold. I had no more than returned the gun to the officer, than a small boy came running down Sixth Avenue and yelled at Martin, "There's a guy holding up the Chink Noodle Parlor." Martin remarked, "I guess this is it," and followed the boy back up the street, while I rode alongside. Arriving at the Noodle Parlor, Martin drew his gun and went in. The holdup was back near the rear end with a small nickel plated gun held on the Chinese owner, while he went through the cash register. At Martin's entrance he whirled around and shot at him. As no bullet came through the glass front I knew he had hit him. Martin shot fast, but planted all his slugs in the holdup's chest. Meanwhile, the holdup emptied his five-shot .32 revolver. Two slugs came through the window. He threw his gun at Martin and it also came through the window into the street. A boy in one of the booths

Eyewitness to Six-Gun Law

began to holler that he was shot while the holdup hung onto the counter and slowly slid down to the floor. He died as he was being carried up the hospital steps. The boy had a .32 slug through the calf of his leg from one of the holdup's bullets and Martin had one through the left breast pocket of his blouse that went through a heavy note book and lodged in the bottom of the pocket. Had the gunman used a heavy gun he would have killed Martin the first shot. After this fight Martin procured a heavy gun. Officer Martin was later killed in a gun

fight with an old classmate of mine but I never heard the details of their fight, or how it started.

Pink Simms told me of being in a gun fight once and being shot through the neck with a .32-20 and he never knew he was hit until the fight was over and he saw blood running down his shirt front. The bullet had missed both jugular vein and spine and he quickly recovered. In another gun fight between a friend of his and another man, Pink said a slug aimed at his partner missed him and hit Pink's saddle horn. It peeled the leather off the steel saddle horn then hit Simms on his heavy double chap and gun belts. He said it did not break the skin, but made him so sick he could not hang onto the saddle horn and fell off in the dust before the fight had ended. It was a 250-grain .45 Colt slug that knocked him from his horse.

Another time Simms and a com-

panion were ascending a flight of stairs in a hotel. The companion was just in front of him when a woman came out at the head of the stairs and aimed an old .45 Colt rod ejector double action at his companion and cut loose. The heavy slug cut a long groove in the staircase bannister then struck the man on the chaps belt. It brought him back on top of Pink, with a grunt, and they both tumbled to the bottom of the stairs. Simms always said he was an authority on the wallop of a .45.

Peace officers will find there is a lesson to be learned from each gun fight, if they will but study the details. Usually the cool head who uses his brains will win. I once had a cop friend in Helena, Montana, named Bill O'Connel. He was half Blackfoot Indian, a tall powerful man weighing over 200 pounds, over six feet in height, straight as an arrow and the best gunfighter on the city police force. Bill and I often hunted together Sundays.

I was a small youngster running

a horseback paper route mornings before school. Each morning I arrived at the *Helena Independent* office, slung a couple of sacks of papers on my horse and took off. I used to roll the papers, kink them so they could be thrown and toss them at front doors as I trotted past. My first stop was always the Weise Cafe where I traded two extra papers for a cup of coffee and two doughnuts.

Bill was on night duty at the N.P. depot, inside the city limits but actually a mile from the main town. An indication of the liveliness of this part of town is that scarcely a porch post in front of the saloon and several eating houses had missed being gouged by a bullet in past gun battles.

After my coffee break I would meet Bill somewhere along his beat and give him a morning paper, then make my rounds, winding up at

home to stable and feed my horse before breakfast. One morning Bill said, "There is something wrong in the saloon across the street," which was located some distance from the depot and near a big fur and hide house. The building was peculiarly shaped, a sort of wedge on the corner, or intersection of a side street. A door entered the tip of the wedge and a line of windows ran along the Helena Avenue side. On the side street was another door. While nothing was visible from the street, everything inside was plainly visible to a man on a horse looking over the curtained windows. I trotted by the place to see what was going on. Two gunmen had everyone lined up in front of the long bar that extended almost the full length of the east side of the building. At the end of this bar there was a break and a short bar against the back or north end of the building. One man held two guns on the small crowd while the other frisked them. Bill told me where he had a sawed off shotgun

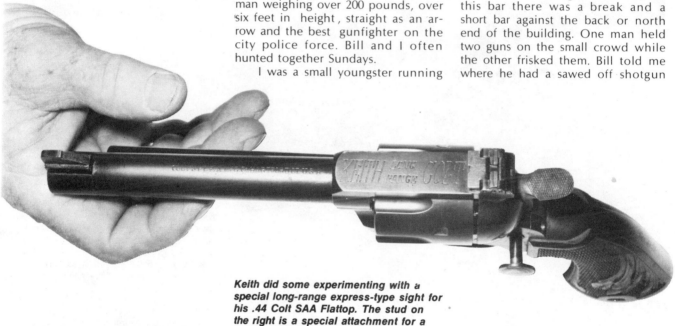

Keith did some experimenting with a special long-range express-type sight for his .44 Colt SAA Flattop. The stud on the right is a special attachment for a fast-draw swivel belt attachment.

and a box of buckshot cached. He said, "I am going in." My orders were to keep the men in there with the shotgun, if possible, until help arrived if he failed.

As Bill went in the front door at the extreme tip of the wedged shaped building, one holdup whirled around and fired, then both bandits jumped over the bar. The others in the saloon dropped flat on the floor. The holdup's slug went through the transom over Bill's head. Bill had his .45 SA Colt cocked and waited. Soon one man's head popped up over the bar; as he fired Bill O'Connel's 250-grain slug hit him square between the eyes. The other holdup ran down the length of the back bar, keeping low out of Bill's vision, but when he attempted to cross the opening between the ends of the two bars at the corner he was exposed and Bill's second slug caught him squarely

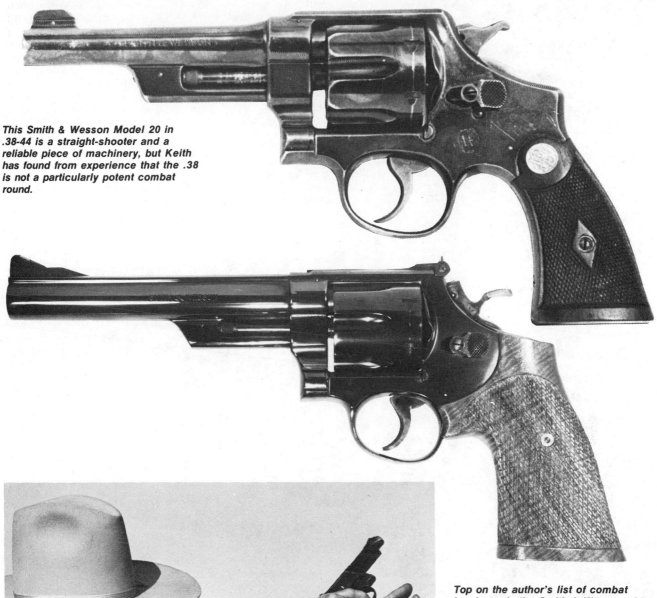

This Smith & Wesson Model 20 in .38-44 is a straight-shooter and a reliable piece of machinery, but Keith has found from experience that the .38 is not a particularly potent combat round.

Top on the author's list of combat handguns is the Smith & Wesson .44 Magnum which he helped to develop in 1953, however its recoil and penetration has caused many police departments to shy away.

through both shoulders and he landed on his face kicking. No doubt he intended firing on Bill from the other bar, thinking Bill would still be watching the place where his partner had been killed.

Bill O'Connel died in the Helena Hospital from flu and pneumonia, while I was flat on my back on another cot, downed by the same ailments. We used to send notes back and forth to each other by the nurses. One morning when I asked for Bill's note the nurse shook her head. I knew he had passed on. So died Bill O'Connel, a man without fear, a terror to evil doers and a friend of lost dogs, stray kids and everyone in trouble or need of help.

Sam Russell had been an old Faro dealer in the Southwest before moving to Helena, Montana, where he ran a one chair barber shop. Sam was a little man, but very fast with a sixgun and deadly with a .45 from the hip. He used to pull the shades down over his front window and instruct me in quick draw work, often shooting short Remington .45 squib loads at the patterns in his linoleum floor covering. He had most of those small squares studded with the hollow base Remington slugs

Eyewitness to Six-Gun Law

that had just power enough to drive them down about flush with the floor. If a cop came along and banged on the front door and wanted to know what was going on, Sam would say, "Go away. I am just giving a kid some pistol instruction."

While I was with a government survey crew in 1917, Sam got into trouble. He was seated at a back ta-

cocked gun in his right hand.

The bar tender told the big man he was up against the real thing. He stood facing the front door where Sam had gone out. Everyone else in the saloon moved over to the back of the room out of line with either door. While the big man watched the front door, Sam Russell came down the alley and kicked in the back door. The big man discovered his mistake too late and whirled to fire at Sam. Russell's .45 slug passed through his gun arm and thence through his body ending that fight in one shot. Sam was given three

his store, getting a few dollars. Then he started for the depot to catch the next train out, but the Frenchman told Myers, who ran a store and the post office across the street. Myers phoned Taplin, the depot agent, and Taplin grabbed his old sawed off shotgun, loaded with buckshot, and ran out on the depot platform to intercept the holdup. When he came in sight, Taplin gave him the contents of both barrels, one buckshot hitting him in the leg. He turned, ducked out of sight and made it back to the hotel where he climbed the stairs and barricaded

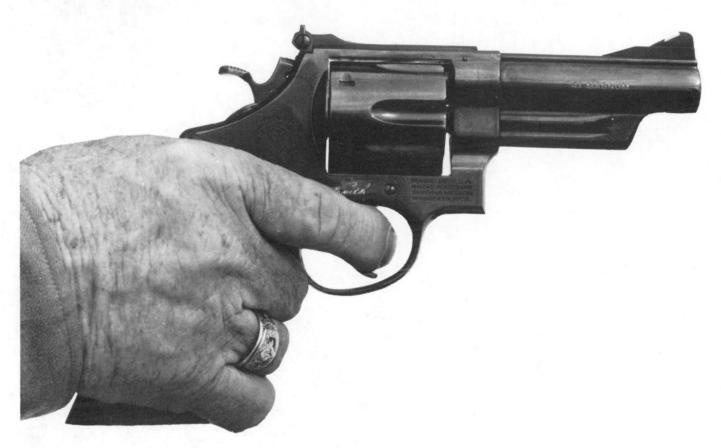

ble in a saloon just above Broadway on the east side of Main Street. A big man came in and ordered a drink for the house. Sam evidently did not hear him or was not paying any attention to what he said. At any rate the big man then yelled at Sam, "Come on you little S.O.B. I said everyone up to the bar." Sam got up and remarked, "Say it with a smile, Mister, and I will be with you." The big man sneered and again called Sam a S.O.B. Sam told him, "Mister, I never took that name from no man and I will be back just as soon as I can get my gun." Sam went across the street to his barber shop. There he cocked one of his pearl stocked 4¾-inch .45 S A Colts and draped a big silk hankerchief over it, muzzle and all, tucking the ends of the hanky back inside his coat sleeve while he held the

years in the State Penitentiary. The Judge confiscated his carved pearl stocked .45. Later when Sam got out, he had a friend steal the gun. I later swapped a .41 rod ejector to Sam for it and its mate and I still have the old guns. Many an old time bar room killing began in similar manner. Some purposely provoked and some getting started almost accidentally.

Another bit of gunplay that occurred while we owned a ranch at Winston, Montana, showed the utter foolishness of anyone trying to hold up a town such as Winston. At one time it had boasted several saloons, but at this time only one remained, along with a hotel, two stores, a rooming house, dance hall, and the N. P. depot.

An eastern gunman came to town and held up a Frenchman in

Keith's latest entry in the big-bore field is the .41 Magnum. It was designed specifically for police usage, and has been considered by a number of departments.

himself in an upper corner room. The little town turned out en masse with their hunting rifles and proceeded to shoot that room full of holes—also the stick-up artist. I had ridden down to Winston, from the ranch, to get the mail when I heard the gunfire. Winston took the episode in its stride, in fact, laughed about it When the room was broken into, the man, badly shot to pieces, was put on a stretcher and on the next train to Helena. He died en route. How anyone could be foolish enough to try to hold up a Western cow town is beyond me. He would never have a chance. 🦂

John Henry Selman

The Man Who Killed John Wesley Hardin.
By Harlon Carter

John Selman, at times in his life, was an outlaw; at other times a respected law enforcement officer. Many have said he was a gallant man, protective of his friends and his family.

Old John Selman (one of his sons was young John), literally leaped into the pages of Western history by killing a bunch of lynchers who by every code of right and wrong he could understand, needed killing. Yet despite periods of desperate achievement, of displays of great courage, he was a rather ordinary product of his times, who doubtlessly performed under the harsh demands of survival as well, but not better than, others less publicized. John Selman was born in 1839 in Arkansas. With three of his brothers he was a Confederate soldier. Two of them died in the war and two went to Texas.

Selman went to Texas to farm, to settle in peace and to raise a family. He became a dirt farmer, a prosaic enterprise filled with routine and hard work. There was no social security, there was no government guaranteed price structure. Men went to the Southwest with a wagon, a plow, a span of mules or horses and, if well-off another to ride. He mostly carried an old gun, likely left over from the disintegration of the Confederate Armies.

In Texas, Selman married the daughter of a decent and hard-working family, Edna de Graffenreid. He worked hard at grubbing a livelihood from the soil of a dry land farm to support his growing family, which shortly contained three sons and a daughter.

He settled near old Fort Griffin in North Texas. Later, at that place, he was raising cattle in partnership with John Larn. He and Larn were successful and as they prospered, made friends, the likeable John Larn was requested to run for sheriff. He was elected. He named John Selman his first deputy.

On one occasion, Commanches kidnaped a boy and a girl. John Selman, with Indian friends from near Fort Griffin, trailed them over 500 miles into the Davis Mountains of West Texas, where they killed the kidnapers, rescued the two children and returned them to their parents. On another occasion Doc Holliday, who later became known for his activities and associations with the Earp brothers at Tombstone, Arizona, was arrested and thrown into jail at Fort Griffin by Selman.

This was a period in Selman's life which gives the measure of the once peaceful and lawful nature of the man deep within, but it is a period writers of Western history and Western tales have not known, or have chosen to ignore.

It was not to last long. A man almost unknown in Western history was to change all that. He was Shorty Collins, who in some way had violated the law around Fort Griffin. When faced by Sheriff Larn, he drew a pistol with apparent intent to shoot the sheriff. Deputy John Selman killed him.

Shortly thereafter, Selman left on a long wagon trip to Fort Worth with a load of buffalo hides and John Larn was accused, by the friends of Shorty Collins, of helping butcher cattle that belonged to other ranchers and of being in league with rustlers. A vigilante committee was promptly formed and called on John Larn at his ranch. He was shot to death by the lynchers and his body hanged from a mesquite.

A hard riding brother-in-law, on a fast horse, overtook Selman who sent his wagon on to Fort Worth with the brother-in-law. Selman rode back to Shackelford County to take the only action he felt reasonable and possible in the death of a friend in such a manner and by such means. On arriving home, he cautiously approached in the night and after long watching from his own corrals, saw a match strike in the darkness, perhaps to light a cigarette. He quietly rode away. He knew who they were and what they intended.

It has been reported that in a very brief period the 11 men who killed John Larn were themselves found dead somewhere on a lonesome road, near a high point or in the dark. John Selman never talked. No man, having knowledge, ever lived.

Jim Gillett was a great Texas Ranger and a good and respected

John Henry Selman

citizen. Gillett said that John Selman was "...an outlaw and a murderer of the worst kind." One is compelled to give weight to such opinion, but there's no denying 13 years had passed since the broken Confederates had returned to their homes, and in those years there'd been no evidence Selman had been more than a sweating, struggling farmer and small rancher. Moreover, Selman was approaching 40 years of age with a wife and four children to care for.

Gillett's opinion may have been widely held, but no man can deny that for Selman to kill and to take the owl-hoot trail so late in life, there had to be the greatest provocation. Justifiable? Hard question, today, maybe, but there's no sign Selman hesitated.

He rode west beyond the Pecos; some say into the Seven Rivers section of New Mexico where he was a leader of outlaws guilty of cattle rustling and murder. No one knows for sure whether he was the same John Gunter or John Gross who were indeed criminal renegades. The Seven Rivers gang splintered after two of them were jailed for murdering lawyer Houston Chapman early in 1879. For the next six months or so, Selman may have been their leader after killing a man named Hart who presumed briefly to take the job. Dissention plagued the gang. Respected citizens formed a "Regulators" scouting party and the country grew hot for rustlers. Pickings were slim. Several were killed. Others just dropped out and rode away never to be heard of again.

Selman—if indeed he were Selman—turned his horse back toward Texas.

Another report says Selman had "...been took North to stand trial for the killings at Ft. Griffin." In any event, Sheriff W. R. Kruger of Shackelford County did not want him returned there to stand trial. He wrote Major John B. Jones, commanding the Texas Rangers at Austin, "Our county is free of mobs and violence and there is nothing here to incite one into action. But I fear the arrival of Selman will be a renewal of the times we have passed through. Without the least show of doing any good, but on the contrary a great deal of harm."

Selman turned west again. Before he could settle down and bring his family out, his wife died; his four children were given out to various families for care. At Ft. Davis or Ft. Stockton, he contracted smallpox and was put in a small tent a mile out of town with some medicine and a barrel of water. Whether deserved or not, fate rarely gave John Selman any choice except to live or die. He lived and for the next ten years, little is known of what he did.

Probably, his life was saved when an elderly Mexican with his only daughter, seeing buzzards lighting on the tent's ridge pole stopped to see what was going on. Finding Selman in a critical condition the Mexican samaritan loaded him into his cart and took him home. It is said that Selman recovered after eating a large bowl of menudo and taking a hot bath with lye soap. Although menudo is first class fare on Mexican ranches, and has a wide reputation for its curative qualities after a night of too much mezcal, this is the first report ever received, and it might be the last, that it had any therapeutic effect in smallpox cases.

Texas law enforcement dropped Selman's case at that time, perhaps assuming he had crawled away and died.

Selman and his Mexican benefactor crossed the Rio Grande into

John Selman, most famous for his killing of John Wesley Hardin, carried his gun on both sides of the law. Here, at age 58, he wears his Colt .45 for the city of El Paso.

Mexico and made their way to Chihuahua more than two months away by wagon and team.

Somewhere on the way a romance sprang up with the old Mexican's daughter. They were married and again her father took on the job helping John Selman. He made the ride deep into Texas to get John Selman's children but only the two little boys, John Jr. and Bud, could be brought to their father.

They stayed in Mexico for several years. The boys went to Mexican schools and were alter boys in the Catholic Church. Selman had become involved in silver mining and was doing well, but again a perverse fate overtook him. His father-in-law died and then his wife.

The two boys were growing up to manhood and wanted to return to their homeland and speak English. Old John Selman, then with his two boys came to El Paso and went to work at the American Smelter. The boys rose to responsible positions but Old John soon drifted into a bit too much drinking and a bit too much card playing—seven-up was his game.

He again married a Mexican girl not as old as his two boys. They left home because they did not approve of his marriage and Old John was elected constable.

Then, it was, John Wesley Hardin came to El Paso. No one seems to have agreed on the kind of life Hardin lived after arriving there but it does seem clear his intentions were law-abiding. He had been admitted to the bar and had some experience as a practicing attorney. There are reports Jeff Milton, John Selman and George Scarborough met Hardin at the train and warned him of the conduct to be expected of him were he to stay in El Paso. Hardin did something he never had done before. He backed down.

These three men by their experience, their positions and their respected character certainly represented the law in El Paso. Hardin had recently served sixteen years in prison for murder. Facts and rumors indicated 40 men had died at the muzzles of his guns.

One can only assume Hardin's true intent was to avoid a break with the law, but he did start drinking heavily and he did get involved with a woman client who later was arrested by young John Selman, an El Paso policeman by now.

On this occasion Hardin was out of town and his woman, intoxicated, hired a buggy and team, took two of Hardin's guns and attempted to shoot up the town. Young John Selman arrested her, seized the guns and $50. Upon Hardin's return, his guns were given to him, but not the $50.

Hardin hunted up old John Selman. After all, young John was still pretty much of a boy and Wes Hardin, for reasons of his own, took his differences to old John by making uncomplimentary remarks about his son. The El Paso *Daily Herald*, August 20, 1895, reported Selman as having replied, "Hardin, there is no man living who can talk about my children without fighting."

In this age of disintegration of families and loss of respect in their homes some people may not understand the warmth and parental affection, the family pride and honor contained in Old John's statement. Most assuredly, he was laying his own life on the line and, no doubt about it, he was threatening the life of Wes Hardin. Hardin undeniably understood that, but he said, "John, I am not armed."

Selman said, "I am armed; go get your gun."

Many reports of varying kinds have been written concerning this exchange. It is certain, however, that tall threats, loud talk and picturesque language was neither the nature nor the mood of either of these two men. Colorful language could have been used, but it is most unlikely. Men willing to kill openly

This modified .44 Colt, SN 42870, belonged to Bass Outlaw. This ex-Texas Ranger who went bad, was killed by Selman in El Paso, Texas.

and quickly do not fritter away their time with loose talk.

Selman said later he sat down on a beer keg at the Wigwam Saloon to await Hardin's return. In Selman's family today they say it *was* the Wigwam. When his son and another El Paso policeman came up, having heard of the likelihood of a fight, Old John told them to get on about their business, that he had a personal affair to settle with Hardin because Hardin had insulted him.

Young John was worried about his 56 year old father who now suffered from an eye injury which impaired his vision at night and who walked with a cane in his shooting hand as a result of the Bass Outlaw fight the year before.

Bass Outlaw was a scrubby little ex-Ranger with a big reputation as a gunman. In a homicidal fit one night, when a madam delayed his favorite girl, Outlaw, half drunk, killed young Ranger McKidrict. Old John was there and was going for his gun while Outlaw shot him twice in the right leg. Outlaw's hurried shooting cost him his life. Selman fired once and it was all over,

though he carried a cane thereafter.

Hardin, however, did not return to the Wigwam. Instead a young barefoot boy came by and Selman told him to get off the street because there was going to be trouble there any minute. The boy replied, "Uncle John, if it is Wes Hardin, I saw him go into the Acme Saloon a short time ago."

The scene was shifted. Perhaps Hardin was engaged in a war of nerves thinking that the longer he waited the more likely Selman would be to get too much to drink. Or perhaps Hardin was once again, at the risk of losing face in El Paso, trying to delay the inevitable.

Selman went to the Acme but he was reluctant to go in until a friend, E. L. Shackelford, urged him to come in for a drink. He was drawn in for the drink and later Selman testified, "Hardin was standing with his back to me shaking dice with Henry Brown. At the end of the bar near the door and while we were drinking I could see Hardin watching me very closely."

Albert B. Fall, who, some 25 years later, was enmeshed in the Teapot Dome scandal, was the attorney for John Selman for the killing of Hardin and next year the attorney for George Scarborough for the killing of Selman. The issue in the Selman-Hardin affair was that Selman's first shot hit Hardin from the back of the head. Fall said he believed Selman when Selman said Hardin was watching, so he went down to the Acme to look over the scene. As he stopped at the Acme's door and looked inside, Fall said, "There was a man standing at the bar and he lifted his head. Then I had the explanation of Selman's statement. For as that man stared into the mirror, I had the illusion for an instant of looking him straight in the eyes."

Here were two old bulls of many battles with plenty of indications each was watching the other in the mirror behind the bar. Neither wanted to give an advantage. Neither wanted to be exposed to the public in taking one. Yet each knew his life depended on winning. It would be a bit silly to say that both men were not comparatively sober. Certainly, both knew the oth-

er and knew better than to underestimate him. Certainly, Wes Hardin knew all the tricks and John Selman said, "I wasn't taking any chances...".

Selman drew and fired, Hardin slumped to the floor without drawing. It was the evening of August 19, 1895. Selman was using a .45 Colt Single Action Army revolver, Serial Number 141805 with a 5½-inch barrel, just like it was available from any hardware or general mercantile store.

A few months later John Selman was killed. The El Paso *Times*, April 6, 1896, reported, "John Selman, the victor of not less than 20 shooting afrays in Texas, the exterminator of bad men and the slayer of John Wesley Hardin is dying tonight with a bullet hole through his body. About three months ago Selman and United States Marshal George Scarborough had a quarrel over a game of cards. Since which occurrence the relations between them have been none too cordial. This morning at four o'clock they met at the Wigwam Saloon and both were drinking."

The fact is no one knows what was said between the two men at that time. They left the saloon together and went into the adjacent alley, several shots were fired and Scarborough re-entered the saloon through the back way as he had gone out and told the crowd he had killed Selman. When they rushed into the alley they saw the prostrate Selman. No pistol could be found. Some surprise was expressed and someone whispered that George Scarborough had killed an unarmed man.

Now, George Scarborough was a brave man and no one accused him of that to his face. Nonetheless, he was held under a heavy bond to answer to a charge of murder. Shortly before Scarborough's trial, a man was arrested in El Paso on some minor offense. On his person was found Selman's pistol. Selman had died carrying a .45 Colt Single Action Army revolver, serial number 36693, 4¾-inch barrel, apparently unmodified in any way. The man claimed he had been standing in the alley and saw one man shoot another. One fell; the other left the scene. He testified, "I reasoned that a dead man had no use for a pistol. And I needed one in my business, so I took the pistol and got away before the crowd came out of the saloon."

So lived and died John Selman. The question exists, would John Selman be prominent in Western Americana today had he not killed John Wesley Hardin? Perhaps not.

Tom Horn

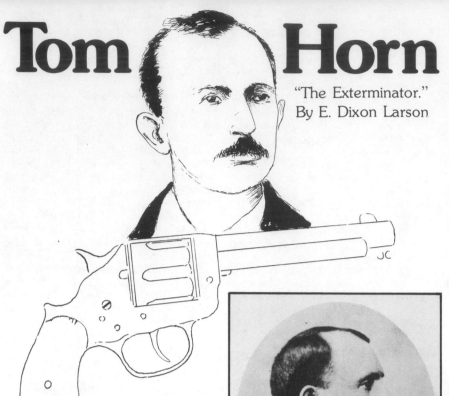

"The Exterminator."
By E. Dixon Larson

Horn in and tagged his double brace of Colt Frontier Model 1878 Double Actions, it can be concluded that these were his tools of the trade from the time Colt introduced the model until they were taken from Horn in 1903. Both are 5½-inch barrels, nickel plated, .45 caliber, serial numbers 1867 and 828. Both are first models with the larger grips. Most of the early ones were shipped to London, but 1867 and the other one, presumably in the same series, was shipped by the Colt Company Nov. 14, 1879, to Simmons Hardware in St. Louis. Of interest is the fact that both are in form-fitting, slim flap-type holsters. Horn apparently preferred the protection of the arms to any advantage in having them exposed and with hammer straps.

Horn later served as a Pinkerton detective with a specialty for tracking down and arresting train robbers. After he brought in "Peg Leg" McCoy, an infamous outlaw, he resigned at the Denver office. Horn liked the luxuries of the *nouveau riche*, such as fine wines and smoking expensive cigars, both of which required a greater income than that of a scout or lawman. This is when Horn changed to his role as a stock detective and rustler exterminator for the cattle barons. He was a clever killer, never leaving any evidence at the scene. He also had endless patience in waiting for his victim. When Horn hit the Hole, only a few stragglers of the Wild Bunch were left, the big namers were dead or gone. Wyoming was the biggest market for a stock detective, consquently, Horn made his headquarters in Cheyenne.

Horn had an excellent physique, six feet in height, 175 pounds, and hard as a rock. In July 1888, he won prizes at the rodeo at Globe, Arizona, as the top ranch hand, and later

Tom Horn had a varied career on both sides of the law. He was a Pinkerton man, hired gun, ranch hand and convicted murderer.

Tom Horn's escape plans made the headlines in the Cheyenne Tribune. The scheme to blow out the wall of the jail was unique, to say the least.

Tom Horn is one citizen of the Old West who hasn't received too much publicity. Horn started his career as a brave and extremely capable government scout, a loyal soldier, and a peace officer. In later years he changed to a hired killer who methodically tracked down his victims, taking no chances. Most of his victims were back-shot from ambush, with no clues left at the scene. Legends from Wyoming to Texas do not credit Tom Horn as making many mistakes, except the big one that cost him his life, on the gallows on November 20, 1903, in Cheyenne Wyoming.

Horn was born in Memphis, Missouri in 1861. At 14, he ran away to start his wanderings. He became a scout with Al Sieber who lived with the Apaches and consquently, taught him many Indian skills, particularly tracking and undaunted patience.

In January of 1875, he hired on as a stage driver of the old Overland Mail Route from Santa Fe to Prescott, Arizona, at a salary of $50 a month. He learned the Indian and Mexican language well and later became an interpreter.

As an Indian scout, Tom Horn was responsible for the capture of Geronimo. Horn's record as a mule skinner during the Spanish American War is very impressive also. Inasmuch as Deputy Sheriff Richard Proctor of Larmamie County brought

SENSATIONAL PLOT TO DELIVER TOM HORN FROM COUNTY JAIL

ONE OF THE BOLDEST AND MOST DARING SCHEMES EVER CONCOCTED IN CRIMINAL HISTORY. A TRUE BUT ALMOST INCREDULOUS STORY

UNAIDED THE TRIBUNE UNEARTHS THE PLAN.

CORRESPONDENCE FROM HORN TO HIS CONFEDERATES OBTAINED BY THE TRIBUNE. EVERY DETAIL ARRANGED. FIVE STICKS OF DYNAMITE TO BE USED IN BLOWING OUT WALL OF JAIL AND EVERYTHING IN READINESS FOR HORN'S ESCAPE. SIGNAL LAST NIGHT THAT PLOT IS COMPLETE

won the world's championship for steer roping and tying.

The story of Tom Horn's work in Wyoming is a strange one. He was, by his own statement, a man who felt absolutely no compunction in taking human life, and would often tell of his adventures which would contain lurid accounts of how he had slain his adversary always in self defense, however. It was fear that he depended on for the success of his peculiar occupation. Consequently, the stock barons continually exaggerated his misdeeds which was to their benefit in keeping Horn a fearful "rustler exterminator." Horn was in Routt County, Colorado when two small ranchers suspected of handling the Wild Bunch's rustled cattle were killed.

Matt Rash and Isham Dart were both killed in the fall of 1900, shot with .45 caliber slugs from the shadows of their own sheds. Horn, upon leaving Routt County, stopped at a

little settlement of Dixon, Colorado where the posse was resting from chasing the purported murderer of Dart. He became involved in a dispute with one of the possemen and received a knife wound in his neck, which left a nasty scar. Horn wounded his assailant making him a helpless cripple for his remaining years. The man threatened to someday kill Horn, but he never caught up with him.

Many believed Tom Horn killed Fred Powell, a small rancher in Laramie, whose cabin still stands on Todd Sermon's ranch out of Laramie City, Wyoming. It was during one of his boastful drunken saloon binges that he confessed to killing a 14-year-old boy, Willie Nickel, by mistake while he was waiting for Willie's father. The confession fell on the ears of U.S. Marshal Joe Lefors. Nickel was a sheep rancher, and his presence had disturbed many of the Wyoming cattle barons who retained the services of Horn.

Horn later denied the confession. He was tried and convicted, a decision that rocked the west, as Horn had many powerful friends in wealthy circles from Denver to Cheyenne:

Horn's influential friends concocted a daring escape plan while he was being held in the Laramie County Jail in Cheyenne. The scheme was unparalleled in criminal daring. The plan was to dynamite the jail and permit Horn's escape, however it was never consummated. An inmate in the jail named Herr, was the weak link in the plan. The *Tribune* reports that Herr was released from the jail two days before the break was to come off. He went immediately to Bosler, Albany County. The second day after gathering some nerve, he returned to

Tom Horn

Cheyenne and "belched up the whole story." The *Tribune* has in its possession, documentary evidence which sounds his story true beyond the peradventure of a doubt.

The *Tribune* carried the story! "Tom Horn is dead." He died as might be expected, with courage, coolness and no sign of faltering. The drop fell at exactly four minutes after eleven o'clock. The visitors were admitted to the jail room at about a quarter to eleven. The newspaper men were admitted to the upper corridor. After a wait of five minutes, Horn appeared in the door of his cell. A moment later Deputy Proctor said "alright if the Erwin boys sing to you Tom?" They sang to the rear of Tom, "Keep your hand upon the throttle and your eye upon the rail." Horn was dressed in a red and white striped negligee shirt, open at the neck, a corduroy vest, dark trousers and low slippers. Horn gave Charlie Erwin some letters to deliver. The drop opened and Horn went to his death. The body was claimed by the Gleason Undertaking Parlor, for delivery to Horn's brother in Boulder, Colorado.

Many believe to this day, Tom

Deputy Sheriff Richard Proctor was responsible for arresting Horn following the Powell murder.

Horn was innocent and that a good man was unfairly hanged. His age was 43.

Tom Horn's guns remained in the Laramie County for many years, later finding their way into a private collection in Albany, County Wyoming.

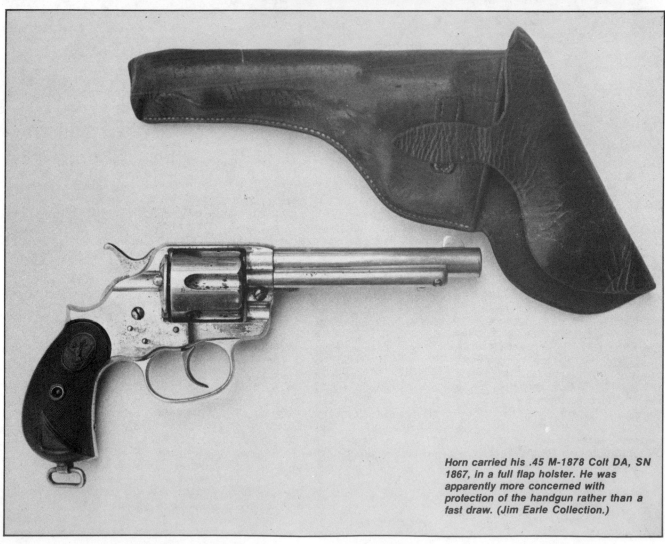

Horn carried his .45 M-1878 Colt DA, SN 1867, in a full flap holster. He was apparently more concerned with protection of the handgun rather than a fast draw. (Jim Earle Collection.)

Charles A. Siringo

Cowboy, Detective and Gunfighter.

By Konrad F. Schreier, Jr.

Charlie Siringo on the trail. Up until he quit working in the early 1920s, Siringo used horses and trains as his prime means of transportation. He was an excellent shot with both pistol and rifle from horseback. (Pinkerton's Photo)

Charlie Siringo was one of the real "wild west" characters, the kind people used to say "still had the hair on." Born in Texas in 1855, he became a cowboy at the age of 11, just after the end of the Civil War.

After pushing cattle around the country for nearly 20 years, he opened a store but finally became a detective for the famous Pinkerton Agency in 1886. He worked for Pinkertons for 22 years, making this part of his life about as exciting as anybody could stand. For a few years after his Pinkerton days, many of which were put in as an undercover agent, he worked as a private detective on his own.

He was not a braggart, or a gunbutt-notcher, despite the fact

This photo was taken of Siringo in the late 1920s, about the time he quit being a lawman. He remained active until his death and acted as a technical adviser in early western movies. (Collection of G.G. Hair)

that he took part in the pursuit or apprehension of scores of bad men. Included are such famous malefactors as Billy the Kid, Butch Cassidy, the Sundance Kid, Flat Nose Curry, and many more of the infamous.

Siringo was a gunfighter by trade, but, unlike most of his breed, he was a readable author. Siringo wrote seven books in all, telling of his many adventures and about the people he had known. He was also a sociable man, and known as a great story teller to his many friends.

Like many westerners of his time and place, Siringo placed a handgun at the top of his personal armament list. He started out using cap and ball revolvers, mostly army revolvers which had come home from the Civil War. When the metallic cartridge revolver came into use, Siringo took up and favored the Colt. 45 Single Action Army six-shooter. The Colts he used, he called "the .45 cowboy pistol", or "Colt's .45", but never a Frontier, Peacemaker or six-shooter. The Colt model he preferred had the standard 4¾-inch or 5½-inch barrel. He felt the 7½-inch Army Model .45 was too long and clumsy for his needs.

He chose the .45 caliber because it was common, and he thought it would stop man or beast cold in their tracks. It could also shoot quite accurately. In the days when Siringo used his Colts, and he used many of them, he used cartridges loaded with black powder. The only complaint he had about them were the clouds of smoke they made. He often "smoked a place up", and once remarked that the white clouds would either attract fire from the enemy he was shooting at or set up such a barrage of smoke it would keep him from seeing his target.

Normally, Siringo carried his Colt .45 in a belt holster; the kind worn on a loop cartridge belt, riding high at the belt line. This kind of rig was well-suited for use on horseback, as Siringo was an expert rider of the rough and tough, fractious western nags. The type of holster he usually used was the old open "Mexican" style, but at times he also wore a "Texas" shoulder holster, or stuck the big revolver in his waistband for concealment.

Charles A. Siringo

This engraving of Siringo was made in the mid-1880s for his book A Texas Cowboy. He is armed with his favorite .44-40 M-1873 Winchester and a heavy knife. Although not visible, it is more than likely he was sporting a .45 Colt single-action as well.

were not as accurate as the longer barreled rifles.

Besides a Colt .45 and Winchester rifle, Siringo usually carried a small "hold-out" revolver. It was a good-quality revolver in the .38 centerfire caliber. He would carry it concealed in his coat pocket, pants leg or anywhere it was most likely to be overlooked when being "disarmed". He usually packed one of these light revolvers in "the city" where his heavy western armament would not have been looked upon too kindly.

Like many men who used firearms as tools of their profession, Siringo was not a bit sentimental about his guns. He would sell one when necessity arose, and considered a good gun his "meal ticket" whenever he ran short of cash. He always knew he could buy a replacement whenever he needed one. As soon as any of his guns got a little tired, it was replaced. Since his life depended on them, this was undoubtedly a good policy. Siringo

Siringo (right) was a technical advisor on many William S. Hart westerns (also pictured). His first-hand knowledge of the lore and ways of the old West give these early movies a look of authenticity that has never been surpassed. (Collection of G.G. Hair)

took meticulous care of his guns, always keeping them cleaned and oiled, and made sure he had clean, good-quality ammunition for them.

One of the earliest mentions he makes of using a gun with deadly effect was when cowboy Siringo defended a calf from a bunch of dogs. The dogs attacked the small cow, and Siringo, who was working the stock on horseback, drew his revolver and fired "to the right and left, driving them off." He knocked down three of the dogs, one unfortunately his own pet who had joined the pack for the killing. He saved the calf. Three dogs out of six shots from a revolver from the back of a moving horse is pretty darn good shooting.

Another demonstration of his sharp-shooting happened many years later while he was working as an undercover detective in Nevada. He was riding cross-country with several criminal suspects he was trying to get the line on, and a coyote ran across the road about 100 yards in front of the party. Siringo pulled his Colt .45 and, from the back of his fast-trotting horse, dropped the moving coyote in its tracks with a single shot.

The next day one of the suspects challenged Siringo to knock a knot out of a board some 50 feet away. Siringo quickly drew his revolver and fired offhand, and his bullet blew the silver dollar-sized knot out of the board. Although his companion tried to persuade him to take a shot at another knot, Siringo refused. Siringo later said, "I had the sense to let well enough alone, as my reputation was made."

This leads to an interesting point about Siringo. He was as good with a rifle as he was with a pistol. Every time Siringo was in the company of outlaws, and fearing an eventual shoot-out with them, he

Siringo's second gun was an inevitable Winchester lever-action rifle, which he considered very accurate and reliable. He began using the original .44 Henry rimfire caliber Winchester '66, but soon graduated to the .44-40 Model '73. When it came on the market, he chose the new .44-40 Model '92. He did not believe in long-range gunfighting until the .30-30 Model '94 Winchester arrived on the scene. Although he mentions people using carbines, Siringo himself did not care for the short-barreled guns and seldom, if ever, used them. He felt carbines

Siringo's personal choice for a sidearm was the .45 Colt Single Action Army with either a 4¾ or 5½-inch barrel.

quickly figured some way to impress them that he was a dead-quick shot. Since not many people were not even nearly as fast or good as he was, his point was well made. Among those who knew him by sight or reputation, he had the distinction of being known as a man who could use a gun well. He was also known as one man who no wise man would ever try to take on. At the same time, however, he did not have the vicious reputation attributed to so many western gun slingers of being ready, willing, able and eager to take on all challengers in a "fair fight". He always preferred a bluff to a shootout.

As a matter of fact, Siringo was a careful, prudent man. He had been shot in the leg when he was quite young, and he didn't like it one bit. He avoided gunfights for the most part, and relied on his reputation of being fast and accurate to keep most men from trying him out. Time and time again he wrote of "getting the drop" on somebody. It seems that with Siringo, getting the drop meant getting his gun unholstered and aimed before his opposi-

the Siringo reputation held up. Scared, the bad guy simply up and walked out, bluffed and afraid to test Siringo's speed and skill. Siringo felt this same man was one of a bunch who later tried to assassinate him by ambush.

Another time Siringo was working undercover, apprehending Colorado gold thieves. The case was closed when a U.S. marshal Siringo had called in, entered the camp he was in, with the leader of the gang. The marshall called on the thief to surrender, and the thief laughed because Siringo was standing there with his rifle butt on the ground. The thief walked over to Siringo and asked him if he was going to do

wasn't proud of such a record, and he didn't make specific mention of shooting any men in his books. He did, however, mention many attempts made to "assisinate" him, and that he always "defended himself". It's a good bet that he finished at least a half dozen or so bad men in his 50 odd years as a cowboy and detective, and wounded several times that many more. In connection with a gold theft case in Nevada in the early 1900s, he said he "defended himself from assisination", killing one thief and seriously wounding another, but regretted that he couldn't have taken both without a fight.

After Siringo left Pinkerton's, he spent a few years working as a lawman in the cattle trade, but in 1922 his health broke down as the result of severe exposure in winter weather. After a serious bout with pleurisy he somewhat recovered, and moved to Southern California. It wasn't long before he got some of his vitality back, and gravitated to Hollywood. He lived near a section of Hollywood called "Gower Gulch", which was the stomping grounds of the motion picture cowboys. Being the kind of person who liked people, he soon came to know a number of the famous, near-famous and working men of the cowboy segment of the film industry. Not the least of his Hollywood friends was William S. Hart, the most famous western movie actor of his time.

As a result of his association with the movie cowboys, many of whom were actors and not real cowboys, Siringo came to have an influence on western films which has lasted to this day. He is at least partly responsible for the fact that the better westerns don't use the ridiculous chatter which some writers allege to have been the cowboy's language of the old days.

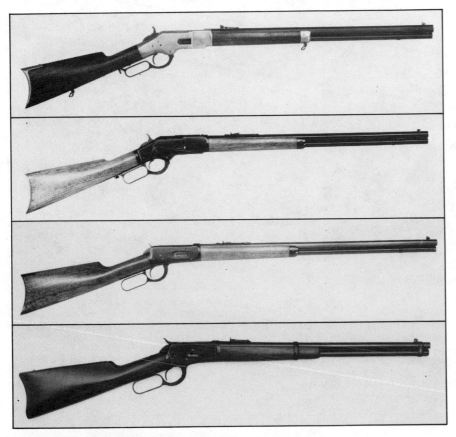

Siringo was always ready to upgrade his armament as improved models became available. His favorite Winchester longarms included (t-b) a Model 66 in .44 Henry, a Model 73 in .44-40, a Model 92 in .44-40 and a Model 94 in .30-30.

tion could. Unlike many a gunfighter of song and story, Siringo unhesitatingly carried his arms ready to use if he felt the need.

Typical of Siringo's many "stand-offs" and "getting the drops on" was one with a New Mexico bad man in the Billy the Kid days. Siringo was eating breakfast with another man in a cafe, when the outlaw walked in and tried to "call him out" for working against him and Billy the Kid. Siringo kept his hand near his "old Colt's .45" expecting the bad guy to draw, but

anything, and Siringo told the thief to give up. That was it—no shooting, although the thief was armed and ready to have some. The $10,000 in gold was recovered for Siringo's mine owner client.

Such incidents colorfully fill Siringo's long career. Once he was about to have it out with a man operating on the edge of the law, (a man who later became a worthy chief of police), when Siringo beat him to the draw so badly, the man put his gun down without resistance. Another time he was after a murderer known as "Mr. Fatty," and he took him in by simply walking in on him with pistol in hand.

This is not to say that Siringo wasn't capable of shooting if he had to. He was just the sort of man who

Siringo became a western technical adviser to many movie makers and stars before he died in 1927. His efforts can still be seen in some of the old William S. Hart silent westerns, which actually have as true a look of the old west as any films ever produced. Siringo showed the movie people how to do their gun slingin' the way he had done it, and seen it done.

To this day, through his books, motion pictures and the stories he told, Charlie Siringo, the cowboy, detective and gunfighter, has created an authentic effect on the modern attitude of the old west, its gunfighters and gunfighting. It is a truly fitting memorial to one of the last of the great gunfighters of the old west.

Faces West

A Gallery of Gunfighters.

Single action Colts and chaps seem to be the order of the day for this sextet of cowboys from John H. Slaughter's ranch and the Chiricahua Cattle Co.

The posse that pursued Black Jack Ketcham rests after their chase. They seem to be ready for immediate action, however, for their Winchesters and Colts are still at hand. The man in the center is C.S. Fly, Tombstone's famous photographer.

This pair of Arizona pistoleros leans casually against the split rail fence and shubbery of the photographer's studio. Colt Peacemakers are their choice.

Tools of the trade. This prospector's Marlin rifle and nickeled Iver Johnson hammerless revolver are as much a part of his kit as are his trusted burro, gold pan and coffee pot.

Cross draw holsters were popular with the Army, lawmen and badmen. This hombre's Peacemaker looks like a part of him, but unfortunately the same cannot be said for his cravat!

This lone cowboy looks like a man who knows his job. He wears his Colt high on his hip in the manner favored by others in his profession.

More Faces West

The boys at "The Cow Boy." It is hard to tell whether this group is leaving or entering the saloon, although a close scrutiny suggests the former.

Taking no chances, this duo of Texas Rangers sports 73 Winchesters, Colt Peacemakers, a Lightning revolver and a fighting knife.

Buckskins, moccasins and a wistful look set off this frontiersman's Peacemaker and Smith & Wesson.

This deputy sheriff obviously likes his "new-fangled" Luger automatic, but his old Peacemaker holster is still good enough.

At the time of this portrait Badman Rube Burrow had little use for his Marlin rifle, Colt Peacemaker and Remington Model 1875 Army.

The bedsheet backdrop suggests that this cowboy was haphazardly photographed in his hotel room. He appears to favor a .32 Smith & Wesson 3rd Model Safety revolver.

More Faces West

This frontier scout was photographed in the mid '70s sporting his typical flowing locks, Smith & Wesson American and Model 1873 Winchester. The army belt plate, embroidered hat and fancy buckskins are personal vanities.

"This is my last poker game" is the handwritten pledge on the back of this picture of a frontier "den of iniquity." President Benjamin Harrison looks sternly down from above the bar, while the man with the small pocket revolver looks cleaned out. No doubt he is the reformed gambler.

This American "soldier of fortune," is taking no chances on running out of ammunition while south of the border. Like his Mexican compadres, he carries a .44-40 Winchester and Colt Single Action.

Equality of the gentle sex on the frontier was never an issue—so long as the "equalizer" was a Colt M-1878 double action revolver.

This 1870s Durango, Colo. silver miner favors a Spencer .52 repeater for his insurance against claim jumpers.

Ɛ *Photos courtesy of: Allen Erwin collection, Arizona Historical Society, Jay Van Orden Collection, Lee Silva Collection and Phil Spangenberger.* **Ɜ**

Nez Percé Reservation Police brandish their .44 M-1875 Remingtons as a warning to lawbreakers. Evidently two of their own didn't heed the warning, as their faces have been obliterated in true Indian custom after they "went bad."

M. C. Goodell,

SALMON CITY, IDAHO.

Frontier Gun Leather

Continued from page 111

exposed stud would slip into the slot on the belt and the gun could hang, muzzle down, thus doing away with the need for a leather holster. This method was somewhat concealable and the pistol could be brought into action very quickly either by sliding it out of the slot, or by merely swivelling the gun into the line of fire. A few of these belts still exist today and command a good price among gun collectors.

Cartridge belts came into use almost immediately after cartridge guns. During the Civil War a Confederate cavalryman's diary told of several men in his outfit who preferred the Maynard carbine and carried them, along with belts that contained 50 loops sewn onto them for the cartridges and expended casings which they were always careful to save.

In 1870 the U.S. Army adopted canvas covered leather belts with 50 loops for their .50-70 Springfields and Sharps. These belts were made by the arsenals as an item of issue, after many officers' reports complained of the inadequacies of the cartridge boxes and pouches then in use. Many soldiers copied the civilian's belts and "unofficially" outfitted themselves with looped belts. Strangely though, the army which is so often the last to "get the word" was ahead of their civilian neighbors on the frontier when they started using the canvas cartridge loops. Leather, when combined with brass, or copper, as many of the early cartridges were made of tends to form

Top to bottom: In 1870 the U.S. Army adopted a canvas-covered cartridge belt which they called the "prairie belt." This belt was patterned after the civilian-used leather belts such as the example in the center. Although canvas is long-lasting and doesn't form verdigris which causes the brass or copper casings to stick in the loops, civilians didn't adopt them until near the end of the frontier era. The dog's head brass plate buckle on the Mills patent belt was a civilian variety. (Author's collection)

One of the few photographs the author has ever seen, showing a "Buscadero"-type rig being used on the frontier. The man is Sheriff Commodore Perry Owens of Apache County, Arizona Territory. He probably adopted this set-up because of the width of the belt used to hold his Colt Single Action cartridges as well as the huge .45-70 cartridges for his Springfield Officer's Model rifle. (Arizona Historical Society)

a green residue and can cause a cartridge to stick in the loop. Canvas does not do this, but for some reason, the idea of cloth cartridge belts never caught on very well with civilians, although they were used to some extent in the later years of the frontier.

Leather cartridge belts of the Old West differ greatly from their modern counterparts. The belts used on the old frontier often carried a man's complete supply of cartridges. With the great distances a man had to travel, coupled with the chances of having to use his guns, it became necessary to carry as large a supply of extra ammunition as possible. Therefore, cartridge belts were made with as many loops as they could hold, generally sewn on in a single row, but some were made with two rows of cartridge loops. Sometimes they were formed by running a strap of leather through a series of slots on the belt as if the loops were woven in. Most belts contained from 30 to 40 loops in the standard calibers of .38, .41, .44, and .45. They were often embellished with the border stamped or rolled tooling and were made from the same weight of leather as were the holsters. Buckles were generally rectangular or octagonal shaped frame type affairs that were longer on the top and bottom than at the sides. They were usually of nickel finish. The buckle and tab were often sewn onto the belt proper which was generally made around three inches in width.

A popular variation of the cartridge belt was the money belt type. This belt looked like any other cartridge belt on the exterior, but on closer examination one would find that the belt proper is made of softer leather than the standard variety. This soft leather belt is folded over, usually on the bottom, and stitched

along the top. One end is also stitched shut with the other end left open. A fellow could carry his silver or gold coins in that belt and feel pretty secure about it.

Regardless of the type of holster that was worn with a belt, it was universally worn over the belt, *not hanging from a slot cut in the bottom of the belt.* This is one of the biggest sins perpetrated by modern western films. The setup with the holster suspended from the bottom of the belt did not come into use until well into the 20th century. In the thousands of photos that this author has seen of cowboys, soldiers, Indians and assorted western types, few pictures or references of such rigs being used on the frontier have been observed. One rig was worn by Commodore Perry Owens and was evidently a special order item, although others could have existed. Commodore Owens used the "Buscadero" rig, as it is now called, because he had two

rows of cartridge loops on his belt. The top row was for the massive .45-70 cartridges for his Springfield Officer's Model Sporting rifle and the bottom was designed for his Colt revolver ammunition. Obviously, any holster that would have to straddle a load like that would be very cumbersome, so some ingenuity was used.

Cartridge belts were worn higher than they are nowadays. They were worn around the man's actual waist or above his hip rather than slung from it. Some men wore their belts looser and lower but the average fellow went for the "high" style. This was slipped through a folded piece of leather that was looped over the horn of the saddle. This was sometimes called the "California" style. With this arrangement, the rifle could hang to the side of the saddle with the muzzle down, or straight across the saddle. It was a practical idea and very popular with many plainsmen.

While discussing carrying arms on horseback, it should be added

Colt Lightnings and Thunderers.

Frontier gun leather has a definite flavor all its own. These old holsters and belts have a character and look about them that seems to tell the story of the settling of the Old West and its many hardships and adventures. For years, they were considered by many gun collectors, as nothing more than old leather. However, this same "old leather" has recently been receiving recognition as a valid part of gun collecting. They are no longer looked upon as "junk items," but as an integral part of firearms history. ☗

Two very typical rigs of the 1870s and '80s period. Both belts are of the "money belt" variety. The top belt was made in Pueblo, Colorado and features sewn-on tabs, and a single loop holster holding an 1875 Remington .44, while the bottom belt utilizes the tapered belt tab method and a formed scabbard type holster which contains a Colt Single Action in .45 caliber.

method is much more practical for riding horseback, or even walking for that matter. Men who favored the crossdraw wore their belts higher also. It's just easier to get to your sixgun if it is about waist high, when you have to reach across your body for it.

Long guns were carried in either saddle scabbards, horn sockets or simply slung across the shoulder or resting on the pommel while riding.

The older flint and percussion plains rifles, along with the big Sharps, Springfields, and other large single-shot arms were generally carried across the pommel sometimes in Indian style soft fringed and/or beaded scabbards of buckskin. There are many of these old buffalo guns around today with the forearm worn away to the barrel as evidence of this usage.

Saddle scabbards were generally used for the easier to handle Winchesters, Marlins and the like. These scabbards covered the majority of the rifle and were sewn or laced along the underside of the sheath. They attached to the saddle by means of two straps. One would connect to the pommel if the rifle was to be carried butt forward, while the lower strap attached to the rear rigging. The stirrup strap would then go over the scabbard.

One other way that rifles were usually carried was where the gun

This Remington illustration from an 1890 Harpers Weekly shows two styles used to transport rifles on the frontier. The Texican uses the "California" saddle horn loop for his Winchester while the Indian prefers cradling his rifle in his arms.

that many revolvers were carried in small pommel holsters or under the flaps of saddlebags. The latter method was popular with express riders in the early days of the west. The 1849 Colt Pocket pistols and "Baby" Dragoons lent themselves to these rigs very well as did the later

The author wishes to thank the following individuals for their assistance in lending items for photography in this article: Dr. Charles Basham, Erich Baumann, Denny Foreman, Garry James and Terry Parsons of Sotheby Parke Bernet, Los Angeles.

Heck Thomas

Continued from page 67

Tarrant County which wanted him to run for sheriff. Heck had some personal problems that caused him to decline all of these offers, however. His wife hated frontier living conditions and wanted to return to Georgia to raise and educate their children properly.

Heck Thomas has been considered one of the most dedicated lawmen of his era. His efforts in bringing outlaws to justice stemmed from a great desire to make living conditions better for the law abiding citizens, he was honest and fair with everyone he met, regardless of which side of the law they stood on and he always gave an outlaw a chance to surrender—even when doing so endangered his own life. On several occasions, this resulted in being wounded in the ensuing fight. But, to Heck Thomas, the responsibilities that went with wearing a badge included giving even known killers a chance to come with him peaceably.

This desire to bring law and order to the frontier caused Heck to decline those more lucrative offers from Texas and look north to Indian territory where several outlaw bands lived, robbed and killed without much fear of reprisal. The law in the Indian territory was enforced by U.S. deputy marshals operating out of Judge Isaac Parker's Court in Ft. Smith, under U.S. Marshal John Carroll's guidance. Jim Taylor, Heck's friend and partner on the Lee brothers hunt, had already put in a good word for him, and even though John Carroll presented a bleak picture for his marshals' lives and income, he accepted a deputy's commission when it was offered.

The next few years were exciting ones for Thomas even though he spent more time in the company of Indians, outlaws and rattlesnakes than he could manage with his family. Another son was born during one of his absences and Isabelle went through her labors with only her children there to help. This was almost the final straw for a gentle-born southern lady. The rift between them stretched almost to the breaking point.

Heck's performance of his duties and reputation as an honest, fearless marshal who deliberately chose the toughest men to track, earned him the respect of men on both sides of the law. It also earned him a transfer to Whitebead Hill, a few miles west of Pauls Valley in Indian territory in 1887. He took his family with him but the primitive living conditions were too much for Isabelle, in November, she told him she was going home to Georgia. Heck agreed, thinking the change would do her good. It's unknown if he ever saw her again for she wrote at Christmas to tell him she wasn't coming back unless he gave up being a lawman. They were divorced the next Spring. He admitted in later years that being a lawman was in his blood, and he couldn't give it up, even to save his marriage.

Law enforcement work has always been dangerous, but it was never more dangerous than during the late 1800's when the frontiers were being settled and tamed. It was in 1887, after the deaths of Deputy Marshals Frank Dalton and Ed Stokley, that the Elevator newspaper printed: "This makes 15 marshals killed in the Territory in two years." Both these young deputies had worked and ridden with Thomas and he had high respect for them.

Thomas was almost an idol to many of the young deputy marshals when he worked out of Judge Parker's court. He was a tall, well-built man, standing just over 6 feet tall, with wavy brown hair and mustache—turned white in his later years. He wore a beard during his years with the Texas Express Company, but by the time he went to work for Judge Parker, he had shaved it off and just sported a full mustache. He habitually wore knee-length boots, corduroy trousers, flannel shirt and a broad brimmed white hat. His horses were among the finest and his firearms were the best available.

The information that is available about Thomas' preference of weapons reveals that he acquired two Colt Single Action .45s shortly after they were introduced in 1873, and wore one or both of them continuously for about 20 years. These were ivory handled and became an integral part of his uniform, recognized by all who saw him. His description was as important to the outlaws as theirs was to him.

These Colt .45s, a decorated .44-40 Winchester Carbine (probably used against the Lee brothers) and his stately bearing were factors in the admiration of young deputies like Frank Dalton. More importantly, was the fact that he rode and fought well, had developed a keen sense of awareness of danger, had an almost uncanny ability to guess where a wanted man would be and was totally honest in his dealings with everyone he met. He prided himself on giving an outlaw a chance to surrender, but if that offer was refused, he shot fast and accurate. Many outlaws lived out prison sentences because of Thomas' reputation as a fast man with a gun—which they respected and didn't challenge.

Frank Dalton's brothers, Grat, Bob and Emmett were law abiding cowboys for many years. Grat and Bob followed Frank into law enforcement as deputy marshals and Emmett was a posseman with them. Several factors led them across the line, but primarily they felt they could get more money outside the law than inside it. Heck had partly been responsible for Frank Dalton being commissioned a deputy marshal by recommending him to Judge Parker. He had also ridden with Grat, Bob and Emmett on occasion. He knew the men personally, and had respect for their gunfighting abilities. He also felt that if he could face them, they would give themselves up rather than pull down on him. Their previous friendship was the basis for his feelings, but from other sources, the opinion was that they had too high a respect for his own ability with a Colt and Winchester. This was never brought to a test, for although he spent several months on their trail, he never was able to corner them. He was close enough that he captured some of their pack animals, camp gear and provisions when they evacuated a camp site just ahead of his arrival. His constant pressure played a big role in their decision to make one last big raid and leave the country and Heck Thomas behind. Even before the sounds of gunfire died down in Coffeyville's streets, Thomas was there—almost, anyway. He had followed them to their camp just below the Kansas border and planned to call on them to surrender at sunup. They left camp hurriedly during the night and made their way to Coffeyville by early morning—Heck was there later that evening.

Wells Fargo Manager Andrews wrote Heck shortly after the Dalton's demise and said: "While it has not been marked by capture, we feel that your work, more than anything, brought about the extermination of this gang . . . and are happy to hand you, from our railway and express pool, a check herewith in the amount of $1500." Emmett, the sole Dalton survivor, stated in his book, written after his release from prison, that Heck Thomas, by "pressing close," persuaded Bob to try that one last robbery. Thomas, according to this youngest Dalton robber, had been the gang's "nemesis."

All of Heck's time was not spent manhunting during the years of 1888 to 1892, however. He had been wounded by bullets in the wrist and side when he and his possemen ordered some moonshiners to surrender. They saw Heck as he had come before their cabin alone, and shot him from ambush. When they rushed out to finish him off, the other possemen shot them. Heck and his wounded prisoner went to Tulsa for treatment from a doctor. A young schoolteacher named Matie Mowbry was visiting the doctor's daughter and when the two met, sparks flashed. Several pleasant weeks were spent in Tulsa and, on leaving to take his prisoner to Ft. Smith, Heck told Matie: "When you are a little older, I'm coming back for you." He visited Tulsa a few more times during the next few years and, in 1892, they were married.

Thomas and several other marshals spent almost full time trying to corral and capture the Doolin gang after the Coffeyville raid. Bill Doolin, George Newcomb and Charley Pierce were members of the Dalton gang, who, for whatever reasons, were not included in the plans for the Coffeyville raid. They formed another gang and recruited others who had ridden with them as cowboys and in the Dalton gang at one time or another.

Bill Tilghman finally traced Doolin to Eureka Springs, Arkansas, in 1896, and captured him. Doolin was kept in the Guthrie jail until he managed to escape July 5th,—only to be killed by Thomas a month-and-a-half later.

During the months Thomas and other marshals were trailing, capturing and/or killing other members of the Doolin gang, Heck switched sidearms. Over the years he had adopted some of the newer models to be developed. In the long gun field, he had used an 1866 Winchester, switched to the '73 Winchester .44-40 and then later used an 1886 .45-90, an 1892 Winchester .44-40 and 1894 Winchester .30-30. Except for his use of a shotgun in the killing of Bill Doolin, there is no mention that he relied much on this type of weapon.

Other than the ivory gripped Colt .45s, there is not much information on the handguns Thomas used prior to the mid-1890s. Sometime during his hunt for members of the Doolin gang, he retired the Colt .45 in favor of the new Colt double-action Navy .38. This cartridge wasn't as powerful as the .38 Special that came along in 1902, but was a popular round at that time. It served as a military cartridge from 1892 to 1911, due in part to the Army and Navy model Colt revolvers.

Underpowered by today's standards and in comparison with the .45 Colt, this pistol and cartridge must have served Thomas well, for he was credited with the capture of over 300 criminals during the 1893-1896 years. The Colt .38 played a big part in some of those captures.

This Navy Colt .38 was given by Heck to Fred Larrance, one of the men who rode with him in his last posse, just before he was elected as Lawton's chief of police in 1901. That same pistol, with its 4½-inch barrel, was later given to the Museum of Great Plains in Lawton, to join the Winchester .44-40, marshal and police chief badges and other momentos.

It seems that Thomas was sufficiently impressed with the performance of the Navy Colt .38 that he bought another one in the same caliber, but with a 6-inch barrel. This pistol was given to his son Earl W., who died in January, 1973. That Colt is now in the John Bianchi (of Bianchi Leather Products fame) Gunfighters Museum, Temecula, California. This was the last Colt owned and used by Thomas.

There is another Thomas pistol in a private collection in Arkansas that is also a double-action Colt—a New Service .44 that has had its barrel chopped to 2 inches. According to the letter of authentication accompanying the pistol—from a former deputy marshal who was a contemporary of Thomas, Tilghman and Madsen—it was carried by Thomas while he and Wells Fargo's Chief Detective Fred Dodge rode the express cars hoping to be present when a robbery took place. The shotgun Thomas used in the battle with Doolin, an L.C. Smith double-barrel, is also in this collection.

According to the history of this shotgun, it had been used by several marshals during the 1890s in their battles with members of the Doolin and other gangs. Bee Dunn used it to kill George "Bitter Creek" Newcomb and Bill Tilghman used it in gun battles with "Little Bill" Raidler and "Little Dick" West. All men were members of the Doolin gang and ended up on the receiving end of lead slugs from lawmen's guns. Raidler was the only survivor, but in prison, developed locomotor ataxia as a result of his wounds and was issued a presidential pardon when it was learned he had only a few months to live. Tilghman personally appeared before the parole board on his behalf and helped him get started in a cigar store business—which he operated the rest of his short life.

By the turn of the century, Heck Thomas had one of the most highly regarded reputations on the frontier. He was elected chief of police of Lawton in 1901 and organized a police department, starting with three men and ending up with 14 on the force at the end of his seven years as chief.

The year Oklahoma became a state, Heck's age, hard life and long years of service caught up with him. He was also in charge of Lawton's volunteer fire department and, while hurrying to a fire one night, suffered a heart attack. Long weeks in an Oklahoma City hospital got him back on his feet but he was never the same tower of strength after that. He tried for re-election in 1909 but failed. He was appointed deputy marshal for the Western District of Oklahoma on January 1, 1910, with headquarters in Lawton, but was limited to serving process papers from a buggy.

A year later, Chris Madsen became acting marshal of Guthrie. On New Year's Eve, five deputies took the oath of allegiance as soon as Chris was sworn in. Heck Thomas was one of these. Bill Tilghman came up from Oklahoma City to join them and the three guardsmen recalled old days and events. Heck was teased by Madsen for wearing such a fancy get-up as the Prince Albert coat he had on. "A funny outfit to wear to go out to capture a bad man," he said. Thomas simply pulled back the jacket to reveal the old standby ivory handled Colt .45 holstered at his hip.

Heck's condition worsened rapidly on his return to Lawton, reaching the point where he was barely able to walk and soon not at all. On August 9, 1912, he wrote Chris: "This malady is troubling me again, and I know I have not the strength to resist it, so no matter what happens don't you and Bill come down here, and no flowers.... No need to answer, for I will not be alive to receive it. Remember me to your children and good-bye forever. Your friend, Heck."

On August 15, he lost consciousness. As a few friends, Matie and their daughters watched at his bedside, age and crippling disease did what no outlaw's bullet was able to do. At 4:00 in the morning, Henry Andrew Thomas died quietly.

Through his efforts, and the efforts of his fellow officers, Oklahoma passed from a raw, rugged, primitive, untamed, lawless land, to statehood, dignity and law and order. Heck Thomas, his firearms—and his proficiency with them—and his courage played a big part in that transition.

211

Billy The Kid

Continued from page 78

burning home. But Dudley refused flatly to interfere with "duly appointed authority," represented, in his opinion, by Sheriff Peppin. He and his men would only be spectators to whatever happened. He then violated neutrality by ordering all McSween men out of the Patron and Montana houses, on penalty of tearing down both houses with his Gatlings. This reduced the McSween forces to the 11 men in the McSween residence—ten men, actually, since McSween would touch no weapon but his Bible. And the McSween house was burning: down one wing of its wide U, across the front, and now along the other wing toward the kitchen.

(Colonel Dudley was severely criticized for his decision. Congress and the president were bombarded with demands that Dudley be court-martialed. Dudley was finally called before a military tribunal, questioned, censured, but not punished.)

The fire had by now driven the McSween ten-man army into the last remaining room of the big house—the kitchen. The chips were down now. Outside the kitchen door was a small yard some 20 feet square surrounded by a waist-high adobe wall. As darkness fell, Murphy-Dolan men manned that wall wherever gunfire from the house could not reach them. They crouched low, guns ready and waiting. Flames from the burning house lighted the yard like a stage . . . .

Morris and Semora were the first to attempt the gantlet. They fell dead, within a few steps. Vincente Romero went next, and died.

Then came McSween. McSween refused to run; he walked out, his Bible in his hands. A dozen slugs hit him. He was dead before his body hit the ground.

Rapidly, one after another, French, Chavez, Gonzales, Skurlock, Salazar and Tom O'Folliard made their runs. Miraculously, all but Salazar made it, diving over the wall into darkness. Ygenio Salazar made it too, finally. Badly wounded, he feigned death while the Murphy-Dolan forces swarmed through and around the house and the bodies; then, hours later, he crawled away and into hiding.

The Kid came last. Ten men had braved that criss-cross hail of fire; five bodies littered the yard. Billy came out fast, two guns blazing, his quick feet dancing over and around the dead. Outside the wall, men stood up, yelling and shooting. One

of those men, Bob Beckwith, caught one of Billy's bullets, and died. A bullet grazed one of Billy's boots, and he stumbled. But another of his bullets hit John McKinney in the mouth; another clipped the ear of a man named Pearce. (McKinney lived, badly disfigured.) Tally one, Beckwith, for Billy.

Three hits, firing two-handed, at a run, over tricky footing. Not as good as the snowbirds story, but—good shooting.

There is no question, from that time on, Billy was an outlaw. With McSween dead, such law as there was in Lincoln County was aligned against the McSween partisans that remained alive, and Billy was the one most bitterly hated. Billy, O'Folliard, Bowdre and a few other hard-core survivors became a "wild bunch," hiding out at times, whooping it up in bars in Fort Sumner and elsewhere when the spirit moved. They stole cattle, gambled, stole horses, anything for meat and a dollar. Billy became *El Chivato,* The Mischievous One, to the Mexican people. He gave them meat, a dollar or two now and then for beans. In return, they gave him shelter when needed, silence and shrugs of the shoulder when anyone asked questions about him.

It was no road to riches. Opportunities for big-time outlawry in that time and place were limited: no train robberies, no bank hold-ups, no big herds driven across the border. Various court records show Billy charged, once with "keeping a gaming table," once with stealing cattle (case "not found"), once with stealing horses (released on $300 bail). He was once reported captured and killed in Santa Fe; was arrested (charge unknown) and jailed once in Albuquerque; burrowed his way out of the adobe jail.

Meanwhile, Governor Lew Wallace issued a proclamation of amnesty to all participants in the Lincoln County War. Some—John Middleton, Fred Wayt and Hendry Brown among them—accepted it and left New Mexico. Hendry Brown later became a peace officer in Kansas. In March, 1879, Billy received a personal invitation from Governor Wallace to come into Lincoln and talk things over. The invitation stipulated that Billy must come alone and tell nobody about the meeting. Billy was skeptical; the word was that Wallace was there under escort of a troop of cavalry. It could be a trap.

But Billy rode in, alone as ordered. The cavalry was there, all right. Billy knocked at the appointed place with a rifle in his hand, a revolver in his holster.

It was a meeting of men from different worlds: Wallace, the firm believer in law and order *A LA* Massschusetts and the Army; Billy, a product of a land where the only law was the gun. But Wallace was quite taken with Billy; a pleasant, well-mannered boy, he thought, but of course misguided, convinced that if he were disarmed his enemies would kill him. Billy must stand trial, he said, for charges existing; but, if convicted, he would be pardoned and given safe conduct out of the Territory.

Billy's reply was, in effect, "The hell with that! I've as much right here as anyone! And whoever thinks different had better come shooting!"

It astonished Wallace. Teenagers in Massachusetts were tough enough to captain clipper ships, but this was a different kind of toughness. The result? Billy rode out of Lincoln, still armed and wary as a cat in a kennel; and Lew Wallace issued a "Wanted" notice:

"BILLY THE KID. $500 REWARD. I will pay $500 reward to any person or persons who will capture William Bonney, alias The Kid, and deliver him to any sheriff of New Mexico. Satisfactory proofs of identity will be required. Signed: Lew Wallace Governor of New Mexico."

Soon after the fight at the McSween house, "Dad" Peppin resigned as sheriff, resenting, he said, Murphy's and Dolan's efforts to "control" him. Then, to the utter amazement of most people, the Lincoln County Commissioners appointed Pat Garrett to fill the Brady-Peppin shoes. After all, who was Pat Garrett?

He was a tall man, 6 feet and some inches; slender; young (born 1850); a Johnny-come-lately from Louisianna via Texas; a cowboy; once a buffalo hunter; recently partner with a man called "Beaver" Smith in a saloon and mercantile business in Fort Sumner. He knew Billy, had shared "rest and recreational" evenings with him in Fort Sumner bars, was rumored to have shared other exploits with Billy on nights when cattle disappeared from various ranges. This was rumor only, vigorously denied, but there were people who wondered if the reason for Garrett's appointment was that he knew Billy's hang-out, hide-outs and habits. Even if true, it was no great slur; many Southwestern (and other) cattlemen were less than choosy about whose calves they branded in their beginnings.

Be that as it may, Garrett went to work with new-broom vigor. On the night of November 26, 1880, a

Garrett posse trapped Billy and several of his pals in an old building near Coyote Springs. Garrett sent one of his possemen, Jim Carlyle, into the building to discuss surrender. Some time later, Carlyle was seen to leap through a window, land running, only to be cut down by a flurry of shots from inside the building. The posse loaded Carlyle's body over a saddle without interference and departed, ending the siege. Who killed Carlyle is another unanswered question, but he is always listed as one of Billy's victims.

Billy had a sweetheart in Fort Sumner, the daughter of a Mexican family, and he made that town a center of his activities. He was among friends there; the town was 90 percent Mexican. One night, after jailing several of Billy's Mexican friends to prevent possible leakage of information to Billy, Garrett and a posse ambushed Billy, O'Folliard, and others as they rode into the village. They killed Tom O'Folliard; Billy and the others escaped. Garrett said O'Folliard "reached for his gun" when challenged, which made the killing proper under the local mores. Score one for Garrett.

There were many skirmishes; chance encounters and planned ones; shots fired; chases. But in December, Garrett and a strong posse cornered Billy and others in an old, one-room, rock house near Stinking Spring. It was bitter cold. As dawn broke, a man came shivering out of the cabin. "That's Billy!" Garrett whispered, and opened fire. The posse made it a volley. The man staggered, turned, and fell back into the cabin. But he came out again, clawing for his gun. He was too far gone. He fell, and died. But it was not Billy; it was Charlie Bowdre. Score two for Garrett.

Or rather, score six. There was neither food nor fire in that cabin, and Garrett's posse was a wall of men around it. Around noon, Billy and three others (Rudabaugh, Picket, and Wilson) surrendered.

In March, 1881, Billy was arraigned in Santa Fe for the murder of Buckshot Roberts at Blazer's Mill. It was claimed at first that this was a federal offense, since Blazer's Mill was inside the Mescalero Apache Reservation. But the actual mill site was owned by Blazer, and this raised the question of jurisdiction. The case was quashed, and Billy was turned over to Territorial authorities to stand trial for the killing of Sheriff Brady in Lincoln. On April 13, he was found guilty and sentenced to be hung—in Lincoln, on May 13, 1881, just thirty days after conviction.

Billy was jailed in a room on the second floor of the old adobe courthouse in Lincoln. Another room on that floor held the Sheriff's arsenal: weapons taken from prisoners, weapons with which to arm a posse. His guards were J.W. Bell and Bob Ollinger. Bell was a quiet, good-natured man; Ollinger was a bully, ribbing Billy about how he would kick, and how Ollinger would enjoy seeing him kick on the gallows. Ollinger chose a double-barrel shotgun from Garrett's arsenal, loaded it with buck, and dared Billy to try to escape. "I'd rather shoot you even than see you hang," Ollinger said. "And 24 buckshot, 12 in each barrel, would tear you up a-plenty!"

On April 28, Billy escaped. Some say a gun was hidden for him to find. Some say he simply slipped his small hands out of the shackles while Ollinger was off to lunch, snatched Bell's gun, shot Bell as Bell sought to escape down the narrow stairs, grabbed Ollinger's shotgun, ran to the window to face Ollinger as he came running, gun drawn, from the restaurant across the street. Pat Garrett was out of town.

"Hello, Bob," Billy said from the window.

Ollinger looked up, his gun swinging—and Billy pulled both triggers. The 24 buckshot did exactly what Ollinger said they would do.

Score two for Billy. He told friends later that he was sorry about Bell, wouldn't have shot if Bell hadn't run; but he was glad about Ollinger...there is no monument for Ollinger. Bell's monument is a bullet hole carefully preserved in the adobe wall at the foot of the stairs in the old Lincoln courthouse (now a Billy the Kid museum) where Billy's bullet hit after passing through Bell's body.

It was generally believed that Billy would flee now, leave New Mexico. But Garrett did not think so. He knew that Billy was seriously in love with the girl in Fort Sumner, and was pretty certain Billy would stay near her.

On the night of July 13, 1881, Garrett and two deputies—John Poe, another ex-buffalo hunter and newcomer to Lincoln County; and Tip McKinney, a friend of Garrett's—rode cautiously into Fort Sumner about midnight. Neither Poe or McKinney had ever seen Billy. Whether intentional or coincidental, this is a fact to remember.

They rode to Pete Maxwell's house, dismounted, and Garrett crossed the porch to Pete Maxwell's bedroom. The room was dark. Maxwell wakened, disclaimed any knowledge of Billy's whereabouts. Garrett sat on Maxwell's bed, talking in whispers.

A man came around the corner of the house, onto the porch. He saw Garrett's waiting deputies, darted into Maxwell's room. "Quien es, Pete?" he whispered. Who is it? or What goes on here?, depending on circumstance and inflection.

Garrett said he recognized the intruder, saw the gun in the man's hand, identified it (in spite of the darkness) as a "self-cocker" (double-action revolver), drew his own gun and fired two shots. But the first shot was enough, he said; Billy the Kid fell dead.

Garrett further identified the gun in his "Authentic Life" as being a .41 caliber Colt "Thunderer." Question: Why would Billy, having used Single Actions all his life, switch now to a new, entirely new model, never issued until January, 1877. It has been said that this was the gun Billy took from Bell's body when he escaped from Lincoln; but there is evidence that Bell's gun (whether "Thunderer" or not is not stated) was found beside Bell's body, that Billy recovered his own guns stored in Garrett's arsenal.

Next day, a hurriedly assembled "Coroner's Jury" (there was no Coroner, no medical testimony) identified the body as Billy's; and authorized burial. The "jury" was all Mexican. The witnesses were Garrett, Maxwell, and Tia Deluvina—a fat, motherly matron who "bossed" Pete Maxwell's house and his servants. Garretts' deputies could not testify as to identity, having never seen Billy.

Was it Billy? Probably so. But Deluvina said repeatedly, much later, that it was not Billy, that it was another boy who had come to her for a meal. He had gone to the main house with a butcher knife to cut meat from a side of beef there, and that she and Maxwell and the men of the jury had said it was Billy "so that Billy could get away." A wild story, but one that has been circulated in New Mexico for more than 90 years by people who "were there" or by their descendants. I myself have talked to men whose fathers "saw Billy years after that killing;" even talked to a man who claimed he was Billy at the age of 90. And maybe there was doubt in his places also. It was not until many months later that Garrett was able to collect Lew Wallace's reward. Wallace, you remember, had stipulated "satisfactory proof of identity." "Quien sabe?"

Interview with a Texas Ranger

Continued from page 162

ing foreclosed on. Frank asked her how much she owed, and he offered to lend her the money. She asked him how she'd ever find him to pay him back, and he told her not to worry about it, that they'd take care of it, so she took the money. They stayed in the barn overnight, and in the morning the people came to collect the mortgage, and the widow paid them off. After Frank and them made sure that the widow had got the mortgage back and burned it, they went out and robbed the money back from the mortgage people.

Q. I think I've heard a version of that story before. Frank James really told you that, huh?

A. Yep, it was funny. He was real proud of that.

Q. Was that when he was still with Jesse?

A. No, that was after Jesse got killed. Jesse wasn't with them then.

Q. Do you remember any other particular incident that you were in?

A. Well, I remember another funny one. My partner and I was riding one day, and I was in front. A couple of niggers tried to get him from behind, but he heard them in the bushes. When we heard something behind us, we never waited to ask anything—, we shot first. Well— he got around and shot one of them, and then the other one. Then he saw something rustlin' in the canebrake, so he cut down on it too. Turned out that it was only a hog in the canebrake that he killed. He got fined $25 for killing the hog, but nobody said nothing about killing the niggers. And you could buy a hog for $4 or $5 in those days too.

Q. There are a lot more questions I'd like to ask you next time, but I'd like to go back to one more for now. Can you remember or just give me a rough idea of how many gunfights you might have been in? Would you say a dozen—two dozen—50—a 100?

A. It's hard to say, but shootin' scrapes? I'd say I wasn't in more than 15 or 20 scrapes a year.

Q. Fifteen or 20 scrapes a year? For six years?

A. Yeah, about that. ♛

George Armstrong Custer

Continued from page 91

a contemporary of similar big-bore black powder cartridges, using 13 grains of black powder to propel a 225-grain bullet at 700 fps. The use of the Webley "RIC" was something of an anomaly, as Custer must have been familiar with the .44 Colt and S&W centerfire service pistols for which he would have had almost unlimited ammunition. The "RIC" was also well-known, having been originated in 1868, and was noted for its smooth double action.

Since Custer was in command of large bodies of troops armed with .45-70 Springfields, he probably did not note the Weblys' pin-rammer ejector and loading gate as liabilities to available firepower. He likely carried them for the same reason that he affected buckskin hunting clothes while campaigning—for a change from military routine, at his own discretion.

Whether or not Custer had retained his Spencer sporter for plains service late in his life is not known. However, it seems unlikely. By 1873, several pictures of him had been taken with both Remington and Springfield sporting rifles, believed to be in .50-70 Musket, or .50 Government, caliber. Custer is shown in a famous photo of himself and Grand Duke Alexis, with a sporter-stocked 1870 Trapdoor Springfield having double set triggers.

This rifle was "sporterized", with a cast-iron pistol grip. No change is evident in the sights or barrel length although the gun must have been lightened considerably. Its .50-70 cartridge was the issue round from 1866 to 1873. A 450-grain bullet started out at 1260 fps ahead of its 70 grains Fg powder. Power was a respectable 1480 ft-lbs. at the muzzle. Carbine loads using a shortened case had also been devised and offered 400 grains of lead and 45 grains of powder, as certain GI carbines couldn't quite chamber the full length .50-70. By 1873, both rounds had been superseded by a newly revised "trapdoor" rifle and carbine in .45-70. Custer evidently preferred the .50-70, or didn't want to replace two expensive sporting rifles which he already owned.

Of these two .50-70 rifles, his Remington rolling block is best documented. The transcript of a letter he wrote to Remington Arms in 1873 gives us much insight into the rifle and Custer's style of hunting:

"Headquarters Fort Abraham Lincoln,
Dakota Territory
October 5, 1873
MESSRS. REMINGTON & SONS:

Dear Sirs—Last year I ordered from your firm a Sporting Rifle, Caliber .50. I received the rifle a short time prior to the departure of the Yellowstone Expedition. The Expedition left Fort Rice the 20th of June, 1873, and returned to Fort Abraham Lincoln, September 21, 1873. During the period of three months, I carried the rifle referred to on every occasion and the following list exhibits but a portion of the game killed by me: Antelope 41; buffalo 4; elk 4; blacktail deer 4; American deer 3; white wolf 2; geese, prairie chickens and other feathered game in large numbers.

The number of animals killed is not so remarkable as the distance at which the shots were executed. The average distance at which the forty-one antelopes were killed was 250 yards by actual measurement. I rarely obtained a shot at an antelope under 150 yards, while the range extended from that distance up to 630 yards.

"With the expedition were professional hunters employed by the Government to obtain game for the troops. Many of the officers and men also were excellent shots and participated extensively in hunting along the line of march. I was the only person who used one of your rifles, which, as may properly be stated, there were pitted against it breech-loading rifles of almost every description, including many of the Springfield breechloaders altered to sporting rifles. With your rifle, I killed far more game than any other single party, professional or amateur, while the shots made with your rifle were at longer range and more difficult shots than were those made by any other rifles in the command. I am more than ever impressed with the many superior qualities possessed by the system of arms manufactured by your firm, and I believe I am safe in asserting that to a great extent this opinion is largely shared by the members of the Yellowstone Expedition who had the opportunity to make practical tests of the question.
I am truly yours,
G. A. Custer
Brevet Major General U.S. Army"

The Black Hills Expedition was not strictly an Indian scouting enterprise, but was also for exploration. Consequently, the expedition included survey, geology, zoology and photography specialists from the civilian world. The force itself numbered 1000 men, 110 wagons, three Gatling guns and one 3-inch rifle cannon. One Mary Jane Canary (Calamity Jane) served as guide part of the way into this area held sacred by the Sioux Indians.

Custer's luck worked both ways on this trip, for in July of 1874, barely a month after leaving, his expedition discovered gold in the Black Hills, at French Creek. This caused a rush that doomed the Great Sioux Reservation, leading to much of the trouble that proceeded and led up to the Little Big Horn. At the time, however, it was a major find. Custer also had good luck on the hunting trail, taking a large grizzly bear at Bear Butte Creek in August. During the expedition as many as 100 mule deer were taken in a day's foraging for meat. All told, 1000 were taken over the two months of the campaign, some 1200 miles of travel through lands hitherto unseen and unhunted by the white man.

Custer was summoned to Washington to testify concerning the infamous Belknap scandals that rocked the Grant administration. Only through his pull with General Sheridan was Custer allowed to finally join his troops at Ft. Abraham Lincoln, on the eve of the Yellowstone Expedition—his last battle.

In 1876 the Cavalry troopers were issued the single shot Model 1873 .45-70 Springfield "trapdoor" carbines. It was a well-made reasonably accurate arm in an effective caliber. It had one main drawback though. After the inside-primed, copper cased service round was fired and the breech opened, the ejector would sometimes cut throught the soft base and fail to remove the case. The only way it could then be removed was by prying the shell out with a knife, a cumbersome process in the heat of battle. The soldiers were also armed with the .45 Colt 1873 single action army revolver and the Model 1860 light cavalry saber. A variety of ammunition boxes were in use at the time but it appears that the 7th favored the Model 1874 Cavalry cartridge loop belt slide which had provision for twenty .45-70 rounds and/or the lamb's wool-lined Dyer Pouch. Each trooper wore one of these assemblies. A small pistol cartridge pouch was worn, on the right front of the trooper's leather belt.

Officers also used the Colt .45 SAA revolvers and the Model 1872 saber, but they often carried their privately purchased long arms on campaign. These might include various models of Winchesters, the Spencers, Rolling blocks, etc.

From contemporary evidence, Custer set out on the Yellowstone expedition dressed in a fringed buckskin jacket, wide-brimmed grey felt hat, and a red cravat. His personal sidearms probably consisted of his pair of ivory-handled .450 Webleys and his favorite .50 caliber Remington Rolling block rifle.

The basic plan for the expedition as laid out by the Commander General Terry, called for Custer and the 7th to proceed to the Rosebud River Creek, where he would determine the direction of the Indian trail. If it went towards the Little Big Horn River he was to follow it and wait until General Gibbon's infantry column reached the mouth of the Big Horn, presumably trapping the Indians between the two forces. Terry added, though, that if Custer arrived first he was at liberty to attack if he deemed it prudent.

Custer was quite sure that the 7th could whip any reasonable force of Indians and made a statement to that effect to several persons. His star was very much under a shadow because of the Belknap incident and he dearly wanted to get himself back in good graces. A smashing, 7th Cavalry victory, he was convinced, would do it. The troops marched out at noon on June 22, 1876. Custer had decided to leave the regiment's Gatling guns behind because the spavined and sickly mules needed to draw the guns and haul the thousands of extra rounds of ammunition required to service these weapons would slow the column down too much.

The morning of June the 25th found a grizzled Custer and his weary regiment in the Valley of the Little Big Horn and Rosebud. Scouts reported that there was "The largest village that they had ever seen on the plains." Custer was unimpressed, remarking that "no village" was too large for the 7th to handle. Indian scouts reported the same information. Previous experience had taught Custer that the Indians invariably overestimated the size of an opposing force, and he decided to discount their information. After a hard 10-mile ride Custer divided his force into three assault squadrons. Major Marcus Reno was ordered to take A, M, and G Companies and follow the trail right to the Little Big Horn. Captain Benteen and Companies D, H and K were to follow a line of bluffs, to the left of Reno's force. Captain McDougal was ordered to take Co. B and guard the pack train, while Custer opted to take Companies C,E,F,I and L and move to the right. He assumed that he would cut Sitting Bull's escape to the north, south or east, and Gibbon and Terry would keep him from fleeing to the west.

Custer and his squadrons broke up and, after a short ride, spotted a small band of hostiles running ahead of them. Some 45 minutes later Custer stopped the column and surveyed the area with his field glasses. He saw hundreds of shelters and campfires, in a camp almost one half mile wide and four miles long, but could find no braves among the Indians lounging around the camp. Custer assumed that he had caught them unawares. He spurred his horse and barked orders to his messenger to tell Benteen to bring the ammunition packs.

Custer soon heard gunfire and assumed that it must be Reno's troops engaging the hostiles. The noise actually was nothing more than a few Cheyenne warriors who had been scouting Custer's movements, and had fired on some of the troopers.

Before he realized it, Custer was surrounded by two forces of Sioux, and was unable to manuever into open space where his men would fight more effectively on horseback.

Reno and Benteen were occupied with hordes of Indians on a knoll some distance from Custer's position and were unable to come to his aid. Armstrong ordered his 230 troopers to dismount on a small hill and thus began the feverish battle against the seemingly endless hordes. The horses were shot and piled for breastworks. Troopers worked their Springfields frantically, (they had left their sabers behind) some of them jamming the cartridges in the breech, rendering the arms useless. The Indians continued the onslaught armed with bows and arrows, lances, trade muskets and a smattering of repeaters. Many troopers, sensing the inevitable outcome, shot themselves rather than be taken and tortured. Slightly more than an hour after it began the battle ended. Custer and his entire command lay dead on the low promontory. The bodies were stripped and mutilated in the Indian fashion, but Custer was left untouched. He had one bullet hole in his temple and one in the left side of his chest. The total number of Indians engaged in the battle must have been somewhere between 6000 and 10,000 . . . an overwhelming force for 230 men even in a defensible position with Gatling guns!

Beset by controversy to the end, Custer throughout his career always managed to rise above the petty slanders of his attackers . . . He was a devoted husband and son; a strict teetotaler and non-smoker who never inflicted his beliefs on others. Custer, complex man that he was, was neither fiend nor saint, just the boyish, energetic, impetuous, rather tragic man that history records. ♟

Black Bart

Continued from page 118

Perturbed, and pretty sure now that the arrogantly indifferent bandit wouldn't shoot at them anyhow, McConnell succeeded in circling back on the stage as Rolleri came on the scene. McConnell grabbed the Henry from Rolleri just as Bart was leaving the stage with a bag full of gold. He shot once and missed, and shot once again and missed.

Rolleri grabbed his rifle back and shot at the fleeing Bart, hitting him in the hand. The bandit stumbled, dropped the bag, picked it up with his other hand, and disappeared into the brush.

Miraculously, once again Black Bart got away clean. But almost as if he had planned it that way, he might as well have left his name and address beside the road, because he left everything else there.

Within hours, Ben Thorpe, sheriff of Calaveras County, was at the site of the robbery, followed shortly by James Hume and his next in command of Wells Fargo detectives, John Thacker.

They could hardly believe what Black Bart had left behind, littered in the brush beside the road; a black derby, a pair of opera glasses, a belt, a razor, a scented handkerchief filled with buckshot, three detachable linen shirt cuffs, and two empty flour sacks.

It was, literally, a Pandora's box of clues, and as it turned out, a direct path to Black Bart himself, for on the handkerchief, faint but still legible, was a laundry mark, "F.X.O.7."

Hume took the handkerchief and other items back to San Francisco and turned the handkerchief over to another of his detectives, Harry Morse. Hume had given Morse the sole assignment of bringing Black Bart to bay.

Not surprisingly for the clues he had to work with, Morse didn't let any grass grow under his feet. There were 91 laundries in San Francisco, and it took Morse eight days to find the right one, for on the eighth day, Morse walked into Ferguson & Bigg's California Laundry and learned that the laundry mark belonged to one of the local shops that acted as agencies for the laundry.

At the shop, a tobacco shop owned by Thomas C. Ware, Morse discovered that the mark was one allocated to Charles E. Bolton, a "Semi-wealthy mining man" who lived just down the street at the Webb House.

Morse had not told Ware that he was a Wells Fargo detective, but rather that he was in mining and wanted to meet Belton, and he glibly persuaded Ware to take him to meet Bolton.

If Morse had been startled before by the rapid turn of events, he was even more startled when, halfway to the Webb House, a dapper gentleman with blue eyes and a bush mustache walked up to them and began a conversation with Ware.

Morse didn't have to be told, but Ware turned and said to him, "This is Mr. Bolton, the man we were going to meet."

Explaining to Bolton that he had a mining venture that he wanted to discuss with him, Morse took Bolton downtown and right into James Hume's office in the Wells Fargo building!

Bolton surely knew, by now, what was in the wind, but he played his hand coolly, becoming appropriately indignant when Hume started questioning him.

When Hume asked him about his wounded hand, Bolton said that he had hurt it getting off a train.

Hume was sure that he had his man, so they got Captain Appleton Stone of the San Francisco Police Dept., and took Bolton in tow to the Webb House to search his room.

Law enforcement practices of the 1880s would make today's police officers turn green. There was no civil rights legislation, and there were no such terms as illegal search and seizure, forcible entry, etc. A suspect was considered to be guilty until proven innocent, and a law enforcement officer had legal authority to do almost anything except shoot a suspect in cold blood.

However, Hume and his Wells Fargo detectives were technically only private detectives. Legally, they could investigate, interrogate, search, disarm, arrest, detain and transport any suspect, and perform all of the duties of a local police officer or county sheriff except book a prisoner into jail.

This legal right was given to Hume and his detective force, and in fact, to any private investigator or private citizen in 1872 by the California Criminal Code, Section 834 ff., which stated, "An arrest may be made by a peace officer or by a private person."

In short, as long as Hume had "reasonable cause" to believe that the suspect had committed a crime, he had legal authority to collar the suspect as long as he took him directly to the local authorities.

This was the reason that Stone was brought into the Bolton case as

rapidly as possible, for Hume and Morse were not about to let their pigeon fly the coop.

At Bolton's hotel room, the detectives found, amongst other things, a suit of clothes that matched the one that the robber was wearing during the Funk Hill holdup the week before, a handkerchief bearing not only the same "F.X.O.7." laundry mark but also the same perfume scent as the one left at the holdup and a half finished letter in the same handwriting as the verse left by the "Po8." They also found a bible, and written inside it, an inscription addressed to Charles E. Boles.

Hume was sold. He knew that he had his man, and he also now knew what his real name was.

Stone put Boles, alias Bolton, under arrest on the spot, and when Boles asked why, Hume said simply, "Because you are Black Bart."

At police headquarters, Hume had Boles put on the black derby that had also been found at the latest robbery, and it fit so well that Boles, never one to lose the wit that had made him famous throughout California and the nation, tried to buy it back from Hume.

Boles was identified by several witnesses as having been seen in the area before the holdup, and Reason McConnell identified his voice as being the same as that of the masked bandit.

Boles was promptly installed in the clink in San Andreas, and that night he finally confessed to the Funk Hill robbery. He also confessed to the other robberies committed prior to 1879, thinking that the statute of limitations had run out on them, but he would not confess to actually being Black Bart for fear of being sentenced to life imprisonment for such a total number of holdups.

Boles also explained that he took the name "Black Bart" from a story which appeared in the Sacramento "Union" in 1871, titled "The Case of Summerfield" and written by a San Francisco attorney named William H. Rhodes, who used the pen name "Caxton."

The next day, Boles took Morse and the others to the site of the Funk Hill holdup and dug the $4000 in loot out of a log where he had hidden it after the holdup. At another spot, hidden beneath a stump, he showed them the double-barreled shotgun he had used.

On Nov. 17, 1883, Charles E. Boles, alias Charles Bolton, alias Black Bart, was sentenced to 6 years in San Quentin Prison on one count of armed robbery for committing the Nov. 3, 1883 holdup, and just 18 days after that holdup, on Nov. 21, 1883, he was admitted to San Quentin Prison to begin his "residence."

The saga of Black Bart, the bloodless bandit, should have ended there but, naturally, it didn't. Black Bart had become a national folk hero, and the news of his arrest and speedy conviction created a flood of front page headlines.

Boles had hardly changed his linen duster for prison stripes before the newspapers began to accuse Hume of having persuaded "Bart" to cop a plea on only one count of robbery just so that Wells Fargo could be sure of having Black Bart salted away and out of its hair for a few years.

In the meantime, in a private interview with Boles at San Quentin, Hume showed him a list of unsolved stage robberies, and Boles identified 29 of them as having been a product of his handiwork, also admitting, at last, that he was Black Bart.

The newspapers picked this up and accused Hume of persuading Bart to admit to all the unsolved robberies just to get them off of Hume's files.

Next, there was a furor over the reward money, and next, Hume and the others were accused of having kept the $4000 in recovered loot from the Funk Hill robbery.

Black Bart's life story was good for more newspaper sales too. Charles Boles was born in New York about 1830. He and his brother, David, followed the tide of gold seekers to California in 1850, returned to New York broke, and went back to California in 1852. David Boles died in 1852, and Charles, broke again, finally settled in Decatur, Illinois. He married and had two daughters and lived an uneventful life until the Civil War, when he distinguished himself in more than one bloody battle before mustering out as a lieutenant in 1865. He promptly deserted his wife and daughters and headed once again for the gold fields, first in Montana, then Utah, and finally California where he eventually took the easy road and began the stage robbing spree which made him a national folk hero.

The furor over Black Bart was good for newspaper copy for so long that it had barely subsided when Boles was released from San Quentin on Jan. 21, 1888.

His release was front page copy again, and never one to let his public down, he had one last chance to display his eternal wit. During an interview, the subject of which was the fact that Boles had said that he would never rob stages again, a re-porter asked him if he intended to write any more poems. Boles quickly quipped, "Young man, didn't you hear me say I would commit no more crimes?"

Hume kept a wary eye on Boles even though he had plastered the state with photographs and flyers giving Black Bart's physical description and method of operation, but in February of 1888, Charles Boles, alias Black Bart, simply vanished from sight.

In July and then early November of 1888, three stages were held up in a style like Bart's, and on Nov. 14, 1888, James Hume issued a flyer suspecting Black Bart of having pulled off the robberies.

It was good for a deluge of national headlines once again, and this time, Black Bart was suddenly "holding up" stagecoaches not only all over California, but all across the West.

Eventually, Hume admitted that he had pretended to suspect Black Bart in the recent robberies only as a ruse to throw the real bandit off guard, saying, "I feel that Bart and this individual who is robbing the stages are not one and the same. Their methods of proceeding are entirely different. He uses a pistol as an intimidator while Black Bart used a gun, a shotgun, in his work. He did not believe in the efficacy of a pistol to frighten stage drivers while he had the greatest confidence in a double-barreled shotgun."

With that, Black Bart disappeared forever without a trace, and though newspapers continued to run articles about his whereabouts for years afterwards, placing him in every state of the Union and Mexico, to this day there is no record of what finally happened to Black Bart, the "Po8", although his obituary was run in a newspaper in, of all places, New York, in 1917.

Like Black Bart himself, the guns that he used have also vanished.

During his confessions to Hume, Boles had told Hume that he had never ever loaded his shotguns during a robbery for fear of hurting someone.

He always used a double-barreled shotgun of the type that was then the "latest" variety, the cartridge type of today which Bart could break down and carry in his bedrole without detection while casing his jobs and while hotfooting it across the countryside afterwards.

True to his image of the lovable Robin Hood robber, Black Bart never owned many guns, simply because he didn't use them, and there is no gun in existence today that can be documented as having been his.

During Bart's first robbery in 1875, he had used a cartridge type double-barrel in his hands, and the other double-barrel that he had slung over his shoulders for effect was an old percussion type. When leaving the robbery, he threw the old percussion double into the bushes. It was found several days after the robbery, but its whereabouts today is unknown.

He sold the cartridge double to a woman for $10 while walking from San Jose to San Francisco. It has also disappeared.

In a magazine interview in 1905, Harry Morse stated that Bart had willed his shotgun to him. Presumedly, this is the shotgun that Boles led Morse to after the Funk Hill robbery in 1883.

What happened to the gun is not known, but strangely, on Aug. 6, 1927, L. O. Head, Vice-President of American Railway Express Co., the successor to Wells, Fargo & Co., presented "Black Bart's sawed-off shotgun" to T. Parker Lyon's Pony Express Museum in Pasadena, California. This would almost have to be the same shotgun that Morse recovered in 1883, but it too has vanished.

T. Parker Lyon moved his museum to a location across from Santa Anita Racetrack, and when he died his gun collection was sold to the Bill Harrah collection at Harrah's Club, Lake Tahoe and Reno, Nevada. Somewhere along the line, Black Bart's shotgun followed Bart into never-never land, for there is no trace of it anywhere in Harrah's collection.

However, in this article and in hundreds of others before it, Black Bart still lives in the history of the West, as James Hume called him, "The most famous stage robber in the world."

John M. Brannan, another old "resident" of San Quentin Prison, perhaps caught up with Black Bart's clever prose, once wrote a song in which he included verses about Black Bart, verses which Bart would have been proud to have written himself:

Yet still there is another
Who well did play his part.
He's known throughout the country
As Highwayman Black Bart.

He robbed the mountain stages
To him it was a pleasure
He seemed to dream of nothing else
But Wells, and Fargo's treasure.

Fitting epitaph for a worthless, wily, old rascal who won the hearts of the West and never harmed a single person doing it. ♣

Belle Starr

Continued from page 144

Belle hired the best lawyers, and in less than two months, Sam had been arraigned, released on bail, and was headed for home to await the time of the trial, March 7.

On the Friday night before Christmas, Mrs. Lucy Surrett, who lived near Whitefield on the Canadian River, gave a dance at her home and invited all the neighbors. Sam was drinking and in a foul humor, but he and Belle went anyway. Frank West, one of the Indian policemen with the posse who had wounded Sam and shot his horse, also was at the dance.

Sam spotted him and snarled: "You are the son of a bitch who shot me and killed my horse that day in the field!" West was denying the charges as Sam drew his six-shooter and fired, hitting the policeman in the neck. As West fell, he reached for his own revolver and thumbed it once. The bullet hit Sam in the chest. In just two minutes, the whole tragic incident was over.

Things quieted down some at Younger's Bend after Sam's death. So much, in fact, that on July 6, 1887, a letter appeared in Indian Territory newspapers which had been written by Robert S. Owen, U.S. Indian Agent for the Five Civilized Tribes at Muskogee, to Belle:"Mrs. Belle Starr, Oklahoma, I.T. Madam: The complaint against you for harboring bad characters has not, in my opinion, been established, and is now dismissed. I hope sincerely that you will faithfully carry out your promise to this office to not let such parties make your place a rendezvous. Robert L. Owen United States Indian Agent"

Early in 1888 Belle chose another husband, Jim July a Creek Indian, 24 years of age who had been educated in the Indian schools. He was scheduled to be tried for horse stealing in February of 1889, and when the time came for him to go to Fort Smith, Belle had ridden with him as far as San Bois, a distance of 15 miles. But then she turned back, and was ambushed on the road back home.

Who waited silently along the lonely trail for Belle?

Jim July was at Fort Smith when the telegram reached him with the news of Belle's murder. He bought a quart of whiskey, swore that "somebody is going to suffer," and rode hell-bent for home, making the 75 miles in nine hours.

He listened to the local tales, but not for long before he accused E.A. Watson, took him at gunpoint, arrested him without a warrant, and took him to Fort Smith in the company of witnesses, including Pearl Younger.

The evidence seemed condemning. Watson had been trying to lease a piece of property from Belle, but she had repeatedly and sharply refused. Rumor, meanwhile, had circulated around the neighborhood that he was wanted in Florida for murder. He was a relative newcomer in the Territory, having lived in that part of the Cherokee Nation a year.

On her way home from San Bois, Belle had stopped at the home of a man named Rowe. Watson was there and the quarrel started again. He made a cutting comment about how often federal marshals came to Younger's Bend to check Belle out. "Maybe officers in Florida would like to know where they could find you," Belle retorted. Watson left the house angry.

Belle's killer had waited at the corner of Rowe's fence row; a set of boot tracks had been found leading from Watson's house to that point, and then back by an indirect route.

Both barrels of Watson's shotgun had been recently fired and in snap judgements, some folks speculated he had decided Belle was going to turn him in. At Fort Smith, United States Commissioner Brizzolara ruled that all the evidence was circumstantial. Watson's neighbors liked him, swore he was a quiet, hard-working man. Only Jim July kept insisting that he be indicted for Belle's murder. When the rumor that Watson was wanted in Florida was checked out, it proved to be untrue. He was promptly released and his case closed.

Some thought the assassin was Belle's son, Ed Reed. He had been drinking a lot since he came to Younger's Bend to live with Belle after Sam's death. And he had been selling whiskey to the Indians. The preceding July, he had been convicted by Judge Parker of stealing horses and was sentenced to seven years in the federal penitentiary at Columbus. Belle hired good attorneys who succeeded in getting him a presidential pardon. Still, Belle was not pleased with her son.

One occasion, particularly, stuck in his craw. He had asked one night to ride the black mare and his mother refused him permission. He stole her horse anyway, returning shortly before daybreak. Belle discovered her horse had been badly abused and ridden hard and she struck Ed with her quirt, several times across the face, furious that he had crossed her. The cuts finally healed, but scars kept the incident raw in his memory. Folks knew he hated his mother, and wondered—but nothing more came of it.

It is told that John Middleton's brother, Jim, confessed years later on his death bed that he had killed Belle for revenge. He said $5000 that John carried in his saddle bags was missing when his body was found on the Poteau River bank. A couple of other names have been bantered around in history when the identity of Belle's murderer is speculated, but the most interesting story surfaces in the investigations of Deputy Marshal J.R. Hutchins.

It was generally known that Jim July had been playing around with a girl at Briartown. Belle, angry at this affront, had told him that she'd not spend her money hiring lawyers to help him when his trial came up.

After Watson had been released, he contacted the deputy and told him he'd been framed by July. Spreading the story that he was on his way to Fort Smith, instead he'd come around to Watson's house about mid-afternoon the day Belle was killed, and asked to borrow Watson's shotgun "to kill a wolf that has been catchin' my chickens." An hour later he brought the gun back. Both barrels had been fired.

A week or so before the shooting, Hutchins learned, July approached Milo Hoyt and offered him $200 to kill Belle. When Hoyt refused him, July rode off shouting: "Hell!...I'll kill the old hag myself and spend the money for whiskey!" July jumped his bond on the horse-thief charge, and Judge Parker issued a warrant for his arrest.

Hutchins must have gotten too close to the truth. The word spread that July intended to kill him. Hutchins was down in the Chickasaw Nation in January, 1892, when an Indian boy came to him, warning him that July had been at his mother's house, asking about the deputy. Hutchins and Bud Trainor determined the route the outlaw had taken towards Ardmore and overtook him at dawn.

Hutchins called for his surrender. July spurred his horse and reached for his guns. Hutchins fired the first shot, badly wounding him and July surrendered. Deputy Marshal Heck Thomas brought him into Fort Smith on the 23rd. Four days later, he was nearly dead. They took him from his cell and he asked for Hutchins, and said to tell him he had a confession to make, an important one. He refused to talk to anyone else about it. Authorities sent for Hutchins, but July died before the marshal could get back to Fort Smith. Perhaps Jim July unwillingly took the real story of Belle Starr's death with him.

The Dalton-Doolin Gang

Continued from page 151

Dunn ranch April 29, 1894. Again, the outlaws responded to the order to surrender by drawing their pistols and firing at the lawmen. Both were killed and the two Colt .45s carried by Creek were taken by Bee Dunn.

Dunn carried the Newcomb .45s only a few weeks before he was killed in a shootout with Deputy U.S. Marshal Frank Canton. Dunn had threatened Canton and, when they met in town, both men went for their guns—Canton was faster.

Canton then took possession of these two fine Colts and carried them the rest of his years as a lawman. To my knowledge, they are still in the family. Mrs. Canton moved to Montana after Frank's death and lived quietly there.

The other Doolin gang member pistol that has been authenticated is a blued Colt Single Action .45 with 5½-inch barrel, serial number 113051. This is an exceptionally well-preserved specimen of a frontier sixgun. It bears the desirable U.S. stamp on the grip frame with "CC3" stamped on the bottom of the grip—and has matching serial numbers throughout! On the left side of the bone grips is stamped the HX—brand and "TJ" (Tom Jones, another alias used by Daugherty) on the right grip. According to the letter of authentication with this .45, it had been owned by Bitter Creek Newcomb and he had put the HX—brand on the left grip while cowboying on that ranch. He had given it to Arkansas Tom when they rode with Doolin on their robberies. The pistol was given by Daugherty to Fred Sutton a short time before he was killed while trying to rob an Arkansas bank. The letter from Daugherty that accompanied the Colt, dated May 18, 1924, stated: "Mr. Sutton, I never want to own another gun as long as I live." Apparently, that feeling didn't last long—about 60 days, to be exact.

Several other members of the Doolin gang were tracked down and given a chance to surrender—none accepted. The last to go was "Little Dick" West who had led the comical Jennings gang briefly after Doolin was killed. West was trailed to a ranch near Guthrie where, on April 7, 1898, he refused the order to surrender and was cut down by slugs from weapons in the hands of Sheriff Rinehart and Deputy Fossett, both members of a Thomas/Tilghman posse. "Little Dick's" cocked sixgun was in his outstretched hand.

Doolin had lost control of his gang sometime before as, one by one, the outlaws were killed or captured. Ol' Yantis was killed barely a month after the fruitless Coffeyville raid. He was followed in death by Jack "Texas Jack" Blake, Charlie Pierce, George "Bitter Creek" Newcomb, Little Bill Raidler and Dan "Dynamite Dick" Clifton. George "Red Buck" Weightman had been kicked out of the gang after he had cold bloodedly killed a preacher (in April, 1895) to get the minister's horse. On January 6 of that year, Doolin had kept Red Buck from shooting Bill Tilghman in the back as that lawman was leaving a dugout in which the outlaws were found hiding.

Red Buck was killed by a posse later in '95 when they surrounded the hideout in which he had taken refuge. He came out shooting and was cut down as if by a lead scythe.

Arkansas Tom was captured after the Ingalls fight, in which lawmen Lafe Shadley, Dick Speed and Tom Huston were killed, and sentenced to 50 years in prison for the murder of Huston. Arkansas Tom had also killed Speed, and Bill Dalton killed Shadley.

Dalton had been a fairly prominent California citizen when his brothers' activities cast doubt on the honesty of anyone bearing the Dalton name. After the Coffeyville raid, Bill's chances for a political career were hopeless. He had been a member of the state legislature and had hopes of running for the governorship. His political party dropped him, however, and the embittered, vengeful Dalton returned to Indian Territory where he soon became a member of the newly formed Doolin gang.

Doolin had missed out on the Coffeyville raid (some say it was due to his horse going lame, others say he was too smart to go to Coffeyville so he pretended his horse was lame and others say he was deliberately excluded by Bob Dalton) and wasn't too eager for another Dalton to be around. Bill Dalton was content to be a member of the gang instead of its leader, though, so he became second in command and stayed with the gang for about 18 months. He was left to his own devices due to an increasingly bad temper, and to show them he was as good a leader as Doolin, he rode to Longview, Texas, where, on May 23, 1894, with a few rag-tag outlaws, he robbed a bank of $2500. He returned to Indian Territory to hide from the law. On June 8, Deputy Loss Hart and his posse surrounded the house in which he and his wife,

along with another outlaw and his wife, were hiding. Hart's .44 Winchester wrote the end to the last outlaw Dalton as Bill jumped out a window trying to escape, firing his sixgun as he ran.

Doolin had married Edith Ellsworth, an itinerent preacher/storekeeper's daughter, in 1891 and built a cabin near Ingalls for her. They had a son in 1893 and Doolin made many night trips to see his son as he lay in his crib.

A bullet in his left leg, acquired as he left the Spearville bank robbery, bothered Doolin so much he went to Eureka Springs, Arkansas, for treatment and rest. Bill Tilghman heard of it and, on January 13, 1896, wired Marshal Nix he had captured Doolin and would bring him back to Guthrie on the next train. When Tilghman took Doolin, the outlaw was carrying a Colt .45 in a concealed shoulder holster (apparently the .45 taken from lawman Lafe Shadley after the Ingalls fight). Even though Tilghman had the drop on him, Doolin made a grab for his pistol and only Tilghman's restraint from shooting and outwrestling Doolin kept the outlaw alive to be taken prisoner.

Doolin remained in the Guthrie jail until July 5th when he arranged a jailbreak for himself, Dan "Dynamite Dick" Clifton and a half-dozen other prisoners. He remained free until August 24 when Heck Thomas ended his career with a double-barrel shotgun loaded with buck shot.

While there were other outlaws and bands of lawless men operating in Indian Territory, they were never as deadly, dangerous or hard to put out of business as were the Dalton and Doolin gangs. The Daltons rode free for less than a year and a half while Doolin operated independent of the law for another four years. Members of the gang were reckless and often brave men who, had they chosen to ride on the side of the law, as the Daltons did before becoming outlaws, could have made significant contributions to the settlement of the frontier. As it was, it took men like Thomas, Tilghman, Madsen and other equally brave, fearless—and deadly—lawmen to make it safe for honest citizens to live in that rough land. As is often the case, the outlaw is what he is, because he chooses to ignore society's standards and restrictions and tries to make a living off others' efforts instead of working for wages. Also as is often the case, they end up as did each member of these gangs: behind bars or in an early grave. Deadly desperados such as these men usually ended up just that way—dead!

219

Texas Rangers

Continued from page 159

are held up by suspenders—an unusual arrangement at best. What holds the shoulder strap in position is a mystery. The carved belt could be holding another revolver on the right hip, hidden by the angle of the photo. One of the great Rangers, he lost his intended bride a few weeks before their planned wedding and he never married. Highly respected, he died at the age of 91 in 1946.

Some did purchase the .30-06 caliber Model '95 but regretted it later, as the action was not adequate for the pressure developed and the cases tended to stretch after the rifle had been used for a time. The odd fact is many Rangers returned to their earlier love, the old 94 in .30-30 caliber, and most Rangers today still swear by it, although the .223 has made considerable inroads among the members of the force.

Other shoulder arms that were used to some extent during the 1920s, included the Model 7 .351 and the Model 10 .401 caliber Winchester self-loader used by Ranger Martin Trejo while stationed in Laredo, and even an occasional Thompson, "appropriated" from some of Al Capone's companions such as those used by Rangers Lee Miller and Warren Smith. The most unexpected is a M-1896 Mauser 9mm pistol, complete with a holster/shoulder stock!

The man whose name became a household word with the demise of two of our most notorious criminals, was Ranger Frank Hamer. Hamer, a legend in his own time, best typified the Ranger that lived through that transition period from the saddle horse to the Model V-8 Ford, cattle thieves to oil field toughs and the 1886 to the Thompson.

As a young Ranger, he had a .30-40 Model '95 Winchester as well as a Model '94 and his favorite "Old Lucky" (a .45 single action Colt) which he always carried, although at the taking of Bonnie and Clyde he used a Remington Model 8 Autoloader.

One Texas Ranger, above all others, can be described as a true gun "buff." Several of his elaborately engraved arms and associated equipment are illustrated but this is only a small portion. This is Captain M. T. "Lone Wolf" Gonzaullas. He joined the Rangers in 1920 at El Paso and was involved in a series of shoot-outs with smugglers along the border towns.

He was deadly with any of his weapons, and carried two guns in spring-loaded holsters and was equally skilled with either hand. His flamboyant personality is revealed in the highly decorated arms he carried during his 31 years as a Texas Ranger. Unlike some men in "fancy togs" he was the real thing.

The Rangers, sometimes in the past described as a semi-military organization, failed to meet such a description when applied to their equipment. Little effort was made to change their appearance from that of the local rancher or cowhand. There was little, if any, uniformity in clothing or other equipment, including firearms, and this facet of Ranger life was particularly evident while in the field. This carried on to the extent that most saddle rifles were carried under the left leg, butt forward—each had his own ideas as to whether the butt was turned toe up or if the comb rode uppermost. On the other hand, in the same group another would have the rifle riding butt to the rear. Some people are sticklers about rifle-carrying etiquette, arguing that one position or the other is the only way to carry the arm for protection from brush, aid in dismounting and ease of getting it into action. Perhaps the horse influenced the rifle position, based on his reaction to having it fired between his ears—or he insisted the shooter dismount—which was sometimes the case.

Some preferred the scabbard on the off-side—butt forward—and grasp the gun as they swing down from the saddle. If in heavy brush, a rifle, butt forward, will create a problem.

By 1920, there appeared a trend to dress up a bit. Coat, vest and tie were the wear in town or on routine patrol. Still there was little in common, hats for example, although usually black, were indiscriminate in style. Some had peaked crowns, others were creased and some were Montana style. There appeared to be no true "Texas" style until the '30s. Leather accessories such as belts and holsters varied to some extent. Some obviously made by the owner, others evidently Mexican in origin with flowered or basket-stamped designs.

Gun belts were mentioned previously in reference to carrying loops for both pistol and rifle ammunition. With the departure of the .44-40 rifle, this was necessary and much in evidence with the .30-40 ammunition used in the 1895 Winchester. To preclude snagging a heavy belt load of 3-inch long rifle ammunition, a belt needed to be 3½ inches wide, which held up the trousers.

Buckles were often plain harness hardware that served the purpose but that was about all. Many a cartridge belt was made by the owner—sewn with two needles and beeswaxed linen thread.

Firearms and leather equipment have always been decorated from time immemorial—a custom which has never changed.

In some way, all equipment served either as a weapon or it supported the mission just as much. An indispensible item was a 30-foot lariat. Often plaited from rawhide, it was indeed useful; it served to keep a Ranger's horse at hand and could do double duty if captured bandits exceeded the number of available handcuffs, or it could be used to drag firewood to camp as needed. Rawhide was susceptible to change if wet and the hard twisted manila 7/16-inch rope was more practical.

Neglected until now, the most important piece of equipment, next to horse and firearm, to the man on his own in the Texas brush was his knife. In the 1800s and up to about the late 1920s, this would be a sheath knife of conventional Bowie design. Prior to 1900, and particularly during the time before repeating arms, it was not only an essential tool of great utility, but a weapon that prolonged the life of many a Ranger. Skill with the 10-inch blade was as important as ability with a pistol or rifle. One can see that with such a knife, 40 rounds of rifle ammunition and 20 for the revolver on the belt, he carried quite a load on his person. No wonder the cowboy learned to open gates without dismounting!

As time progressed, the Ranger's equipment turned more and more toward the Mexican craftsman. Carved ivory or silver pistol grips became common, as well as silver belt buckles, keepers and tips. Arms were engraved, and the author knows of one fully nickel-plated Model '97! How that shotgun must have reflected light. It must have been carried as a challenge to any bandit who had the nerve to take it up. This gun, incidently, was taken off of an outlaw, but was to serve another owner for years.

Today some Rangers carry, or at least own, matched single-actions, and a considerable number have changed allegiance to the .45 automatic, engraved with silver and gold grips encased in the finest of twin carved steerhide holsters.

Today a near uniform exists. The white Stetson remains and the black boots and white shirt, but a tailored tan gabardine suit goes with it. This is, of course, for city jobs and the cowpunchers work clothes reappear if a horse is being trailered into the mesquite. It seems that they still have cattle thieves in Texas—but not many. ♣

Henry Starr

Continued from page 172

for the seven robbery convictions and another five years was added for the Pryor Creek train heist for a total sentence of 15 years and seven days. On January 23, 1898, Starr left Fort Smith to begin the sentence at federal prison in Columbus, Ohio.

Starr was a model prisoner and read extensively during his confinement. He enjoyed the classics and he studied philosophy and other subjects—even ballistics. He was an ideal prisoner and convinced prison officials, friends and his mother that he was a reformed man. In the fall of 1901, the Cherokee National Council requested an unconditional pardon for Starr from the president of the United States. The warden of the prison also vouched for Starr's being rehabilitated.

The next spring Henry's mother took this resolution and a number of affidavits and testimonials to Washington D.C. There she petitioned her son's case to President Theodore Roosevelt. Roosevelt sent a wire to Henry at the prison, "Will you be good if I set you free?" Starr, of course, promised to be good and his sentence was commuted to end on January 16, 1903.

In 1892 another gun was built that was to come into Starr's possession. It was a Colt single action Army .41 caliber with a 4¾-inch barrel and nickle finished. This gun, serial number 148049, was shipped November 22, 1892, from Colt to E. C. Meacham Arms Company in St. Louis, Missouri. Meacham Arms was a wholesaler of guns and other sporting goods. How this arm traveled from St. Louis, Missouri to the Indian Territory is unknown.

The story behind this gun is that it came into Starr's hands before he was captured in Colorado Springs and he possibly had left it with Ed Reed (who was Belle Starr's son) or it could have been Reed's gun which was given to Henry after Reed had been killed and Starr had been pardoned.

Henry Starr had possession of this Colt later and gave it to Katherine Reed's husband just three weeks before he was killed in a bank holdup. Fred, who was Katherine Reed's husband said that Reed was good with a gun, but Henry Starr was much better.

After his release from the Columbus prison, Starr returned to the Territory and worked in his mother's restaurant for a few months. He married a pretty young lady, a school teacher who had some recognition on a national scale, as she was the girl in a very popular photograph of the time entitled, "The Cherokee Milkmaid". Miss Ollie Griffin had been boarding with Henry's mother and she and Henry met there. He finally settled down to become a real estate salesman.

When Oklahoma became a state, Arkansas wanted to extradite Starr for the Bentonville bank robbery 13 years before. They had not been able to extradite him from the area while Oklahoma was still the Indian Territory. Henry sent a friend to the governor to try to avoid extradition, but not knowing what the governor would do, he "took to the tall and uncut." What he did not find out until he was back on the scout and in hot water again, was that Governor Haskell "had turned down the application, (for the extradition) upon the opinion from the Attorney General, that there was no authority for extraditing members of the five civilized tribes, to any state or territory for a crime less than murder."

In the winter of 1907 and '08, two banks were robbed in Oklahoma and two in Kansas and Missouri. These were all daylight jobs and the newspapers laid them all to Starr. "The papers claimed I was in all of them and had me in four different places at the same time."

He and his old friend, Kid Wilson, who was out on parole from his sentence in the Brooklyn Federal Prison, got together again and in February of 1908 they bought two Winchesters and 500 rounds of ammunition at Bartlesville. From here they headed north and on the afternoon of Friday, the 13th, they hit the bank at Tyro, Kansas. A posse started out from Tyro, and near Wann, Deputy Sheriff Amik and Mr. Dabney had their horses shot out from under them which slowed the posse down. Meanwhile, a party had set out from Wann. These posses were so jumpy that they were actually shooting at each other at times. There were also posses out from Deering and Caney. The hub bub of the chase lasted about 60 hours and luckily no one was killed. The bandits had made it to their old haunts in the hills around Hominy Creek. This job stirred up a total of $2450 in rewards offered for the capture dead or alive of Henry Starr and Kid Wilson.

Starr attempted to negotiate a proposal to turn himself in, in Oklahoma, providing he would not be "dragged to other states". Governor Haskell refused the proposition and in April, Starr and the Kid left Oklahoma. They moved on into New Mexico and stayed there with a friend until June. Late in June the pair were in the small town of Amity, Colorado, and its small bank to quote Starr, "looked too good to pass up." They withdrew $1000 and headed for the hills. After spending several weeks in the mountains, the partners broke up. Wilson left and disappeared and nothing was heard from him or about him again. About all Starr had to say about his leaving was that "Wilson wanted to quit for good."

Starr moved on to New Mexico where he spent the summer and fall. "I rode a little every day to keep my horse in trim, practiced shooting with the same regularity and occasionally tried my gun on antelope." In January, he moved on, settling at Bosque, Arizona in the Maricopa Mountains. In the meantime his wife had tired of his absence and his inability to remain respectable and divorced him. She took their son and moved to Deurey. Here he made the mistake of trusting a real estate man in Tulsa and it put him back in the hoosegow. He asked this man to sell his Indian allotment and send him the money. The supposed friend told S. W. Fenton, an officer for the territory of Oklahoma. of Starr's whereabouts, and Fenton went to Colorado and he and Sheriff John Simpson of Powers County, went into Arizona and arrested Starr and returned him to Lamar, Colorado.

He was taken to Pueblo and kept in solitary confinement from June 8 to November 24, 1909, when he was moved back to Lamar for trial. Starr pleaded guilty and was sentenced to do 7 to 25 years in the Colorado State Penitentiary at Cannon City. He was to serve the time here under Warden Thomas T. Tynan who was the instigator of prison reform that was picked up by several states. On September 24, 1913, after serving less than 4 years, he was paroled by the governor of Colorado. The terms of his parole were that he was to report once a month and not leave the State of Colorado. Again, Starr had served his time as a model prisoner.

Starr tried to live up to the terms of his parole. He opened a short-order cafe in Holly, Colorado near Amity. People were afraid of the known bandit and the business did not make it. He had become enamored with the wife of a Holly merchant and when the business failed, they left Colorado together. Colorado put out a warrant on him for parole violation and that old Bentonville bank indictment was revived.

It was about this time that H. S. Holliday, a special officer for the

Henry Starr

Kansas City Southern Railroad arrested Starr at Lake Charles, Louisana. According to the information at hand, Henry was released after "He promised Holliday that he would arrange it so that Holliday would get one of his guns, the guns being at Starr's sister's home in Oklahoma." After Starr was killed in 1921, Holliday obtained the gun from Starr's sister. This gun was a Colt .38, Officer's Model, serial number 423218, with a barrel length of 7½ inches. The gun is now in the excellent J. M. Davis Gun Museum in Claremore, Oklahoma. It was obtained from Holliday while he was a deputy sheriff in Kansas City, Missouri.

From September 1914 through about the middle of January 1915, there was a rash of Oklahoma bank robberies.

The law was at a loss on who the culprits were in these jobs until a witness in the Carney job identified a photo of Starr. A $1000 reward was put out for Starr, and officers began scouring the Ozage Hills, Bigheart Mountains, the Verdigris and the Big Caney Valleys as well as other known Starr haunts. They did a lot of traveling for nothing as Henry Starr and his Colorado mistress were living in a five-room bungalow with all the comforts, at 1534 E. Second Street, Tulsa, Oklahoma. The sheriff lived less than two blocks from the bungalow and the mayor only four blocks away.

It was here that Starr planned a type of job that no gang in history had ever tried. They rode into Stroud, Oklahoma about 9 a.m. on March 27th, tied their horses at the stockyards and with one man staying with the horses, the other six proceeded up the street to rob two banks at the same time. They took only $1600 from the Stroud State Bank as the big safe was locked and the cashier did not have the combination. The First National Bank paid off better with $4215. After picking up the money the gang was moving down the street with their hostages, when some of the townspeople began to fire at them. Starr was using Samuel Lee Patrick, vice-president of the bank, as his shield when he spotted a horse buyer by the name of Guild coming around the corner with a shotgun. Telling Patrick, "stand aside and let me get that bastard up there," he fired one shot from his Model 8 .35 Remington autoloader which went through Guild's coat and singed his vest.

As Starr laughed, a slug caught him in the left thigh shattering the bone; the slug had come from a sawed-off .30-30 that 17-year-old Paul Curry used for killing hogs. As Starr went down he tried to return the fire, but was partially paralyzed in the area of his waist. Curry chambered another shell in the Model '94 Winchester and shouted, "Throw away that gun or I'll kill you!" Starr dropped his .35 Remington.

Curry ran for the railroad tracks at the stockyards; here he put the .30-30 to work on Lewis Estes hitting him in the neck and breaking his shoulder. Estes managed, with help, to mount his horse, but about a mile and a half from town he became too weak to ride and fell. The others took his horse and rode on, leaving Estes behind.

Some of the townsmen had picked Starr up and were carrying him to the office of Doctor John Evans, when somebody yelled, "Look out! They're coming back!" Those carrying Starr dropped him and headed for cover. When the alarm proved false, Starr was taken on to the doctor's office. While the doctor was treating his wounds, Starr asked, "What did the kid shoot me with?" When they told him it was a hog gun, he said, "I'll be damned! I don't mind getting shot; knew it had to happen sooner or later. But a kid with a hog gun—that hurts my pride."

Starr asked young Curry what he was going to do with the reward money. Curry said that it would go for his education. "You're all right, boy", Starr told him. Starr gave Doctor Evans his $500 horse, and apologized to Patrick, the bank vice-president, and gave him the Model 8 Remington.

Starr admitted having been a part of most of the Oklahoma bank robberies since his flight from Colorado. He was moved to the jail where many friends and relatives tried to visit him.

He pleaded guilty to the Stroud robbery and was given 25 years in the Oklahoma State Penitentiary. He served his sentence as he did his others—being a model prisoner. He obeyed all the rules, worked in the prison library, taught classes in spelling and composition to the other prisoners and worked with the prison chaplain. All his efforts at acting like a reformed man paid off again and he was paroled in February of 1919, only 3½ years after receiving a 25-year sentence.

The Bentonville robbery of 1893 was was again posing problems, as Arkansas again tried for extradition Governor J.B.A. Robertson denied the request. Starr got back to Tulsa and when friends told him "there's more money in the motion picture business than in robbing banks," he managed to get into the flourishing movie business by acquiring a quarter interest in the "Pan-American Motion Picture Company" of Tulsa.

Henry went at the business with the gusto he had shown in his bandit trade. He made a movie, "Debtor to the Law", which was an immediate success. It was the story of his Stroud double bank job. He was the "Evening Starr" in a couple of later pictures, and was supposed to have netted $15,000 for this, but was unable to collect.

Starr was offered a job in California, staging a bank robbery for a movie and working as a technical director for other westerns, but unfortunately, that Bentonville bank charge was still extant and he could not go to California for fear Arkansas would start new extradition proceedings. During his tour with his movie he had met a 23-year-old Sallisaw girl by the name of Hulda Starr (no relation) and they were married in February, 1920. They moved to Claremore to make their new home.

Starr and three other men drove around Harrison, Arkansas on February 18, cutting all of the telephone and telegraph lines. They then pulled their "high-powered touring car" up in front of the Peoples National Bank. As the robbers entered, waving their revolvers, 60-year-old W. J. Meyers, former president of the bank, slipped unseen into the vault. This oversight was to prove to be Starr's downfall as there was a 73 Winchester hidden in the vault for just such an occasion.

Henry picked up about $6000 that was out in the cashier areas of the bank. More money was stored in the safe and G. C. Hoffman, the cashier, was ordered to open the safe. As he was doing this, Starr bent to watch him closely and Meyers fired a round from the 73 Winchester, which struck just below the ribs in the right side and passed out through his spine, paralyzing him. The rest of the gang fled without gaining a cent, as Starr had stuffed the money in his pockets. About two miles out of town they stopped, set their car afire and they escaped on foot. Starr refused to divulge the names of his companions and they were never caught.

Starr, feeling certain that he was not long for this world, sent a telegram to his wife telling her that he was dying. In his 30 years of robbing he had robbed more banks than the James' Daltons and Doolins combined. He boasted, "I've robbed more banks than any man in America." Not many men would question the validity of his statement. ♦

John Slaughter

Continued from page 177

disturbed by another shotgun blast, but Chacon had departed leaving behind enough identity to prove he was indeed Augustine Chacon, the bandit, who had come with the intention to kill John Slaughter.

John Slaughter's six-shooter sometimes found other uses besides shooting at outlaws. By a fluke of fate, he once won a poker pot consisting of thousands of dollars, by using his gun as a paper weight! The much publicised incident has become a forgotten chapter in Southern Arizon's history. But those who are old enough to remember the wily old rancher still chuckle about it.

The old Gadsden Hotel in Douglas, Arizona was the gathering place for a number of card games held by local ranchers and businessmen of the area. It was the number-one hostelry for miles around. It seems that any time the exchange of large sums of money are taking place, that eventually it reaches the ears of those hoping to acquire it. For two card sharks, known to have taken many an innocent person to the cleaners, it seemed that rancher Slaughter would be an easy victim.

When the tin-horned gamblers arrived, they learned first hand that John Slaughter played with the best of them and furthermore, was handy with his gun, standing for no tomfoolery. So after some research on their part, the card sharks sought out a fellow named George Spindles as the ideal man to manipulate a game of poker with, and have Slaughter in the game.

George Spindles was a sort of cross between Will Rogers and Jesse James. He was an old cowboy and ranchman who was well liked by everyone who knew him. But somewhere in his make-up was a streak of the devil. He was exactly the right sort of man to bring John Slaughter into a poker game with strangers. In Slaughter's earlier life, he played poker among the Texas Rangers, Minute Men of Texas, soldiers of the cavalry, and many cow camps. He was known to be a high bidder of stakes, a good winner, and a good loser as well. Slaughter knew just when to bluff, and when to raise the ante.

The card sharks plan called for some strategy that would not arouse any thoughts that the game was bent on a fleecing mission, so it was decided that Spindles was to be dealt the top hands. After the game, he was to split the winnings with the two card sharks. Now and then the strangers would win a hand, and so would Slaughter. The whole thing began with a feeling of friendship and sportsmanship. But as the night grew, so did the size of the pots. So adept were the strangers with cards, they knew and could produce any card in the deck with the least sleight of hand. The higher the stakes, the more liquor was brought up from the bar below, however Slaughter was too involved to do much drinking; and was much too shrewd to become inebriated.

As the game grew to a climax, the center of the table had on it quite a few thousand dollars. For everytime a bid was made, Slaughter upped the ante. He sat there with a very poor hand, and as he did many times before, built the pot to such dimensions, that usually everyone else dropped out, before they lost their shirt.

Now in accordance to the strategy, the two card sharks were to toss in their cards and pass, meaning they were no longer in the game. George Spindles sat there with a red glow on his face, holding a royal flush, dealt to him by his new companions. Things became extremely electric, and much winking and cues went on between Spindles and his henchmen. Slaughter commonly sat there with his well-known catfish grin. The weather was extremely hot and the windows were wide open. Suddenly a breeze came in and distrubed the paper money. Beside Slaughter was a heap of money which also fluttered in the breeze.

At that moment, Slaughter slammed down a large denomination of paper currency. At the same time, he jerked out his six-shooter and laid it on his money beside him. Spindles reflexes over-acted instantly. He threw down his cards, and cussed the dealer for dealing him a lousy pair of deuces. Slaughter swept in the huge pot. The night was late, so the game was over. Spindles later said he knew John Slaughter was going to use that six-shooter, though it turned out he was merely using it as a paper weight to keep the money from blowing off the table. The sharks left, very disgruntled, never to return to Douglas.

John Slaughter had a brand new Marlin rifle, in .45-85 caliber. It was the first Marlin rifle he had ever owned. Slaughter liked the feel of it and noted it was very accurate, so early one morning he put his old Henry rifle in the corner and stuck the Marlin in the boot of his saddle. As usual he was up long before sunrise. He had a lot of help, and rode over his ranch, assigning each hand with work for the day.

The day before, news reached Slaughter that a bank had been held up in Nogales, Arizona on the border to the west of the Slaughter ranch. It didn't disturb Slaughter much. He was no longer the sheriff, but if he were summoned for help he would favorably respond. Arthur Finney was a gay young blade from Texas, who fashioned himself as quite a desperado. He was hampered by having a "peg leg" from some previous accident, and it seemed to make him down on the world. He hated everyone it seemed. He made his big mistake by riding to the border town of Naco and stealing a fine horse and saddle from a respected rancher named Marion Williams.

The new-fangled gadget called the telephone had just made its first appearance to Arizona. The U.S. Customs office had one on the border, and the line ran to Bisbee, the Slaughter ranch and a few other points where it was deemed most in need. The poles were iron and quickly rusted with the rains and weather. They were about 12 feet in height and about four inches in diameter. Soon after Finney's escapades at Nogales and Naco, Judge Williams of Bisbee called John Slaughter that a man answering the description of "Peg Leg", was headed for the San Bernardino Ranch. Orders were to take him dead or alive, as he was considered armed and dangerous.

Mrs. Slaughter had called her husband to the phone, and while he was conversing with the judge, one of Slaughter's Mexican cowboys ran into Finney. Finney cussed out the Gringos and thought he won the Mexican's confidence. All he wanted was a good saddle horse. The Mexican assured him to wait there and he would bring him one. But it would take sometime before he would be back. Finney thought that was fine, as he needed to catch some sleep anyway. So he hobbled his horse and layed down under a shady tree, and was soon asleep.

In the meantime, the Mexican cowboy found John Slaughter and told him about a man with a "Peg Leg" who was on the ranch and wanting a horse. They immediately set off to find Arthur Finney. Slaughter came upon Finney as quietly as possible. He saw his horse and caught a glimpse of him sleeping under the tree. Finney had with him a Winchester rifle. The outlaw had his six-shooter in his right hand, and covered it with his body, so that if he were surprised, all he had to do is raise slightly and fire.

Slaughter crept up to Finney with his Marlin ready for action. He carefully reached over and grasped the outlaw's Winchester throwing it behind himself. Finney's reflexes instantly caused the sleeping man to roll into a sitting position, at the same time cocking the hammer of his pistol. John Slaughter shouted, "You are under arrest!", firing at the same time. Finney fell back dead, shot through the heart. The coroners report cited him as 28 years old.

Miles away the Klondike gold rush was going on, also the Spanish-American War. For John Slaughter it was just another day in his life. 🐛

The Pinkertons

Continued from page 71

local criminal element.

Criminals were prone to arm themselves "to the teeth." Four pistols (revolvers) were often carried on the person. Nothing was as handy as an overlooked derringer in 41 rimfire caliber, either a single shot Colt or one of the popular two-barreled Remingtons in the event one was captured. A spare or two was usually in the saddle bags (loaded of course) if mounted, or in the carpet bag when going by stage or train.

On the East Coast the criminal and Pinkerton alike would normally carry concealed weapons, being in a more *civilized* atmosphere than in the unruly West. In the West the Colt's, Smith & Wesson's and Remingtons were openly displayed and provided an insight to the owners intentions and potential ability in defending himself—or more than likely his inclination to cause some trouble.

As *civilization* spread over the land, it brought improved arms. The Remington double-barrel hammer shotgun was replaced by the new Winchester Model 1887 10 or 12-gauge lever-action shotgun. It provided a total of five rapid shots—and quick reloading—if the first shots proved inadequate in bringing a quick conclusion to the event. The Model 97 that followed was even faster, with its slide action and six shot capability, five in the magazine and one in the chamber.

With the turn of the century and the arrival of the semi-automatic pistols such as the Remington, Colt, Savage, Smith & Wesson and Harrington and Richardson, the era of the "gangster guns" arrived.

The Savage, based on the designs of Elbert H. Searles of Philadelphia, was undoubtedly the superior design. In any event the Savage pocket models took over extremely well, in spite of the fact that Colt won out after intense competition for an Army contract for a .45 caliber auto. Savage, a much smaller company, had not been involved in side arms until the prospect of the Army contract came up.

With considerable acumen, Savage started an intense advertising campaign for their Model 1907 .32 caliber.

Colt had come out with its .25 and .380 caliber automatics the same year, but it was 1912 before the Savage .380 was introduced.

The slogan "ten shots quick" apparently appealed to the public and 80,000 .32 caliber 1907 Savage

pistols were sold. Aiding Savage's effort in their advertising were such well known names as Buffalo Bill Cody; Captain Crossman, top gun writer of that day; Bat Masterson heartily endorsed the gun, and Savage even had a book prepared by Masterson, available for the asking. And, not too surprisingly, *both* William A. Pinkerton and William T. Burns were greatly impressed with the merits of the Savage pistols. Savage gave wide publicity to the expert's comments in their advertising.

Although many of these remarks may have been encouraged by the gift of a silver plated Model 1907, complete with mother-of-pearl grips, there is no question as to the outstanding workmanship and quality of these arms. Without a doubt they were quickly attained by practically every plainclothes officer including the Pinkertons. Superiority over the long popular .36 Navy Colt was too obvious to deserve discussion. The only fly-in-the-ointment was that every gangster owned two!

Savage was to produce the 1915 and 1917 models as well as some .25 caliber pistols. The Model 1917, available in 1920, was never turned out in the quality inherent in the 1907 model, and arrived when prohibition was to spawn small wars among the rival rum-running gangs of the time.

Public sentiment turned against the pistol, and the laws directed against "pocket automatics" and the coming depression led to the last of the Savage automatics by 1928.

The Savage pistols were excellent weapons, near the ultimate in design that would be too expensive to produce today, due to the time consuming fine tolerances and finishes incorporated in these arms. Inspection reveals these are among the finest of contemporary arms of the period. Only Colt survived the period. Their .32 and .380's were issued in World War I and II to Generals as personal arms, and to nurses for their own protection in areas of the South Pacific during WW II.

Remington's Model 51 Automatic produced from 1918 to 1934 was a most comfortable pistol to hold, and performed well but was never overly popular. Being produced from 1918 to 1934, it no doubt absorbed some of the sales that would have otherwise gone to Savage.

By 1930, numbers of Lugers, Mausers, Astras, Brownings, and Berettas had joined our domestic arms, which already included a goodly amount of WW I "battle lost" Model 1911 .34 Colts. These were 9mm in the majority, along with pocket pistols in .380, .32 and .25 caliber. Although long popular in Europe

and for that matter most of the world, the .380, .32 and .25 calibers were never used in the U.S. as issue police arms, but were often carried as "hideout" guns. Even today the .380 is considered very minimal in stopping power.

Probably of all the foreign pistols of this period, the Browning Hi-power was best suited for police work. One major advantage was its 13-round staggered magazine over the old favorite 7-shot 1911 Colt.

During this period near the change of the century, the Colt self-cocking, New Navy revolver made from 1877 to 1912, showed the lines of the modern double-action revolver. Adapted by both the Army and Navy, it was also favored by peace officers. It was six-shooter chambered for the .38 Short and Long Colt and .41 Short and Long Colt.

A series of competition Smith & Wesson arms, starting in 1880 with the double-action hinged frame, 5-shot in the Smith & Wesson .38 cartridge double-action with a barrel length of 3¼ to 6 inches, entered the field of police arms. A .32 caliber of the same type was produced during the same period. There were a large number of variations in size and caliber.

Allan Pinkerton, who contributed so much to the establishment of law-and-order throughout the United States as well as serving his government during the Civil War, although some may question the effectiveness of his analysis of garnered intelligence passed on to General McClellan, was to pass away on July 1, 1884.

The Pinkerton operation continues to this day and employs a total of over 13,000 full-time and 10,000 part-time personnel. However, the character of its operations has wandered far afield since those days when Allan Pinkerton finally placed the beautiful southern spy, Mrs. Rose O'Neal Greenhow in prison, and then, along with their father, William and Robert planned the strategy against the long list of desparados that ranged from Black Bart in California to the Midwest with the Reno Brothers, the Daltons, the Youngers, Frank and Jesse James, the McCoys, and Butch Cassidy's "The Wild Bunch."

Without the Pinkertons, our history would have read a great deal differently, undoubtedly much to the worse. The nation owes an everlasting vote of thanks to this dedicated group, devoted to the welfare of their country, that risked their lives as a mere matter of daily routine; many of whom were unfortunate enough to die in the performance of the assignments. ♟